BEYOND THE BALLOT BOX: REDEFINING SELF-GOVERNANCE IN A NEW ERA

Reclaiming the People's Role and Confronting Entrenched Power in American Democracy

Alan Hillsdale

Table of Contents

INDEX

FOREWORD

The Constitution of the United States was written over two hundred and forty years ago. Amendments have been few, organizational add-ons many, but the conceptual framework remains undisturbed.

But, during the time elapsed since its writing there have been dramatic changes within the Union. Little of the communication, information storage, transmission, transportation, or social and business environment of today existed in 1776. The high-powered nation we live in is radically different from the relatively new agrarian society that existed when the Framers made the decisions that became our Constitution. The 1770s population was about 8 million people; today, it is about 330 million.

It is remarkable that the Constitution functions at all today. That fact must be taken as proof that the founding principles were generally sound enough to get us this far. It provided the vital framework under which the nation was able to rise, in many ways, to the rank of world leader. The Constitution created a governance structure of which Americans are proud.

It was the first of its kind, an experimental foray into a virtually unknown world of great freedom, using a creative form of government tilted away from both autocracy and democracy.

ENTROPY

In nature a condition called "entropy" is always at work.

In scientific terms, entropy means "an organized system inevitably deteriorates." The dysfunction in the governance of our Republic that we observe today is the product of the harsh grind of entropy. Entropy dissolves human structures, and the process is irreversible. The structures have to be rebuilt, but then entropy, like déjà vu, starts all over again. It should come as a surprise to nobody that entropy would mercilessly apply its rasp to our constitution and government.

Spotting institutions struggling because of entropy isn't difficult. The Catholic Church is an instructive case model. One of the oldest institutions on earth, it has had to reconstitute itself repeatedly over its lifespan, in battles sometimes waged with encyclicals and sometimes with guns, as was the case when Garibaldi's soldiers put an end to the papal states. Its battles were, and are, with modernism, a word used to describe the societal changes relentlessly grating on its fixed religious structure. Pope Pius X, in 1907, declared modernism "the synthesis of all heresies."[1]

---

[1] Quotations and references from" The Irony of Modern Catholic History," by George Weigel

The impact on the conservative old Church of Progress, the modernization of civilization, and the societal trend toward liberalism has been dramatic over the past century. In its "collision with secular modernity," it has had to concede a less hostile attitude toward the death penalty, divorces, abortion, and, most recently, to deal with headlines and lawsuits stemming from sexual abuse committed by its clergy. Its aging policy and administrative decisions are out-of-step, and in some cases in direct confrontation, with the evolving intellectual stance of society.

The Second Vatican Council modernized the Church to some degree in the 1970s, but the bastion of Christianity has backed down slowly, changing little and searching for a balance. Meantime, in the last half of the 20th century ordinations dropped 50%, with the average age of priests jumping from 46 to 60. The Church is writhing under the inexorable grind of entropy, and a resolution is not in sight. The relentless force of progress, beating against the firm and stationary old-order bastion structure of that venerable religious institution, will, at some point in time, force reconciliation between the two. What that reconcilement will look like is anybody's guess.

To quote author George Weigel, "Rather than killing Catholicism, the encounter with modernity has helped the Catholic Church rediscover some basic truths about itself. Even more ironically, the Church's rediscovery of those truths might, just might, put Catholicism in a position to help secular modernity save itself from its own increasing incoherence."

The case model of the Catholic Church is worth keeping in mind when considering the effect of entropy on the government of the United States of America.

ENTROPY AND THE CONSTITUTION OF THE UNITED STATES

The complex and vital life processes of our nation, operating within the framework created in 1776 by the Constitution, have moved forward in two-plus centuries of steady growth, supercharged by occasional spurts of rapid advancement. Those life processes were fashioned in the Agricultural Era, the Industrial Era, and the Financial Era and are being reshaped once again in the Technological Era now under way.

The three branches of government created by our constitutional framework today govern a rapidly-moving, instant-communication, high-technology-impregnated economy of 330 million-plus people, generating the largest gross domestic product in the world. Ground down by the inexorable rasp of entropy, however, elements of the three Framer-created check-and-balance branches have shifted away from the conceptual framework of the Constitution, and in some aspects, founding principles have been intentionally violated. This nation's government is truly suffering its own "collision with modernity."

Modernity thrust upon our Constitution the notion that government does not exist solely to manage the affairs of the nation and to provide its fundamental security. Government, modernity posits, possesses massive financial powers that should be focused on improving the welfare of The People. The 20th-century encroachment by this modernity concept, which was unheard of in 1776, has wreaked havoc on the form of government conceived by the Framers.

Our Constitution is a Ford Model T. It was beautifully designed and dependable, the most amazing vehicle of its time! Now it's old, hasn't had any maintenance, and we're getting by with it, but it's running awfully rough. The old Model T just won't get us to where we must go, given the heavy traffic and the way people drive nowadays.

SOME CONSTITUTIONAL PRINCIPLES HAVE BEEN IGNORED, SOME VIOLATED, SOME ARE NO LONGER FUNCTIONAL

One constitutional principle has failed: the principle that each branch of government should act as a check-and-balance on the activities of the others. The Ballot Box check-and-balance does not perform its function of correcting the non-performing Congress. Other checks-and-balances have degraded into a state of sullen ineffectiveness. Some were originally placed in the wrong hands or are now situated improperly within the organization. The rush of progress has simply outgrown some, rendering them obsolete. Critical new checks-and-balances, unanticipated or unrecognized by the Framers, have long been needed to halt the relentless slide of government performance. The failure of Constitutional checks-and-balances and the absence of badly needed new ones are a glaring weakness, the effects of which are plain to see for any who take the time to look.

While the Constitution has remained intact, governance carried out within its framework has been purposefully altered, propelled by new political party thinking as to the proper role of government and how it should best be organized. A huge administrative function has been superimposed on the original government, a function never considered at the time of the Framers and for which there was obviously no provision in the Constitution. The Framer concept of limited government has been burst asunder by a political party's impassioned thrust of the massive Administrative State into the Framer-prescribed government body without as much as a kiss on the Constitutional cheek.

Further, another party-fueled thrust has breached the constitutional check-and-balance barrier separating the Framer-conceived three branches of government. Encroachment of one branch on another, coupled with the abandonment of constitutional principles by the branches, has birthed the dysfunctional government that rankles us today.

Much of the turmoil of current-era governance had its origin in the inability of the Framers to envision entropy and build a workable mechanism to adjust the Constitution to changing conditions. The processes they established for constitutional change are cumbersome and structured inappropriately, but their main failing was the placement of authority for constitutional amendment in the wrong hands, those of the political elite. To quote an ancient analogy, the processes for constitutional change "put the fox in charge of the chicken-house."

3

With The People denied the right to make changes to their own governance control document, it should come as a surprise to nobody that the Constitution has not been amended to bring it current.

THE FRAMERS MADE AMENDMENT DIFFICULT ON PURPOSE

The Framers purposefully made the Constitution difficult to amend. They were putting into place a new form of government that, for its time, was an aggressive quantum leap forward. Looking back from our vantage point at the conditions existing then and the complex political battles then being waged, it is amazing that they were able to produce a system as well-conceived as ours. They made some critical errors and didn't provide well for the inevitable future change, and for system entropy is excusable. Their laser-like focus was on their number one priority, creating a system of government they could get approved in the very difficult political environment of the thirteen states. It was a monumental task, and we should be thankful they succeeded.

From the discussions in the Federalist Papers, it is clear that among the politicians of that time, there was great angst that the then-existing Confederation might collapse because of untenable weaknesses in the Articles of Confederation. The Framers were consumed with finding a solution acceptable to thirteen highly independent states. The best they could do was agree upon and implement a new government system that would allow the nation to correct its dangerous situation and move forward. The goal was the survival of the nation by establishing a strong central government and correcting the deadly errors incurred in Confederation. They could only hope that what they created would accomplish that, and in the process no doubt gave up a number of wish-list items of lesser importance.

Making it easy to amend the Constitution was considered a fundamentally bad idea because the Framers didn't want to give those thirteen states an "easy way out." But it is brutally clear that being unable to correct dysfunctional government, a curse placed upon us by their inflexible Constitution, is far worse. They should have given more thought to a popular saying of that era: "A young man will rapidly outgrow his new suit."

A MAJOR REMODEL OF OUR DEMOCRATIC REPUBLIC IS PROPOSED

This Republic has reached that point where we, The People, must say loud and clear that we will not allow our government venture to fail. WE WILL MAKE THE NECESSARY CHANGES!

Ours is a system of self-government. We know, from a thoughtful examination of the nation's Constitutional Amendment history, that if The People don't do it, it will not be done. But the Framers left no constitutional door open to The People.

The government of the United States is one of the largest organizations of its nature on earth. It is extremely complex and cumbersome. Determining the best way to analyze its endless array of inter-related dysfunctional attributes while maintaining content cohesion has been an intellectual challenge. So, too, has been deriving understandable solutions that will hopefully be acceptable to the average citizen, who probably has no background in organizations and systems but who must knowledgeably participate in making final Constitutional decisions. Very little of the government is functioning properly today.

Any revision of our Constitution must obviously be the work of groups of people dedicated to that task. Revision decisions must be made by vote of The People. All one lowly author can hope is to stimulate the minds of those who will lead and of those who will vote.

DON'T APPLY YESTERDAY'S SOLUTION TO TODAY'S SITUATION

The three-branches-of-government democratic republic structure, "the Constitutional Framework," with its built-in checks-and-balances, established a classic new model for its time. With time's passage, government organization and process deficiencies (some constitutional inheritances, some the product of entropy, but most the inevitable result of relentless political striving) have combined to produce our state of dysfunction. Those organization and process deficiencies have sprouted the seeds of constitutional doom.

There are adherents to the Constitutional Framework who believe strongly that reverting government back to strict conformance with the original plan will solve all of our ills. We dare not pursue that course because the environment in which government operates has changed dramatically, and the government we work with today bears a scant resemblance to the original creation. The Framer creation fit circumstances that existed almost two hundred and fifty years ago, as different as night-and-day from what is in place now. Rather than applying yesterday's solution to today's problem, we would be more rational in custom-designing a solution for today's situation. In doing so, however, we must, of course, retain those Framer principles that we judge to be solid.

Our political and governmental dilemma largely stems from a functionally-obsolete Constitution. Its state of obsolescence has been aggravated by the concerted actions of politicians overlaying a radical structural concept in gross violation of the Constitutional Framework and who then cheated by not amending the Constitution itself. This Book will identify and define the afflicted conditions and propose solutions. Those solutions must necessarily address the deficiencies of a badly-abused and degraded Constitution by redesigning it to fit the needs not only of the present but, more importantly, of the future.

BET ON STRENGTHS, USE PROVEN PRINCIPLES

The biggest single risk from Constitutional change would be the abandonment of the principles that have made our country great. There is a proven edict in business strategic planning: *Always bet on strengths; avoid betting on weaknesses*. That simple edict applies, in spades, to decisions regarding our nation's controlling document.

Many of the principles the Framers employed in developing our Constitutional Framework of government are valid, proven over time, and *if employed properly* in a constitutional revision, will guarantee that the resulting new Framework not only functions as desired but will be as true to the original plan as practical. There were many principles applied by the Framers, but many of the most important were never written into the Constitution. Some Framer principles, as would be expected, have proven over time to be ill-conceived, even destructive. Those will have to be ruthlessly removed.

DON'T PERMIT CONSTITUTIONAL CHANGE FOR POLITICAL GAIN

Political events that distress activists often generate a flurry of noise aimed at inciting a constitutional amendment to rectify the event that caused the distress. In the 2016 election, the Democratic Presidential candidate achieved a majority of votes cast. The Electoral College, however, gave the win to the Republican candidate, who was widely hated by the political elite of both parties because he was a disrupter and a significant threat to their comfortable positions. Proponents of pure democracy perceived that outcome to be unfair, which engendered a hue and cry to disband the Electoral College as being a non-democratic process.

The Electoral College, which was not expected by the Framers of the Constitution to be a lasting structure, has weathered the passage of time surprisingly well. In the Presidential election, it amends the pure majority vote of citizens by intercession of the States to create a joint result. It is the structure of a Republic, whereas a Presidential election by direct vote is the process of a pure Democracy. Those who wish to wield the political power of voters from heavily-populated states will inevitably launch an attack on the Electoral College, which was put in place to prevent them from doing exactly that. The Electoral College has worked well as an equalizer and is a vital structure in a state-based nation with immense geographic population imbalance.

Noisy reaction to political events is to be expected. Nonetheless, a document as important as the Constitution should never be changed based on an emotional reaction to a short-term outcome that some may view as unsatisfactory. The Constitution certainly should not be attacked for *political advantage,* which almost always has been the motivation behind efforts for its amendment. Constitutional amendments can today be activated *only by the political elite*.

Hard-core issues that have considerable history and can be analytically related to other unsatisfactory effects are matters that might be considered for potential Constitutional amendment. By placing the Constitution under the control of The People and separating it from political activities, we will be betting that such problems can be resolved dispassionately.

FAITH IN THE CONSTITUTION, A GREAT AMERICAN STRENGTH, IS ALSO A BARRIER TO CHANGE

One thing is certain. The average American has great faith in the Constitution. Many feel that its long-term stability, which has stood the test of time, is the foundation for the success of the nation. That faith is also the reason there is reticence to make changes. Given the realities of today's polarized political climate, the faith of the People in their Constitution could be the glue keeping the polarized nation from falling apart.

Faith in the Constitution has blinded citizens to the fact that it has been systematically violated and has dramatically eroded before their eyes. To accept constitutional revision, the Voters must come to grips with the fact that a solid intellectual connection exists between their low opinion of Congress and the crying need for constitutional revision of that branch of government. They must understand that the nation's poor government is a constitutional problem that can't be solved merely by electing a different President or a different political party. They must come to understand the impact of entropy, which may never before have been brought to their attention. They must use similar reasoning when evaluating the need to cancel the unwarranted position afforded the Media. The average citizen probably doesn't spend much time worrying about the Constitution. It is, to most, an American Fixture akin to the Statue of Liberty.

Despite dogged faith that the Constitution is a bulwark of American success, most opinion surveyors conclude that Americans know something is very wrong in their government. With no success, citizens are trying to affect correction using the one vehicle at their disposal: the ballot box. A large segment of our citizens is fundamentally rational and pragmatic. It is a reasonable bet that they will transfer their affection for the Constitution to a new document if they themselves have been involved in its creation.

WHAT IS THE PURPOSE OF THIS BOOK?

The book aims to provide **The People** (and that is how it refers to our citizens throughout its pages) with an assessment of the dysfunction in our government and an analysis of its causes. It tries to avoid putting too much attention on *the problems*, which are large and endless. It *focuses on solutions*. The solutions proposed are based upon proven principles of management and authority delegation. Citizens should be able to easily relate them to observable conditions.

That approach should help to promote comprehension. The People need the comfort of knowing there are ways to work themselves out of our morass and will welcome an opportunity to evaluate some real proposed solutions. At this juncture, however, People cannot go back to sleep and certainly cannot rest on their laurels because the problems we face are very threatening.

The analysis uses well-established management rules about authority, delegation, and, the other side of that coin, accountability. Government is, of course, nothing more than management on a large scale. It is hoped that the approach to analysis will raise discussions high above the opinion level and give readers a credible foundation in broadly-accepted principles to help their reasoning process.

This book is about self-government. The People must take charge of their country and resolutely take the steps necessary to make their government function. It proposes that The People, for the first time, make the owner's decisions for their nation, decisions that are their sole responsibility as owners. It proposes a path forward and suggests methods that could be employed. The right and obligation of The People to do that is rationally clear but legally cloudy.

This book does not propose the abandonment of our democratic republic plan; it builds on what the plan gives us. Its sole purpose is to motivate The People to make their government function properly. It doesn't abandon checks-and-balances; it relocates and resets those important controls and suggests new controls needed. It focuses on improvements that dampen the role of political parties so that the needs of The People and the Republic are given first priority in all decisions. It proposes ways to involve The People in the decisions that are their sole responsibility but from which they have historically been wrongfully excluded. It proposes changes to government functions that will remove the poor performance and highly objectionable behavior we observe and create real government accountability to the citizens, where none exists today.

This book posits that the dominant responsibility of government, to make the operating decisions of the nation, must be the point of focus for dramatic improvement of government. It proposes that the main strategy of The People must be to achieve high decision quality. Relentless actions to implement that strategy will produce dramatic results.

And, most important of all, it proposes important ways to remove various internal threats to the continued existence of our self-government, such as the media/political party threat and the threat from internal totalitarian factions.

FINAL THOUGHTS

Our self-government has perennially been described as "Government of The People, by The People, and for The People."

Our nation is not self-governed the way that descriptor implies. The only involvement of The People in government is voting at the ballot box. The power to govern was totally and completely delegated constitutionally to those elected, who, in concert, operate what this book frequently describes as a "monarchy republic." The People cannot be said to conduct "self-government" because they were granted no constitutional power to modify government structure or workings and no power to hold government accountable.

The will and ability to govern ourselves effectively is the responsibility of The People. True self-government requires an entirely new approach. How about this as a rally statement?

> *Never give up faith in The People. It is their Republic. Challenge them to think for the nation. Make sure they are well-informed with factual information. Construct for them the proper processes to consider, vote, and impose their will.*
>
> *Then, believe that their intelligence and self-interest will produce judgments that are vastly superior to those made any other way.*

It is worth while creating a mental picture of what our scoured and remodeled Authority Structure should look like and how it should function. Throughout the book, descriptive phrases are used, like "high-performance decision bodies." This nation actually has the substance, the capability, and the intellect to create a new form of democratic self-government that is so remarkable in its functionality and performance that it will cause other nations to sit up and take notice. To have a goal lower than that is not adequately challenging our people.

CHAPTER 1

DYSFUNCTION IN THE U.S. GOVERNMENT

CONTENT:

SECTION 1: EVENTS OF RECENT HISTORY

SECTION 2: THE STATE OF DEMOCRACY WORLD-WIDE

SECTION 3: HOW WE WILL APPROACH THE ANALYSIS

FOREWORD

We will begin with a discussion of the current dysfunction in the governance of our nation and how this book's analysis of symptoms and causes will be carried out.

Because of the complex nature of interrelationships between the various parts of our republic system of government, be forewarned that some topics will be revisited from time to time in other Chapters. Also, be aware that the breadth of the topic of discussion is huge, so many worthy topics will be given short shrift or may not be mentioned at all.

SEARCH FOR COMPREHENSION

Events of recent history produce endless headlines shouting out the degeneration of government performance in our country. We are daily exposed to a litany of distressing behavior, conditions, and events.

Understanding those conditions is not easy because media reporting is selectively factual and designed to slant our conclusions in one direction or another. True comprehension does not allow becoming overwhelmed or distracted by short-term conditions and events and the media hoopla they generate. The citizens, sadly, are unlikely to find much true comprehension from media coverage.

The search for real comprehension must revert to our government system and the practices embedded in it. That is where one will find the causes of the behavior we observe. Causes will sometimes be found in the Constitution itself. Ours is reputedly a system of self-government, which implies that the citizens shape and drive the outcomes. That should wave the first red flag in the comprehension search.

To evaluate, a person needs reliable benchmarks or standards against which government can be compared. Since the government is nothing more than a huge management organization, our analysis will use as a standard the rules of management and organization that are well intrenched in the many huge U.S. commercial organizations. You will encounter in our discussions frequent references to the rules of delegation, to owner/manager responsibilities, and to the principles of decision-making, including strategic planning.

Many readers probably have no practical experience or background in those disciplines to apply, so this book has increased the levels of detail when discussing and applying such standards. The point, for the non-corporate readers, is that well-established standards exist, they work, and they have been developed and tested over long periods of time in thousands of organizations.

Our system, democratic self-government, is a very complex undertaking. Accordingly, we introduce here a planner's credo that will be repeated ad nauseum:

"For every complex problem, there exists an obvious and simple solution. AND IT'S DEAD WRONG!"

Readers with no planning background should interpret that to mean "if the problem is complex, expect that the solution will also be complex." Solutions like communism are popular because they provide quick-and-dirty answers to gullible and uninformed persons who want something that sounds intelligent when they use it in discussions.

Comparative Analysis of Democracy Index Ratings

Understanding Democracy Through the Lens of Global Transitions

The Democracy Index, published annually by the Economist Intelligence Unit (EIU), evaluates the state of democracy across the world. It categorizes nations into four regimes: "Full Democracies," "Flawed Democracies," "Hybrid Regimes," and "Authoritarian Regimes." With the United States classified as a "Flawed Democracy," understanding how other nations have transitioned between categories provides crucial insights into the structural and cultural dynamics influencing democratic performance.

The U.S. as a Flawed Democracy

The United States, ranked 30th in the 2023 Democracy Index, is classified as a "Flawed Democracy." While it scores high in the electoral process and civil liberties, its low ratings in political culture (6.25/10) and government functioning (6.43/10) reflect challenges such as polarization, declining trust in institutions, and legislative inefficiency.

Comparing the U.S. to nations that have successfully transitioned to "Full Democracy" or regressed into "Hybrid Regimes" highlights the factors driving democratic evolution or decline.

Case Studies of Transition

1. Norway (Full Democracy, Rank 1)

Norway consistently ranks as the world's top democracy, with near-perfect scores in electoral processes, political culture, and government functioning. Its democratic resilience offers lessons for the United States:

- **High Political Trust:**
  Norway's citizens exhibit exceptional trust in their government, attributed to transparency, low corruption, and a social welfare model that reduces inequality. Public participation in policy decisions is actively encouraged.

- **onsensus-Oriented Politics:**
  The proportional representation system fosters multi-party collaboration, minimizing polarization. Politicians focus on long-term policies rather than short-term electoral gains.

- **Lessons for the U.S.:**

  - **Combat Polarization:** Adopt electoral reforms that incentivize coalition-building rather than majoritarian dominance.

  - **Build Institutional Trust:** Enhance transparency and accountability mechanisms to rebuild public confidence.

2. South Korea (Flawed Democracy to Full Democracy Transition)

South Korea transitioned from "Flawed Democracy" to "Full Democracy" in 2020, driven by reforms addressing public dissatisfaction and political scandals.

- **Civil Society Mobilization:**
  Large-scale protests, such as those in 2016 demanding President Park Geun-hye's impeachment, showcased citizens' commitment to accountability.

- **Judicial Independence:**
  Judicial reforms ensured greater independence, curbing corruption and promoting equality under the law.

- **Technological Integration:**
  South Korea's e-governance initiatives improved public service delivery and reduced bureaucratic inefficiency.

- **Lessons for the U.S.:**

  o Encourage grassroots movements to demand accountability.

  o Invest in digital tools to streamline governance and improve public access to information.

3. Hungary (Full Democracy to Hybrid Regime)

Hungary's dramatic regression from "Full Democracy" in the early 2000s to a "Hybrid Regime" highlights how democratic erosion occurs when institutional safeguards weaken.

- **Media Control:**
  The ruling party consolidated control over the media, stifling dissent and manipulating public opinion.

- **Judiciary Undermining:**
  Judicial reforms weakened checks and balances, allowing the executive to dominate.

- **Centralized Power:**
  Hungary's move toward an authoritarian leadership style under Viktor Orbán eroded democratic norms.

- **Lessons for the U.S.:**

  o Protect judicial independence and media freedom as pillars of democracy.

  o Avoid political centralization by strengthening local governance and federalism.

4. Brazil (Hybrid Regime to Flawed Democracy and Back)

Brazil's democracy has oscillated between "Hybrid Regime" and "Flawed Democracy," reflecting the fragility of democratic progress in the face of political corruption and populism.

- **Corruption Scandals:**
  Political scandals, such as Operation Car Wash, undermined public trust in government institutions.

- **Polarization:**
  The rise of populist leaders exacerbated divisions, weakening democratic norms.

- **Judiciary as a Stabilizer:**
  Brazil's Supreme Court played a pivotal role in safeguarding democratic principles preventing total regression.

- **Lessons for the U.S.:**

    o Strengthen anti-corruption frameworks to restore public faith in governance.

    o Utilize a neutral arbiter to balance executive overreach.

Key Indicators of Democratic Health

Comparing these cases highlights critical factors that influence democratic performance:

1. **Electoral Integrity:**
   High-functioning democracies prioritize free, fair, and transparent elections. Gerrymandering and voter suppression, as seen in the U.S., undermine electoral integrity.

2. **Civil Liberties:**
   Protecting freedoms such as speech and assembly fosters public trust and engagement. Attacks on press freedom or the right to protest, even indirectly, erode democratic standing.

3. **Institutional Accountability:**
   Nations like Norway excel due to robust checks and balances, whereas Hungary demonstrates the consequences of weakened institutions.

4. **Cultural Cohesion:**
   Political polarization, often exacerbated by social media, poses a significant threat to democracy. South Korea's emphasis on unity contrasts sharply with the fragmentation seen in the U.S. and Brazil.

What the U.S. Can Learn

The U.S.'s classification as a "Flawed Democracy" reflects challenges common to many democracies but also points to specific areas for improvement:

1. **Address Polarization:**
   Encourage electoral reforms that reduce partisanship.

2. **Rebuild Trust in Institutions:**
   Combat misinformation and enhance transparency to counteract declining public confidence.

3. **Strengthen Democratic Norms:**
   The People's safeguards against executive overreach and judicial politicization must be prioritized.

4. **Invest in Civic Education:**
   South Korea's success demonstrates the importance of an informed citizenry. Promoting civic literacy can empower Americans to engage constructively in governance.

SECTION 1
EVENTS OF RECENT HISTORY

ANALYSIS OF 2016 ELECTION RESULTS

At the time of this writing, 2019, an analysis of the 2016 unexpected Federal election outcome leads to two broad conclusions. The conclusions are the base-line rationale for this book:

1. A significant segment of the voting public was upset with what they were seeing in the conduct of the nation's governance.

In the 2016 election, the voters took radical steps in an attempt to effect change. Their venting may have been aimed at the political class, at the non-performance of the legislative branch they have always held in poor regard, at the unimpressive economic performance of the republic over recent decades, or at the departing Presidency (with whom the defeated Democratic candidate was closely associated), or at the pitiful lack of government progress addressing matters demanding attention.

Their venting may also be traced to the general citizen's lack of financial progress in recent years and the economic anxiety that seems to be present in large segments of the population.

Readers will have their own opinions as to the reasons, but the takeaway conclusion must be that the election reflected an attempt on the part of the Voters to invoke basic change.

2. It is a reasonable conclusion the upset Voters did not trust professional politicians to carry out the needed changes. They selected the outsider, the non-politician, the "disrupter" candidate.

That those Voters would take a risk on an inexperienced candidate with a "disrupter" platform suggests that they were totally aware that the government was not functioning and were blaming the dysfunction on the political class. It also suggests that they clearly understood that *their only means of affecting change was through the ballot box, using the President and political parties as the change vehicles.*

The upset Voters saw the Trump candidacy as the only one that came anywhere close to addressing their concerns. They did not see a professional politician candidate in either political party who could be depended upon to do what they thought needed to be done.

That reasoning supports the conclusion that the target of the voters in the 2016 election was, in fact, the political class.

Those conclusions turn our focus to the system fashioned by our Framers. It was to be government "of the People, by the People and for the People." But, in designing it, the Framers left The People with only one means to affect needed change: **THE BALLOT BOX.**

The "by the People" part of the old slogan is pitifully weak, and the weakness is constitutional. In the system designed by the Framers, The People can go to the ballot box. They are allowed to pick from a political party candidate menu presented to them. That's what they can do. THAT'S ALL THEY CAN DO!

In designing government "of the People, by the People, and for the People," the Framers granted the political elite total rights to run the government and even to make changes to the controlling document that is the sole property of The People......**THE CONSTITUTION.**

THE FRAMERS LEFT THE PEOPLE WITH THE BALLOT BOX. <u>NOTHING ELSE!</u>

"Government of the People, by the People, and for the People" is a slogan that should be restated. It is, more correctly:

"GOVERNMENT OF THE PEOPLE, BY POLITICAL PARTIES, AND FOR THE POLITICAL ELITE."

POST ELECTION DEVELOPMENTS

Post-election 2016, the sole objective of the Democratic Party has become **"DESTROY TRUMP!"** One stimulant giving rise to that response is the emotional reaction of Democrats to the voter rejection of their party. Another, perhaps more important, is the fight-back impulse of swamp critters whose comfort and security are threatened by the Disrupter with his "Drain the Swamp!" slogan.

The Democratic response has been a spewing of party hatred of the person Trump and his policies and promoting the resolute belief that he must be destroyed at all costs. Comparable to a "jilted lover" he has become the living, highly visible, and hated symbol of both their rejection and the threat to their comfortable position of power.

POLITICAL REACTION TO THE TRUMP ELECTION WAS ASTONISHING

The negative reaction from Elected Persons substantiates the conclusion that the target of voter venting must have been the Political Class as a group. Trump's election as President was, surprisingly, not even wholeheartedly supported by Republican party stalwarts. **Politicians of both political parties felt very threatened by his agenda.**

The furor made brutally clear that Donald Trump was the dull ax the voters used to try to chop down the political elite cherry tree. Democrats, especially, are exhibiting all the human reactions one might expect from those who felt most threatened by the cherry tree chopping. Their undisguised emotional vindictiveness, eclipsing all sense of reason, flies in the face of the time-honored political practice of placidly accepting the People's election choices.

Decision theorists warn us to "beware of emotional responses." Emotional decisions and reactions are usually highly irrational. **The consequences of emotional decisions may not be obvious for some time,** *but they will inevitably make their appearance.*

POLARIZATION AND THE IMPOTENT LEGISLATIVE BRANCH

Developments following the 2016 election have glazed the already-solid polarization between the two political parties. The realization that the Framer-designed Legislative branch of government is in deep trouble has hit home.

Despite Republican majorities in both houses, in the four years following the 2016 election, only one major piece of legislation, tax reduction, was passed and signed into law. In the preceding eight years of the Obama administration, only one major piece of legislation became law: the Affordable Care Act.

Both of those major legislative efforts were achieved without a single support vote from the opposition party, classic "tyranny of the majority." Both implemented the basic dogma of the enacting party. In later chapters that discuss decision-making, the role party dogma plays in poor government decisions is examined at length. But even more disconcerting, those "tyranny of the majority" party votes demonstrate that the Nation's government, with the impetus of polarization, is sliding down a slippery slope, away from democracy and toward totalitarianism.

In the 2018 mid-terms the Democratic Party gained control of the House of Representatives and has evidenced the same non-performance characteristics as their predecessor Republican Party**, suggesting that the legislative malaise and inertia we observe is not party-instigated**. Rather, the political elite of both parties are focused on keeping party representatives elected and in their seats by employing similar techniques, and in the process are paying scant attention to the needs of the nation.

Intense polarization, a party-and-media propaganda-generated condition, exists without a doubt, but it is also **a symptom of other illnesses deeply imbedded in the political system**. Those illnesses will be examined in later chapters.

HOW IS THE NATION'S GOVERNANCE FUNCTIONING?

National progress since the 2016 election, mimicking the history of the predecessor Obama administration, derives from Presidential Orders. President Trump worked to fulfill his campaign promises using Orders as tools at his disposal, as did his predecessor, President Obama. **Presidential Orders that are not the implementation of legislation represent a dramatic move away from democracy. They constitute basic and fundamental authoritarian governance.**

As he pursued those, President Trump's political opposition engaged in obstructionist/attack activity: the Special Counsel appointment, vendettas, opposition to Presidential appointments, Presidential Order litigation, investigations of key personnel in the Executive branch, and finally, attempted impeachment. None of that political activity is beneficial to the Nation. It is in-fighting that serves only to harden the party divisions of a bi-polar country and diverts Elected Person focus away from their fundamental reason for existence.

The disrupter Trump has not received enthusiastic support from his own party in pursuing his campaign promises. **That fact has made it clear that the Swamp is infested by critters of both parties, an infestation best described by the monicker "the Political Elite."** It further supports the conclusion that the voters are very aware of what is happening, and that their election of Trump had fixed the political elite in their cross-hairs.

The political elite of both parties have a common vested interest. **Political elitism is an institutional phenomenon. The political elite are the royals of the "monarchy republic" form of government created by the Framers.** The Framers, in Article I, Section 8 of the Constitution, gave each House the right to "determine the Rules of its Proceedings," and Article V denied citizens any route to amend the Constitution. Those provisions gave the government a monarch's latitude and authority and eliminated true accountability to The People, who have no rights or routes to affect change.

WHERE TO LOOK FOR SOLUTIONS IN THE GOVERNMENT WASTELAND

The grim picture before us is of a government and political system within which few functions are behaving properly. The People have mentally given up hope for salvation from the two political parties, which, housing the political elite, are focused solely on pursuing strategies and tactics that reduce their personal re-election risk.

Signs are that voters are again searching for Presidential candidates exhibiting a "savior" mantle and aura in the hope that such a person can lead the country out of its governance quagmire. That was unquestionably their goal in the Trump election. **If you are a voter with one tool--- the ballot box ----you use the ballot box. That's what you have; it's the only tool available!**

But voters also know that a successful Presidential candidate, even one possessing celebrity-level credentials and a credible management background, can only achieve what "the system" will allow. Without denigrating or applauding Trump's leadership, we make the point that the political elite is well-positioned to defeat any president with a "change" agenda. The political elite hold aces!

Voters understand *the system*. **They know that all they can do is vote and hope. However, credible surveys suggest they would be amenable to a different system.**

The Constitutional plan of using the ballot box as a check-and-balance against the performance of individual legislators, and of the Legislative branch, HAS FAILED.

Although voters are using the ballot box choices available, it is not producing a solution for them. The voters will not find a "savior" leader through the political-party-focused election system. No savior leader can fix the intrenched and defective Monarchy Republic created by the Framers, or make it produce miracles.

Surveys signal the voters are searching for an answer. They are mentally prepared to consider rational proposals that address the Nation's government problems.

After all, "doing the same thing over, and over, and over again, but expecting different results" is the definition of insanity.

SECTION 2
THE STATE OF DEMOCRACY WORLD-WIDE

Analysis of breakdowns in our Republic's ability to govern itself effectively, the subject of this book, begins with a look at the state of democracy worldwide and applies that assessment of world democratic government conditions to our own situation.

Although we describe our government system as a "republic" and are offering a comparison of the conditions within world-wide democracies, that comparison is not irrational. The Framers designed and implemented a "republic," but in the ensuing years, democracy practices have overtaken and subordinated the Framer republic plan. Most citizens of our nation today refer to us as a "democracy," as most of our practices are more democratic than that of a republic.

Our governmental dysfunction is not unique. Democratic government is having difficulty in modern society world-wide. Democratic nations, large and small, are struggling. The obvious question raised is, "Is the democratic system of government failing, or is what we are observing merely the impact of other forces on it?"

The past two or three decades have ballooned electronic communication to levels never imagined. The intercommunicability of people is undoubtedly an important factor influencing their opinions about government, as well as governmental behavior.

It is interesting to note that authoritarian governments are flourishing. One might speculate that their apparent relative stability is traceable to totalitarian control over citizen thought, communication, and the repression of critical inter-personal opposition. Perhaps more important, such governments have the ability to limit what other nations know about their internal functioning, by "controlling the message." The view that such governments are flourishing may well be manufactured rather than real.

As an opinion, the tendency of democratic nations to apply simplistic solutions to their complex situations or to apply someone else's solution to "our problem" is the root cause of turmoil. Political decision-making is the Achilles Heel of the democratic system of governance. Democracy is a complex form of government so structure-of-democracy decisions are usually of the "copy-cat" variety. Politicians are not "rocket scientists" when it comes to organization and process design.

DEMOCRACY'S TRAVAILS

In a Wall Street Journal report on January 21, 2020, author Gerald F. Sieb observed, "It has become more difficult to knit together cohesive societies and governing coalitions."[2]

Sieb cites world events that signal democratic difficulty: the British government's struggle to implement Brexit, foundering for three years and through three prime ministers; Canada's problems forming a minority government; the exit of Angela Merkel in Germany and the probable collapse of her ruling coalition; the drift of India away from secular rule toward religious sectarianism; the difficulties of Israel in forming a government after multiple votes.

Sieb pinpoints as underlying causes the eroded trust in government, the rise of populism (fueling anger toward the political elite), and the splintering of democratic society by information technology.

WORLDWIDE STATISTICS

The source of the following selected status is the Democracy Index Report from the Economist Intelligence Unit, 2023 edition.[3]

The Report classifies forms of government into four categories, reported in the following table as "Percentages of Global Population."

Authoritarian	37%
Full Democracy	8%
Flawed Democracy	37%
Hybrid Regime	18%

The United States is classified as a "Flawed Democracy," ranking 30th in the group, and its performance has regressed by 4% since the previous tabulation.

Using a scale of 10, the Report rates components of the Flawed Democracy of the United States as follows:

Electoral Process and Pluralism	9.17
Functioning of Government	6.43
Political Participation	8.89
Political Culture	6.25
Civil Liberties	8.53

---

[2] "The Messy State of Democracy, Gerald F. Sieb, The Wall Street Journal January 21, 2020
[3] Economist Intelligence Unit, "Democracy Index Report 2023"

After readers have recovered from the shock of seeing that their vaunted nation and its government is classified way down the grossly unflattering segment list called "Flawed Democracy," a label that would never have entered/her mind from listening to the President speak or other general internal political commentary. Questions about "How can that be?" crowd into the mind.

A look at the scale of 10 statistics quickly reveals the reasons for the Flawed Democracy classification. They are the "Functioning of Government" rating of 6.43 out of 10 and the "Political Culture" rating of 6.25. Those produce the second shock to the reader …… the realization that the ratings are precisely what he/she would have applied based on personal observations of what is happening in the country.

And, the high marks given for Electoral Process, Political Participation, and Civil Liberties are certainly understandable, given the endless fooforaw of elections and the enjoyment by the citizens of the benevolent freedoms granted under the Bill of Rights.

All in all, those ratings look "right on the money."

GENERAL OBSERVATIONS

In a recent Pew Research Center Survey, it was determined that 51% of people in 27 countries are dissatisfied with how democracy is working for them. We are not alone!

Democracy is a very complex way to govern a Nation. Concepts generated centuries ago in democracy's infancy but still rigidly applied have long since outlived their usefulness. It is this book's position that the fixed organizations and systems utilized by democratic governments fail to perform because they poorly connect the swirling mentality of the masses of humans populating a nation with its problem resolution. The involvement of voting citizens in the affairs of their nation is grossly ill-conceived and inadequate. Politics, as practiced in most democracies, is a snarky melodrama in which villains preach and parade to create trust. Once in office, they are mostly revealed as anything other than the honorable servants they profess to be.

The decision-makers who should be guiding and involving the citizens have neither the skills nor the ethics to perform such functions. Democracies thereby become iron-clad fixtures immune to improvement or correction, left to run on their own until they "hit the wall."

Democratic government, often called "self-government," is a massive human organization. Such governments are unsuccessful if they fail to correctly involve their various components; they are successful if they do. The most common error is failing to produce high-quality decisions, making the governance irrational.

Democratic election processes are also a root of government turmoil. If democracy is failing, then the officials produced by the election systems are inadequate for the task of governing.

Government non-performance starts with election systems and those elected. **Popularity is an incredibly poor criterion for choosing hired management.**

But even the most qualified and competent elected persons will fail if the government's democratic assembly process is dysfunctional. Decision processes, required to be executed in unwieldy assemblies of huge scale, fail during the voting. Always, the quality of decisions made in government defines the quality of its performance.

Earlier, it was said, "The definition of insanity is doing the same thing over and over and over again but expecting different results." That saying neatly describes the general view of American democracy.

Comparative Analysis of Governance Systems and Entropy

Understanding Governance Through the Lens of Entropy

Entropy, the inevitable decline of organized systems into disorder, is not a phenomenon unique to the United States Constitution or its governance framework. Across history, numerous governance systems have grappled with the slow decay of their foundational structures. By examining other systems—such as the Roman Republic, the Ottoman Empire, and constitutional monarchies like the United Kingdom—we can gain valuable insights into how entropy manifests in governance and, critically, how it can be managed or mitigated.

The Fall of the Roman Republic

The Roman Republic (509–27 BCE) offers a textbook example of entropy in governance. Originally founded on principles of checks and balances, with a mixed constitution blending elements of monarchy, aristocracy, and democracy, the Republic thrived for centuries. However, as Rome expanded, systemic cracks began to emerge:

1. **Overexpansion and Administrative Overload:**
   Rome's vast territorial acquisitions outpaced its governance structures. The Republic's political systems, designed for a small city-state, struggled to manage a sprawling empire. This parallels the U.S. governance framework's challenges in adapting to the rapid expansion of modernity, population growth, and technological advancement.

2. **Erosion of Institutional Integrity:**
   Political norms, such as term limits and the sanctity of republican offices, were increasingly flouted. Figures like Sulla and Julius Caesar exploited legal loopholes to amass personal power, undermining the Republic's foundational principles. Similarly, modern critics of U.S. governance point to the erosion of norms that safeguard the balance of power among branches.

3. **Rise of Populism and Factionalism:**
   Populist leaders appealed directly to the masses, bypassing traditional republican institutions. The Gracchi brothers' reforms, while addressing economic inequality, polarized the Senate and led to violent political conflict. This mirrors the polarization in U.S. politics, where populist movements have highlighted the tension between institutional governance and direct appeals to the electorate.

Key Takeaway:
Rome's inability to adapt its governance to a larger, more complex state led to the Republic's collapse into autocracy. Without mechanisms to recalibrate its system, entropy overwhelmed the Republic's structures.

The Stagnation of the Ottoman Empire

The Ottoman Empire (1299–1922), one of history's longest-lasting empires, also struggled with entropy, particularly during its later centuries:

1. **Centralization and Decay of the Devshirme System:**
   Initially, the Ottomans thrived on an innovative administrative system, including the recruitment of talented non-Muslims into government via the devshirme system. Over time, nepotism and the loss of meritocratic principles weakened the bureaucracy. This resonates with modern concerns over bureaucratic inefficiency and the politicization of public administration in the U.S.

2. **Economic and Technological Lag:**
   While European powers industrialized, the Ottomans clung to outdated economic and military systems. Their failure to modernize administrative and fiscal policies exacerbated their decline. Similarly, the U.S. Constitution, though innovative for its time, faces increasing strain in a globalized, technological era without significant structural updates.

3. **Inability to Respond to Regional Autonomy Movements:**
   As the empire aged, regional governors and provinces sought greater autonomy. This decentralization eroded central authority, leading to internal fragmentation. In the U.S., similar tensions arise between federal and state governments, particularly on divisive issues such as healthcare, immigration, and voting rights.

Key Takeaway:
The Ottoman experience underscores the dangers of failing to modernize and adapt governance structures. Resistance to change, whether due to tradition or vested interests, accelerates entropy's impact.

The Resilience of the United Kingdom's Constitutional Monarchy

In contrast to the Roman Republic and the Ottoman Empire, the United Kingdom provides an example of resilience against entropy, largely due to its adaptability:

1. **Gradual Evolution of Governance:**
    The UK's unwritten constitution allows for continuous, incremental adjustments. Landmark developments such as the Magna Carta (1215), the Glorious Revolution (1688), and the Parliament Acts (1911, 1949) reshaped governance while maintaining stability. This flexibility contrasts with the rigidity of the U.S. Constitution's amendment process.

2. **Balance Between Tradition and Innovation:**
    While retaining symbolic traditions like the monarchy, the UK has embraced institutional reforms to adapt to modern challenges. For example, the House of Lords' power was curtailed to reflect democratic principles. The U.S. could draw lessons from this balance in updating its governance while preserving its foundational ideals.

3. **Strong Civil Institutions:**
    Independent institutions, such as the judiciary and civil service, have played a critical role in mitigating political instability. In the U.S., public trust in institutions has eroded, highlighting the need to rebuild their credibility as a counterweight to entropy.

Key Takeaway:
The UK's ability to evolve without discarding its foundational principles demonstrates the importance of flexibility and adaptability in governance. By embedding mechanisms for reform, the UK has effectively managed entropy over centuries.

Lessons for the United States

These historical case studies offer actionable insights for addressing the entropy within the U.S. governance framework:

1. **Institutional Flexibility:**
    Like the UK, the U.S. must create mechanisms for incremental constitutional and systemic reform, avoiding the pitfalls of rigidity observed in the Roman and Ottoman systems.

2. **Meritocratic Leadership:**
    To counter bureaucratic stagnation, the U.S. could adopt principles akin to the Ottoman devshirme system—emphasizing merit over political allegiance in appointments.

3. **Modernization Without Abandoning Core Values:**
   As seen in the UK, reforms should modernize governance while preserving foundational principles like checks and balances, federalism, and individual rights.

4. **Addressing Polarization:**
   Drawing from the Roman experience, fostering cross-party collaboration and depolarizing political discourse is crucial to maintaining a functional democracy.

SECTION 3
HOW WE WILL APPROACH THE ANALYSIS

Section 1 provides a summary of the political and governmental environment of the United States at this time, and Section 2 notes that democracy, as a system of government, is not flourishing world-wide and not functioning well in the United States.

We conclude that our voters understand the political and governmental environment and have decided that the problem is the Political Elite. They are attempting correction using the only tool at their disposal, the ballot box, searching for a Messiah to lead them out of the wilderness.

Sorry, folks! That route will produce no correction. The definition of "insanity" explains why.

Correction is stymied by the requirements for amending our Constitution, defined in Article V, which place amendments totally under the control of the hated Political Elite. The People are blocked from making the changes needed to correct the performance of their government, which is unassailable by citizens and boxed in a fortress controlled by the Political Elite.

Political Elite control is enshrined in our constitution. It can't be corrected by changing Presidents. The Framers positioned the inmates to run the asylum and gave them the only set of keys.

Section 2 discusses the turmoil being experienced in democracies worldwide. It concludes that the organization and processes of democracy are generally outdated and rigidly employ practices not well conceived and not based on proven organizational management principles. Political party management is a force common to such governments, and contention is the usual assembly atmosphere.

Many a democratic nation is finding that broadly accepted democratic organizations and concepts borrowed from other nations do not produce good government.

HOW WE WILL APPROACH THE ANALYSIS OF OUR CONSTITUTIONAL SYSTEM

There is no magic wand to create comprehension, nor is there a fairy godmother to wave the wand. Instead, solutions will have to be developed the hard way by ordinary humans, using whatever tools and resources they have available.

The most important tool at our disposal is **the five functions of ownership/management**, which are "Plan, Organize, Staff, Direct and Control." Those responsibilities were first published in the 1950s and establish the foundation of sound reasoning whenever analysis of defects in organizations and human systems is undertaken.[4]

Although labeled the "five functions of management," they are more accurately "the five functions of ownership." '" Management "is composed of persons hired by owners to conduct management activities on their behalf and to whom authority is delegated. Owners make a conscious decision to delegate to their hired management a defined portion of their five ownership obligatory functions. In the process, they delegate to management their authority to carry out specified activities on the owner's behalf.

Rational owners retain unto themselves the functions critical to determining the outcome, functions they dare not delegate, including their right to modify any arrangement within the organization at any time.

The Framers of our Constitution delegated all powers to the government. The Framers were well aware that the owners of the Republic were The People. Nonetheless, they gave to the government all powers, including those that must always remain the sole responsibility of the nation's owners, The People. The Framers failed to treat the country's stake-holders fairly or properly. They failed to rationally and ethically divide the five critical functions between The People and their Hired Management.

Government in our Nation is conducted by elected persons who are managers *hired by The People.* Our hired management operates under constitutional instructions that were implied to be those of The People but which were, in fact, the terms of a bargain between the then-existing Federal Government and the thirteen states. The People apparently did not individually vote to approve the constitution, the aforementioned bargain. The constitution's provisions were conceived and written by those who would, without question, become the hired management in the new government to be created. **If ever there was a conflict of interest, that was most certainly a critical one.**

---

[4] Koontz, Harold, and O'Donnell, Cyril.: Principles of Management" (1959)

Much of our government's non-performance is traceable to the Framers' failure to delineate between the rights and duties of the owners of the Nation, The People, and the role and function of their hired management.

The Framers gave the government total authority to do all things necessary to run the country and left The People with only the right to vote, a pitifully weak sop. Readers are reminded that The People are the owners of the nation, and that elected government is nothing more than a collection of hired management that is supposed to serve them. The People were totally excluded from governance participation by giving them no right to change government form or function through amendment of the constitution. That, in turn, vested total control over the government in the hired management, which has been identified as the root cause of the nation's travails.

THE NATION IS OWNED BY THE PEOPLE

We will work from the basic documented truth that the Nation is owned by The People, first stated in the Declaration of Independence, second paragraph:

> "That whenever any Form of Government becomes destructive of these ends, it is the Right of the People to alter or to abolish it, and to institute new Government, laying its foundation on such principles and organizing its powers in such form, as to them shall seem most likely to affect their Safety and Happiness."

The Introduction to the Constitution of the United States contains language that firmly states The People ordained and established the constitution.

Although not specifically stated as such in any constitutional documents, there is no conclusion to be reached other than that the Elected Persons who conduct government are management hired by The People. Citizens are not conditioned to think that way. We are trained to be subservient to government, so viewing elected persons as "hired management" is a strange concept for us.

But as The People, that great body of citizens who own the United States, we must don the Owner's hat and shoulder the Owner's responsibilities. That is the first and most fundamental act of self-government. If The People are not willing to shoulder their Owner's duties, **they are, by definition, incapable of self-government.**

It also means that The People, in managing their Nation, must become accustomed to viewing and treating elected officials as what they truly are……. "HIRED MANAGEMENT!" To be steeled mentally to perform their owner's duties, The People will have to change their view of, and treatment of, those elected to government. Rather

than being placid and subservient party supporters, The People must become demanding.

For emphasis and reinforcement, throughout this Book, we will capitalize the name of the Nation's owners whenever the term is used: **The People**!

MANAGEMENT THEORY AND PRACTICE WILL BE HEAVILY EMPLOYED

Throughout, the five functions of management/owners will be referred to in tiresome repetition. The best way to evaluate the non-performance in an organization is by determining which of the five functions are not performing. When that has been done, the path to a solution usually reveals itself.

We will also use other time-honored principles of management, such as the rules of delegation, the essential balance between authority and responsibility, and the fundamentals of decision theory. The principles and processes of strategic planning, which is a foundation for a rational management decision-making structure, will be brought to bear wherever appropriate. None of those are the creations of this author. Persons who have spent time in management and pursued its vagaries are very familiar with them.

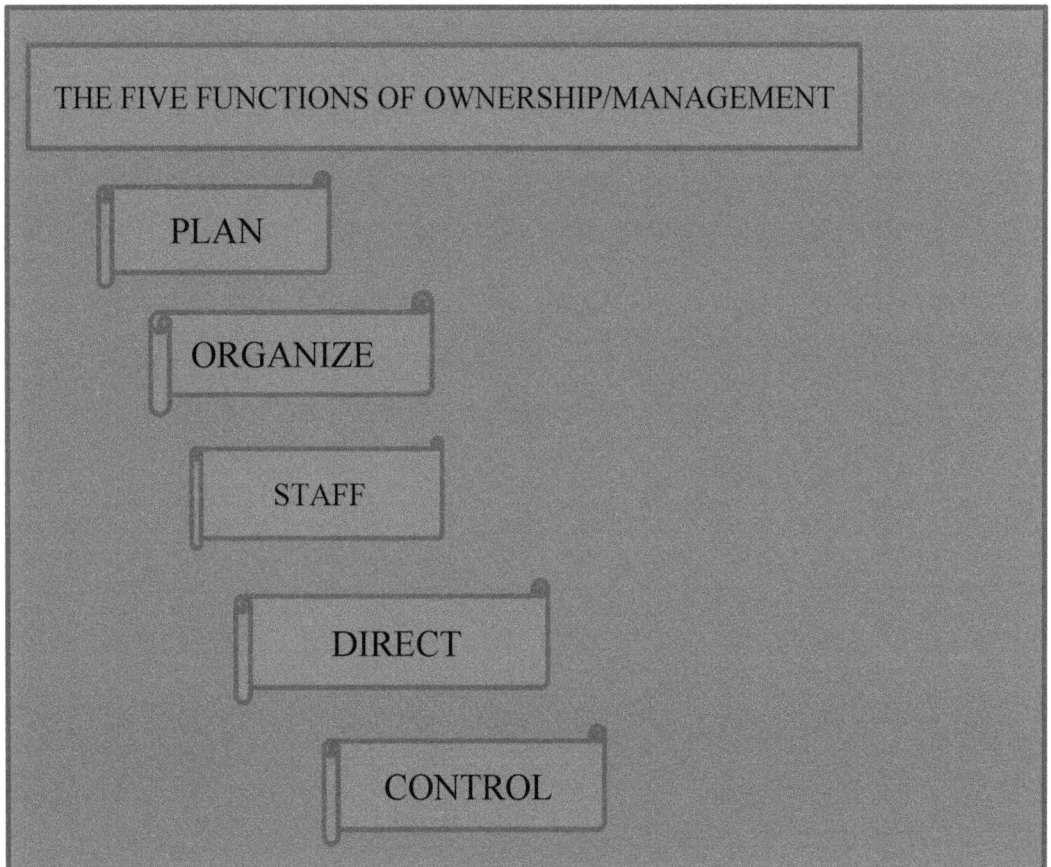

THE FIVE FUNCTIONS OF OWNERSHIP/MANAGEMENT

PLAN

ORGANIZE

STAFF

DIRECT

CONTROL

CHAPTER 2

> ## "TRUST"
>
> CONTENT:
>
> SECTION 1: TRUST, THE DEMOCRACY GLUE
>
> SECTION 2: TRUST IN THE U.S. GOVERNMENT
>
> SECTION 3: SOLUTIONS FOR OUR NATION'S TRUST DEFICIENCY

FOREWORD

Politicians, from the very beginning, strove to define the fundamental attributes of our nation's unique system of government. All manner of terms and descriptions have been "run up the flagpole," and some have become imbedded in our everyday civic lexicon.

The Declaration of Independence leads off with a discussion regarding the "unalienable rights" of Life, Liberty, and the Pursuit of Happiness. The Constitution talks about Justice, Tranquility, and the Blessings of Liberty. We call the First Amendment the "Bill of Rights" because of our pride in the Freedoms it bestows upon the citizens. Even the least-informed among us talks proudly about "the right to speak your mind out."

Democracy requires a common agreement on fundamental values that define "what we stand for," the values upon which self-government is based. Those values underlie the trust upon which the "government of the People, by the People, and for the People" must be anchored. Without agreement on fundamental values, successful self-government is unlikely.

As we watch our country becoming increasingly divisive and incoherent, we get the feeling that some essential ingredient was never firmly anchored in place or new ingredients have been introduced that degrade those that were our foundation. Something vital is clearly missing, something more fundamental and important than all of the beliefs and values we regularly haul out for patriotic display.

Could it be the Founders and Framers missed something truly important?
You bet they did! It is trust that ingredient essential to "government by the people," a government reliant on the morals and ethics of the nation's citizens, and a government built on the principle of our nation's citizens working together.

SECTION 1
TRUST, THE DEMOCRACY GLUE

ACHIEVING TRUST, DESPITE A BROADLY DIVERSIFIED POPULATION

A great leap of faith was taken when our nation decided to install a republic system of the national government to bind together the people of the then-existing thirteen states. The nation bet that it could meet the governmental objectives by building and maintaining national cohesion despite a widely diverse citizenry.

Countless languages, religious faiths, levels of education, and understanding were then present in regions of varying economic foundations. There existed a wide range of ethnicities, different ways of making a living, and a plethora of other diversity factors. To build self-government and maintain a democratic nation on such a human foundation, a strong common ground of values and beliefs was needed.

On the other side of the coin, there were independent nation needs that begged for a strong common ground, needs that draw people together in support of self-government, but that aren't classified as "values and beliefs."

For example, our nation is geographically remote from the rest of the world, and other nations aren't always friendly, creating a common need for defense. Cohesion against the rest of the world in a variety of commercial situations, trade, or law is another common ground. At the time of Confederation, America was in the process of violent separation from its mother country, Britain. Out of that turmoil blossomed a pervasive hatred of monarchies and widespread distrust of the goals of great powers. That old tribal instinct came into play, the urge to gather in force of numbers, displaying an "all-of-us-together" mentality.

But still, our nation's body of citizens contained a multitude more differences than similarities.

TRUST IS THE FOUNDATION OF CIVILIZED SOCIETY

Civilized society came into being when groups of individuals submitted to commonly-agreed-upon rules. An individual must believe that others will abide by the prevailing rules before he/she will be willing to associate with them. That belief condition is called "trust."

As civilized societies advanced and governments were established, society's accepted rules were codified into law and enforced with misbehavior penalties. There was common recognition that some would not willingly comply, but there was also faith that those could, and would, be dealt with by the remainder. Democratic governments sprang out of the "trust" that is the basis for civilized society.

Author Thomas G. West writes, "Because all men are created equal, just government can only be founded on the unanimous consent of individuals who want to protect their rights, **which are insecure outside of civil society.**"[5]

THE TRUST REQUIREMENTS ARE HONESTY, DEPENDABILITY, AND TRUTHFULNESS

Trust is a summary condition, a positive conclusion about others built on an assessment of the trust requirements. **The trust requirements are honesty, dependability, and truthfulness**.

Other requirements may be added, but those three are fundamental. Absent any one of those requirements, we do not trust others. For trust to be present, all three must be rated positively.

Forthcoming Chapter 17, which discusses the Freedoms granted in the Bill of Rights, observes that the Framers, supporting 100% unfettered delegation of freedoms to The People, must have had immense faith in the citizen ethics and morality of their time. It is reasonable to assume that "ethics and morality" were the very same honesty, dependability, and truthfulness stated to be the basis for trust, magnified by an individual's definition of morality.

Our nation's level of trust has ebbed in the 250 past years because the components of trust, "honesty, dependability, and truthfulness," have diminished in society.

TRUST IS A FUNDAMENTAL REQUIREMENT FOR DEMOCRACY

Trust is unimportant in authoritarian governments that rule by force, but absolutely critical for democratic governments whose power flows from the consent of the governed. It is not an overstatement to say that "trust" is the glue that holds democratic society together.

A "leap of faith" was taken that generally-accepted civilized societal rules could be expanded to become the basis for self-rule democratic government and that citizens would willingly submit to the rule of such a government. Freedom, a foundational social strategy of our nation, derives from the belief that the factors comprising the "trust" requirement (honesty, dependability, and truthfulness) predominate among the people. Security is the cornerstone foundational requirement for freedom. Security is the conviction that others in society will not harm the individual.

---

[5] West, Thomas G. "The Political Theory of the American Founding"

The government is organized to administer the affairs of a nation. Democratic self-government is a complex process with many working parts. It is daily subjected to the pressures and forces generated out of human activity conducted within the nation's boundaries. **Democratic government is only as successful as its conceptual framework will permit, and trust in it will endure only as long as it functions as intended**.

It is interesting and sad that the Framers did not highlight the fundamental requirement of "trust" in the Constitution. In personal statements outside of the Constitution, they often talked about that basic foundation but failed to inscribe it in our founding document.

For example, John Adams opined: "Our Constitution was made only for a moral and religious people. It is wholly inadequate to the government of any other."

Benjamin Franklin concurred: "Only a virtuous people are capable of freedom."

INTERPERSONAL TRUST

So, our form of democratic government could only function to govern a "virtuous" people. The Framer delegation of freedoms to citizens in Amendment 1, the Bill of Rights, has been previously noted as reflecting the apparent Framer belief that the level of morals and ethics present in the society of that time justified granting a high level of individual freedom.

A democratic government based on freedom cannot succeed if trust among the citizenry is not in place. Self-government is built on the principle that the needs of all are superior to the needs of the individual. It requires a conviction that "the right values," as principles of government, can be developed that will be accepted as common ground for all citizens to "get behind and support."

But most of all, democracy requires a belief that fellow citizens are basically dependable, good people who will work together in self-government for the common interest, and who will do what is necessary to make the system work. Our common term, "dependable good people," would seem to be a way of saying, "We trust each other."

The foundation for democratic self-government is trust in other people, a fundamental belief in our fellow citizens. If citizens together create a democratic government, it must be based on "trust." If trust diminishes to the level of "inadequate," force will inevitably become the means of achieving agreement.

The low level of "trust" evident among citizens today signals that the freedoms delegated by the Bill of Rights no longer rest on that essential foundation.

SECTION 2
TRUST IN THE U.S. GOVERNMENT

According to Kevin Vallier's Dec. 19, 2020, article in The Wall Street Journal entitled "Why Are Americans So Distrustful of Each Other?[6]"

"The U.S. is the only established democracy to see a major decline in social trust. In other nations, the trend was in the opposite direction. From 1998 to 2014, **social trust increased in Sweden from 56.5% to 67%, in Australia from 40% to 54%, and in Germany from 32% to 42%. Meanwhile, the U.S. is becoming more like Brazil, where trust is around 5%.**"

He further states, "In the early 1970s, half of Americans said that most people can be trusted. Today, that figure is less than one-third."

Vallier explores several politically popular causes of distrust and concludes that, while those may impact trust levels, they are not root causes. He provides the following summation:

"If the decline in social trust in the U.S. can't be fully explained by corruption, ethnic diversity, or economic inequality, what is driving it? One likely candidate is political polarization, which hasn't been as well studied as those other factors. Some social scientists are convinced that polarization increases political distrust, and it may play a role in increasing social distrust too."

This book's comments pinpoint efforts to promote racial tension as a currently employed attack strategy to diminish Trust. Evidences of authority (police, the court system) are also under organized attack. Elsewhere in this book, the alliance between the Media and the Political parties for the purpose of totalitarian-type mind control has been identified as another major cause of diminished trust. **It is clear that a multi-pronged totalitarian effort is under way to erode the trust underpinnings so vital to our democracy.**

The old bogeyman, entropy, has worked its degenerative effect on the ethics and morals of our Nation's population. We know that is true merely by comparing the "Puritan" ethics of the 1700s with the "woke" ethics of the 2000s.

The need for a strong moral and ethical foundation extends well beyond the realm of government and democracy. It is the essential foundation for a thriving society. **Ethics and morals are the foundation upon which sound interpersonal and business relationships are based.**

---

[6] Kevin Vallier, Dec. 19, 2020 article in The Wall Street Journal." Why are Americans so Distrustful of each other?"

Given that The People do not trust their government, do not trust many of the institutions operating within their self-governed nation, and do not trust the opposing political party, it is unlikely that the **current form of government** can survive in our nation.

The rising incidence of social disorder, disrespect for authority, and disrespect for government among the citizens/owners of the Nation on the one hand, and the lack of ethics of many in government, its slide toward totalitarianism, its polarization, and the underhanded behavior of its political party/media propaganda machine on the other hand, have accelerated mistrust in recent years.

The incidence of conditions such as those described is likely to accelerate further as the ethical foundations necessary for self-government continue to break down.

Fortune Magazine devoted its April/May 2021 issue entitled "Trust and Consequences: Why It's Time for a New Era of Accountability in Business" to discussions on the subject of trust, stating that widespread concern about the subject is present among citizens.[7] In a companion article, author Matt Heimer, "Moment of Truth: Why Accountability Matters More than Ever," quotes the following statistics attributed to the Edelman Trust Barometer:[8]

> Percentage of Americans who trust their own employer: 72%
> Percentage of Americans who trust business in general: 54%
> Percentage of Americans who agree that business leaders
> are purposely trying to mislead people: 56%

Those are not reassuring statistics. Ill-advised recent moves by businesses to take public political positions will further damage the public's opinion of their trustworthiness. In doing that, businesses classify themselves as "political factions," thereby cloaking themselves in the trust reputation of the political party with which they have aligned. The reputation of a business that walks that path is not likely to be retained, let alone be enhanced.

If it has not fully evaporated, the trust of institutions and authority so essential to self-government today in our nation is perhaps best described as nothing more than "a thin mist." The logic of working together has dissipated, wilting under relentless attack.

---

[7] Fortune Magazine April/May 2021 Issue. "Trust and Consequences."
[8] Matt Heimer, "Moment of Truth: Why Accountability Matters More than Ever," Fortune April/May 2021 Issue.

2018 Pew Research Center Survey	
WIDELY SUPPORTED DEMOCRATIC VALUES	% of Americans Who Say "Describes the Country Very Well"
Republicans and Democrats work together on issues	19%
Elected Officials face serious consequences for misconduct	30%
Campaign contributions do not lead to greater Political Influence	26%
Gov't is open and transparent	30%
News Organizations do not favor a party	30%
Judges are not influenced by political parties	43%
Rights and freedoms of all people are respected	47%
Tone of Political Debate is respectful	25%
News Organizations are independent of government	43%
Everyone has an equal opportunity to succeed	52%
People agree on basic facts even if they disagree on politics	34%
Gov't policies reflect views of most Americans	36%
Views of those not in the majority on issues are respected	40%
Balance of power between gov't branches	55%
People are free to peacefully protest	73%
Military leadership does not publicly support a party	60%

The question is, "What is the current level of trust in government in the United States?" To answer that, we will utilize the above-displayed 2018 Pew Research Center survey of Widely Supported Democratic Values.[9] **60% to 84% of Americans say the values employed in that survey are "Very Important."**

The survey provides opinion research on a range of "Widely-Supported Democratic Values" selected by the survey group. **Even if those are not the best selection in the opinion of individual readers or deemed by them to be the most important, they support a general conclusion that Elected Officials do not reflect the Nation's values.**

That same Pew Research Center survey states, "Views of Congress remain extremely negative: Two-thirds of Americans say they have an unfavorable view of Congress, compared with 30% saying their view is favorable." The unfavorable public view of Congress has been persistent in the 2000s to date.

Those data make it clear that citizens exhibit a high level of distrust of their Elected Officials, which must be a wake-up call to any person evaluating our self-government.

---

[9] Pew Research Center April 2018 "The Public, the Political System and American Democracy"

But what must be a matter of even greater concern is that citizen mistrust is not just as narrow as Congress. The mistrust extends to most everything associated with our system of government.

WHY IS THE GOVERNMENT FAILING TO MEET THE TRUST STANDARD?

Trust is a critical ingredient in successful self-government, the glue that holds the pieces together. The requirement that citizens trust the government they have created is fundamental. **Failing to trust what was created is an acknowledgment that the creation effort is a failure.**

When trust evaporates, the logic of working together for the common good evaporates with it. Dissention sets in. That neatly summarizes our current situation. The low level of trust among citizens, between political parties, and our government signals that the glue that holds democracy together is badly fractured, a condition that must be addressed, or our nation's government could collapse.

Congress consistently fails to meet the fundamental requirement of "trustworthy." Citizens have very little respect for Congress. It seems to be the centerpiece of government mistrust.

> Paul Bedard, Washington Secrets Columnist, in a Jan. 6, 2020 article, quotes a Gallup survey showing that only 12% of Americans rank ethics and honesty of House Lawmakers as "high.**" In that survey, the only occupation ranked lower was car salespeople.**

Our Constitution imposes no moral or ethical standards on citizens or government, nor does it prioritize such values. By taking no position, our base document leaves our citizenry without enshrined direction concerning the primary factor upon which self-government is dependent. **There is a critical relationship between the morals and ethics prevalent in society and the level of trust present in the nation.**

Could it be that the Beverly Hills people are correct when they quote their old business saying, "A fish stinks from the head?" Could it be that the behavior and values of our elected persons have been accepted by the citizenry as "appropriate" and worthy of copying? Probably not, given the low respect citizens have for Congress. It is unlikely that citizens would copy the behavior of members of Congress.

Under our Constitutional provisions, citizens may decide whether or not to be moral and ethical. Morals and ethics are thus deemed to be a matter of individual choice, a "freedom," *rather than a fundamental requirement for effective self-government, an obligation of citizenship, or the foundation for a happy and secure society.*

There is a positive side. At least the Framers did not consider the "freedom to be immoral or unethical" of sufficient importance to warrant its inclusion in the Bill of Rights, along with Freedom of Speech and the rest.

We can never know what would be the nation's ethical and moral standards today had the constitution strongly emphasized the importance of such values and tied their importance to the success of our form of government. Given citizen knowledge of and support for other values enshrined in the constitution, one can reasonably conclude that had they been included as constitutional standards, the morals and ethics of our nation would largely reflect those standards. The impact the Constitution has on citizens is remarkable.

LACK OF TRUST IN GOVERNMENT REFLECTS CITIZEN "GUT FEELING" AND LOW COMPREHENSION

Trust is to democracy what breathing is to a human. Smooth and regular, we know the human is alive and well. Absent or ragged, the human is dead or close to it.

Lack of trust in government is a "vital sign" that should attract citizen attention, like the wail of an ambulance.

And yet, it does not! American citizens bitch about government but repeatedly vote for the same people and the same parties at the ballot box. It is almost as if their attitude is, "It's not my problem."

Citizen behavior signals that they view voting as a right of citizenship, a patriotic duty, and reject the idea that they have any other responsibility. The follow-on conclusion is citizens haven't thought about their true obligations under "self-government" or "government of the people, by the people, and for the people." There is a major disconnect between general citizen attitudes and true reality, and that disconnect is not surfacing on party platforms.

Our citizens behave like automatons. They have been very well role-trained by their political party and the media! Most citizens display no alarm about their lack of trust in government. Mistrust of government has been there "forever." It is suspected that citizens focus their mistrust on "politicians," who they see as having a set of morals and ethics different from their own. **But the new ones they elect are party members, comic-strip repetitions of the ones they elected before!**

This unsatisfying analysis tells us that the political organization and environment are so complex the average citizen really doesn't understand much about it. They are voting on quick-and-dirty "gut feelings" derived from a little bit of information.

The People know something's wrong, don't like a lot of what they see happening, and are disgusted with the government, but all they can do is vote. So, bitching is about the only other thing left, and they are certainly doing that. Our political system demonstrates no ability to identify and find a solution for such problems. Citizens are waiting around for somebody to suggest something.

DO THE ELECTED PERSONS GENERATED BY OUR ELECTION-BASED "STAFFING" SYSTEM PRODUCE THE MISTRUST PROBLEM?

If citizens associate their mistrust of government with the politicians being elected to the legislative branches, and they do, that topic is worthy of some discussion.

The People have no direct control over party candidate selection, and their election decisions are distorted by the strong influence of political parties, which are the elephant in every precinct election room. Every political candidate's total loyalty is dedicated to his/her party sponsor. Regardless of what candidates say, they have forever been willing to put their party's interest ahead of the interest of the nation. **Political candidates are self-promoters who fit neatly into the role that politics requires of them.**

Parsed from Jennifer Senior's article "Maybe Congress Needs More People from the College of Hard Knocks"[10] is the following:

"According to the Congressional Research Service, more than one-third of the House and one-half of the Senate have law degrees." *Citizens do not generally regard lawyers as paragons of virtue.[11]*

Eight senators and 42 House members have doctoral degrees. All senators and 95% of House members have a bachelor's degree.

"A kite-string of initials behind the name does not improve the performance of an elected person. There doesn't seem to be any correlation between good government and educational attainment." [12]

The educational profile of House and Senate members does not match the educational profile of citizens as a group. And yet, with all that education, elected persons are not competent to produce good government. Is it any wonder they are viewed as a "political elite" and that government is viewed as inept? **The People look at Congress and see a privileged political class: "Oh, they're all in their ivory tower; they don't care about us."[13]**

This Section began with the heading question, "Do Elected Persons generated by Our Government's staffing" System Produce the Mistrust Problem?" and followed with commentary regarding election system performance. Are we electing people who are total

---

[10]Jennifer Senior, "Maybe Congress Needs More People from the College of Hard Knocks," Article Las Vegas Review Journal Dec. 26, 2020
[11] Author observation.
[12] Jennifer Senior
[13] Jennifer Senior

misfits for the tasks that must be performed? Or, is it possible politicians such as those we are now electing could produce good government if they were properly managed, directed, and controlled and denied the ability to engage in self-serving actions?

The question restated: "Is the mistrust problem the result of what our election system produces, or is it a Congress inside-management problem?

REASON SUGGESTS IT'S A CONGRESS INSIDE-MANAGEMENT PROBLEM

It was discussed earlier that education levels among elected persons are very high. Elected persons are generally intelligent. **There is no reason to believe that such persons could not perform in an organized, directed, and controlled environment.**

The lack of such an environment in the Houses of Congress results from the Framer error of constitutionally granting the two Houses the right to set their own "rules of proceeding." Mistrust of Congress is the general citizen assessment of those two bodies, not of the persons that have been elected. The answer to the mistrust source question is "It's a Congress inside-management problem," traceable back to that highly inappropriate constitutional provision, the Framer self-interest that generated it, and the House leadership self-interest that continues it.

> Political parties in assembly-dominant positions, as permitted by the Framer error, create the inside-management problem. Under proper direction, competent supervision, and operating under an appropriate set of rules, **it is *highly probable*** that the existing House members could be managed to produce acceptable results, even given the type of person the election system is producing.

That is not to say that the present profile of elected persons is our best choice. That issue will have to be addressed sooner rather than later. **However, eliminating Congress' authority to set its "Rules of Proceedings" is the critical action necessary to dramatically improve elected body performance. Improved Congressional performance will, in turn, go a long way to lowering the level of mistrust.**

CONGRESS HAS ALL AUTHORITY NEEDED TO REVERSE THE GOVERNMENT TRUST DEFICIENCY

Probably the most damning aspect of government trust emerges from considering what each house chooses as its focus. The Framers gave the two houses carte blanche to manage themselves and everything in sight, which allowed them to unilaterally decide where they place their focus and spend their time.

Government has the power to do most everything. The People, however, expect it to focus on important issues affecting the nation and its citizens. Not only does it have the power, but dealing with the important issues affecting the nation and its citizens is its reason for existence. **It has the power and the duty to eliminate its own "Trust" problem. The fact that it has chosen not to do so must be laid at the feet of its conflicted self-management.**

It is suspected a significant percentage of elected persons blame the lack of trust in government on "voter ignorance." If the lack of trust emanates from voters who "just don't understand," why would the government spend time trying to solve the trust issue?

Elected persons ignore the bad opinion voters have of them, have reconciled themselves to the notion that public opinion of Congress will continue to be low, and have decided not to be concerned. **Their lack of panic stems directly from the reality that all the voters can do is reject them at the ballot box.** *And at a 90% re-election rate, why worry?*

Lack of trust in government stems from voter realization that government is just not performing the functions that are its reason for existence.

And government is not performing the functions that are its reason for existence because of its realization that the Voters can't do anything about it!

Although most of the lack of trust stems from the Constitution's provision "Each House may determine the Rules of its Proceedings," Article 1, Section 5, second paragraph, an apparently large segment of voters disapprove of making changes to the document to correct!

Wake up, Citizens!

SECTION 3
SOLUTION PROPOSALS FOR OUR NATION'S "TRUST" DEFICIENCY

This Chapter makes clear that there was, truly, a critical ingredient missing in the Constitution!

A clear discussion about the critical relationship between "Morals and Ethics" and "Trust" sets the stage. The critical missing ingredient is a Constitutional position establishing a moral and ethical basis for the nation and its people, and an equally firm and clear statement regarding the importance of Trust in democratic self-government.

With apologies to readers, reference will be made here to proposed new Constitutional bodies called the Guardians of the Constitution and the Constitutional Convention. Those proposed bodies won't be examined in detail until somewhat later in this Book. Solutions to the Trust issue under discussion here require that the proposed role of those new bodies be introduced.

Following are important tasks associated with establishing morals and ethics as The People's intended foundation for society and self-government.

A. ESTABLISH MORALS AND ETHICS AS THE BASIC FOUNDATION FOR SELF-GOVERNMENT

If our nation intends to succeed in self-government, and if strong morals and ethics among citizens are fundamental to self-government's success, then morals and ethics must become the foundation for the nation's value system. Citizens have historically responded to clear Constitutional direction.

That "Direction," from the citizens to the nation, is merely a beginning. It must be made real (fulfilling the "Organize" responsibility of the nation's owners) by the implementation of changes to the law respecting the Authority system, the education system, the judicial system, the Media, and other national functions through which constitutional values are communicated to The People, instituted and maintained.

Reinforcement can be aided greatly by regularly focusing public attention on statistical assessments of the nation's progress (the "Direct" and "Control" responsibilities of the nation's owners), which will also serve as performance measurements for government bodies and for elected persons performance incentive payments.

B. IMPOSE THE HIGHEST MORAL AND ETHICS STANDARDS ON ELECTED PERSONS, NON-ELECTED SOCIETAL LEADERS AND CONSTITUTIONAL OFFICERS

The highest performance standards for morals and ethics, with commensurate penalties, must start with the imposition of standards on the nation's elected persons and civic leaders. Those who hold themselves forth as being worthy of an elected position or are leading citizens occupying positions of stature must, at all times and in all situations, be accountable for their moral and ethical behavior. "Positive example" from those viewed as, or consider themselves, to be "leaders" is a fundamental requirement. Poor past examples have become major contributors to society's moral and ethical decline, with a corollary negative impact on self-government.

It is proposed that abiding by moral and ethical standards in leadership positions be raised constitutionally to high levels, with violations considered Treason against the nation. Such a course makes it necessary that determinations regarding treasonous acts be removed from government politics and media gossip and elevated to the constitutional butt-kicking level.

C. TRUST IN GOVERNMENT MUST BE INDEPENDENTLY RATED AND APPROPRIATE ACTIONS TAKEN

Given that The People do not trust their government or the opposing political party and do not trust many of the institutions operating within their self-governed nation, it is unlikely that our Democratic Republic can survive in its current form. The incidence of social disorder, disrespect for authority, and disrespect for government among the citizens/owners of the Nation on the one hand, and the lack of ethics in government, its slide toward totalitarianism, and the underhanded dealings of its political party/media propaganda machine, on the other hand, have accelerated in recent years. Unless put in check, the rate of incidence is likely to accelerate further as the ethical foundations of the nation continue to crumble.

The People should measure trust in government deliberately and methodically, with the intent of establishing trust measurement as a principal evaluation of government effectiveness. Obviously, the measurements would pinpoint segments of government that are causing problems for the purpose of enforcing accountability and identifying organizations needing correction, but the main purpose is to provide performance information to the voters. The measurements should provide input to the Authority structure for planning decisions about how to improve self-government.

It is proposed that every two years, an independent firm be contracted by the Guardians to conduct a survey of citizens regarding trust in government. The survey

results would be communicated to The People as a part of developing a well-informed voter group.

This is one of those critical measurements that should produce no reward for expected good performance but generate a brutal reaction to bad performance. For example, whenever such a survey finds the trust level falling below some high-standard percentage, a purge of elected officials should be Constitutionally launched.

D. INCREASING CRIME RATES IN VARIOUS CITIES SIGNAL MANY STATE AND LOCAL GOVERNMENTS ARE PROBABLY DYSFUNCTIONAL

The Framers delegated 100% freedom and significant fundamental rights to citizens based upon their faith in the morals and ethics prevalent in the society of their time, which was then rated "virtuous." They understood that the self-governance model they created could only succeed with the existence of a "virtuous" citizenry. **The Framers, however, failed to establish a constitutional focus on the virtuosity of The People.**

The level of lawlessness (a prominent measure of changes in virtuosity) in the nation varies from city to city. It is highly probable that national statistics of morals and ethics are negatively skewed by the performance of ten or so cities. Applying the "a fish stinks from the head" business metaphor; one must conclude the level of citizen morals and ethics directly reflects the quality of government.

There is, further, a high probability that governments at the city level suffer from dysfunctionality of the same type and nature as that which afflicts the federal government. If true, that would indicate ineffective charter documents and a lack of functioning accountability.

Political party activities and self-interest are distracting such governments and rendering them incapable. It further suggests that in such cities, local citizens have a weak path of correction and that the ballot box is dysfunctional.

The following is proposed:

1. The Constitution should include provisions that ensure state and local governments govern in a manner that produces a moral and ethical citizenry. **State and local government dysfunction cannot be permitted to degrade national performance.**

2. Negative achievement in one locality negatively affects many other components of the nation and its governance. Always, the cause is dysfunctional local government, and the cause of that is lack of enforcement of accountability. But despite that, there is no constitutional provision for Federal intervention.

3. This book takes the position that The People have a responsibility to ensure that state and local governments function properly. The quality of state and local government should be constitutionally made the operating responsibility of the Federal Government to ensure conformance to constitutional standards.

4. The performance of state and local government should be measured by independent surveys. Two years of selected crime rates, court and incarceration statistics, homeless rates, traffic violations, school educational achievements, and other important measures are needed. Events of civil disorder, which are the waving flags of ineffective government, should receive special attention. The surveys would be carried out under the direction of the Federal Government and reported to The People.

5. State and local governments evidencing poor results would then receive a review of charter documents to isolate weaknesses and arrangements made for new charters to be written, providing the means for citizens to enforce a broad range of accountability measures on local government.

The Federal Government should be accorded crisis-level authority to discharge local elected politicians, call new elections, and institute changes emulating those established Federally. Law enforcement in such cities would be Federally reinforced. Federal authorities would guide all democratic functions of the city until correction is achieved.

It is much more efficient and productive to attack the national morals and ethics problem in small pieces, jurisdiction by jurisdiction than to bet everything on a nationwide fix. The People must recognize that not all states and cities are capable of self-government, and may not be competent to overcome a lack of morals and ethics prevalent among citizens.

E. CREATE A MORALS AND ETHICS SCORE SYSTEM TO DISPLAY CITIZEN BEHAVIOR FOR PUBLIC USE

Unacceptable moral and ethical behavior among citizens reflects a lack of clear standards and the means for enforcing personal accountability.

If The People decide that moral and ethical improvement is required for the continuation of American self-government, they then must fulfill their "direct" and "control" responsibilities. A moral and ethical citizenry is there for the taking. Required is an action plan and the will of The People.

The key to improved moral and ethical behavior is accountability. Establishing accountability requires credible public information regarding individual behavior. Presently, there is little information available to the public as to which citizens are not moral or ethical, and what has been their objectionable behavior. There is no penalty for being immoral or unethical unless the actions happen to also be "illegal." In order to establish accountability, it is necessary for the public to know who has not met standards and what standards have been violated.

Today, our democracy grants great freedom with very limited or no personal accountability. That underlies disreputable citizen behavior and America's poor performance in achieving ethical improvement from those incarcerated for crime. Our nation usually does not publicly expose individuals who commit immoral or unethical acts unless they are illegal. Immoral and unethical people have the ability to remain incognito, seamlessly melded into the population. And, because a person is not likely to be publicly exposed for immoral or unethical acts, no incentive exists for that person to change behavior. As such persons proceed through life, immoral and unethical acts frequently balloon to egregious criminal behavior.

The lack of morals and ethics among the population is the "root cause" of anti-societal and trust-destroying human behavior. Public records exist of acts that reach law enforcement or the court system, but unless an investigator has great capability and time, such acts are not likely to be revealed to the public. Following are some examples:

1. Participation in public assemblies that degenerate into mob violence and illegal behavior under the guise of the "right to peaceably assemble."
2. Ostensibly non-violent crimes, such as the production and sale of narcotics, prostitution, thievery, inappropriate internet behavior, outright illegal activity, fraud, etc.
3. Violent behavior, crimes, and organized crime activity, including gun-based.
4. Unsafe and reckless driving habits and law violations such as speeding and intoxication.
5. Engagement in various forms of monetary larceny.
6. Legal actions of all kinds, including enforcement of penalties for moral and ethical lapses.

What is needed is a public record of all moral and ethical violations of individual citizens, public records readily available to all that do not result in criminal conviction.

Fortunately, there exists, in the commercial practice of the nation, a model that can be copied to collect and report citizen morals and ethics for accountability purposes. As imperfect as it is, the FICO credit scoring system has reduced credit granting to mathematical precision based upon organized and reliable tabulation and reporting of individual credit performance. Its existence has beneficially impacted the credit behavior of the public. The nation's financial system successfully relies on the credit scoring system to guide its allocation of consumer credit, and individuals utilize it to aid personal decision-making and evaluate their own self-management.

Reliable information is available in the public records, sufficient to compile a data base on each citizen's moral and ethical misbehavior, which could be later expanded as required. The technical capability needed to launch such a rating program is readily available. In its present form, the information is broadly scattered and exists in a variety of places.

A Morals and Ethics Scoring System is proposed, using the credit rating model, to provide government and citizens with information on the quality of individual citizen's moral and ethical behavior. It is a tool The People will find invaluable in the exercise of their "Control" responsibility.

Implementation of a Morals and Ethics Scoring System would open up a wide range of opportunities, the most important being the institution of actions that combat untrustworthiness. It will allow the government to trace back the sources of tendencies among abusers. It will allow the use of public shame as a motivator for change. It could be used as a basis for classifying citizenship into varying categories.

If The People want a moral and ethical citizenry upon which effective self-government can be based, they must take decisive steps to achieve that condition. An automated reporting system would introduce accountability for individual actions within the Freedoms constitutionally granted and become the means for achieving behavior change.

F. EXPAND THE DEFINITION OF TREASON TO INCLUDE ACTS IN VIOLATION OF CONSTITUTIONAL PROVISIONS

Treason was very narrowly defined by the Framers in Article III, Section 3: "Treason against the United States shall consist only in levying War against them, or in adhering to their enemies, giving them aid and comfort."

As commentator Bill Maher astutely observed, "Americans are such silly people!" That observation is a corollary to Alexander Hamilton's question of whether or not we possess the ability to govern ourselves. Self-government, as constructed by the Framers, imposes no requirement that The People deal effectively with reality.

It has become painfully obvious that destruction of our self-government is much more likely to come from enemies inside the nation than from those outside.

To quote Pogo, yesteryear's famous swamp comic strip character, "We has found the enemy, and they is us!"

It would be helpful if the Constitutional definition of Treason addressed the source of most attacks on our democratic government's functioning. It should focus on internal threats destructive to our self-governed Nation, taking specific aim at known and identified threat sources, and abusive political practices that denigrate government.

It is recommended that the People establish an entirely new approach to Treason as a way to induce behavior supportive of The People's chosen form of government and to provide punishment for activities that threaten it. It should set heavy penalties on citizens, elected persons, and those in positions of influence or power by establishing long-overdue morals and ethics standards and by making their violation a treasonous act. It should also be labeled as treasonous, actions subversive to The People's chosen economic, governmental, and political forms.

G. THE NATION'S CAPITAL PUNISHMENT SYSTEM NEEDS A COMPLETE REMAKE

Individuals who have a propensity to commit cruel crimes cannot be trusted in society. The centuries-old governmental solution has been to lock them away for the safety of the citizenry. The worst offenders have been executed, making the fix permanent.

Our nation boasts the highest per-capita percentage of incarcerated criminals in the world, the inevitable by-product of morals and ethics regression under ineffective government. Our nation also has the highest level of argument concerning the purpose of capital punishment, the inconsistent application of legal principles, and the interests of the prison guard union. Most noteworthy is the inability of our vaunted legal profession, with its heavy involvement in court cases, the judicial system, and the Houses of government, to provide any solution whatsoever for this national problem.

This author will limit further discussion by suggesting that the Well-Informed Electors make revision of the capital punishment system a priority National Imperative. The involvement of citizens in the formulation of a new system just might put the nation on the right path.

Trust-Building Mechanisms: Lessons from Global Success Stories

Restoring trust in democracy requires more than introspection—it demands actionable reform inspired by proven mechanisms worldwide. Trust, the cornerstone of effective governance, can be rebuilt by empowering citizens, increasing transparency, and fostering inclusivity. The following trust-building initiatives from successful democracies offer replicable models for the United States.

Citizen Assemblies: Ireland's Model for Deliberative Democracy

Ireland provides a compelling case study on using **citizen assemblies** to address contentious issues. This trust-building mechanism involves randomly selected citizens representing a microcosm of society who deliberate on complex topics. Two landmark examples include:

- **Marriage Equality:** In 2015, citizen assemblies paved the way for Ireland's referendum on same-sex marriage, fostering constructive dialogue and building societal consensus.

- **Abortion Legislation:** A similar process informed Ireland's decision to legalize abortion in 2018, an outcome backed by a public referendum.

How It Builds Trust:

- Inclusivity ensures that diverse perspectives are represented, mitigating feelings of marginalization.

- Transparent deliberation processes demonstrate respect for public input, increasing trust in government decisions.

Applicability to the U.S.: Citizen assemblies could address polarizing issues like immigration, healthcare reform, or gun control. Implementing state-level or local assemblies could also reinvigorate civic engagement at grassroots levels.

Participatory Budgeting: Brazil's Democratic Innovation

Introduced in Porto Alegre, Brazil, **participatory budgeting (PB)** allows citizens to directly influence how public funds are allocated. Residents gather in local assemblies to propose, debate, and vote on community projects, with approved initiatives funded through municipal budgets.

Key Outcomes:

- Improved infrastructure in low-income areas.
- Greater transparency in public spending.
- Enhanced civic engagement and accountability.

How It Builds Trust:

- PB ensures citizens have a tangible impact on local governance, fostering ownership and reducing skepticism about government inefficiency or corruption.

- Annual cycles of participation create consistent opportunities for dialogue between citizens and government officials.

Applicability to the U.S.: Cities like New York and Chicago have experimented with participatory budgeting, but expanding these programs nationally could bridge the gap between government action and public expectations. Targeting underserved communities could address systemic inequalities, a root cause of distrust.

Transparency Laws: Scandinavia's Commitment to Open Governance

Scandinavian nations, frequently ranked as the world's most trustworthy democracies, have institutionalized **transparency laws** that ensure public access to government information. Notable examples include:

- **Freedom of Information Acts (Sweden, Finland):** Citizens have the right to access government documents, fostering openness.

- **Lobbying Regulations (Denmark):** Strict laws mandate disclosure of lobbying activities, reducing undue corporate influence.

- **Whistleblower Protections (Norway):** Strong legal frameworks encourage reporting of corruption or abuse without fear of retaliation.

How It Builds Trust:

- Transparency reduces the perception of secrecy, a common factor in eroding trust.

- Openness encourages public participation and vigilance, deterring misconduct.

Applicability to the U.S.: The U.S. can strengthen existing laws like the Freedom of Information Act (FOIA) by reducing bureaucratic hurdles and expanding disclosure requirements. Enhancing lobbying transparency, particularly at the state and local levels, could also curb undue influence by special interest groups.

Combining Mechanisms for Maximum Impact

Each of these mechanisms addresses distinct facets of trust erosion:

- Citizen assemblies tackle polarization and foster inclusivity.

- Participatory budgeting combats perceptions of government inefficiency and elitism.

- Transparency laws enhance accountability and deter corruption.

When integrated into broader governance frameworks, these initiatives create a culture of mutual respect and accountability between governments and citizens.

For the United States to rebuild trust, it must adopt mechanisms that:

1. **Empower Citizens:** Encourage direct public involvement in decision-making processes.

2. **Ensure Transparency:** Eliminate barriers to accessing government information and hold officials accountable.

3. **Promote Inclusivity:** Create platforms where diverse voices are heard and valued.

Trust, once lost, is challenging to recover, but adopting proven mechanisms from global democracies offers a practical path forward. By borrowing from these success stories, the U.S. can reimagine governance to better reflect the will and confidence of its people.

CHAPTER 3

THE POLITICAL PARTY SERIES, PART 1

CONTENT:

SECTION 1: HISTORY OF PARTIES AS POLITICAL FUNCTIONS

SECTION 2: BUSINESSES VENTURE INTO TURBULENT POLITICAL WATER

SECTION 3: THE NATION'S IDEOLOGIES REQUIRE CONSTITUTIONAL TREATMENT

SECTION 4: TOTALITARIAN ENCROACHMENT IN OUR DEMOCRATIC REPUBLIC

SECTION 5: THE ELECTION SYSTEM QUANDRY

FOREWORD

Ancient tribal instincts are indelibly tattooed on the psyche of man. Something embedded there compels people to cluster in groups when experiencing fear or when driven by aggression.... the "safety-in-numbers" compulsion.

Back in the time when brute force was the commonplace problem-solver, humans clustering in factions was not only the way to survive, it was also the way to wield the hammer of oppression. Human society has risen above brute force, the theory posits, but the need to subjugate others remains a fundamental human drive, and the "weight of numbers" clustering motivation is still dominant. Sophisticated political factions are today's "civilized" brute force, the preferred subjugation method that humans will employ if allowed.

In democratic governments where a "voting majority" is the preferred brute force objective, politicians gather in political parties to achieve voting majorities that can wield the hammer of oppression. Party dogma, which members obey and evangelize as though decreed by Divinity, reeks with fervor. Heaven on earth, to politicians, is a "voting majority."

Is it now the standard that democratic government can be accomplished only by a majority of the "enlightened," who dominate and drag along the "primitive" remainder? Apparently so!

How is it, in a nation that sings the praises of its "one person, one vote" principle and worships at the altar of equality, that domination by a political party is not only tolerated but joyfully celebrated by a high percentage of the population? And why is it that huge numbers of small-group non-political clusters have been permitted to use their size and resources to influence elections and officials, thereby greatly diminishing the effect of the one-person-one-vote principle of which our nation is so proud?

We are a Nation whose fight for independence was driven by hatred of the Monarchy's abuses. Where is that same hatred evidenced by our citizens, who stand idly by and allow political parties and political factions to wield monarchy powers? Is submission of a democratic nation's government to a political party "true democracy," or is it nothing more than thinly-disguised totalitarianism?

This Chapter will develop the background information to examine these distressing contradictions, because it goes to the core of problems wobbling our Nation's incoherent system of government.

SECTION 1
HISTORICAL REVIEW OF PARTIES AS POLITICAL FUNCTIONS

BACKGROUND

At the time of the Framers, the word "faction" meant "political party." In the time elapsed the meaning of the word has changed. "Political party" is now the broadly-used term. "Faction," today, probably most accurately describes smaller groups that have political involvement. In any event, that is how we will use it in this discussion.

Readers should take the time to read Federalist #10, in which Madison discusses the "faction" (political party) issue. Washington, Jefferson, Madison, and Hamilton each publicly demonstrated a fear of factions because of their negative impact on self-government. Those Framers opposed allowing factions to operate, but did not Constitutionally decree that, instead leaving the door open for factional involvement in government by their fatal Article 1, Section 5 provision referenced repeatedly here.

There were no political parties in Congress in the immediate aftermath of the signing of the Constitution.[14] Article 1, Section 5 permits each House to "determine the Rules of its Proceedings," an ill-advised Framer grant of absolute internal control to the Political Elite, which was an anchor of their "Monarchy Republic" plan. It paved the way for the elected to

---

[14] Wikipedia

launch political parties, vehicles they could then use to control Congress. In our Framer government plan, "Congress" was made the dominant branch, but political parties were a feature neither constitutionally authorized nor welcomed.

Constitutional delegation, to their Monarchy Republic creation, of a group of vital rights and powers that belong solely to The People was the crucial Framer action. It laid the foundation for the Framers' Monarchy Republic. In every Monarchy, royalty governs the citizens, who have no power. In our Framer-conceived Monarchy Republic, citizens were permitted only the election decisions that would select the President and congressional members who would run the Monarchy Republic. The elected persons produced by that process control the operations of the government with no interference from the voters. Even though the political elite was democratically elected, that form of government is a de facto "Monarchy" because citizens have no meaningful role and no power.

The operations of government, including organization, were not pre-designed by the Framers. They delegated the design of the operational structure to the incoming elected politicians.

A student of large organization performance, Alfred D. Chandler, in his 1962 book "Strategy and Structure: Chapters in the History of the American Industrial Enterprise," states, "Unless structure follows strategy, inefficiency results."[15] The government created by the elected political elite differed substantially from the Framer strategy because the Framers failed to outline the structure desired, granted totally unwarranted powers to the elected representatives, and failed to deny the formation and use of political parties.

These brief commentaries provide insight as to what happened when the post-constitution elected politicians designed the operating structure of our Legislative assemblies. By "dumping" that responsibility onto them and providing no guidance, the Framers allowed elected representative self-interest to dominate the decisions concerning operating process and organization. **The structure did not then follow strategy, and Chandler's chosen word, "inefficiency," does not seem adequate to describe the outcome.**

THE LEFT WING AND THE RIGHT WING

In the evolution of this nation's government, the Democratic Party has come to be known as the "Left" and the Republican Party as the "Right."

---

[15] Chandler, Alfred D. "Strategy and Structure: Chapters in the History of the American Industrial Enterprise." (1962)

The terms "left" and "right" originated in 1789 during the French Revolution, and derived from the seating arrangements for the supporters of the King (who sat on the right) and the supporters of the revolution (who sat on the left). In the elapsed time people have come to associate the Left with liberalism and the Right with conservatism.

It is politically possible to blame today's polarization on the French Revolution's antagonistic seating arrangement!

Left-wing parties are composed of liberals, progressives, socialists and communists. Ideologies of the Left-wing are unlimited abortion, absolute gun control, no death penalty, unchecked immigration, high taxation coupled with free social services, and massive authority exercised by a large centralized government. Left-wing parties lean toward liberalism and central control.

Right-wing parties are made up of conservatives, traditionalists, reactionaries and fascists. Right-wing ideologies feature limited taxation and regulation, the upholding of morals and personal accountability, and are politically postured in diametric opposition to the Left on abortion, gun control, the death penalty, and immigration. Right-wing parties espouse limited government and high levels of personal freedom.

The left and right wings have solidified as hard fixtures in the American legislative process, which is based upon "contention." Most elected persons are lawyers who modeled the legislative process after their most familiar environment, the courtroom. The contentious sides, rather than "plaintiff" and "defense," became "party in power" and "opposition," and operational routines were based upon court-room processes. Political parties fit themselves into those two sides.

This book describes our form of government as a "Monarchy Republic," rather than referring to it simply as a "Republic." The revised label is more accurate. **By our nation's constitution all power was vested in the Political Elite, shouting "Monarchy!"** The People have no rights concerning government except to elect or unseat those who occupy designated elected positions. (Chapter 9 will examine the Monarchy Republic concept in detail.)

The guarded and secure box we call the Monarchy Republic protects within its walls the political elite who manipulate the levers of power, and excludes all others. The secure box was conceived by the Framers, but installed by the initial occupants of the two Congressional assemblies. **To solve our government dysfunction citizens must think outside of that box to find solutions.**

The Political Elite of our nation today include appointed autocrats accountable to no one, and elected officials re-elected endlessly, also accountable to no one. Currently-experienced 90% re-election rates have converted elective seats into incumbent possessions of miniscule turnover. Our Political Elite are a replication of the authoritarian royalty of old.

EMERGENCE OF THE "POLITICAL ELITE"

Out of our Monarchy Republic operating environment, a government state of mind has emerged, a state labeled by author Emily B. Finley[16] as "democratism." She describes the "democratism" mindset as an "imaginative and idealistic concept of popular rule that disdains ordinary people and looks to a cadre of so-called experts to operate the levers of power. In this state of mind, "democracy" and "the people" are rhetorical cover for the will of the elites.

Readers may want to review the Covid administrative fiascos of 2020 to 2022 to refresh themselves on how democratism works.

Under Finley's "democratism," political elites employ the façade of democracy to mask their actions with an appearance of legitimacy. The façade is verbally enhanced by reference to the events of 1776, using words such as "freedom," "free speech," and "democracy." Behind the republic façade, totalitarian decision-making by political parties and by so-called "experts" in the Administrative State is the true production of government.

---

[16] "" Democracy by and for the Elites," Wall Street Journal article Sept. 26, 2022. Dr. Finley is author of "The Ideology of Democratism"

Dr. Finley states Alexis de Tocqueville predicted that, eventually, an "immense and tutelary power" would replace genuine popular rule in America. **The People would accept their tutelage because of their belief that "they themselves hold the end of the chain."** de Tocqueville's prediction seems to be well advanced today.

Monarchy Republic government and its companion state of mind, Democratism, describe our nation in its current transition from Democracy to Totalitarianism. Political Elite rule, of course, is a carry-over from authoritarian government, discussed in depth in the "Battle to the Death between Democracy and Totalitarianism," forthcoming Chapter 5.

SECTION 2
BUSINESSES VENTURE INTO TURBULENT POLITICAL WATER

Political Parties are organizations of diverse membership. It is not unusual for members to have beliefs that transcend the party, so both U.S. political parties contain smaller factions clustered around sub-set beliefs or goals.

The Democratic Party contains a major left-wing sub-set called "Progressives" and other smaller factions. The Republican Party contains a significant far-right cadre known as the "Tea Party" and smaller factions.

Smaller factions content themselves with pursuing their goals and beliefs from the power structure of the major party they support. Both political parties of our nation cater to smaller factions, each representing a collection of members gathering around a common interest. Labor Unions, including those whose membership includes government employees, are prominent public political factions but not by any means the only ones. The U.S. Chamber of Commerce is an influential political faction representing businesses.

Business managements have historically steered clear of public involvement in politics, viewing the risks of such a course as far exceeding potential benefits. That posture is changing in the present polarized political climate. In recent developments, distressing to democracy believers, corporations and other business organizations have become politically active by lending their often-powerful business name and presence to a public position on a political issue.

In many businesses, vocal employee groups rail on management to take a political position on issues they deem important, pushing those managements into hazardous political water, and in the process converting the commercial business into a political faction. If employee groups are successful in such efforts, they will have enhanced their political clout dramatically.

Thus, another vote-accumulation attack on the one-person-one-vote fundamental of democracy appears to be well under way, aligning business corporations with political parties. The trend further degrades the value of the individual vote, and with it, democracy.

THE CITIZEN VIEW OF POLITICAL PARTIES

Only the politically sophisticated among us ever stop to think about the legitimacy of political parties in our governmental structure. In the memory of most, political parties have always "been there," dominating the political landscape. A government without political parties, to the average citizen, would be unrecognizable. To question the legitimacy of political party existence might, by many, actually be considered radical!

So, check your knowledge about the history of our form of government: **Did you know that The People and the Framers did not approve and provided no support for the formation of political parties? Political parties are neither mentioned nor sanctioned in the Constitution. They were consciously avoided by the Framers!**

Political parties are attractive to elected persons because of the "simple majority" vote rule, which was installed by those same early politicians as the bill passage benchmark of the two Houses. At the 50% majority vote bill passage, often called "tyranny of the majority," House majority control was thereby set at a level low enough to provide impetus for the formation of political parties

Although political parties are elected-member power-focused political union businesses operating within the assembly structure of government, **they are subject to no governance. Their power stems from majority-attainment through the ballot box, but they have no**

accountabilities except to the voters who elected them. They have been granted, by the members of the two Houses, an incredible power position in government.

As far as is known by this author, our citizens have never voted approval of the use of political parties, such as those operating within our government.

All the rights and privileges enjoyed by political parties are free to them, with no strings attached. They have the capability of wrecking our nation, and if they do that, the worst that can happen to them is the loss of majority rule at election time. If political parties are not the worst construct ever foisted on government by the politicians of a nation, they certainly must rank near the top of the list.

Political parties were the creation of elected politicians. They are political trade unions within which politicians with similar beliefs and objectives congregate. They do that to improve their personal welfare, by permitting them to exert control over their employer.

Business managements have historically steered clear of public involvement in politics, viewing the risks of such a course as far exceeding potential benefits. That posture is changing in the present polarized political climate. In a recent development, distressing to democracy believers, corporations and other business organizations have become politically active by lending their often-powerful business name and presence to a public position on a political issue.

In many businesses, vocal employee groups rail on management to take a political position on issues they deem important, pushing those managements into hazardous political water, and in the process converting the housing business into a political faction. If employee groups are successful in such efforts, they will have enhanced their political clout dramatically.

Thus, another vote-accumulation attack on the one-person-one-vote fundamental of democracy is under way, as business corporations align with political parties. The trend further degrades the value of the individual vote, and with it, undermines democracy.

Political parties do not exist to improve the welfare of the nation. Making the role of elected representatives easier, and easing their challenge in achieving legislation approval, were important benefits to elected persons.

WHEN POLITICAL PARTIES GAIN CONTROL OVER GOVERNMENT, THEY DO SO BY TAKING THAT CONTROL AWAY FROM THE PEOPLE AS A WHOLE.

THE RATIONALE FOR THE FORMATION OF POLITICAL PARTIES

Professional politicians have no concern for the best interests of the nation. The paths they choose benefit themselves, including the path of party affiliation. They are focused on power, the congregation of which allows them to impose on all citizens their notions of how things should be done. The political party is their business sword. From the political process, party members hope to gain public recognition that can be further leveraged for personal gain.

By these devious and circuitous routes, our early political elite converted the Republic's Houses of Congress into institutions vulnerable to control by any political party that can corral more than 50% of the voting members. By achieving majorities in both Houses of Congress and securing the Presidency, a political party can install a de facto totalitarian government.

The simple majority vote was established within the assemblies by elected politicians as the benchmark for bill passage without citizen voters ever approving the idea. Considerable space will be devoted in future chapters to the problems of a simple majority vote. **Such a dramatic change to the democratic republic form of government described in the Constitution should properly have been written into the Constitution, but the Framers had built in a huge constitutional loop-hole that made legal politician-conceived arrangements such as political parties ……perhaps not abiding with the Republic's principles, but legal!**

THE TWO - FACED ALEXANDER HAMILTON

"Factions" were decried at great length by the authors of the Federalist Papers, the most prominent being Alexander Hamilton. When the Constitution was under consideration by the states, the Federalist Papers were published as a series of political opinions in its support. Factions were viewed by prominent thinkers such as Hamilton as a substantial threat to government, a view that time has validated.

Alexander Hamilton later organized and led the Federalist Party, the first major political party of the United States. **Even the revered Hamilton was willing to subordinate the nation's best interest to his own. He was not above forming a political party, which he knew to be a threat to democracy, to further his personal political goals.**

The drive of politicians for power and personal goal achievement will overcome the interests of the nation every time! That is the reason assembly voting process restructure, and control by The People over the entire government decision process, is so necessary. **The People's self-government, to survive, will require Constitutional control mechanisms that protect the nation against the self-serving actions of the politicians operating within its structure.**

POLITICAL PARTIES ARE AUTHORITARIAN

1. Their goal is to establish a system where a minority can exert disproportionate influence over democratic decisions, undermining the principles of majority rule. Any attempt to gain party control within a democratic government is a totalitarian action. Assemblies controlled by a totalitarian entity representing but a fraction of the voting citizens is not democracy!

2. Political parties exist to impose their own philosophy of governance on the nation. That is an autocratic goal accomplished by the use of the majority hammer. **The philosophy of governance is solely the business of the nation's owners and its People. Governance philosophy should be a deeply-considered decision made by the vote of the owners and not ever result from party practice or party manipulation.**

3. The political party is a business unit of a union of elected persons. It exists to use government assemblies as factories where the party product is produced and marketed. Successful product delivery buys the re-election of party members. Such business activity is totalitarian because it uses The People's law-making facilities to benefit a self-interest trade group.

   Elected Assemblies of government were not intended to be factories for the sale and delivery of party products. They exist to produce the decisions of democratic government for all of The People, and other existence reasons are not relevant.

Political Parties are composed of **citizens banding together**, following the leadership of politicians, to elect the number of members required to establish party voting control over individual Houses of Congress. **They are the direct consequence of the constitutional provision "Each House may determine the Rules of its Proceedings" and the assembly-manufactured rule of bill passage by simple majority vote tally.**

The higher the bill passage majority vote benchmark, the lower the likelihood of political party existence. When the assembly voting majority is set at 50%, the benchmark is low enough that it is feasible for political parties to elect the number of assembly members needed for control.

Gaining a voting majority in Houses of Congress allows political parties to pass laws structured to reflect their political ideology, even extreme variations to the vaunted "democratic republic" government ideology and the "free-market, free enterprise" economic ideology of our nation. Within their ranks political parties will employ democratic voting, and they will play the democratic game, **but they are authoritarian gatherings**. Their existence is destructive to democratic government.

Political parties operate within the constitution of the nation that houses them. In Communist nations, of course, the constitution is custom-designed by the Communist party to eliminate political competition. Communist countries carry the political party notion to the ultimate. They only allow one party to exist. In democratic nations, political parties exist in the manner and to the extent permitted by the constitution or assembly rules of the host nation.

As will be discussed elsewhere in this book, **whether or not to allow political parties to exist and function is a discrete "organized" decision to be made by the owners of the Nation, The People.** That decision may not be delegated to the government by The People. It is an issue The People of our nation have not ever had an opportunity to decide by vote.

SECTION 3
THE NATION'S IDEOLOGIES REQUIRE CONSTITUTIONAL TREATMENT.

The political ideology of the United States is that of a Democratic Republic. Its economic ideology is a Free Market and Free Enterprise Economy. Most will agree that those are high among the values that underlie the economic success of the United States. But you will not find them mentioned in the Constitution!

This book will focus substantial attention on vital matters that, in a self-governed democratic nation, are solely the responsibility of The People. The nation's political and economic ideologies top that list. They are primary and basic statements to be enshrined in the Constitution, statements that cannot ever be allowed to become a ballpark for hired management political play.

Owner decisions of that nature should be re-evaluated by The People on a constitutionally-set long-cycle basis. Once set, they should no longer be the permitted subject of debate. Such an approach rids The People of endless political argument about matters already decided, matters for which there is nothing to be gained by re-examination.

THE NATION'S DEEP-SEATED VALUES AND BELIEFS ARE NOT CONSTITUTIONALLY ENSHRINED

Unfortunately, our Framers failed to constitutionally enshrine many of the nation's deep-seated values and rules. One glaring failure was not defining our ideologies and not expressly prohibiting other ideologies. Invigorated by the opportunities left open to them by that Framer oversight, today, political parties freely promote ideological proposals radically different from those of our Framers or those accepted as common beliefs that underlie our society and form of government.

The result is endless, senseless, divisive political arguments about matters that are solely the business of The People as the nation's owners. Once decided, such critical rules should not be permitted continuous argument under Freedom of Speech.

The implications of the foregoing statements warrant deep consideration. **Attacks on democracy from internal factions are always more threatening than those from external enemies.** Uncertainty and argument about the nation's fundamental posture continuously drives a democracy toward totalitarianism. It diminishes the control of The People, unnecessarily mis-focuses the nation's inhabitants, and provides ammunition for endless internal dissention. Our constitution has provided no defense against such destructive and dangerous time-waste.

In a freedom-based democracy, freedom must not ever extend so far as to permit individuals or factions to attack, or attempt to replace, The People's guiding principles. Scheduled reviews by The People, after long time intervals like 50 or 100 years, is a much better approach for consideration of drastic change than is endless day-to-day political argument, or politically opportunistic action. Establishing certainty concerning the fundamentals of society is a factor underlying stability.

Never spend national time arguing over matters already decided!

LACK OF RESPECT FOR POLITICIANS

Our Senators and Representatives are neither widely admired nor respected by the voters. Since the formation of our Republic, that has been the case, yet nothing positive has ever been done about that painfully obvious sign of distress. The Administrative State, the formation of which was a political party solution to the perceived lack of quality among elected officials, was a political run-around, the purpose of which was to avoid confronting the elected person's quality issue. A stronger argument can be made that the Administrative

State had, as its main goal, a switch from a democratic government to an authoritarian government.

Much of the following content has been parsed from a recent article by Lewellyn King.[17]

1. There are three barriers that keep good people out of politics: money, the primary system, and media scrutiny.

2. The system is inherently corrupt. A candidate must be prepared to spend much of his/her career raising money, **then must bend judgment to accommodate the will of donors**.

3. The primary system produces candidates who are extreme and appeal to the fringes. Those candidates progress to shape the party itself. Although postured as favoring grass-roots democracy, in fact primaries favor those with rich friends who will cough up.

4. If you run for office, you become a public plaything. Everything you ever wrote or said can and will be dredged up.

Author King ends with this observation: "If primaries continue as they have, the fringes triumph. Just look at the Congress --- a smorgasbord of wackiness."

ABUSIVE PARTY PRACTICES: USING TOTALITARIAN TECHNIQUES TO GAIN AND MAINTAIN POWER

In his book "The Naked Communist: Exposing Communism and Restoring Freedom," Author W. Cleon Skousen identifies "The 45 Goals of Communism Today," a comprehensive summary of strategies and tactics employed by totalitarians in their organized drive to undermine democracy. Many on the list will be discussed under various headings.[18] **Most are continuously being employed by opponents of Democracy in the United States.**

A totalitarian regime in power always establishes control over "the message" to the public for the purpose of controlling the intellectual distribution of its values and beliefs and to publicly present its government exactly as the regime desires. To that end, control over all communications media is imposed as "standard operating practice." **No opposition viewpoints are permitted.** Totalitarian regimes do not want a well-informed citizenry. Their objective is a compliant, mind-controlled citizenry.

Importing that successful totalitarian strategy into our United States democracy, political parties have joined forces with media companies to establish the required political mind-control. The party message is fine-tuned and consistent, and with the substantial help of

---

[17] Lewellyn King, Inside Sources .com. Article "Why do we get such lousy politicians? Because running for office is ghastly," Las Vegas Review Journal, July 23, 2023

[18] 'The Naked Communist', W. Cleon Skousen, Izzard Ink Publishing

media cohorts, opposition views are not given public exposure. There is little outright evidence of collusion between the political parties and their media partners. Both will deny its existence vociferously, but the actuality of collusion is clear to anyone watching mainstream television or reading mainstream newspapers.

The totalitarian strategy of mind-control is being pursued masterfully by political parties in concert with their media propaganda arms, and that is happening in a nation that ballyhoos "freedom of speech."

Mind control is established through consistent messaging, which is an incredible tool to gain political success. If you have a discussion with party members, you will be able to quickly discern the level of mind control of which each member is the victim. It is astonishingly high.

Polarization is the off-shoot of political party/media mind-control operations. Mind-control is a totalitarian strategy that is subversively employed by political parties to support their "control" drive. It is one of the practices, threatening to democracy, that must be constitutionally outlawed. In a self-governed democracy it should be permitted only if specifically authorized by the People.

The incessant drum-beat of the message from the "right" and the message from the "left" has relentlessly herded our citizenry into two groups, and goaded hostility between them. **Murky thinking about "freedom," coupled with inept governance, has produced polarization. Polarization is the big wooden Hero Medal awarded to The People of this nation for granting governance-subject communication freedom to political parties and the media.**

Rather than stepping back to analyze cause-and-effect, citizens are willfully participating in the polarization hostility. Those are not the actions of wary citizens focused on high-quality self-government.

Our forefathers, Washington and Madison, decried factionalism in their time, a time when the dominant and intrusive electronic media, to which we are everyday exposed, had not yet been invented. They understood the threat of factions but decided to do nothing except talk about the problem. The Framers were correctly focused on creating a federal government that could bind together the thirteen independent states and did not get side-tracked into attempting to solve peripheral problems. But the government they fitted us with was not interested in or capable of following through to complete what the Framers began. One does idly wonder how the Framers would have reacted had they witnessed the media political behavior we observe today.

The media is best understood if it is viewed as a huge conglomeration of private industry participants positioned between the only two managerial functions of democratic self-government that matter. Those two functions are the voting citizens, who are the owners of the nation, and their hired management in government, who must determine and execute their direction. The free flow of vital information between those two critical functions being essential cannot be warped by blockages or distortions caused by the third-party media conglomerate that has been granted a preferential in-between position. Self-government cannot succeed as long as the huge media communications blockage exists between the only two Authority Structure functions that matter.

This book rates the media as the biggest threat to our form of government, a threat created by the Political Parties but actualized by the huge and monopolization-intent media.

SECTION 4
TOTALITARIAN ENCROACHMENT IN OUR DEMOCRATIC REPUBLIC

Following is a list of functions or activities within our nation that are either independently totalitarian or are being conducted by political parties for totalitarian purposes. **Readers should note that all are made possible by the grant of Freedom but are carried out to undermine our freedom-loving democracy.**

As can be seen from this summary, the level of totalitarian encroachment is very significant.

1. Creating Unrest to Degrade Public Opinion of Government

Totalitarians use indirect methods to undermine democracy. Indirect methods have the advantage of disguising the goals of the perpetrators and perhaps the perpetrators themselves.

A major strategy employed by totalitarians is fostering social unrest to sow the seeds of distrust in democratic government. The cause used as a reason for the unrest is incidental; any cause that will attract backers and media attention will do.

A tabulation of totalitarian activities whose general purpose is to stir up anti-democratic or anti-government feelings would include pitting one race against another as a way to foster dissatisfaction with the quality of governance, opportunistically using events to promote negative feelings toward and resentment of government functions such as policing; under the guise of "correcting history," tearing down important symbols of democracy to focus attention on things Democracy has done wrong, actually or ostensibly; demonstrating in opposition to government-function decisions or processes; desecrating monuments that are symbolic of the nation's history; denigrating traditional values such as morals, ethics, and religion, by creating "woke" or "progressive" factions and promoting their message.

Those activities are going on daily and are widely covered by the Media. Their connection to political party posture is very abstract and seldom mentioned.

2. Manipulating the Message to Citizens Through the Media

Controlling the communications media has long been a key totalitarian strategy. Totalitarian factions always control the message so that citizens receive only the laundered version. Within democracies, political parties and their affiliates attempt to follow that same principle by entering into illicit arrangements with the media, wherein messages are manipulated to present a party perspective and mute those of the opposition.

In our nation, both major political parties have entered into alliances with friendly newspapers, networks, and media personnel to present their interests favorably, a fact that is clearly visible to observers. Radical political factions, usually sub-sets of a major party, are very active. Media censorship, a form of "manipulating the message," is becoming more and more prevalent.

3. Using Political Parties to Control Government

Political parties are totalitarian entities formed by politicians as a way to control the assemblies that were formed to be the seats of democratic self-government. **They do so by establishing the party as an in-between group lodged between The People, as owners of the Nation, and the Hired Management conducting government.** In that position, there is no direct communication between the boss (The People) and the Hired Management. All communication is filtered through the political party intermediary, thus blurring The People's direction and much of the direction of government.

When a party has established majority control, it has been vested in a totalitarian-bent position. It will (among other things) foster totalitarian decision-making, introduce radical political practices, amend assembly processes, attempt to change national direction, fail to control critical business of the nation (such as the national debt), use the nation's assets to support party goals and implement programs that further the interests of the party rather than those of the nation.

4. Infiltrating Non-Government Institutions to Degrade Democracy

Political Parties, when in a position to do so, infiltrate non-government institutions in the nation by inserting people supportive of their ideology into key positions so that the party message is faithfully distributed. Education is today a principal field of totalitarian endeavor, as instruction material is deployed, the purpose of which is degrading democracy and often promoting notions not generally supported to install a radical mindset in future citizens of the nation. Influencing elections, the justice system, the immigration system, and the labor force are equally important political party activities.

As a threat to our nation, the most critical of those is the infiltration of the education system.

5. Structuring Departments, Bureaus, and Agencies as Totalitarian Functions

The creation of the Administrative State converted a large segment of the U.S. government from democratic to authoritarian. Management there is not elected, yet departments, agencies, and bureaus of the Administrative State have been delegated immense authority by our elected assemblies. **Laws are written permitting Administrative State units to write, implement, and adjudicate law concerning legislated matters.**

At question is not the justification for the existence of departments, agencies, and bureaus. **At question is the powers delegated to them that warrant the designation of "totalitarian."**

Viewed separate from the democratic government that supports them, an impartial observer could not distinguish units of our Administrative State from comparable units in the communist governments of Russia or China.

James Madison warned: "The accumulation of all powers, legislative, executive and judiciary, in the same hands.......may justly be pronounced the very definition of tyranny." Were Madison to view today's Administrative State, he would rate much of it "tyrannical."

6. Undermining Democracy by Denigrating Morals, Ethics and Religion

Self-government, employing democracy and freedom, requires a moral and ethical citizenry. That fact has been known and restated repeatedly since the time of the Framers.

Many organizations, religious or otherwise, have historically made improvement of moral and ethical behavior a feature of their outreach programs. They provided critical education to the public, installing in our culture the values upon which social and business rules and practices were initially, and are still, based.

To weaken that important foundation of democracy and self-government, totalitarian organizations are working hard to undermine morals, ethics, and religion as national values. They have devoted massive effort to the denigration of religion, to removing critical morals and ethics instruction from education to fostering media communication that promotes radical alternative lifestyles and values, and to moderate punishment for such activities in the law and court system. Denigrating morals and ethical values erodes positive attitudes among the citizens, making them susceptible to degenerative suggestions that produce a negative effect on national behavior.

7. Converting Decision-Making from Democratic to Authoritarian

Increasingly, critical decisions in government are being made by individuals, rather than by vote of elected bodies. Our government organization contains no watchdog person or organization dedicated to ensuring that democratic process is faithfully employed, and elected persons have proven to either not know, or to not care, about democratic process. **Democracy demands that all decisions affecting the nation or its citizens be made by elected assembly vote.**

Delegation by Congress of major decision authority to unelected Agencies, Departments, and Bureaus of the Administrative State, Executive Orders issued by the President, and a range of non-democratic activities within political parties and the Houses of Congress all function to further the conversion of democracy to totalitarianism.

The fatal Framer decision granting self-management to our elected assemblies has made possible Congressional decisions to transfer their responsibilities and authorities to unelected Federal bureaucrats. Abandonment of democratic principles is commonplace in the nation's government, aided and abetted by judges whose decisions support the presumed superior knowledge of the bureaucracy. As Kimberley Strassel observes in her Wall Street Journal article, "Lawmakers see only benefit in outsourcing their dirty work."[19]

A ray of light has been shone on this critical matter by the Supreme Court. In a decision of great importance rendered in June 2022, the Court declared the "major questions doctrine," previously mentioned in a handful of court decisions, to be a living, breathing principle. The federal bureaucracy is not permitted to impose programs of "major economic and political significance" on the country absent clear legislative authorization.[20]

---

6. "The Justices' Message to Congress" by Kimberly A Strassel. The Wall Street Journal, July 1, 2022.

While welcomed, the recent Supreme Court decision, in and of itself, will take ages to affect the operations of government. A more direct and decisive approach supported by the weight of democratic authority is required.

8. Providing Health Care and Welfare to Make Citizens Indebted to Government

To generate voter support, political parties utilize totalitarian strategies to make citizens reliant on the government. Prominent among those are programs providing public health care, education support, and welfare. Those costly benefits endear the political party to the beneficiaries, creating blocks of captured voting citizenry using money provided by the remainder of the citizenry.

SECTION 5
THE ELECTION SYSTEM QUANDRY

We are focused on the Constitution and the U.S. Government, a prominent feature of which is the election system. That System in the United States is a huge and integral part of its democratic process. It's the vehicle by which the persons needed to fill official positions in government are sorted out and elected by the voting public. It is also the only meaningful vehicle where discussion of the "What needs to be done" strategy takes place.

As is true of most aspects of the nation's governance, because of the vastness of the voter group, the involvements of regional and municipal governments, and overall voter vulnerability to the bifurcating and incestuous influences of political parties, that intellectual chasm is an invitation to become hopelessly mired.

The discussion here will, therefore, be curtailed to top-level matters that fit into our overall constitutional and governmental concerns.

TRUST IN THE ELECTION SYSTEM

Chapter 2, "Trust, the Democracy Glue," contains much information on the importance of Trust in self-governed democracies. The election system demands a critical trust element called "faith." The current low level of citizen trust in our nation's government is a matter of great concern.

Doubts about election integrity have been present for ages. History records periods in the 1800s when election fraud was rampant in cities like New York, at a time when local politicians were active, corrupted, and controlling. Fast forward to the 1980s. Doubts reached high levels then and in successive time periods, peaking with the 2000 extremely-close election of George W. Bush, which brought us the "hanging chads" controversy and a final election ruling by the Supreme Court. The 2020 election, lost by Donald Trump, brought with it his charges of "stolen election," culminating with the Jan. 6, 2001, citizen storming of the U.S. capitol.

These events are happening at a time when trust in government is at an all-time low, stoking citizen concern about the overall state of the union. Only 44% of Americans have a "great deal" of confidence in the vote count. Political polarization is intense. Support for the system is evident from party voters only when a tight race has gone their way. It is clear that the election system needs to be improved to a level of universal support.

The election system is old and poorly conceived, riddled with inefficient ideas and processes seeping into it from the government and from a variety of political and regional jurisdictions. Its major problem is "too many cooks with their fingers in the soup," far too many jurisdictions making rules concerning it, and too much influence from political parties. Voter accountability is non-existent. The lack of concrete constitutional guidance from The People leaves the election system devoid of basic principles upon which a modern, highly-supported democracy can be based.

ELECTION SYSTEM AREAS OF DYSFUNCTION

Dissecting our entire complex voting and election system is well beyond the scope of this Chapter. Changes to such a system will require extensive research and study, which is the topic of a forthcoming Chapter. The key issue for this book is recognition of the need for action by The People. The author has chosen to constrain discussion to a few areas of the voting and the ballot system to lay the groundwork for the approach proposed.

Citizen Voting Responsibility

1. **Voting is a responsibility of citizenship**. The constitution does not state that, and establishes no penalty for citizen voting non-performance. Voting is treated as a citizen's discretion rather than a dead-serious obligation.

2. Because of poor citizen participation, the nation is subjected to endless voting improvement projects emanating out of government, but instigated by political parties for party advantage. Various methods of making voting "more convenient" to citizens are a current party focus. Most such projects breed voter disdain and decreased election integrity.

   A. It is not the job of government to promote increased voting by citizens. The job of government is to penalize citizens who fail to vote. That is the direct path to increased citizen voting participation. Why are we playing "nicey-nicey" with something as basic and fundamental as voting?

B. Voter convenience is not vital to the nation, but election integrity certainly is.

C. All political party efforts to increase voter participation are self-serving, generally employing poor concepts. They bath election system improvement efforts with the odor of self-interest conflict.

D. We suggest The People establish a new national voting system founded on a stiff reduction-of-citizenship penalty for not fulfilling the obligation to vote. Balancing accountability with privilege is rudimentary.

Government Elected Persons Cannot be Involved in Setting Election Rules.

1.Election Systems are "Vital Infrastructure" in a democratic nation. As such, their construction is the sole responsibility of owners, The People. Governments, for which elections generate staffing, must always be held at arm's length from election processes, permitted no involvement or influence. Allowing inmates to run the asylum has never been successful.

2. Political Parties are gatherings of voters of common belief under the direction of elected persons. Their purpose is to achieve sufficient representation to control democratic assemblies.

3. Political parties in the United States are not constitutionally authorized. They are the trade-unions of elected persons. They are totalitarian organizations whose avowed purpose is control over the governance of a democratic nation so they can infuse into it their own beliefs and programs.

4. Election Systems of our nation have been administered by governments. Governments are controlled by political parties. Election systems are, therefore, controlled by political parties. The People must solely control election systems, with governments and political parties banned from election system proximity.

Political Party "Position Locks" in Election Systems Must Be Scoured Out

1. The political parties have secured for themselves entitlement positions on printed ballots. Each party and party candidate(s) is the ballot voting choice presented to The People, usually with limited (or no) alternatives.

2. This has occurred despite the percentage of voters who identify with a political party dropping steadily (now Republicans 26%, Democrats 30%). The percentage of

voters identifying as Independent is climbing persistently (now 44%).[21] The largest voting block is Independents, but they are denied any way to vote their wishes. Small parties and non-party candidates are denied ballot access.

3. Some believe the aforementioned statistical trends reflect sharply reduced trust in government, but rejection by voters of what they consider a rigged and unfair election system is the more likely cause of increasing "Independent" voter registration. Some observers analyze the independent group statistics by their political party voting preference, a very poor approach, since it reveals only what party an" independent" would select if given a choice of two. **No effort is under way to find out what Independents really want, why they reject the election system, why they chose the independent route, and what corrective actions they desire.**

4. The Primary Election vote is another position lock of the political parties. Primaries are nothing more than a means for a political party to select the candidates it will present on a general election ballot. A government voting system is totally inappropriate for such an effort since Primary elections are strictly party affairs in which the government has no stake.

5. The political parties have, through control of government, been able to shanghai the government voting system for their own use. In the process, they are able to incorrectly communicate that political parties are an integral element of government.

   The two political parties are at the heart of this untenable situation, and voters have no non-party route. They content themselves by expressing political party rejection, declaring themselves "independents."

6. Some way must be devised to give The People control over the election ballot system, wresting it from governments and the political parties and opening up routes for those not aligned with political parties to express their choices.

SOLUTION PROPOSAL

We propose a new election process that addresses inherent problems. A later chapter will provide details of the proposal.

1. To eliminate the conflicts of interest between the political parties and of government, we propose that the Election System be established as a stand-alone Vital Infrastructure organization, separate from the government and managed solely by The People. All conflicted parties would be barred from participation.

---

[21] Gallup Poll January 7, 2015 (Jeffrey M. Jones)

2. The election process is just one more function in our system of government bedeviled by the actions of political parties. Getting rid of the political parties needs to be the nation's highest priority. It would immediately force a total restructuring of election processes.

3. We suggest a new two-pronged national planning system called National Imperatives and Financial Measures, selected by the voters. Those elected would be required to successfully carry out the Imperatives and Measures. It is also recommended that heavy citizen involvement in a President-led "legislative priorities and decisions" planning process be instituted. Let's get the horse out in front of the cart! **The People must decide what needs to be done, not political parties.**

4. An entirely new election approach is suggested, wherein voters are presented with, say, six candidates for each elected position, given in-depth information and the opportunity to listen to and examine each, and be told to make the selection based on the candidate's ability to contribute to the "What needs to be done" proposals.

5. The "Election Commission," as a Vital Infrastructure unit, would have widely-increased responsibility, made necessary by the exclusion of government and political parties from the election process. In this project, The People must lead, not follow!

   A. We suggest the U.S. Treasury fund the election process, eliminating private money all together. Treat the cost as a "management finder's fee" because that is exactly what it is.

   B. Candidate location, selection, and vetting would be performed by the Election Commission, which will identify candidate talent to be focused on "what needs to be done." The nation needs to rid its government of miscast people and lawyers, replacing them with talented problem-solvers.

   C. An entirely new employment and compensation arrangement for elected persons is strongly recommended. Term limits, one-time service, strongly focused duties, employment contracts, and heavy incentive compensation are proposed elements of the new approach.

This brief overview demonstrates that any new organization for government decision-making must eliminate the many interest conflicts that presently burden ours and take a creative approach to finding people capable of dramatically improving the decision process, which is our strategy for creating high-performance self-government. The approach starts with determining what has to be done and then fitting the staffing to the tasks.

CHAPTER 4

THE POLITICAL PARTY SERIES, PART 2

CONTENT:

SECTION 1: THE IMPACT OF PARTY DECISIONS ON GDP

SECTION 2: THE NATION'S ASSEMBLY DECISION-MAKING

SECTION 3: AIDING THE DECISION PROCESS WITH NATIONAL IMPERATIVES

SECTION 4: WHAT IS THE PATH FORWARD?

FOREWORD

National decision-making is not simple, employing such democratic accepted rules as exist, but the difficulty is simply a hill that must be climbed. Democracy is founded on voted decisions, either by The People themselves or by elected persons in the assembly. The degeneration of our democracy has resulted from failure to abide by those rules. This book will religiously observe them and construct methods for better applying them.

Defining the requirements and expectations of decision-making is an obligation of The People, and the results are to be issued as "direction." Decision-making, for a nation such as the United States, must be planned and organized from start to finish, with nothing left to chance. And the process instituted must be tightly controlled by The People, not ever left in the hands of the hired management. Of all government operational rules, those for decision-making are the most important. The results are that critical!

The ownership position of The People dictates they alone must design and control the Authority Structure decision-making process. Any other approach is not "self-government." Because high-quality decisions are a top national goal, the chosen decision process will dictate the organization of government and the Authority Structure.

Dumping decision-making on the laps of elected politicians with the cheerful instruction "Here, you figure out how to do it!" is the height of managerial stupidity, a certain formula for disaster. And decisions in a self-governed nation should never wind up being the playground of self-serving political parties. If The People must control decision-making in their self-governed democracy, what could be more irrational than turning that job over to political parties?

SECTION 1
THE IMPACT OF PARTY DECISIONS ON GDP

Opening comments on this segment of the Political Party Series focus on the great attention that needs to be paid to governance structure and organization because of its effect on the decision process.

Why do you think the observed endless political machinations of elected persons are considered important enough to warrant the investment of effort and time?

The answer is that under our government scheme, involvement in making decisions is the road to power. For elected persons, power is the road to personal glorification. To gain that end, public exposure of the processes of power is essential, making the time and effort to achieve it justifiable and necessary.

Future elected persons will participate in government solely as heavily-involved voting participants in a People-proscribed democratic decision process. All diversions, particularly the personal pursuit of power, must be denied them. **Their job structure and duty will be to cast the most deeply-considered vote possible to fulfill a very high level of responsibility to the nation and the people who elected them.** We think the liberal use of incentive bonuses is the best path to achieve that level of focus. Decision-maker focus is the dominant requirement for high-quality government.

There should be no reward for elected persons other than those provided contractually, no promotability, and no progression through government service. Elected persons will serve their agreed-upon time, hopefully earn considerable incentive pay, and return to private life. The approach is designed to eliminate any striving for power and permanence from the minds of those hired to vote for the decisions of the nation.

With that introduction, an examination of government decision-making will be carried out.

There is an endless political discussion about the widening gap in income distribution between societal segments, lack of wage growth, the inadequacy of government-provided medical care, the inability of elected persons to control the national debt, and a range of other matters needing attention by the government. There is little discussion about our gross ability to pay for improvements to the citizen welfare. "How can the nation afford those?" is the question.

The cheerful answer of our political parties is, "We'll just build up the national debt to pay! This is important for our re-election!"

The accepted measure of our nation's economic progress is Gross Domestic Product, or GDP as it is popularly known. GDP measures the nation's production, which ultimately produces its wealth.

The nation's GDP measures production that, properly taxed, should generate enough revenue to pay for what the nation needs or wants to achieve, and the cash to fill the nation's coffers.

GDP growth is the best measure of how well our country is doing economically. GDP growth is also a very good measure of how well our government is governing.

HOW WELL HAVE WE DONE AS A NATION IN GENERATING GDP?

Over the past seventy years, as revealed by the vital GDP statistics readily available on the internet, some force has begun to drag down GDP growth.[22] That conclusion becomes clear from the reported trends. The negative impact of government decisions is the obvious cause of slowing economic growth. The most significant GDP-influencing decisions of government in the past century were the formation of the Administrative State and the installation of various expensive social programs paid by the taxpayers. Those government decisions directed resources and focus away from production, thereby decreasing national efficiency.

The 40-year time period, 1980 to the present, was selected to demonstrate the growth of productivity in our country. The Administrative State was fully established by 1980. Since that date, GDP growth has been "weak with a negative trend." Growth has slowed, arguably because of the weight of government spending decisions on the economy.

---

[22] Bureau of Economic Analysis Data

SUMMARY OF U.S. GDP GROWTH OVER THE PAST 70 YEARS

- In the 70 years SINCE 1950 there were 25 years when annual GDP growth exceeded 4%. **That happened in 36% of those years.**

- 1980 is the approximate date when implementation of the Administrative State was effectively completed. In the 40 years since 1980 there have been 7 years when GDP growth exceeded 4%. **That occurred in 18% of those years, a serious decline.**

- **Most telling, since the year 2000, there have been zero years when GDP grew more than 4%.** Since 2005 there have been zero years evidencing growth higher than 2%.

- **Most government planning is now based on a 2% GDP growth rate assumption for the future. Acceptance of a mediocre-growth future is now built into the national psyche.**

There is, of course, another perspective. **Perhaps growth slowed because high GDP growth has not ever been a national imperative!** The imperatives of today are party-driven. Parties spend their money on social goals aimed at capturing voter support. Our party politicians do not want to be held accountable for increasing GDP growth because doing so would diminish the financial resources available to pursue party agendas.

GDP growth, the critical measure of how well a nation is doing financially, is never a topic of political discussion. Political parties rank their re-election priorities ahead of the welfare of the nation and do not discuss those issues unless forced to do so.

Poor economic performance since the year 2000 signals a weak future for our Nation. Slow GDP growth during that quarter-century has produced slow wage growth for the working population. It is one of the causes of the gap between the "haves" and the "have-nots," although not by any means the only cause.

SLOW GDP GROWTH HAS SERIOUS NATIONAL SECURITY IMPLICATIONS

Our GDP trend is alarming. Communist China, with a population four times as large as the U.S.A., has grown its GDP in excess of 7% annually for many years. If the trend continues, within two decades, the U.S.A. will be a has-been power in a world dominated by Communist China.

The difference between Chinese and U.S. economic performance is not the result of different political systems. IT IS THE RESULT OF A DIFFERENCE IN THE QUALITY OF GOVERNMENT DECISION-MAKING.

China makes decisions, and the United States does not. The Chinese focus on decisions that improve their country's position and performance. **Decisions made by the U.S. are for the purpose of improving political party re-election prospects.** *China has a well-designed strategic plan to advance the country's interests.* **We do not. We have programs to improve party election prospects.**

2% growth is acceptable? In a country as great as ours, 2% growth must be rated ABJECT FAILURE. There is no other way to describe it. Twice that growth number, 4%, would be barely acceptable performance for the United States.

The People must set the national imperative for GDP growth! The hired management then has responsibility for achieving the goal. Every government decision would be made based upon whether nor not actions being considered will drive the nation toward achieving the national GDP objective. Having national imperatives clearly does tend to put the horse in front of the cart!

WHAT IS CAUSING SLOW GDP GROWTH?

Our g*overnment's decision-making process is deeply flawed. The cumulative effect of our poor decisions is slow (and slowing) GDP growth.*

Poor decisions, lack of decisions, flip-flopping of political party dogma and political programs every few years, lack of clear and agreed-upon national goals, weak policies such as out-sourcing business overseas to take advantage of cheap labor costs, and diversion of resources to expensive and non-productive party-promotion programs, all are weighing down national economic performance. We are a "dithering" nation, trundling along without a road-map or defined destination and overlaying one mistake with another. But the political parties are doing just fine, thank you!

Our "Ship of State" is trying to sail, but dragging a huge anchor. Government programs are not supportive of or coordinated with a set of national goals. The nation's programs are random political pot shots fired at party-beneficial targets. **True national goals do not exist**.

In the 200-plus years following the adoption of our Constitution, we reaped the huge financial benefits of westward development in a large country blessed with vast tracts of unused land, massive raw materials, ethical and motivated people, and endless freedom-based opportunities. A powerhouse nation admired by the world emerged.

The wealth generated by that rapid expansion masked deep flaws in the system of government. There were, of course, incredibly strong positive forces embedded in the Constitution that laid the foundation for rapid growth and economic development. Prominent among those are high levels of personal freedom, a small, constrained government, and the Free Market and Free Enterprise economic system. For many years, in the generation of GDP, those positive forces outweighed the negative effects of poor decision-making in our political party and political-elite controlled Monarchy Republic government.

The 200-year boom of westward expansion is now history. Indications are that our Nation is at a major fork in the road. The "freedom momentum," inventiveness, and the general drive of the citizenry continue to generate economic steam, but the drag of poor government is slowing the ship of state. Sick GDP growth is clear proof of that conclusion.

What the Nation decides to do at this fork in the road will determine its future. We had best be sure we choose wisely. **We still have a choice, but the time clock is ticking. The choice must be made by The People, most certainly not by political parties or the hired management.**

SECTION 2
THE NATION'S ASSEMBLY DECISION-MAKING

Steered by the Party system, vast national effort and huge sums of The People's money are being bet on self-serving political party programs or on ideological goals that may be popular with party factions and poorly-informed voters but do nothing to produce the GDP growth essential to our People's welfare. And while following that disastrous course, our nation is piling up a mountain of debt.

The enduring political argument is "The decisions were made via the democratic process; therefore, they were the will of the people." What is described in the preceding paragraph is the failure of the planning and decision processes of the nation by blindly relying on the self-serving actions of political parties. **The fact of the matter is that the decisions of our nation were just the will of one party in power. That doesn't mean the decisions were the *will of the people. It simply means one party acquired a voting stick big enough to beat the opposition into submission and impose its own will!***

That is why being "in power" is the overarching party need. It gives the party an opportunity to impose its "superior system beliefs" and the all-important ability to spray financial benevolence about to enhance its re-election prospects. Party focus is always on re-election, never on the welfare of the nation.

Our nation can make a turn-around only if government focus is fixed squarely and solely on the nation's welfare. Putting the party ahead of the Nation, our totally irrational way of governing produces warped and corrupted decision-making. That is the unrelenting curse of the party system and the underlying cause of our nation's poor GDP results.

If there is such a thing as a "superior system," it would not have party origin because that kind of system has the active support of but one-third of the population and blind acquiescence from the other two-thirds. A "superior system" would be one in which, after an organized national dialogue, our citizens developed "our best direction judgment," written as statements of intent and supported by all. A superior system of authority would then direct the nation to achieve the decided imperatives.

> *Political parties will never provide an answer to poor government decision-making.* The reason is THEY ARE THE FUNDAMENTAL CAUSE OF POOR GOVERNMENT DECISION-MAKING.

GIVEN THE FREEDOM TO ORGANIZE OUR ASSEMBLIES, ELECTED PERSONS DECIDED TO FORM POLITICAL PARTIES FOR VOTING CONTROL.

It was under Article 1, Section 5 constitutional provision that Elected Representatives and Senators, in the period immediately following the signing of the Constitution, decided to congregate as political parties to establish assembly voting clout.

Political parties were not the idea of the Framers and were not the idea of The People. Neither of those groups has ever voted on the political party approach to government. They were solely the construct of elected officials, created to give them a hammer that would aid in their drive for assembly power and control.

> **Of all the organization and delegation decisions made by nations in the history of mankind, the Framer constitutional decision incorporated as Article I, Section 5, Para. 2 ("Each House may determine the Rules of its Proceedings.") must rank as the most ill-conceived. Existing processes of our legislative branches, including decision-making processes, are all the result of that Constitutional provision.**
>
> **Readers must remember that, in a self-governed nation, a constitutional arm of the citizens must control and direct the Authority Structure decision process. If that control does not exist, neither does "self-government."**

A political party is a trade union of elected officials. Trade unions exist to amass leverage for use against the employer. They are not the "friend" of the employer. They have one purpose, which is to serve the interests of their union members.

Because the employer of our elected officials is The People, the parties had to enlist supportive voters to solidify backing for their union control effort. From their position of superiority, they were able to convince citizens to support their party system.

Legislative branch organizations and procedures that have evolved in the last two-plus centuries are a mish-mash of compromises devised within their assemblies by the elected persons. The procedures were not devised for the purpose of delivering to The People the finest decisions known to mankind. And, predictably, they never have!

USING PLANNED FORWARD DIRECTION TO IMPROVE DECISION-MAKING

Commercial enterprises have developed sophisticated strategic planning processes to generate what are usually called "Corporate Objectives." Usually five or less in number, they define the important goals to be accomplished by the enterprise over a long-term forward period and, once developed, guide the planning process and overall decision-making. **They rank as the most important business decisions of the enterprise.**

The purpose of Corporate Objectives is to provide the enterprise with FOCUS, shutting out all phantom competing notions, ensuring that the swirling indecision effect of lacking direction is eliminated, and allocation of resources is totally rational. Decisions are made against the test of whether actions under consideration support the achievement of the corporate objectives.

Much has been said about the political party system and its disastrous effects on our nation's forward momentum. **Absent from the political process is any meaningful long-term focus**. In a nation the size of the United States, most every major effort covers a time horizon much longer than four years, which merely measures the time space between Presidential elections.

NATIONAL IMPERATIVES ARE NEEDED TO POINT THE NATION FORWARD

It has been mentioned that Communist China has excellent strategic planning, while the United States contents itself with relying on the political parties for what passes as planning, following the majority party lead, and governing by reacting to whatever occurs. China has a dozen or so objectives that it pursues relentlessly, all falling within its "grand strategy," putting our nation in an on-going defensive and reactive posture.[23] Most are familiar with the Chinese "Belt and Road" initiative, which fulfills one of their important national goals.

---

[23] Rand Corp Article "Interpreting China's Grand Strategy" by Michael D. Swaine and Ashley Tellis

OUR "POOR DECISIONS" PROBLEM HAS ITS ROOTS IN THE CONSTITUTION

An old Beverly Hills business metaphor is worth quoting: "A fish stinks from the head." In our nation, the odiferous head is party-system government.

The cause of organizational non-performance will always be found at its top. In the case of our country the waft of poor government is excreted by Congress. To be more specific, it is the odor of a slather of poor decisions and avoided decisions, generated by a lack of an overall agreed-upon sense of direction, compliments of the party system.

The pungent odor originates from an ostensibly innocent provision in the Constitution, Article I, Section 5, Para. 2: "Each House may determine the Rules of its Proceedings."

An implication of the aforementioned provision will immediately pop into the mind of thinkers: Given the propensities of elected politicians, granting assemblies of them full authority to manage themselves without direction, control, or accountability is indeed putting the inmates in charge of the asylum. **The likelihood of a good outcome approaches the zero bound.** The only citizens likely to think this is a good path to follow would be the party faithful and the Elected Politicians themselves.

ALTERNATIVE PRINCIPLES UNDER WHICH ASSEMBLY PROCESSES CAN BE CONDUCTED

Elected Assemblies in countries that practice democracy can be managed by employing two opposite processes:

1. "Contention" is a process in which assembly conclusions are reached between factions of members who oppose each other. Its decision process utilizes vote purchase techniques like bargaining, trading, coercion, and force to achieve a majority vote resolution.

2. "Cooperation," in which assembly conclusions are reached by participants working together using planning, investigation, and problem-solving to make rational decisions that are believed will produce optimal results.

HOW DID "CONTENTION" BECOME OUR ASSEMBLY DECISION PROCESS CHOICE?

The Framer separation of Government into three independent branches, checking-and-balancing each other, created an atmosphere of "contention" rather than of "co-operation." Elected persons introduced the contentious courtroom environment into the processes of the two Legislative branches. Political parties, converting government to a competitive resolution process, instituted "contention" as the operating mode of the Legislative branches.

"Contention" was not the choice of The People. It is not a specific provision in the constitution. Its implementation was adopted under the disastrous Article 1, Section 5 provision, "Each House may determine the Rules of its Proceedings." As the choice of political parties, its selection was obviously the wish of the dominant lawyer assembly faction.

The largest faction of our politicians are lawyers. "Contention" is the courtroom atmosphere with which lawyers are most familiar and comfortable. Applying it to the government workplace was likely a "programmed decision" on their part.

This discussion carries a warning to The People concerning the severe risks of allowing democratic assemblies to be dominated by factions of any type. Both subjects, "factions" and "programmed decisions," will receive particular attention later in this writing.

The judgments of a faction-dominated assembly will inevitably be warped. That conveys a challenge to The People. They must make a discrete decision as to which of the previously mentioned assembly alternatives shall be used to derive future conclusions and write laws.

The word "decisions" is often used to describe the bargained conclusions of elected assemblies. The descriptor "decisions," is inaccurate for that purpose, however.

A "decision" is reached by the application of reason and logic using factual information. The result achieved in our elected assemblies, by bargaining, trading, and utilizing whatever leverage is available, more closely resembles a "marketplace bargain" than a "decision." But the Elected Persons comprising an assembly were given the right to reach conclusions any way they chose, and that is what our nation ended up with.

EXPERT OPINIONS AND VIEWS REGARDING ASSEMBLY DECISIONS

Authors Maria Turpin and Mario Marais, in their 2004 book "Decision-making, Theory and Practice,"[24] describe their "views" of several types of decisions. One of those types, The Political View, describes political decisions as follows:

> **"The political view sees decision-making as a personalized bargaining process driven by agendas of participants rather than rational processes. People differ on the organization's goals, values, and the relevance of information. The decision-making process never ends, but remains a continuous battle between different coalitions.**
>
> **Influence and power are wielded in a deliberate manner and to further self-interest. The goals of coalitions are defined by self-interest, rather than what is in the best interest of the organization as a whole."**

That rather damning view very accurately describes "Contentious Assembly Processes" and how political parties "make decisions" in our elected assemblies. Is it any wonder the quality of decisions in our government is so poor?

SECTION 3
IMPROVING THE DECISION PROCESS WITH NATIONAL IMPERATIVES

This book repeatedly discusses the critical weakness in our government's decision-making. An ancient Strategic Planner's saying applies to the U.S. government decision process very succinctly: **"If you don't know where you want to go, any road will take you there!"**

The importance of a strong sense of direction for any country is obvious. Well-governed nations determine where the country should go and then decide how to go there. Operating decisions are made against defined strategic goals. **For such nations, the government focus is on goal achievement.**

Look no further than China for a working example of the effective use of national imperatives. There is much to dislike about the Chinese communist government, but there is much to admire about the directional focus that drives its rapid GDP growth and its rise in

---

[24] Turpin, Maria and Marais, Mario (2004): "Decision-making Theory and Practice," ORION, 20.10.5784.20-2-12

power. **Chinese long-term objectives are clear to all, as are their implementation strategies. Their strategic planning is first-class!**

Of course, China has no polarization problem because only one political party exists and no media problem because the one-party exercises tight control over the media. And there is no contention about "where we are going and what we want to achieve" since one party decides all of that. **But they do make the important directional decisions, and they do execute them!**

We don't want their political system. We certainly don't want their administrative process, which trends toward bungling. We don't want their authoritative approach. But we certainly could benefit from their focused strategic direction, which moves the country forward cohesively and relentlessly.

FORTUNATELY, DIRECTIONAL FOCUS IS NOT THE PROPERTY OF ANY PARTICULAR POLITICAL SYSTEM. IT CAN BELONG TO ANY POLITICAL SYSTEM THAT IS WILLING TO USE STRATEGIC OBJECTIVES AND INSTALL A "MUST-DO" CULTURE.

OUR NATION CAN HAVE DIRECTIONAL FOCUS, AND THERE IS NO MYSTERY ABOUT HOW TO GET IT.

PARTY GOALS PRODUCED IN ELECTIONS ARE NOT NATIONAL IMPERATIVES

If one begins with the basic truth that national strategic objectives (or "imperatives") would set a clear direction to focus a Nation's decision-making and operating performance and that determining those imperatives is arguably the most important decision process of a Nation, then an examination of our current dysfunctional decision process becomes very relevant.

Most large businesses and non-business organizations in our Republic manage themselves by making current decisions against an agreed-upon set of long-term objectives. Those objectives, derived in a rigorous strategic planning process and adopted by all, implement the "planning" responsibilities of the nation's owners. Defining strategic objectives is the means to communicate their "Direct" responsibility.

Well-conceived and agreed-upon imperatives become the framework against which the operating decisions of a country are made. **Agreed-upon direction eliminates the curse of indecision and endless argument. It provides certainty**, allowing all attention to be focused on "what we must do." The process of setting and achieving strategic goals builds national cohesion.

A party's promotional goals, designed for election success, do not translate into the longer-term aspirations of the nation. It would be an accident of the first order if a political party happened to stumble on our nation's long-term imperatives when searching for something that will snag enough voter interest to *put the party in power*. **Getting the party's candidates elected and putting the party in power is the purpose of political party planning. Identifying the nation's aspirations has little or nothing to do with that.**

When an election has been held, no national agreement has been reached concerning major actions needed or problems that must be solved. No national "will" was created, no national "sense of direction" was established, and no national "commitment" was put in place. Do not be swayed by a party leader's self-justifying shouts of having "a mandate from the voters." The party planning process was party-centric. The resulting goals were party goals, and the party was elected by votes of only a minor percentage of the nation's owners.

What is popular with party faithful is usually not what is needed by the country. The notion that political party leaders have magical insight into the needs of the country is shredded by the realization that they really don't care about the country's needs; their job is to get their party into power. The voting system is popularity-based, not rationality-based. When did you last see a political party campaigning on a platform of fiscal sanity?

Elections are the democratic way to select individuals to serve in government. The foofaraw of the election process is mainly generated by and for candidates. Elections aren't an appropriate setting for determining national direction. Poking at critical "what we must do" national direction decisions in political party elections is totally irrational, but that is what emerges when the planning process has been abandoned to political parties by The People.

THE NATIONAL IMPERATIVES WOULD GUIDE
GOVERNMENT ACTION

Chapter 15 of The People's Direction and Control Series will discuss the importance of observing "the proper order of things" in top-level decision-making. It is improper to preempt that discussion here (thereby violating the proper order of things, so to speak), but its relevance to the current discussion is important enough to justify a brief propriety over-ride.

> The "what to do" decisions of the Nation must be made first, and the "how to do it" decisions follow. That discipline in the decision process "keeps the horse in front of the cart," as the old saying goes.

Totally absent from our national governance is any process for deriving a consensus answer to the critical question, "What do we need to do?" As a nation, we do not establish objectives or imperatives. We have values, we have beliefs, we have principles, we have elections, we

87

have political parties shouting at us, and we have a constitution, but our country's processes do not contain a rational planning-based process to define "What must be done."

Chapter 16 of The People's Direction and Control Series contains a proposal by which the National Imperatives, our nation's statements of "What must be done," **would be determined by The People to establish for the nation the needed sense of direction.**

GET THE HORSE OUT IN FRONT OF THE CART!

Our "directional" conversations consist of considering proposals put forth by political parties, which are self-serving totalitarian entities trying to attract interest in programs that support their party goals. Party proposals serve that party's purpose only. They are not, and will not ever be, an agreement among The People about "What must be done and where must we go" as a nation.

Under the constitution's provision that allows each Legislative branch to "determine the rules of its proceedings," both Houses turned control of the chamber over to the majority political parties. Signaling that they didn't see any real value in national direction-setting, they abandoned that critical activity to the political parties.

In the order of disciplined decision-making, they positioned the cart squarely in front of the horse. Bass-ackwards, as the saying goes.

DIRECTION-SETTING IS THE PEOPLE'S OBLIGATION, THE EXECUTION OF THEIR OWNER "PLAN AND DIRECT RESPONSIBILITY." The People must not ever delegate that to the hired management in government, and it most certainly should not be put in the hands of the hired management's trade unions the political parties.

SECTION 4
WHAT IS THE PATH FORWARD?

Improved government decision-making distills to a choice between (a) establishing a cooperative and owner-controlled process of producing quality decisions for the nation or (b) continuing to use the Legislative branch contention process of contriving negotiated bargains.

That conclusion brings to the fore our citizen's perspective of democracy, the political parties, and how they observe government being conducted. **Citizens have difficulty envisioning self-government carried out in any manner other than the endless contentious and unproductive political party hassle with which they are familiar. Thinking "outside of the box" is difficult-to-impossible for most citizens.**

There are a few signals that The People (or at least a considerable percentage of them) are aware of the factors discussed in these Chapters. Somehow, they have developed an increasingly pessimistic attitude toward political parties. The depth of citizen comprehension is difficult to measure. One sign of developing citizen pessimism is the number of voters choosing to register as "Independent." Those voters now outnumber registered Republicans or registered Democrats and, according to pollsters, will decide the 2020 election.[25]

Registered Independents are mostly not truly independent, so we are told. Registered Independents tend to favor either the left wing or the right wing but are frustrated with the party toward which they lean. It is not known the extent to which their ballot choice, always a choice between the two major parties, reflects the favoritism propensity of independents. If you have a ballot choice between two parties, it is necessary to pick one, whether you like it or not. Independents may truly not favor either political party, and they may register as Independents to register a revolt against the party system.

Nor are registered Independents a political party. Independents are merely a classification reserved for voters who have "opted out" of the party system. Independents tend to be young, under 40 years, an age group that is heavily biased against political parties.

Registered Independents, it is believed, will favor the proposals in this Book, which can be distilled into a quick summary. **It is entirely possible for voters registered as independents to formally demonstrate rejection of political parties.**

**CONSTITUTIONAL ACTION PLAN
ELIMINATING POLITICAL PARTIES TO IMPROVE GOVERNMENT DECISIONS**

- DEVELOP PEOPLE-GENERATED NATIONAL IMPERATIVES THAT GOVERNMENT MUST ACHIEVE.
- DEVELOP PEOPLE-GENERATED FINANCIAL MEASURES THAT GOVERNMENT MUST ACHIEVE.
- DEVELOP CONSTITUTIONAL RULES TO CONTROL OR ELIMINATE POLITICAL PARTIES.
- ESTABLISH AN ELECTED CONTROL BODY TO ENSURE THE PEOPLE'S INSTRUCTIONS ARE CARRIED OUT.
- DEVELOP AND IMPLEMENT A PEOPLE-DEVISED AND GOVERNMENT FUNDED CANDIDATE SELECTION AND VOTING SYSTEM TO REPLACE POLITICAL PARTY ACTIVITIES.
- ESTABLISH CONSTITUTIONAL CONTROL AND SUPERVISION OVER LEGISLATIVE BRANCH PROCEDURES TO ENSURE FOCUS ON QUALITY DECISIONS

----

[25] Gary Martin, Las Vegas Review Journal, November 4, 2019

CHAPTER 5

THE POLITICAL PARTY SERIES, PART 3

CONTENT:

SECTION 1: THE MORTAL BATTLE: DEMOCRACY VS. TOTALITARIANISM

SECTION 2: THE POLITICAL FACTION ISSUE

SECTION 3: ESTABLISH CONSTITUTIONAL BARRIERS AGAINST TOTALITARIAN ACTIVITY

FOREWORD

We, whether you regard us to be a "democracy" or a" republic," are supposedly committed to decision-making utilizing democratic voting principles. The extent to which citizens are involved in decision-making marks the difference between democratic government and authoritarian government.

Our nation's need for greatly improved government will be best met by improving the quality of its decisions, which ultimately determine the success of the nation and the welfare of its people. Improved authority-structure decision-making requires two actions: Eliminating a host of structure problems, poor practices, and activities that pollute the existing decision process and ensuring that the critical directional decisions are made by those who have the most at stake, The People.

"Government of the People, by the People, and for the People" is our nation's slogan. It was the "right" goal, but it turned out to be nothing more than a slogan. The People were given no power to conduct "government by the People." Being able to elect government officials but not being able to correct the performance of government can hardly be described as self-government.

From the beginning, totalitarian forces have been working to replace democratic government CONTROL. Our elected democratic bodies, with their political parties and constitutionally-granted self-management, have proven inept guardians of our governance system.

The "battle to the death" between democratic and totalitarian ideologies is the subject of this chapter. CONTROL, the motivation and weapon of democracy's deadly enemy, totalitarianism, is given special attention. Under the concepts of a democratic republic government, all control decisions require approval by a democratic vote.

SECTION 1
DEMOCRACY VS. TOTALITARIANISM

THE MORTAL BATTLE

The years since the launching of our Republic have been scarred by constant and never-ending internal political battles for CONTROL over the political system and governance, **battles fought between democracy and various non-democratic internal threats.** A range of threats exist.

The true meaning of "Government by the People" is 'The People alone exercise control over government." The Framers created and constitutionally installed a variation to the "democratic." form of government called a "Republic." A Republic selects those who govern through elections but vests those who govern with total power. Citizens have one role, and one role only....to elect those who govern. Such a system, a democratic variation, is not "Government by The People." It is "Election by The People." It is useful to consider the wide range of variations within the government classification "democracy," variations that are generally not discussed.

Democracy features government by democratic vote, with total control belonging to the citizens. Within the category labeled "democratic," small-to-wide differences in philosophy and process are commonplace.

Totalitarian government, on the other hand, is authoritarian. Its decisions are made by one or a few individuals, and ultimate control is vested in them. **Totalitarians achieve total control of government so that one or a few can impose authoritarian methods and ideas. Within the broad category called "totalitarian," small-to-wide variations of approach are common.**

This Chapter will focus on the two major governmental systems, democratic and totalitarian, and ignore the varieties of approaches within each. The two major systems have developed antagonism, flowing from constant battles between them for dominance.

The Framer grants of "freedom" opened the door for that existential battle in our nation. The grant and structure of total freedom make the democratic system extremely vulnerable to internal attack. Our democracy is a weak bastion, and it has taken no steps to insure or defend itself against such attacks. To those bent on subverting democracy, freedom is fertilizer. They take advantage of the freedom and population ignorance to cast the weed seeds of tyranny. Absent a weed killer, those weeds soon dominate the political field.

The many battles for control have produced nothing for our nation except time wasted and a monumental diversion of focus. The reason the battles occur is the failure of the Framers, and all who followed them, to build into our constitution provisions that deny anti-democratic forces any operating latitude. By failing to protect against that internal threat, "freedom" was accorded a value much higher than that given the continued existence of our "democratic republic government."

This final Chapter, Part 3 of the Political Party Series, will address the on-going totalitarian threat to the continuation of our democratic republic government from two directions:

1. It will examine the effect of freedom facilitating the totalitarian attack against democracy in government and propose defenses permitting the survival of both freedom and democracy.

2. It will examine ongoing totalitarian actions within the nation by "political factions" and their warping effect on the democratic process.

THREE CONSTITUTIONAL PROVISIONS SET THE STAGE FOR THE EXISTENTIAL BATTLE:

Because of the absence of the weed-killer called "accountability," "Government of the People, by the People and for the People" matured as an over-grown weed-patch. A monarchy republic, generally viewed in disrepute by The People, it functions as "Government of the People, by Political Parties, and for the Political Elite."

The Framers well understood that a long reign for their Monarchy Republic could be secured by instituting the following three constitutional provisions. The government they designed was trumpeted as being based on democratic processes, and in fact many were employed, but the final government, which they called a "republic," is fundamentally a monarchy.

1. The First Amendment "Bill of Rights," granting broad freedom to citizens, opened the field for planting the weeds of tyranny by control-driven individuals and political factions. The Bill of Rights granted broad freedoms but established no commensurate accountability on the part of citizens. It contains no defense against

those utilizing the freedoms to promote tyranny. **There is no weed-killer in the First Amendment.**

2. The Constitution's Article 1, Section 4 provision declaring that "Each House may determine the Rules of its Proceedings" is another ill-conceived freedom grant. This provision gave control-oriented elected persons the freedom to plant the weeds of totalitarianism within the Houses of Congress. Their first act was to permit self-interest political parties to control government, thereby implanting an aggressive crop of tyranny weeds. **Article 1, Section 4, ignores the need for weed killers.**

3. The Constitution's Article V transfers away from The People who own the nation the power to amend their own Constitution, granting that critical power to government functions that are ultimately controlled by the political elite. Article V guaranties endless continuation of the Framer Monarchy Republic governance arrangement by denying The People any route to amend their own constitution. **There is obviously no weed killer in Article V.**

THOSE CONSTITUTIONAL PROVISIONS GUARANTY ENTRENCHMENT OF THE POLITICAL ELITE IN THEIR MONARCHY REPUBLIC

One must wonder why "Government of the People, by the People, and for the People," that wondrous slogan, never became a reality in our nation. It must have been nothing more than a public relations ploy designed to divert voter attention away from the Monarchy Republic that is our true form of government. The Monarchy Republic is totalitarian, as are all monarchies. The fact that those who manage the Monarchy Republic were democratically elected and that democratic processes are employed here and there within the Assemblies does not change the fundamental character of the government. In the fashion of all monarchies, the People were left with no power.

CONTENT OF THIS SECTION

1. This Section will examine the totalitarian attack on democratic government by "political parties" and propose actions for democracy's survival.

2. It will examine totalitarian actions across the nation by "political factions," with their warping effect on the democratic voting process. Corrective actions will be proposed.

Did the Framers not realize that democracy and totalitarianism are mortal enemies in a fight to the death? They must have because the British monarchs they hated so intensely were classic totalitarians.

> Democracy is based on broad freedom, which makes it incredibly vulnerable to subversion from within. Freedom is considered a vital attribute of democracy, but unfortunately, by granting internal totalitarian factions freedom of operation, various routes to democracy's destruction were opened wide to them.

Democracy and Totalitarianism are situated at the opposite poles of the political spectrum. For whatever reason, the Framers did not seem to comprehend that future threats to their "democracy" would be internal, mounted by authoritarian factions of our own people taking advantage of that which Freedom makes available. Perhaps they thought that totalitarianism was a permissible political outcome under the concept of Freedom, an extremely radical interpretation of that democratic right. In any event, they installed no constitutional barriers to protect their freedom-based Monarchy Republic from the internal totalitarian enemy.

No weed-killer there, either.

SUBVERSION FROM WITHIN

Using elected persons to design government is like asking corporate employees to invent the propulsion system for jet aircraft. With apologies to corporate employees for the probably inappropriate comparison, we make the point that it would be a miracle if elected officials had the skills and knowledge to design government.

We recognize totalitarianism by its distinguishing attributes: *its aggression, its restraint of freedom, and its focus on centralized control by a few*. By way of contrast, in a democracy, control vests solely in the hands of the citizens. When the control is total, "government by the people" has been instituted. **If The People's power is only to elect or terminate elected officials, that version of democracy arguably does not qualify as democracy and clearly is not "government by the people."**

Totalitarian interests, given operating freedom, pursue their take-over goals by installing totalitarian processes whenever the opportunity arises, usually without disturbing the underlying democracy. Although citizens (including those elected) should be qualified to do so, they are not able to readily identify totalitarian activities. **Ignorance, in a democracy, is also a fertilizer for totalitarian weed growth.**

The internal subversion threat is not as simple as just "freedom," however. Freedom can be retained in a democracy by making certain it cannot be taken away by internal enemies or other elected persons or be lost through operating weaknesses. That certainty must be established through Constitutional provisions. The result will be a democracy with freedom exclusions.

Democratic government cannot be allowed to be a political party tennis-ball or to wander aimlessly under self-management. It has to be tightly disciplined by its owners, its duties directed, and must be made to take the unpopular actions that political parties and elected persons want to avoid. It must be designed so The People can set its direction and correct course if they have erred. Those demands require that it be under constant scrutiny by The People. Assembly's internal freedom of operation, given the kind of officials we elect, lays open the immense possibility of mismanagement. Knowledgeable outsiders hired by The People, are needed to do the system designing and provide assembly management.

WHY HAVE ELECTED OFFICIALS NOT INSTALLED DEMOCRACY PROTECTIONS IN OUR NATION?

Readers will, by this time, have become bothered by a nagging thought. Since the 1780s, tens of thousands of elected officials have paraded through the halls of Congress. With kite-strings of initials behind their names, they were self-promoters who could convince voters that they are the answer to the nation's problems. Then why is it those tens of thousands could not have been depended upon to recognize threats to government and install democracy protections?

There is, of course, the possibility that many elected to Congress did not possess the ability to distinguish democratic practices from those of totalitarianism. The kite-strings of initials behind an elected person's name apparently don't include a "democracy expert" credential. There is also the probability that the elected are not able to divine how protecting democracy could boost them into their personal "Hall of Fame."

A new constitutional definition of Freedom is needed. It would contain, in addition to others, the following protective provisions:

1) Totalitarianism is a major threat to Republican Democracy, so its existence in the nation is not permitted. Citizen involvement of any kind in anti-democracy activity is a treason offense against the nation.

2) After a 50-year period has elapsed, and every similar span of time thereafter, the citizens may reconsider our form of government as against alternative forms, including totalitarianism, and make a voted choice.

3) Totalitarianism, any type, shall have no Free Speech rights in the nation.

4) Educational systems shall instruct the threat of totalitarianism as a part of civics training concerning our nation and its Constitution.

5) All elected persons, and all management persons in the nation's Authority Structure, shall receive totalitarian characteristics and deficiency instruction before assuming duties, and swear an oath of totalitarian opposition.

6) The goal of the nation is to maximize Freedom, but recognizes that there are limitations. Freedom cannot extend to the support of any activity that constitutes a threat to our selected form of government.

We think it likely, despite the flag-waving and patriotic trumpeting that garnishes the behavior of persons occupying the elected office, that mostly their motivations are neither wholesome nor patriotic. Their driving motives are more likely personal, of the "personal life-plan advancement" variety. Observing their behavior leads to the conclusion that seeking political office is a self-serving entrepreneurial venture with one overriding goal …. to enhance the life prospects of the elected person through whatever benefits serving in an elected office brings.

> To explain human behavior, in the 1950s Abraham H. Maslow, a well-known American psychologist and philosopher, introduced a "conceptual ladder of human needs" that came to be known as Maslow's Hierarchy.[1] The ladder is based on the principle that, after physiological needs at the base of the hierarchy have been met (such as food and shelter), human drives are elevated through two additional definable stages (love/belonging, and self-esteem) to self-actualization, which is the final stage, the ultimate goal of human striving.
>
> It is probable most elected officials will be found in the middle/upper echelons of Maslow's Hierarchy, around the "love/belonging" level. There they seek acceptance, recognition, and confidence from their peers and others. They are under way in their drive toward the goal of self-actualization, and their role as an elected person is the vehicle to get them there.

If that hypothesis is accurate, elected persons are not in Congress to advance the nation. Rather, Congress is a place for them to pursue their personal drive toward self-actualization. In that mode, political parties, voters, and legislative processes are merely tools they use advantageously.

Elected persons attempting to climb the hierarchy make great party members. They try, with the aid of the political party, to "make things happen." "Be a good party member, don't make waves or do anything stupid, and the party will help you reach "Self-Actualization."

But the thinking reader will also note that party-oriented elected officials seeking self-actualization, are not good foundation-stones for democratic government. Good government is founded on elected officials whose sole purpose is to serve the nation. Perhaps that explains why elected officials have made no effort to protect our democratic Republic against authoritarian incursion.

BEWARE THE SLIPPERY SLOPE!

Russia is a prominent totalitarian nation. In September 1959, one of its leaders, Nikita Khrushchev, visited the U.S.A. to address the United Nations. A viral social media quote currently in circulation attributes to him the 1959 prediction of a "socialist state" to replace our democratic government, a prediction that also contained the famous statement "We will bury you!"

In a speech to the Orange County Press Club in 1961, entitled "Encroaching Control," Ronald Reagan alleged that Khrushchev had said, "We can't expect the American people to jump from Capitalism to Communism, but we can assist their elected leaders in giving them small doses of Socialism until they awaken one day to find they have Communism."[26]

Our democratic republic government has degraded over time because it is excessively vulnerable to authoritarian attack from within, allowing the Reagan-described process to flourish. It morphed Congress and the Presidency into today's hybrid mixture of democratic government and totalitarianism. The morphing continues, its speed seemingly accelerating.

One suspects that the older a democratic-type government is, the greater will be the percentage of non-democratic practice present in its operations. Democratic elections produce officials skilled in party politics and achieving popularity but strangers to the principles of management and the rules of democracy. A factor contributing to our long path of democratic degradation has been the inability of mentally manipulated and poorly informed citizens to recognize the blatantly totalitarian practices of elected persons. **Policing of government by citizens and by the media has not been successful in our nation.**

It would seem that failed democratic governments are almost always replaced with totalitarian rule. To view the process, follow the events now unfolding in the Republic of Panama.

DEMOCRATIC GOVERNMENT IS DIFFICULT

Dedicated, well-informed, moral-and-ethical citizens are essential. They must be committed to doing what is necessary to make their democratic system of government function at a superior level and must develop the insight to comprehend what is needed.

Survival of democracy requires that citizens establish powerful defenses against all internal threats to their self-government, totalitarianism being prominent. The main defense must be a constitutional denial of freedom to engage in such activities. That approach requires a

---

[26] Reuters World May 11, 2020: "False Claim: Nikita Khrushchev 1959 Quote to the United Nations General Assembly"

revision of the democratic definition of "Freedom" to a new definition that allows for freedom's essential exclusions.

THE NEVER-ENDING BATTLE BETWEEN "DEMOCRACY" AND "TOTALITARIANISM" RAGES

Totalitarianism and democracy are direct opposites. They are mortal enemies in constant and endless confrontation. One or the other will persevere, in every nation where they contest, and they contest in every nation currently under democratic government.

History informs us that human striving for control is relentless and never-ending. Battlefield graveyards attest to that truth.

The political control battles of our nation have run uninterrupted for more than two centuries. They have produced a government by "contention and opposition" rather than a government by "co-operative consideration and decision." Those battles produced our totalitarian two-party political system and the endless unproductive controversy and polarization associated with it. It produced a huge Administrative State, a massive violation of the constitution's basic beliefs.

A surprising number of U.S. government decisions are today made in a non-democratic manner. Those decisions make clear how our government is steadily yielding ground to the internal authoritarian enemy. Left on their own, democratic processes will inevitably drift toward authoritarian practices.

Eliminating the existential threat of internal subversion by installing planned Constitutional barriers will ensure the battle to the death between democracy and totalitarianism, will be short-lived.

CONCLUSIONS

The following highlighted statements summarize key points from the above discussion. They are important enough to warrant highlighting:

FREEDOM IS A FUNDAMENTAL OF DEMOCRATIC SELF-GOVERNMENT.

- **CONTROL, WHICH IS THE ANTITHESIS OF DEMOCRATIC SELF-GOVERNMENT, IS THE GOAL OF THOSE PREFERRING AUTHORITARIAN GOVERNMENT.**

- **CONTROL IS ALWAYS ACHIEVED BY A PROPORTIONATE REDUCTION OF FREEDOM.**

- **CONSTITUTIONAL FREEDOM IN A DEMOCRATIC NATION CAN NEVER BE ABSOLUTE. ABSOLUTE FREEDOM LEAVES THE NATION VULNERABLE, AND UNABLE TO SURVIVE RELENTLESS ANTI-DEMOCRATIC ATTACKS FROM WITHIN.**

FREEDOM-BASED SELF-GOVERNMENT CAN SURVIVE ONLY IF ANTI-DEMOCRATIC ACTIVITES ARE LABELLED AN *EXISTENTIAL THREAT*, AND APPROPRIATE CONSTITUTIONAL BARRIERS ARE ERECTED TO DENY SUCH THREATS EXISTENT RIGHTS WITHIN THE NATION.

SECTION 2
THE POLITICAL FACTION ISSUE

This Section will examine another internal threat to democracy called "political factions" and how their activities affect democracy's functioning.

Political parties and the multitude of smaller political groups supporting them were all called "factions" in the Framer time. At the time of Federalist Paper #10, often referenced in this Book, the word "faction" was used to describe political parties. In the two centuries-plus that have elapsed, the large factions operating within government came to be called "Political Parties," and the smaller politically-active groups outside of government were labeled "Political Factions." Wikipedia defines "factions" as common-interest groups operating within a larger entity.

In their reason for existence, most common-interest associations of people in our nation (meeting the broad definition of" faction") are non-threatening. Non-political associations exist for a wide variety of business, altruistic, religious, professional, pleasure, sport, or fraternal purposes. They are no threat to the nation's form of government and are positive contributors to the lives of citizens.

Swarms of common-interest organizations within our democratic Republic that were brought into existence for non-political reasons (including corporations formed for business purposes) subsequently chose to use their position to influence or control a political outcome. Organizations following that path decide to use their size or reputation, their money, their membership voting bulk, the loudness of their voice, or any other advantage they possess to influence the direction of the public, political parties, candidates, elected persons, and government. Those who have chosen that route can be massive in size and immense in impact. Walt Disney Company and the Teacher Employee Unions are prime examples.

When such gatherings use their membership bulk for political influence, they can have a profound effect. Democracy is modified, and not positively, by such actions. Such factions move their members from the one-person-one-vote citizen group and relocate them into a "factional disruptor" group. Their members, individually and in total, unite to become a bulk force that erodes, even eradicates, the one-person-one-vote fundamental.

We have chosen to call organizations formed for non-political purposes but which choose to engage in political activity "POLITICAL FACTIONS."

James Madison made remarks in 1787 aimed at what we would today call "Political Parties." It appears to mirror the general view of our citizens in 2022:

> **"Complaints are everywhere heard from our most considerate and virtuous citizens, equally the friends of public and private faith, and of public and personal liberty; that our governments are too unstable; that the public good is disregarded in the conflicts of the rival parties; and that measures are too often decided, not according to the rules of justice, and the rights of the minor party; but by the superior force of an interested and over-bearing majority."**

HOW DID THE FRAMERS DESCRIBE FACTIONS?

Factions utilize their inherent advantages to influence or achieve control. Nothing has changed in the two-plus centuries since Madison's assessment. Political parties are totalitarian organizations that have been permitted to operate within a democratic government. They are labeled "totalitarian" because they attempt to impose their beliefs by control.

In a self-governed democracy, control is exercised by The People, never by a political party or faction.

DEMOCRATIC PROCESSES THAT ARE VULNERABLE TO FACTION-WIELDED POWER

In general, the many political factions within our nation act in support of a favored political party. Their strategy is to use advantages conveyed by their inherent position for political influence or control. By employing the faction's bulk power, its leaders can bolster the control drive of a favored political party, which is to implant a totalitarian (control-focused) function in our democratic government. In return, they seek favored treatment.

In doing those things, political faction leaders hope to gain reputational enhancement within their faction for personal aggrandizement and internal stature purposes. The drive for self-actualization among faction leaders is present and strong! Maslow would be nodding his head and muttering, "I told you so!"

The following four are democratic processes vulnerable to the actions of political factions:

1. Each political faction member who votes to support a faction's political position decreases the national count of free citizen voters and increases the national count of captured "political faction voters." Citizen votes, thus converted to political faction votes, dilute the "one person, one vote" count, which produces negative effects on the nation's decision process. The effect is the dilution of "government by The People," which works its way upward to undermine the nation's governance.

2. The second of the four is the election process, where political factions exert heavy influence to elect candidates that favor their political position.

Various enterprises, originally formed for business or other purposes, are choosing to become involved in the political scene, thus earning the "political faction" label. The impulse to do that flows from various leadership and group motivations. The weapons wielded by political factions are their hefty public persona and money raised from employees or associates. But even more powerful is political faction leadership that swings employee or member votes to influence political thought or direction, actions are often undertaken to enhance leadership power or control within the faction. Private enterprises, many of which are prominent in the business scene, can wield awesome influence when choosing to become political factions.

Political factions dilute and undermine democracy. Their actions are a serious negative influence on the decisions of the nation and need to be dealt with as a force affecting the nation's "decision quality" strategy.

They do that by reducing the value and influence of the vote of individuals and magnifying the impact of large-block voting. Bolstered by large money contributions from those same factions, elections can be swung in the direction desired.

3. The third of the four is the process of government, in which political factions influence political parties and elected persons to gain favorable legislative treatment or support of a favored political direction. Money and votes are the weapons wielded to gain the ear of elected politicians, influencing them to favor the specific interests of the faction over that of the citizenry. The oversized influence of political factions on the voted decisions of Congress must be a matter of great concern to voters.

Political faction activity dramatically reduces the quality of decisions made by elected bodies of government.

4. The last is public opinion, where political factions use their money, the advantage of their position, or any other advantage they possess to influence the general public via Media advertising and other forms of communication.

That practice deeply contributes to the low level of political comprehension prevalent in the nation by increasing the number of biased voters and reducing the percentage of well-informed voters in the population. The intent of the practice is the degradation of the nation's democratic decision process.

THE IMPACT OF POLITICAL FACTIONS ON CITIZEN VOTE AND ON THE "ONE PERSON, ONE VOTE" PRINCIPLE

Readers, evaluating the impact of faction political activity, should consider which of the following would be their preferred environment for our democratic self-government:

a) All national citizens vote as individuals, with no citizen members of a political party or faction, no citizen committed to supporting such an entity, and with the nation totally obedient to the "one person, one vote" rule.

   OR:

b) The bulk of national citizens vote as members of one of the many thousands of existing political factions and will vote for their faction's narrow interest. The bulk of the nation's voters is, therefore, "factional disruptor" voters, supporters of their faction, subordinating the national interest (high-quality decisions) to the interest of their chosen faction.

If environment (b) is the choice, the national quality-decision goal supporting "government by The People" will have been ceded to the many Political Faction Disruptor groups. The term "government by The People" will become "government by self-interest voting blocks." They constitute thousands of entities, each diluting the vote value of the non-aligned citizens.

Nobody knows what the outcome of such a governing arrangement would be, but it certainly will not be the democratic self-government our citizens desire. The ordinary citizen will not be happy with such an arrangement.

SHOULD POLITICAL FACTIONS BE PERMITTED IN THIS DEMOCRACY?

Achieving high-quality democratic self-government requires suppression of anti-democratic activities in favor of a government based, to the extent possible, on purely democratic principles and processes. Political factions are just one of the multitudes of such activities within our nation, and a clean-up to achieve "government by the people" is badly needed. Denying anti-democratic activities operating room is vital. Achieving quality governmental decisions by placing all decision-making under the control of The People is merely cleaning up democracy's decision process. Establishing the one-person-one-vote principle by eliminating vote-aggregating activities would be a huge step forward in improving the critical government decision process.

For successful self-government decision upgrading, important voting decisions must be made by persons possessing substantial levels of knowledge. Citizens will want the nation's elected persons who participate in decision-making performing with focused patriotic commitment in an atmosphere free of influence, so that there can be no excuse for not producing quality decisions. **Factional forces of all types exist to warp the judgment of decision-makers, thereby undermining the exercise of well-informed free will.**

Citizens should view political factions as private armies (or mobs) operating within a democratic nation. Many citizens view assemblies of people, including Political Factions, as "freedom in action," as permitted by the Bill of Rights. They never stop to answer the baseline question: "Are such assemblies positive contributors to our self-government decision process?"

Factional political activity is not a superior way to provide the government with input from The People. It is an approach that produces more problems than solutions. There are more productive ways for people to communicate regarding issues than by participating in a direction promoted by special interest factions of one kind or another. **There can be no more potent representation for The People than through special facilities operated within their own Constitutional Authorities.** Removal of such people-to-government communication from today's channels requires that organized communication facilities and processes be initiated allowing The People to individually address issues, a proper and necessary companion to the "one person, one vote" concept.

Constitutional Authorities, as proposed in this Book, are the "planned replacement" of existing political parties and factions and the street activities of gatherings, which are the present means of stimulating Authority Structure action. The purpose of a Constitutional feedback process is to eliminate the elected person's middle-man role of "elected representative." Organized communication systems are always more appropriate in self-government democracies than is the mob route.

IS THE "RIGHT PEACEABLY TO ASSEMBLE" APPROPRIATE FOR POLITICAL FACTIONS?

The right peaceably to assemble was a "simple solution to a complex problem," authorized in the 1791 Bill of Rights, at a time when communication alternatives were few. It was installed to meet a basic requirement for a functioning democracy by ensuring that citizens can communicate with the government.

The Framers addressed that need with what was then available. They did not invent the "public gathering" vehicle, which is ancient and believed to be of tribal origin. The Framers merely adopted it as a permitted political process.

Political factions are commonplace citizen organizations engaging in political activities that are destructive to a functioning democracy.

Most political factions are organizations, originally formed for a non-political purpose, which added political activities along the way. Eliminating political involvement of such organizations would not remove from society their valuable civil contributions, which would rightfully create resentment. It is their "political activities" that need to be put under control, not the organizations themselves.

The solution is to deny all factions the right to engage in political activity without a permit issued by the Election Commission, a route that would provide Constitutional Authorities with a way to regulate them.

BUSINESSES BECOME POLITICAL FACTIONS!

Businesses have historically avoided political involvement. Those who focus on their reason for existence and steer clear of politics are not threats to democracy. But businesses that attempt to use their public position for political effect or control, or their organization resources for influence, have made themselves **political factions.** In that inappropriate mode, they do become a threat to democracy.

Nations have been down the political faction road before. Although not a pure comparison, Medieval England provides a valuable perspective. Monarchs there dealt with a power structure of Counts, Dukes, Earls, and Barons (roughly comparable to the business corporations, trade unions, and educational organizations of our time), each of which conducted regional governance and controlled legions of subjects. Monarchs were forced to cater to that power structure because of its capability to exert damage to the monarchy. In the latter stages of England's evolution, the titled aristocracy ("Peers," in the English lexicon) congregated into a parliamentary assembly called the "House of Lords" and were granted limited powers as the second but unelected House of Parliament.

Recent centuries in that nation have been consumed with mulling change proposals and writhing in indecision concerning those still-powerful factional medieval leftovers in the House of Lords that remain a pain in the rectum of the English government.

The course of action for our nation is clear. An internal power-structure of politically-active businesses, trade unions, and other organizations is marching us down the medieval England road toward an outcome better avoided. Businesses should focus on their reason for existence and be denied the right to heft their bulk advantages politically, like a club, for the purpose of distorting the democratic decision process. Each may retain, however, the right to take political action regarding government matters directly affecting their own business.

CORRECTING THE UNDEMOCRATIC CONSEQUENCES OF POLITICAL FACTION ACTIVITY

Since the beginning of time, tribal humans have congregated. Always, it is an attempt to influence an outcome by wielding the club of numbers. Ordering U.S. citizens not to congregate would be about as constructive as ordering water not to flow downhill. But the human propensity to congregate is not the cause of political factions, and it merely provides a convenient and existing political vehicle that can be used to distort the democratic "one person, one vote" rule and thereby throw a wrench into the orderly gearing of democracy.

Political factions are a product of and a subset of the party system, which is itself a tribal throw-back. Without political parties, political factions have little political leverage.

Readers should view Political Factions as a facet of the totalitarian drive for control that is the mortal enemy of democracy. Their motivations are totalitarian rather than democratic.

Madison, in Federalist #10, stated "There are two methods of curing the mischiefs of faction: The one, by removing its causes; The other, by controlling its effects." To purify the functioning of democracy, our nation needs to focus on removing the political causes of dysfunction, but also must set up barriers that reduce political faction activities.

HOW WILL THE PROPOSED AUTHORITY RESTRUCTURE WORK TO "REMOVE POLITICAL FACTION'S CAUSES"

Many parts of the political system of the United States were basically unplanned. It is composed of many moving parts, almost all of which have resulted from the original delegation to the Legislatures of the States. The parts put into use by the States were ad hoc creations of citizens, elected or otherwise, or borrowed from other democracies.

Throughout this Book, proposals are advanced to dramatically change existing governmental organizations or processes. Implemented, they would permanently modify politics at the grass-roots level where Political Factions sprang into life. With those changes implemented, in most cases, Political Factions would become redundant, but that is no guaranty they will disappear.

a) Factional influence on the election and political behavior of assembly members, is today achieved with a polluted mixture of money, media, and cumulative faction-influenced votes. As strongly proposed in this Book, constitutionally-selected candidates, supplemented by-elections managed and financed by The People's Election Commission, would eliminate the need for candidate advertising, fund-raising, and vote promotion, which are the influence force- fields of political factions.

b) The proposed restructure of the House of Representatives is to convert it into a considerable number of smaller decision assemblies, with The Guardians of the Constitution managing individual assembly decision processes. The purpose is to create decision bodies designed and managed specifically to perform decision functions. Implemented, the proposal will make political parties redundant in those assemblies. This Book strongly advocates constitutional denial of any right for political parties to exist.

c) **Political factions evolved as a voting force in the election system of our nation because politicians must endlessly run for re-election**. Proposed term limits for elected persons will eliminate the need for Political Faction re-election support. Eliminate endless re-election, and the many factional activities that support it will disappear.

d) Compensation programs proposed for elected assembly members would include substantial bonus awards for personal and assembly performance. That change to the rewards system has the purpose of focusing assembly members on producing quality decisions. It will have the effect of making elected persons less vulnerable to outside influence.

d) **Functional and reliable forums will be installed, under Constitutional Authority supervision to invite and facilitate interested citizens ' input regarding issues needing consideration by the nation's Authority Structure. By that means, an**

important democratic need will be met without all of the ancillary political hoopla present today.

Citizens will influence decision-makers with reason rather than faction-supported lobbying, money, shouting, advertising, or vote influencing. Coupled with the proposed constitutional management of assembly decision operations, the planned interface of citizens with the decision process of government will set a path toward eliminating political influence-peddling.

SECTION 3
ESTABLISH CONSTITUTIONAL BARRIERS AGAINST TOTALITARIAN ACTIVITY

The mission of totalitarian entities is to replace democracy with authoritarian government. Communism is the prominent alternative political system. **Totalitarians gain control by taking it, piece by piece, from The People via activities of the democratic government in place.** When totalitarian individuals or entities establish control over any governance process or function, they will substitute autocratic decision-making for democratic voting.

Elected persons have delegated substantial control over the Houses of Congress to political parties, which are regarded as totalitarian entities. The total amount of control within the nation is finite, meaning that any amount granted to political parties has to be taken from The People.

The five functions of management/ownership, "Plan, Organize, Staff, Direct, and Control," are used in this text to discuss the responsibilities of authority. The People, who are the owners of the nation, have the first and foremost responsibility to carry out those five functions. The People may choose to delegate authorities and responsibilities to the government or may retain and execute them, **but must retain and execute those deemed "vital."**

RECLAIMING CONTROL TAKEN FROM THE PEOPLE

The decision re-focus will be on those places in the authority structure where, historically, the decisions of the nation are made. "Government of the People, by the People, and for the People" cannot become a reality unless The People assume total control over the decision process and the Authority Structure.

> It is the proposal that control over the nation's decision process be assigned by The People to the Guardians of the Constitution under a directional mandate to install and oversee the Authority Structure. The Guardians will not make any of the Nation's governance decisions, but will instruct the decision process to be employed, and assign specialists to actually manage the decision processes of the elected assemblies.

Decisions concerning re-delegation of control within the Authority Structure would be made or approved by the Well-Informed Electors, the voting body of The People.

Delegating all assembly "control" to elected persons, which was the strategy of our Framers, does not create democratic self-government. It created a self-contained and all-powerful monarchy conducted by officials who happened to have been elected democratically. Their election may have been democratic, but the resulting government they designed is not.

When considering the reclaiming of control by The People, Readers may say, "You can't possibly do all that!" **But to create a self-government that functions efficiently, we can and we must.** It is merely a matter of developing a plan, committing to it, and executing it. The following statements identify the broad actions necessary.

1. Constitutionally Define Totalitarianism as the Existential Enemy of Democracy

Totalitarianism is an authoritarian practice introduced into government and public institutions without fanfare by replacing specific democratic processes with those that do not employ democratic principles. It may be, and usually is, inserted to function within an otherwise democratic setting. The ultimate purpose is, over time, to convert democracy to some form of authoritarian government, usually communistic.

An authoritarian practice may also be introduced into an otherwise democratic process by an ignorant leader/manager, merely as a matter of personal style, like or dislike, and even with the thought of improving government efficiency.

It must be banned from practice within our Authority Structure by Constitutional provision to deny its use by individuals or by factions or in functions operating anywhere so that it cannot gain a foot-hold.

This Book introduces a plan designed to put The People in control of all facets of decision-making within the nation's Authority Structure. **The control group in our nation's Constitutional Authority Structure, executing the decision-making plan for the People, will be the Guardians of the Constitution.**

The People will direct the Guardians to tightly manage the government's strictly democratic decision processes. That control will identify, prevent, and eliminate totalitarian practices and guide the decision process to a new, high-quality level.

Democracy cannot be a government wherein show-off leaders make unilateral decisions so they can demonstrate personal superiority. Driven by the need for power and to demonstrate the superiority of authoritarian government, totalitarian leaders tend to become very aggressive. Russia and China provide good examples. Voted decisions are much more constrained, well thought out, and safer for the nation. If the process is properly organized and controlled, democratic decisions are more rational, of much higher quality, and therefore produce better results.

Accountability for the maintenance of democratic purity is essential. Totalitarian activities would become constitutional "treason against democracy," subject to Level 1 penalties.

2. Our Constitutional Definition Shall Exclude Freedom to Engage in Authoritarian Political Activities

Our nation will continue to foster individual freedom to the extent possible, because it is a fundamental foundation of democracy, but acknowledges that total Freedom is neither practical nor possible. A new definition of Freedom, defining its exclusions, is needed as a prominent constitutional provision.

Citizens, elected officials, and organizations would be denied freedom to engage in totalitarian discussions or any totalitarian activities. Proposals for any government other than the Democratic Republic, as constitutionally defined, will be Treason. Organizations that work to modify or interfere with democracy will be deemed treasonous.

It is important to think clearly. It is totally inappropriate for our citizens to spend time mulling totalitarian proposals or discussions. **The People will have decided what form of government our nation will utilize, and once that decision has been made, the discussion is over.** The subject may be raised by The People fifty or one hundred years downstream, at which time the attractiveness of an authoritarian government alternative can be openly and publicly examined.

If The People establish a high-performance democratic self-government, authoritarian alternatives will be of no interest. Meantime, the attention of citizens should be focused on achievement, specifically of the National Imperatives, the Financial Measures, planning decisions and legislation, revising the nation's legal code, the constitution, and the creation of new Imperatives and Measures for a nation dedicated to high-performance government.

3. The Guardians of the Constitution is Designated to Root Out Totalitarianism and Establish Control over the Decision Process

The Guardians of the Constitution will, in addition to their other duties, administer the nation's Authority Structure processes, searching for totalitarian activities and ensuring they are rooted out and replaced with pure democracy. Particular attention will be paid to the nation's education system.

The Constitutional actions to be carried out by the Guardians shall be approved by the Well-Informed Electors before implementation.

4. Political Parties Shall be Designated Totalitarian

In our self-governed democracy, any factional effort to establish control of or excessively influence governance must be designated a totalitarian action.

In the government of our nation, the instrument of the Control drive has historically been the political party. Political parties are totalitarian factions formed by elected officials who, because of a permissive Constitution, were allowed to operate freely. Because of the always-destructive control drive of elected officials, Political Parties must be banned from our nation and its self-government.

Elections have been the playpen of Political Parties and are designed solely to accommodate them. The People's Election Commission, a proposed Constitutional Authority function, would be designated to install new free election operations, including candidate selection, campaign management, the voting process, and election financing.

5. Factions Shall be Licensed

Factions are common-purpose gatherings of individuals. If such a gathering engages in political activity, it shall be designated a "Political Faction." Factions would be forbidden from engaging in political activities except those relating to the business of the faction itself.

The People's Election Commission will be designated to identify Political Factions operating within the nation, maintain all records concerning them, license them, and control their activities so that they cannot warp the one-person-one-vote rule. Any Faction permitted to operate politically will do so under a license from The People's Election Commission.

CHAPTER 6

THE ELECTED ASSEMBLY SERIES, PART 1

CONTENT:

SECTION 1: CURRENT CONDITION OF THE LEGISLATIVE BRANCH

SECTION 2: ELECTION SYSTEM AND BALLOT BOX SICKNESS

SECTION 3: REPRESENTATION

SECTION 4: LEGISLATIVE BRANCH ACCOUNTABILITY

SECTION 5: DYSFUNCTION IN CONGRESS AND UNINTENDED CONSEQUENCES

SECTION 6: THE ADMINISTRATIVE STATE

FOREWORD

The current furor and heat of political discourse emanates from deep-seated system and performance problems in the Congress of the U.S. government. The legislative branch is ineffective, unable, or unwilling to act. It spends virtually all its time on committee work and political party activities, the main purpose of which is party promotion and party member re-election.

The House of Representatives is the focal point of the sickness but not the only point. The Senate is not a model of superior performance either.

This Chapter examines the present government operating environment and discusses Legislative branch activities that are propelling compensatory reactions in the two other branches of government. Reader grasp of that organizational inter-play is essential to an understanding of what is now occurring, and to the formulation of solutions. The intent is to help readers tie their own observations to the relevant analysis.

SECTION 1
THE CURRENT CONDITION OF THE LEGISLATIVE BRANCH

THE "FEEL" OF THE COUNTRY HAS TURNED DECIDEDLY NASTY

Some would say legislative malaise has never harmed the Republic, that it is trauma often previously experienced and overcome. Over time, they say, this too shall pass. Some even opine (in a sneering tone mirroring their very negative opinion of the Legislative branch) that the Nation runs better when Congress is inactive.

Our democratic Republic churns on, essential services ostensibly in place and government business apparently being attended. A closer look reveals that very little governance is produced in the Legislative Branch. And, amid the raucous political aggression, the "feel" of the Nation has turned decidedly nasty, the rhetoric aggressive and pointed. Concern for the Nation's welfare has risen markedly among the citizens, and faith in our form of government has reached a low point.

THE COUNTRY IS POLARIZED

The book Foreword summarizes the political situation. Readers may consider it worth re-reading, in that the material presented there lays the groundwork for this discussion.

There is ever-increasing heat to the political discourse, stoked by an extremely partisan media. Mid-Term elections in 2018 gave control of the House of Representatives to the Democrats, with the Senate and Presidency remaining in Republican hands. The 2020 election gave the Democrats a slim majority in the House, with the Senate virtually in a dead tie, but a Democrat won the President's office. The 2022 mid-term election gave a slim House majority to the Republicans, with the Senate marginally controlled by the Democrats.

There is disagreement about everything. Disagreements have become more vitriolic and personal. While in the majority, the Democrats spent their time investigating and attacking Republicans. Republicans, assuming the 2022 election House majority, indicate that they will reciprocate with the same actions.

The government-centered bi-polar condition has spread dramatically among the citizenry. Members of one political party now view members of the other as enemies, not in full possession of their faculties. The citizen state of mind is antagonistic, reflecting the actions of the government.

Common courtesy has been replaced with an attack-dog attitude. The Democratic Party, in control, pursued their vindictive attacks on the ousted Republican President Trump, with a focused intent to destroy him. The sense of common purpose that once typified the legislative forum and allowed bi-partisan agreements to be made has evaporated. The most powerful committees of the House continue to spend their time trying to find a path to legally attack the deposed Republican Trump, even though their formal impeachment effort failed.[27] The Republican party, now controlling the House, is aiming their cannon at President Biden.

While this is happening, governing in the legislative branch is locked in stand-still mode. Presidents have become more and more totalitarian. President Biden's dictate, canceling roughly a half-trillion dollars of student loans without a formal vote of Congress, tells the whole story.

THE VITRIOL IS NOT MERE PARTY POLITICS

Symptoms of the disorder are popping up in many other parts of government. Ours is "government based on contention," where disagreement is the foundation of the system, but historically, polarization has been rare. Political polarization is a dangerous illness. From an analytical viewpoint, the country's polarization is a condensation of sicknesses that go back as far as the original Constitution plan.

> **Rarely does a citizen squirm with as much discomfort as when witnessing loud and insistent political polarization. The discord is telling us something important. If we, The People, don't solve the polarization there will be an unpleasant price.**
>
> **We are, after all, a self-governed nation. At least, that's what we are told. And self-government has always meant "all of us together."**

PAYING HEAVILY FOR POOR GOVERNMENT IS NOT SMART MANAGEMENT BY THE PEOPLE

The cost of our government is astronomical. **The financial cost of poor government is measured by the annual increases in the national debt.** Paying huge sums for poor government is evidence of stupid management on the part of The People, another negative vote on the question of whether the citizens of this Nation are capable of self-government. Although the comparison is not pure, one should consider that a business operating in such a manner would not long exist, and the shareholders would be wiped out. Our Democratic

---

[27] This text was written in the early months of the year 2020, and discusses conditions of that time.

Monarchy's performance is not a loud tribute to The People's self-government skills if, indeed, self-government is what we are practicing.

It is becoming increasingly evident that the Republic is in danger. Within government, the rules of democracy are being ignored. The threat to the survival of our democratic government is real. Absent a solution of some sort, which will have to come from The People, the mounting acrimony could very easily spin off into a crisis.

Our slide toward totalitarian control is already well advanced, and its take-over would terminate democracy. Our foreign enemies are well aware our government is in extreme disarray and are using every tool at their disposal to build dissension among our citizens. Foreign enemies (at least those that are totalitarian) would expect to benefit greatly from an alliance with a totalitarian replacement for the U.S. government.

What was to be "Government of The People, by The People, and for The People" has solidified as "Government of The People, by the Political Parties, and for the Political Elite." The Framers gave The People no Constitutional path to correct the problem of dysfunctional government. **That necessary correction is not going to be easy.**

THE PEOPLE'S OPINION OF LEGISLATIVE BRANCH PERFORMANCE

Surveys tell us voter dissatisfaction with the performance of the legislative branch is very high.

Only 20% of those surveyed say the work of Congress is good or excellent. 47% say Congress is doing a poor job[28].

Voter dissatisfaction with the government is centered on the Legislative branch. That it is the center of government disintegration is clear to all. **Given the level of citizen dissatisfaction, if we were a true self-governed democracy, correction would have begun long ago.**

SECTION 2
ELECTION SYSTEM AND BALLOT BOX SICKNESS

"INCUMBENT LOCK"

In a truly self-governed democracy, citizens would express their displeasure by voting for high turnover among elected representatives. What is happening in our democracy is

---

[28] Rassmussen Poll, May 14, 2019

completely the opposite. **Despite intense citizen displeasure with Congress, Congressmen and Senators are being re-elected repeatedly!**

In the House of Representatives, the highest re-election rate in modern history was 98%. Nowadays, it rarely drops below 90%.[29] Washington Post correspondent David Broder calls this glaring symptom of dysfunctional democratic self-government "incumbent lock," meaning nothing is likely to dislodge an elected member once he/she has won a seat.

Re-election in the Senate is less certain, with the lowest rate in the past 50 years being 55% in 1980. **But Senate re-election, too, has averaged over 90% in recent times, an incredibly damning statistic!**

There is a major disconnect between public opinion of the performance of the members of Congress and the actual election results of those bodies. It is obvious that the ballot box and election system are not performing their functions in the manner required.

Various reasons are bandied about for irrationally-high re-election percentages: gerrymandered districts, incumbent advantages in raising campaign money, the franking privilege, the ability of incumbents to earmark money for projects benefitting voters, etc. Wide name recognition is among the incumbent advantages mentioned.

No question, those are factors that affect outcomes, **but they do not support the high re-election rates being recorded**. Obviously, something else is in play.

The influence of political parties in the voting process, and political party alliances with the media, are causes that underly the high re-election percentages.

Voters are electing a political party; individual candidates are of minor importance. The Framer ballot box check-and-balance on government is a broken process.

THE FRAMER CHECK-AND BALANCE PLAN INCLUDED THE BALLOT BOX

The Framers employed newly-discovered "sciences of politics" when they constructed the Constitution under which our government operates. Among the new (and unproven) ideas they utilized was "checks and balances,"[30] a system where one branch of government monitors the actions of another.

The voters, at the ballot box, were supposed to execute check-and-balance on those they elected. The Framers set the term for Congressmen at two years, Senators at six years, and

---

[29] "Do Members of Congress Ever Lose Re-election?" article by Tom Mures July 13, 2019
[30] The Federalist Papers, Number 9

Presidents at four years, under the theory that having Elected Officials face the Voters frequently would promote an active ballot-box accountability plan.

The Press was expected to keep voters informed on the performance of Congress and Elected Representatives. The information thus distributed was expected to motivate voters to impose accountability on incumbents. As an incentive to carry out that expectation, the Bill of Rights granted the Press important Constitutional protection, commonly referred to as "Freedom of the Press."

That grant will be revisited later in conjunction with other topics. Rather than fulfilling its role as honest reporters of information regarding elected officials and government, a critical expectation of the Framer plan, the media has gone in the opposite direction. It has become the propaganda arm of chosen political parties.

> **The Framers made a constitutional bet on the private-enterprise Press, that it could be depended upon to fulfill the critical role of providing the dependable and unbiased information flow needed to make the voter check-and-balance system work.**
>
> **The Press, and its successor (the Media), by aligning with political parties and economically prostituting themselves for gain, destroyed the Framer plan.**

Re-election rates are at such high levels that "incumbent lock" has become the term used to describe the tenure of elected persons in Congress. **High re-election rates are clear evidence that the Framer box-and-press-reporting accountability model is not performing.** The People are gazing in horror, eyes wide and mouths open, at the political charade in Congress. The People are gazing in horror, doing a lot of complaining, and turning off the television news in disgust. But they continue to re-elect the same people, over and over and over again!

There is a currently-popular definition that applies: "Stupidity is doing the same thing over and over and over again but expecting different results." When citizen behavior becomes that of a mere party-addict, common sense is "gone, gone, like the landlord's smile" of country music fame.

THE ROOT CAUSE OF BALLOT-BOX CHECK-AND-BALANCE FAILURE: POLITICAL PARTIES!

The failure of the ballot box to fulfill its Elected Official performance check-and-balance function can be laid squarely at the feet of political parties. They exert a deadly influence on the voting process. **Their unholy alliance with the Press has magnified their influence to a level where they are now the dominant citizen voting-decision factor.**

Ballot box accountability relies totally on the Voter's ability to assess the performance of elected representatives. Voters are expected to cast out those not performing, which would punish individual elected persons for the non-performance of the House of which they are a member. **If those expectations were being met by the system, every election would reject 50% of incumbents, bringing election results into line with the public's survey opinions of congressional performance.**

Evaluation of an Elected Person requires voters to have quality factual information upon which solid judgments can be based. Because of media/political party alliances, the information provided by the media is so biased and of such poor quality that our Voters must be rated "poorly informed." A quick look at ballot box decisions leads to the conclusion that voters spend little time evaluating the performance of their elected persons or connecting it to the performance of the Congress they detest. Instead, they tend to vote the "party line" and their own emotions. Candidates who represent their party of choice are highly likely to receive their vote, regardless of performance considerations.

The Framer check-and-balance plan has been sabotaged by the political parties, whose elected-person-created non-constitutional role dominates voter decisions at the ballot box. In the process, Congressional accountability (which was very weak to begin with) has been scuttled. **Voters have one goal: to keep their favored political party in power. The 90% re-election rate is the result.**

Voters understand something is very wrong in our government, but still focus on party re-election.

Apparently, voters do not connect their dissatisfaction with elected government to political parties. Yet, in a 2018 Pew Research study, 61% of respondents said the design and structure of government needs significant changes.[31] One would have to conclude that voters are not blaming parties or incumbents for the performance of government. The "design and structure" of government is the cause of the poor performance.

There's enough blame to go around. Our voters are the key players in the ballot box check-and-balance breakdown. We tend to excuse away their performance by blaming it on the forces that influence them. Based on their performance, it is a struggle to drum up conviction that voters are capable of self-government. They seem to see their self-government responsibility as faithfully voting for their chosen political party!

A national commitment to establishing true democratic self-government will require, among other things, restructuring the minds of the voters. But the cause of poor voter behavior is

---

[31] Pew Research Center, April 2018, "The Public, the Political System and America Democracy"

not hidden, it is there for all to plainly see. **The education of the voter is being conducted by the Media!**

FAILURE OF BALLOT BOX CHECK-AND-BALANCE HAS ELIMINATED ACCOUNTABILITY OF ELECTED PERSONS TO THE PEOPLE

"THE LEGISLATIVE BRANCH ACCOUNTABILITY GAP"

In both of the Legislative houses, true accountability to the Voters does not now exist in any form whatsoever. We refer to that system condition as "the Legislative branch accountability gap." The absence of public discussion of that issue is deeply disturbing.

Fact linkage seems not to be followed by the voters. Media discussions never mention the legislative body accountability issue, despite deep voter frustration with legislative branch performance. One would not, of course, expect to hear a media discussion about the failure of the ballot box as a Constitutional check-and-balance or the role in that breakdown played by the political party/media alliance. Political parties and their media cohorts do not want those topics to be examined.

The result of compromised media coverage, as might be expected, is a very poorly-informed voting public.

SECTION 3
REPRESENTATION

Imbedded in our system of self-government is the principle that elected persons are "Representatives" of the voters. The Framers labeled the lower house of Congress the "House of Representatives" and its members "Elected Representatives."

The Constitution is silent regarding the meaning of "representative." By employing the term "representative government" perhaps the Framers intended nothing more than to convey the notion that the House of Representatives was a body whose function related closely to the citizens in each voting jurisdiction.

In the absence of a constitutional definition, however, a plethora of opinions have arisen among the populace as to the true meaning of "representation" and what those opinions mean to the functioning of elected persons in the lower House. Many opinions prevailing among the citizens appear to be the product of over-active imaginations.

This book expends considerable space on the widely-acknowledged non-performance of Congress and of elected persons. It searches for the system factors that have brought about those failures. **Congressional non-performance is both system-based and human-based.**

In a self-government democracy, elected persons are management hired by The People to perform governance functions on their behalf. Terms of employment of elected persons should reflect practices prevailing in the Nation's labor market, with the elected person's government functions clearly and precisely defined. **Conflicting employment duties like "representation of the citizens" and "committed to the responsibilities of office" as against "obedience to a political party" and "retaining the elected seat" lead to the list of reasons why our elected persons perform so poorly.**

DIFFERING NOTIONS ABOUT REPRESENTATION

There are as many notions about the meaning of the word "representative" as there are people using the term. Two centuries of practice have embedded in the public mind a range of opinions concerning what "representation" means.

If a block of voters elects an individual to represent their constituency, history, and opinion being what they are, the likelihood is very high that those voters will claim they have a "call" on the elected person, or, if you will, an "ownership interest." In the minds of voters, an election obligation was created for the representative to cast assembly votes that reflect the thinking of the voting constituency. Some authors suggest that the total obligation of an elected representative is to the voters. Some believe an elected representative should even look like, and think like, the voters of the represented constituency. The term "my representative" describes that voter's belief rather well.

It is vital that citizens have effective representation before government. This author does not dispute the view of the voter who consecrates representation as an entitlement conveyed by citizenship. Concern focuses on the best way to provide voters with effective representation. **The Elected Representative is arguably the worst vehicle available to carry out that essential democratic function.**

TWO CONCEPTUAL MODELS OF REPRESENTATION

Academic thinkers have proposed that the obligation of an elected representative to the voters of a constituency can be best analyzed by posing it under two conceptual "models."

a) <u>The Trustee Model</u>: In this theoretical configuration, the elected representative in Congress is viewed as a "trustee" for the interests of the voters of the constituency. The representative, under this thinking, makes the best independent judgment possible in each matter before Congress, but is not obligated to attempt to vote on a given matter as he/she thinks constituents would.

b) <u>The Delegate Model</u>: In this theoretical configuration, the elected representative is expected to act strictly in accordance with the beliefs of constituents. The representative has no right to act independently, and is bound to knowing and representing the constituency position.

The two conceptual models compare the role of the elected representative solely from the perspective that the voters own (employ) the representative and, therefore, have the right to control what he/she does. If the representative was the employee of constituency voters, making a choice between the two aforementioned models would suffice. The relationship between the voters and their elected representative is not, however, an employer/employee relationship.

Citizens are hopelessly confused by the lack of constitutional definition, the on-going argument concerning the elected representative function, and years of political practice that have magnified the confusion.

Citizens may be excused for taking proprietary attitudes toward representation. After all, the election of a representative and his/her subsequent assembly voting record is the only existing way by which voters can influence the government.

ELECTED REPRESENTATIVES ARE TORN BETWEEN THREE MASTERS

While the voter may view the elected person as "my representative" or "my senator," the reality is that each elected representative is torn between three masters. Three groups exercise ownership rights over elected persons, resulting in an extremely conflicted employment arrangement.

> **In the real world, the three masters who assert ownership rights to an elected representative or senator are:**
>
> 1. The constituency whose voters elected the official.
>
> 2. The political party of which the elected person is a member.
>
> 3. The government of the United States, owned by The People as a whole, which created the function the elected person carries out, and signs his/her paycheck.

WHICH ONE OF THOSE IS THE ELECTED PERSON'S TRUE "MASTER?

Of the three aforementioned masters the voter constituency has probably the weakest claim. At the current 90% re-election rate, representatives are not at great risk of rejection for voter displeasure. **The odds are just one one in ten that a representative will not be re-elected.** The voters cast their ballots to produce a political party majority government, so party association is the dominating factor in the representative's re-election. Voter opinion of the elected person's performance is believed to be a minor re-election consideration, rarely of importance.

And, the government that signs the paycheck is also not a great worry to an elected person. Each House of Congress was given the Constitutional right to "determine the Rules of its Proceeding," which shields those bodies from outside interference. Elected persons, as a group, are the masters of their assembly domain. As Congress is one of the three Framer independent branches, the Houses have incredible insulation. Although the government signs the paycheck, it exercises almost no oversight and exerts few demands.

That leaves the political party as the most powerful of the three masters of an elected person. The individual Elected Representative is beholden to his/her political party, relying on the party for re-election support. Re-election of his/her political party will likely carry him/her to victory at the polls. In the world of today, the true "master" of an elected person is clearly the political party.

CONFUSION STEMS FROM AN ABSENCE OF RUDIMENTARY EMPLOYMENT FUNDAMENTALS

From the time of the Signing, basic employment fundamentals have not been applied to the jobs of those elected by The People to participate in government on their behalf. The Democratic Monarchy created by the Framers places assembly-elected persons in a position elevated above the reach of everything except the ballot box.

The managerially correct approach would be to treat all elected persons as The People's hired management, responsible for participating in government in the manner The People determine appropriate. **The Voters vote on the employment decision, which is the election or rejection of a candidate. The employer of the elected person is the government of the United States, which is owned by The People. The government is the reason for hired management's existence. It signs the paycheck. The elected person must be obligated to only one "boss," and that "boss" must be the government. Neither the voters nor the political parties should have employment direction rights over an elected person.**

Basic employment principles would require members of hired management to execute a contract of employment with the employer who signs the paycheck, a contract that specifies the job requirements and defines permissible employee behavior. It would demand the hired management demonstrate fealty solely to the employer, and be denied allegiance other than to the employer upon penalty of termination. **Until The People devise such an employment contract, conflicted performance by elected representatives will not abate.**

"MY ELECTED PERSON" IS NOT AN APPROPRIATE WAY TO PROVIDE THE PEOPLE WITH "REPRESENTATION"

"Representation" of the voters is an issue completely separate from an elected person's employment purpose.

A voice for the individual citizen, which is called "representation," is very important in democratic self-government. **However, using an elected person to give citizens that voice is an inappropriate way to meet their needs.**

The government, as the employer of the hired management, will want elected persons to obey one master only --- the government that employs them --- and will want the elected persons to think about one thing only --- making the best decisions possible. **They are there to participate in the democratic decision aspect of the governing process and nothing else. That approach is called "focus."**

Extraneous demands, such as from constituent representation or from political parties, do nothing whatsoever to further The People's goal that elected persons focus on the decision process to produce the best decisions possible. Quality decisions must always be the "holy grail" of government and are, therefore, the desired result to be achieved by the employment contract.

To accomplish that, The People must establish their own control mechanisms that are totally independent of the government itself. Government cannot be permitted a mind of its own, and it must do what The People intend. **This book proposes establishing People-elected organizations, congregated into a people-representative group called "Constitutional Authorities," to assist The People with defining their intentions and carrying them out.**

Under the proposed plan, The People will possess all power to direct government and will do so. The government will execute. Constitutional authorities will receive their direction from The People. What better "representation" could The People ever acquire?

The approach will require the separation of "representation" from the functions of government. The representation will be housed in a special Constitutional organization directed by The People, permitting voters to properly and powerfully magnify their voice. "Government by The People" will be satisfied with nothing less!

THE POLITICAL PARTY CANNOT BE THE DOMINANT MASTER OF ELECTED PERSONS

The conclusion reached earlier is extremely concerning that the elected representative is harassed by three "bosses" and that the dominant "boss" of the elected representative currently is the political party. That pinpoints the principal reason why our legislative bodies are so dysfunctional and underlies its polarization. Eliminating political parties and putting elected persons under employment contracts with their employer, the U.S. Government, will go a long way toward resolving the elected person's (and the Legislative branch's) confusion and non-performance because drawing the terms of the contract will require clarification of the issues.

Eliminating the elected person's "representative" responsibility will eliminate the existing "three-boss" work conflict. The People must reduce the elected representative and senator's responsibility down to a "focus on democratic decision-making" by making government their sole master. That will clear up elected person's behavior problems, particularly if it is reinforced with appropriate employment contracts under Constitutional Authority oversight.

Assembly members and senators should, in our form of government, be selected by the voters in a pure "staffing" decision process, one that hires them to perform in the critical assembly duty of "decision-maker."

As such, they would be contract employees of the U.S. Government, and denied fealty to any other influence. The U.S. Government must, in turn, be controlled solely and unquestionably by The People, certainly not by a Political Elite or by a political party.

All relationships, obligations, and influences that have muddled the essential "one boss" principle must be eliminated. A reasoned employment agreement is an important part of the solution.

ACCOUNTABILITY OF ELECTED REPRESENTATIVES AND OF THE LEGISLATIVE BRANCH ARE TWO SEPARATE ISSUES

Voters do not see their Elected Representative's performance as the cause of government dysfunction. The scream can be heard from afar, "It's not our Representative that's the problem, you idiot, it's government!"

That rant contains more than a smidgeon of truth. It throws light on the question of why voters continue to endlessly re-elect their representatives and why Congress is plagued by "incumbent lock." Although Washington is a mess the citizens deplore, ***voters have no way to change the government itself***. And, as the rant states, voters do realize that expecting their individual Elected Representative to correct the non-performance of their government body is an unreasonable expectation, given the current organization and process.

Voters know their only recourse is to the ballot box. Through the ballot box, voters can change individual Elected Representatives, but they can do nothing about the performance of Congress. Following that line of reasoning, the acknowledged non-performance of Congress cannot be laid at the doorstep of the voters.

If our Congressional performance is rated "poor," the blame falls on the political elite and the political parties. In the background, however, the Constitution's provisions have set the scene for that breakdown.

Performance of the Legislative branch of government is heavily affected by the breakdown of the Framer ballot box check-and-balance accountability plan. The Legislative branch demonstrates clearly what happens to the performance of an elected body when the voters cannot correct non-performance or, stated differently, cannot enforce accountability.

That reasoning tells us that direction and control by The People must include oversight of the legislative function. This book proposes that be accomplished by vesting total control over the government decision process in the Guardians of the Constitution, who will act on behalf of The People, and by making The President responsible for activities of all legislative bodies.

Constitutional Authorities, in the hands of The People, will ensure the will of The People is enforced.

SECTION 4
DYSFUNCTION IN CONGRESS AND UNINTENDED CONSEQUENCES

ELECTED REPRESENTATIVE RISK AVERSION AND ITS EFFECT ON LEGISLATION

Except for initiatives emblazoned in media headlines by a political party for vote-attraction purposes, or unless an initiative gives a political party a compelling advantage with the voters, legislation to address major national needs will not be considered by Congress. Totalitarian party leadership does not allow proposed legislation on such matters to go to the floor.

Elected members of Congress have, over time, become more and more risk-averse. **The needs of the nation pale to insignificance, in their minds, when compared with the need to assure their own re-election.** Major legislation conveys election risk to political parties and to elected persons who support it, laying them open to personal accountability at the ballot box. Their answer is to do nothing, which eliminates any chance The People will hold them accountable.

There has been created, because of party-fostered risk aversion, an indolent "political elite" of long-term legislators who live off the largess of The People, but contribute little.

Party legislative initiatives have only one purpose: to curry voter favor for the majority party's benefit. Initiatives that might produce the opposite effect are rapidly discarded by the majority party, *regardless of the initiative's importance to the Nation.*

It has been known and discussed for years that the Social Security system will go bankrupt in the foreseeable future, but needed correction is not legislated. The national debt has risen to levels twice, precipitating a down-grade in the Nation's credit rating but producing no government action. Budget deficits are huge and growing, yet no attempt to stop the deficits or debt growth has been made. Every year, there is a loud political furor over funding the government for the next year and re-setting the debt ceiling, but the causes of fiscal stress go unaddressed.

Those statements are clear evidence of the legislative branch's lack of accountability to The People.

LACK OF FOCUS ON LEGISLATION HAS DIVERTED CONGRESSIONAL ATTENTION ELSEWHERE

Rather than confronting the Nation's problems and opportunities, the houses of Congress occupy their time micro-managing the appointment of ambassadors, department heads and judges, holding hearings, conducting political investigations, and overseeing the activities of the Administrative State. Most activity is attention-attracting, party-based and party-centric. It is administrivia that conveys the impression of productivity, garners reams of publicity, and evidences low re-election risk, but does nothing for the Nation.

The ability of the legislative bodies to manage themselves and set their own rules (Article I, Section 5, second paragraph) has resulted in a variety of practices that reduce re-election risk but stymie effective governance. Through a mass of committees and subcommittees, Elected Representatives have decided to spend endless time monitoring the Departments, Bureaus and Agencies of the Administrative State, which have evolved as the true legislating and governing functions of the Nation.

No way exists, under the provisions of the constitution, for The People to change anything governmental. Election statistics prove that elected persons are virtually immune to losing their seats in Congress. Thus, citizen check-and-balance on the Legislative branch has withered to nothing, thereby eliminating its accountability to The People. **Essential accountability can now be installed only after future Constitutional Amendments are initiated by The People.**

All routes to amending the constitution are controlled by the political elite, the most important of whom reside in Congress. Readers should devote considerable thought to the huge barrier represented by the Constitution's Article V.

Elected persons completely understand what is said here, hence their selection of the low-personal-risk non-performance course.

Legislative branch misdirection has produced firstly its own dysfunction, and, secondly, compensating reactions in the Executive and Judicial branches, which act to keep the country functioning in the face of a non-contributory Congress. "For every action, there is an equal and opposite reaction," according to Newton's Third Law of Motion. Notable and concerning reactions are the rising number of totalitarian edicts from the so-called Fourth Branch of Government (the Administrative State), which revels in authority defaulted to it by the Legislative branch. ***Considerably more disturbing is the emergence of a strident and authoritarian Presidency.***

> Entropy-generated breakdowns in the elected Legislative branch have resulted in an inappropriate migration of critical decisions to unelected Administrative State organizations, and to an autocratic Presidency. That movement toward totalitarian government is noteworthy. The People must consider it high priority that decision out-migration from the center for democratic government decision-making, the Legislative branch, to various totalitarian decision points, be halted and reversed. This realization fits hand-in-glove with the goal, expressed frequently herein, of significantly improving the Nation's decision-making.

FOR EVERY ACTION, THERE IS AN EQUAL AND OPPOSITE REACTION

Reactions to Legislative branch performance regression within the existing three-pillar governance structure of the Republic are worthy of review.

A. INTENSE PRESSURE ON THE PRESIDENCY

> Pressure for authoritarian Presidential action, and a President's willingness to act unilaterally, have increased dramatically in recent time because of the absence of legislation emanating from the House and Senate. To quote Aristotle, "Nature abhors a vacuum." Another branch of government will inevitably be sucked into the vacuum created when one branch vacates its constitutional responsibility. The Executive branch and the Administrative State, and to some degree the Judiciary, have taken over duties abdicated by the Legislative branch.

Where needs existed that should have received legislative attention but did not, the three most recent Presidents, Barack Obama, Donald Trump, and Joseph Biden, considered it expedient to take Executive Action. Executive Action is promptly labeled "autocratic" by the opposing political party and often generates an avalanche of lawsuits somewhere in the Nation to halt implementation. **The unelected third branch of government, the Judicial branch, then becomes the Nation's resolution body.**

It is particularly distressing that persons qualified to be President may not know fundamental democratic rules. Three presidents in a row have either not known the rules or chosen to violate them. Executive Action is purely authoritarian, the direct opposite of the Democratic Republic government envisioned in the constitution. There never has been, in our Nation, one person responsible for overseeing government, and the three branch check-and-balance creation of the Framers has not ever performed that function.

The demand must be to create a government wherein all decisions for matters affecting the Nation or its citizens are made by a democratic vote of duly elected persons. To create the organization required for that approach, proposals in this book restructure the President's job to eliminate totalitarian decision-making and make him/her responsible for managing government and planning its decision operations and execution. Associated with that is remodeling the legislative assemblies to fit them for advanced decision processes because, under true democracy, the volume of decisions they make will be very high. The existing Legislative branch structure and organization is the barrier to effective governance.

The key to establishing effective self-government is The People gaining control over the decision process of the Nation. That move is necessary to ensure success. **Self-government means that The People make the decisions themselves or delegate the decisions to the Nation's Authority Structure, always retaining total control over decision performance.**

So, the failure of one branch to perform its function initiates a reaction in the other branches. A roil of unproductive activity erupts, accompanied by great media furor and efforts involving many times the number of people that would have been needed to properly deal with an issue in the first place.

Working through to resolution is a time-consuming litigation-oriented process with the Nation in stand-still mode. The national cost of that massive process inefficiency is seldom discussed and never calculated. Citizens shrug and accept it as "the way things are, politics as usual." The political elite are happy with those processes, which provide them heavy media exposure and an opportunity to make political hay at little risk to themselves. Any groups that attempt to initiate correction are promptly labeled "extremist."

The net result is a decisive shift away from democracy and toward totalitarian government. Whenever democracy fails, authoritarianism becomes its alternative.

B. PRESSURE ON THE JUDICIAL SYSTEM

Many are cases where an appointed judge in the unelected branch of government, in a courtroom in Lower Podunk Center, has halted actions affecting the entire Nation ordered by a duly-elected American President.

But that is not the greatest concern. Presidential orders violate the most basic fundamental of democracy, that decisions affecting the country and its people should be made by the democratic vote of elected assemblies. The President should be the implementer, not the decision-maker. Public resistance to President-ordered Covid mandates, none of which were democratically decided, is revealing.

The People are entitled to better. But to achieve "better," it has become clear that The People will have to make "better" happen. The political establishment has the authority to enact Constitutional Amendments, but since such Amendments would be detrimental to them, prospects are zero. Correction can't be achieved through the ballot box. And, if the political establishment had intended to correct the Amendment situation, they would have done so long ago.

It will be up to The People.

C. EMERGENCE OF A POWERFUL FOURTH BRANCH OF GOVERNMENT

This Series contains an exhaustive examination of the Administrative State, so we will not delve deeply into that topic here.

Behind the constitution-busting creation of the Administrative State lies the problem of a Congress incapable of dealing with the massive number of laws required by our Nation. That issue will be addressed in the Government Decision-Making Series, Chapters 8 to 10, where analysis is conducted and solutions are posed.

The forces bringing about dysfunction in the Legislative branch are also forces that enhance the power of the Administrative State, which is often referred to as the Fourth Branch of Government. Administrative State power is derived through legislation that delegates to Administrative State organizations, law-making and judicial authority that should not ever be delegated and should not ever be housed in one function. That impropriety was a companion to changes in the functions of the Legislative branch, which has abandoned its constitutional role of legislating and is instead spending its time overseeing the Administrative State through an expanded committee system.

Such changes violate Framer-imposed separation of powers between the branches, shifting rule-making power from the Legislative branch to the Administrative State, which is not a member of the three-branch Framer creation, and the abandonment of legislation in favor of government by Presidential Order. Legislative dysfunction does, in fact, produce unplanned consequences elsewhere. The need for organizational role purity and enforcement of it, are the reason for many structural changes to government proposed here.

Except for initiatives emblazoned in media headlines by a political party for vote-attraction purposes, or unless an initiative gives a political party a compelling advantage at the polls, legislation to address major national needs will not be considered by Congress. Totalitarian-bent party leadership does not allow proposed legislation on such matters to go to the floor. **Permitted party legislative initiatives have only one purpose: to curry voter favor for party benefit.**

The proposals of this book include organization changes that will cure the aforementioned dysfunction.

Elected members of Congress have, over time, become more and more risk-averse. The needs of the nation pale to insignificance, in their minds, compared to the need to ensure their own re-election. Major legislation conveys election risk to political parties and to elected persons who support it, exposing them to accountability at the ballot box. Their answer is to do nothing, which eliminates any chance of The People holding them accountable.

There has been created, because of risk aversion, an indolent "political elite" of long-term legislators who live off the largess of The People, but spend their time on mundane matters.

CHAPTER 7

FOREWORD

"Executive branch administrative agencies exercising power to create, adjudicate and enforce their own rules." (Ballotpedia definition of the Administrative State.)

A Government re-organization approach, first launched in the late 1860s to address a range of government performance concerns, has expanded into a mind-boggling bureaucracy now commonly labeled "the Administrative State."

In order to set the stage for an examination of governmental and constitutional turmoil caused by the evolution of this huge block imposition on the Framers' "limited government" plan, some historical background and commentary are offered. Many organizations within the group are well known, perform important services under any form of government, and would be independently managed. The concerning feature is that none are under the direct supervision of The People.

SECTION 1
HISTORIC ORIGINS OF THE "FOURTH BRANCH OF GOVERNMENT"

T he government envisioned by the Framers was limited in nature and scope. The Framer era was slower-paced and less complex than any that followed. A government structure planned for the horse-and-buggy environment of the late 1700s is not likely to be a good fit with the 2020s rockets-and-electronics economy.

Elected officials who were challenged to organize the first congress took liberties in their implementation of the Framer plan. As is usual with all untested plans, the Framer plan subsequently revealed its critical gaps, inadequate detail, and questionable provisions.

> *President Woodrow Wilson, in the 1880s, was one of the first to promote the idea that government should be carried out by professionals, schooled for the tasks they would perform, and free of the turmoil of politics. He was said to be a man of progressive thought.*

By the 1880s, entropy, accelerated by political abuse and self-management within the Houses of Congress, was producing noticeably poor performance in the House of Representatives. Political decisions, which produced both the Framer plan and the legislative branch organization, were coming home to roost, as they generally do.

His administration's Pendleton Act of 1883 established the Civil Service Commission to overthrow the then-existing "spoils" system, under which jobs in the federal bureaucracy were doled out based on party affiliation rather than merit or skill. The second Administrative State Agency launched, the Interstate Commerce Commission, was established in 1887 to regulate the railroad industry. Agencies and Commissions initiated to solve the problems of that era are still with us today.

There was a time gap of nineteen years before the Federal Meat Inspection Act and the Pure Food and Drug Act were passed in 1906. 1913 brought the Federal Reserve Act and the formation of the Federal Reserve Bank to manage the nation's money supply. In 1914, the Federal Trade Commission was formed, and the Clayton Antitrust Act was passed, resulting in substantial bureaucracy additions.

The next major explosion in the long Administrative State build-up took place in the 1933-1939 era. The Great Depression, in the aftermath of the stock market crash of 1929, caused immense hardship for the people of the United States, mentally conditioning voters to elect candidates who proposed radical solutions for the nation's problems. Voters, after all, have only one means to affect needed change… through the ballot box.

Democrat Franklin Delano Roosevelt's New Deal in 1932 was embraced by the voters. It produced a flurry of progressive legislation and a slather of new Federal departments and agencies, such as the Securities and Exchange Commission, the National Labor Relations Board, the Federal Communications Commission, the Federal Deposit Insurance Corporation, and the Social Security Administration.

During World War 2 and the recovery period that followed, the nation was focused on other matters. Today's commonly-used label, the Administrative State, was coined in 1948 by political scientist Dwight Waldo to describe the agencies, commissions, bureaus, departments, and other support functions that had been created. **They, at that point, were radically altering the form and function of the federal government.**

Troubling social unrest in the 1960s produced yet another wave of laws and the inevitable new agencies or bureaus. This wave was aimed at eliminating discrimination, leveling out perceived inequities, and correcting corporate practices viewed as being unfair to consumers.

President Lyndon B. Johnson's Great Society of that era birthed a new batch of bureaucratic control functions possessing administrative power. The Environmental Protection Agency, the Consumer Product Safety Commission, the National Highway Traffic Safety Commission, and the Occupational Safety and Health Commission were among those creations.

> *Assembly of what is called the Administrative State was virtually complete by the 1980s. The Administrative State was not solely the construction of the Democratic Party, its primary proponent. During the 1970s, Republican administrations continued down the same path, adding bulk and number to the agencies, bureaus and departments.*

One would be correct in concluding that the massive reorganization was the product of the Political Elite rather than of a political party. Elected officials in Congress were the instigators and primary beneficiaries of the transfer of governance responsibilities from the elected bodies to the agencies, departments, and bureaus of the Administrative State.

It is noteworthy that this massive change to the function and structure of the government of the United States was accomplished without one word of change in the Constitution!

Of organizational importance is the fact that, although most elements of the Administrative State are supposedly monitored by Congress, this massive structure stands totally devoid of direct supervision from officials elected by The People for that express purpose. It remains under the general supervision of the House of Representatives!

SECTION 2
THE ADMINISTRATIVE STATE IS A MASSIVE GOVERNMENT ORGANIZATION

In raw size, the Administrative State, the hugest Constitutional violation ever, is an add-on apparatus so large and powerful it is now often referred to as "the Fourth Branch of Government." It is so invasive of the two legislative branches that it dislodges and relocates functions in an organizational disruption that has relentlessly modified government operations.

It is composed of huge independent self-ruled entities eerily reminiscent of the lordships and earldoms of the monarchical era's feudal society. It is a fitting add-on to the Monarchy Republic creation of the Framers, as it follows the same organizational thinking.

> It is of such raw bulk that it deserves highest ranking on the list of organizational forces affecting government performance. Those who reject the need for constitutional updating use the argument that the plan of the Framers, regarded as a plan of genius, should not be subjected to tinkering.
>
> That argument loses its steam at the first description of the Administrative State, because the original Framer plan was blown asunder by its impact. There is not as much left of the original Framer plan worth protecting as many suppose.

The exact number of organizational units comprising the Administrative State is not easy to pinpoint. The count depends on the definitions used. When its departments, agencies, bureaus and other organization components are added up, according to the Federal Register, the count is 454. That number does not include the Military.

To get a sense of its mass and complexity, review an Agency or two from the List of Federal Agencies of the United States.[32] You will find, for example, that the Department of Health and Human Services (one of the sixteen Agencies whose head person is a member of the Executive branch) lists 111 individual organizations within its structure. The U.S. Department of Energy lists 75. The sixteen Agencies that make up the Executive branch do not publish their subsidiary organizations, and it is doubtful many will bother to count, but there must be at least 1,000 individual component organizations within those sixteen.

---

[32] Wikipedia, List of Federal Agencies of the United States

Each Agency is a self-contained fiefdom housing every support function needed to meet its own needs. The Agency group includes only those whose head person is a member of the Executive branch and does not include all the remaining 400-plus bureaus and what-not that comprise the U.S. Government's Administrative State.

NATIONAL PRODUCTIVITY IMPACT

As of 2021, the count of civilian government employees was 2.85 million. Included in that number are Veterans Affairs employees and members of the Military, together totaling about 760 thousand. It would appear the civilian federal government employee count is about 2.1 million, which does not include 560 thousand civilian contractors.

The 2015 Code of Federal Regulations totaled 178,277 pages in 237 volumes.[33] At yearend, there were 3297 new rules in the pipeline, and 218 were "economically significant," meaning an annual impact of $100 million or more. Clyde Wayne Crews Jr. of the Competitive Enterprise Institute estimates the 2015 cost of compliance with regulations, absorbed by U.S. businesses and citizens, was $1.9 trillion.

The Administrative State has been added to the Framer-designed government structure over the past 150 years. Its impact, and that of the policies it generates, on the nation's economic efficiency is arguably the principal reason that U.S. GDP growth has lagged and languished on a downward trend over the past several decades. The drag of this huge apparatus on the U.S. economy is very heavy.

ITS FORMATION WAS A POLITICAL STRATEGY

The annexation of the Administrative State to the elected U.S. government branches could hardly be described as entropy-correction. Readers will recall that the House of Representatives was the Framers' darling. For political considerations, they gave it an unwarranted position and power. The formation of the Administrative State, a radical modification of the Framer favorite, must be viewed as a blatant political repudiation of the efficacy of the original Framer concept. **It exists because of the operational failure of the Framer Legislative Branch structure and concept.**

The politicians of the last half of the 19th century and those of the 1930s did not want to modify the House of Representatives or the Senate in any way. No attempt was made to amend the constitution. Those two assemblies have historically been the seat of power of the political elite who run the Framer-created Monarchy Republic, with which politicians would obviously avoid tinkering.

---

[33] Clyde Wayne Crews, Competitive Enterprise Institute, 2015 annual study.

Change proponents conceiving this organization chose to ignore the true causes of poor legislative branch performance, such as the imperfections imbedded in the original Framer legislative assembly design, the ill-conceived internal processes introduced into the Houses by the political elite themselves, weaknesses in the candidate selection and election system and the main course, the political parties.

In justifying the need for Administrative State formation, proponents blamed the poor performance of the House of Representatives on the quality of the elected representatives.

Nothing has been done since the 1880s to upgrade the quality of Elected Representatives, of course, and that topic is not publicly discussed anymore. One must conclude that placing blame on the quality of elected representatives was nothing more than a smoke-screen designed to take political advantage of deep-seated citizen disrespect for elected representatives and for Congress as a whole.

The real reason for the formation of the Administrative State was to affect a change in democratic governance by reducing reliance on elected assemblies by moving high volumes of decision-making to non-elected bureaucrats located outside of the democratic vote process. As such, it was another long slide down the greasy slope, away from democratic government and toward totalitarianism.

In forthcoming Chapters, recommendations will be made to break up the existing House of Representatives into a substantial number of smaller assemblies, each focused on a specific segment of the nation. Readers should, when considering that proposal, hearken back to the contents of this Chapter and assess the commonalities of the two situations. Give particular thought to the arguments common among citizens today who oppose changes to the Constitution.

THE ADMINISTRATIVE STATE CONCEPT IMPLEMENTS POLITICAL THEORY THAT IS CONTRARY TO FRAMER PRINCIPLES

Apparently, in the mid-1800s the behavior of the corps of elected representatives was held in disrepute by various intellectual and political factions. At the time, supervision of the government administrative processes was carried out by politicians, favoritism was rampant, and competence was generally lacking. The need to eliminate assembly self-management and procedure development was as apparent and pressing then as it is today but was totally ignored.

The Progressive view of that time was that the Constitution plan had become obsolete.

Progressives felt strongly that the role of government needed to be continually adjusted to meet the requirements of each new age. They advocated that government be carried out by professionals, schooled in the tasks they would perform, and free from the turmoil of politics.

> Their base case was reasonably accurate, and remains so today. Progressives were also correct in concluding the popularity-based election system was producing representatives unfit to perform in a government assembly. As a solution, governments headed by parties of the "Progressive" persuasion imposed, piecemeal, an organization of government completely different from that envisioned by the Framers.
>
> As is generally true of politician-produced organization changes, selected aspects of their need analysis were accurate, but the correction plan was poor. Their solution violated too many principles of organization and management to have much chance of operational success. The politically-contrived solution ignored true constitutional causes, such as dysfunction in the politician-managed Legislative branch, ignored the political party impact on performance, and ignored the "three-boss" job conflict that has historically caused elected representatives to appear incompetent. Most critical, it ignored the clear need for constitutional amendment.
>
> Administrative State formation was just another political "simple solution to a complex problem that is dead wrong!"

The Progressive solution was the initiation of "the Administrative State." Time passed, and then America suffered a violent economic disruption. During the financial Depression of the 1930s, the citizen demand for fundamental change reached a level that could not be politically ignored. The ballot box was the only change vehicle available to voters, who used it to elect a political party with a corrective agenda. The irresistible force (national need for government aid) met the immoveable object (the inflexible constitution). The irresistible force merely ignored the immoveable object and executed a political run-around. **Employing constitutional rules promulgated for their Democratic Monarchy, the elected political party implemented critical organization and system change by legislation, pretending the constitution did not exist.**

The absence of a constitutional definition of The People's stakeholder rights permitted elected politicians to legislate and implement radical changes that are the sole right of The People. It was carried out as though those radical changes were nothing more than the discretionary actions of the government. The Framer's constitution left the legislative door wide open to the formation of the Administrative State.

The Progressive chosen path for correction, that of ignoring the constitution rather than amending it, was an unfortunate political choice. Going that route tainted the effort with a whiff of unconstitutionality and an unpatriotic taste that does not ever seem to dissipate. The sorely needed corrective actions, badly conceived and executed, have produced negative consequences just as destructive as the problems they were designed to cure. **And the problems that needed curing were not cured. They are still with us, still degrading government performance.**

The most serious consequence of the political path chosen for the formation of the Administrative State **was politically depositing our written constitution into the waste-basket of irrelevancy.** In succeeding years, parties have continued ignoring our fundamental document. Thinking persons will understand that this result was caused, in the main, by an inflexible constitution not controlled by the nation's owners, The People. But even more important was the power vested in the majority party that allowed them to legislatively install a new and highly questionable government organization structure through legislative action supported by perhaps a mere one-third of the voting population.

ADDITION OF THE ADMINISTRATIVE STATE CHANGED THE FRAMER FEDERAL GOVERNMENT CONCEPT

The massive new weight on government imposed by the organization structure called the Administrative State and the resulting reallocation of power within government, dramatically changed the role and behavior of its branches. That, of course, was the intent of those who implemented the reorganization changes.

The Framer model, "small-government incorporating high levels of delegation to the citizens," was replaced by the progressive model, "big-government employing high levels of central control."

It is interesting that, when imposing the new organization on the existing government, the proponents didn't change the Framer "high level of delegation to the citizens," who still enjoy unconstrained freedoms and rights without accountability. That left the nation muddled under an incoherent and contradictory authority structure.

It is difficult not to view the Administrative State formation as a waterfall event in the inexorable flow of our democracy river toward the totalitarian ocean. **"Control-focused central government with decisions made by individuals," the governance model of totalitarianism, was instituted in the Administrative State.**

With the delegation to Commissions, Agencies, Departments, and Bureaus of the power to make rules that have the effect of law, to administer those rules, and to internally adjudicate the rules, the daily activity of the Legislative branch and the Judicial branch was substantially reduced. **That shift in the location of power shattered the sanctity both of the Framer system and of their separation and non-delegation doctrine.**

The House of Representatives happily responded to the exodus of legislative decision responsibility by raising its total number of Committees to 46 and changing its focus to overseeing the activities of Administrative State organizations. In doing so, the House assumed responsibilities that arguably belong in the Executive branch, where Administrative State organizations should report and where organization principles dictate that legislative support organizations should be housed. And, because it felt it could justify its existence by committee work, to reduce incumbent re-election risk the Congress sharply slowed down the process of enacting law.

Legislation changed as well. Laws passed today make sense only in the context of the Administrative State operations. The Affordable Care Act, for example, granted the Department of Health and Human Services power to formulate laws governing health care. **It was a law that authorized the DHHS to make the laws of the Affordable Care Act.**

There is one over-riding principle that emerges from this discussion. Because branches of government are a place where those in power can easily violate the nation's principles, The People must take firm steps to control their political actions.

Politicians are exposed to all sorts of notions and forces and are susceptible to them. Internal check-and-balance has not protected the citizens against illicit political actions. The number of them shows politicians cannot be trusted to put the Nation's interest first, nor can they be trusted to operate ethically.

The People's future authority structure must, therefore, incorporate strong monitoring and control over the actions of those operating within the government. That is the conclusion supporting the policy decision to have The People's Authority structure control all aspects of the government decision process.

SECTION 3
CONSTITUTIONAL VIOLATIONS INVOLVED

Many feel strongly that the current disorder in our system of government stems from overlaying the "Fourth Branch of Government" on to the three-branch Framer structure. **The base-line authority that made possible the massive government-authorized reorganization creating the Administrative State should have been constitutional.**

Royalty is a feature of every monarchy. The recent passing of Elizabeth 11, Queen of England, and the crowning of her heir to the throne reacquainted us with the rituals and pageantry of that ancient form of autocratic rule.

The Administrative State's political changes were not built into the constitution. The formation of the Administrative State, which was intended to cure existing disorders, did not cure them; it aggravated them.

The Administrative State is not a constitutionally authorized concept. It was cut out of the same phantom bolt of cloth as was our political parties. It was not ever a constitutionally-defined program of The People. **Like the party system, it was a totalitarian idea conceived and implemented by the political elite under the banner of "political mandate," supported by perhaps one-third of the voters.**

The Administrative State is a network of administrative agencies, departments, bureaus, and organizations that have been granted legislative, executive, and judicial powers. **Those powers, housed in authoritarian organizations that received no such authorization in the Constitution and do not employ democratic assembly voting, crucified whatever integrity our republican democracy possessed.**

But even more egregious are the actions of the Supreme Court, which, by failing to enforce the separation of powers, allowed the Fourth Branch of Government to flourish. **The Supreme Court,** *the branch positioned by the Framers to act as a check-and-balance against constitutional abuses*, **failed to function.**

It is an inescapable conclusion that the Supreme Court cannot be relied upon to resolve organization and power distribution conflicts within the government. Political pressures are too intense for the Court to perform that function. A solution, creating a people-controlled and politically-shielded Constitutional Authority that will manage the formulation of those decisions, is proposed in subsequent Chapters. The decisions would be the sole responsibility of The People, removed totally from the government and from the Supreme Court.

EMERGENCE OF THE "DEEP STATE"

One would have thought that the party politicians who conceived and implemented the Administrative State would have had some clue about the unintended consequences of overlaying that structure on the three-branch government concept of the Framers. Either those party politicians did not comprehend the probable consequences, or if they did, they gave their power goals higher importance. Political parties are consumed with carrying out their business plan and achieving their own goals, and if unintended consequences in the nation result from the process, too bad!

Frequent mention is made in this Book of the tendency of democratic governments to slide inexorably toward totalitarianism, following the greased path of least resistance. **The Agencies, Bureaus, and Departments created under the Administrative State concept are classic authoritarian organizations whose creation accelerated the totalitarian slide within our federal government.**

Hiring professionals to conduct the administrative functions of government, thereby supplementing or replacing the function of elected assemblies, set the stage for power delegation to a new cadre of authoritarian government organizations. The number of organizations involved and the power of their processes birthed the label "Fourth branch of government."

Most importantly, those actions imbued in the intellectual elite, staffing those organizations a belief that they were the experts, that elected persons were inferior, and that theirs were the opinions that mattered. Today, we often hear the political claim that elected decision-makers must "honor the science." That highly-advocated state of mind denigrates the democratic principle and has given politicians a way to deny personal responsibility for decisions by claiming, "We listened to the experts." **The catch-all label for Administrative State employees evidencing such propensities and for their other political activities became "the Deep State."**

The level of independence and power enjoyed by organizations of the Fourth Branch of Government has severely damaged our constitutional framework. Agencies act unilaterally and undemocratically on a wide range of matters affecting the rights of citizens. The C.I.A., elements of the Military, the Department of Justice, and to some degree the F.B.I., using the cloak of "required secrecy" or "national security," deny citizens knowledge of or access to activities concerning which voters in a "self-governed" nation are entitled to full information. This grants those organizations freedom from oversight by the Press and by the other branches, but most inappropriate of all, oversight by the owners of the nation.

Powerful Administrative State organizations are greatly feared, and for good reason. They are essentially a law unto themselves.

BLATANT POLITICAL ACTIVITY BY EMPLOYEES OF AGENCIES, DEPARTMENTS, AND BUREAUS

Politically-aligned-and-motivated government employees have been exposed as working behind the scenes to use their positions and the power of the administrative function itself to promote the interests of their political party of choice. As such, they have defined their organizations as "political factions," a topic of considerable discussion elsewhere in this document. Recent political furors exposing Deep State operators in the F.B.I. and the Department of Justice reveal how damaging such activities can be.

The actual extent to which party politics has permeated the work force of the Administrative State is not clear. What is clear is that there is no functioning control over such activities within the existing U.S. Government.

If its employees engage in party politics, the Fourth Branch of Government becomes an internal threat against U.S. self-government. Unless brought under control, party politics within the Fourth Branch will inevitably expand until Government by The People no longer exists. That theoretical milestone has probably already been passed.

AN ADDED ROLE: PROVIDING GOVERNMENT SERVICES TO THE PEOPLE

The Framer concept was to combine a limited, but all-powerful, central government with a high level of delegated freedom to self-reliant citizens. The Constitution and its amendments reflect that concept.

The Framers viewed government as a self-contained body that would write and enforce the laws to govern, manage certain vital infrastructure, and provide for the nation's defense.

The Framers of the Constitution, in 1778, did not consider the providing of services to be a function of government. The constitution is silent on the subject.

Today, Federal, State, and Municipal governments provide a wide range of services to the public. Examples are unemployment insurance, health insurance, student loans, business financing, home financing, pensions, and pension services. There are many.

From the perspective of organization performance, inserting the new function of "providing services to the population at large" into the constitutional small-government structure has produced dangerous unintended consequences. Surprise, surprise!

POLITICAL PARTY SELF-ENDEARMENT STRATEGY OF PROVIDING SERVICES HAS DEMOLISHED THE FRAMER "LIMITED GOVERNMENT" SCHEME

"Government providing services" changed the behavior of Elected Representatives, who now propose to voters all manner of services funded with the money of other taxpayers. That, in turn, changed the behavior of political parties inhabiting the Legislative branch, giving them an entirely new vote-purchase tool; it introduced immense party pressure into the voting system, degrading the effectiveness of the ballot box; it destroyed the organization concept of the Framers, violating the walls between the three branches; it migrated to the government involvements in business that would ordinarily have been solely the purview of the private sector, blowing apart the Framer "limited government" scheme; it imposed immense and endless pressure on the Federal budget; it dramatically changed the attitude of The People, who now see the government as existing to look after their needs; and it inserted government into the everyday lives of The People.

SERVICES PROVISION WAS NOT A DECISION MADE BY THE PEOPLE

The decisions to provide services were made by political parties, ostensibly authorized in an election, thereby fulfilling the party business plan of increasing voter support and installed using the hammer of majority vote. Such massive changes to the role of government demanded specific approval by The People, and under no circumstances should they have become the play-pen of political parties.

Our nation headed down that rocky road because the Framers failed to anchor in the constitution the inherent control rights of The People, instead granting those rights to the elected persons in government.

The constitution performs its most vital function when it designates The People to make the critical decisions of the nation, and creates the organization structures by which that can be accomplished. Thinking citizens, considering this book's proposal to form Constitutional Authorities that perform a variety of functions on behalf of The People, will understand that their purpose is largely citizen control over a government that is unable to control itself.

Politicians in government should not ever be permitted to buy votes using the money of The People.

SECTION 4
CONCLUSIONS REGARDING THE ADMINISTRATIVE STATE

The People, as owners of the nation, have the responsibility to Plan, Organize, Staff, Direct, and Control the U.S. government. Defining what the government will do, the organization and framework within which it will operate, and how its decision-making is carried out is the core of that responsibility.

The government would be organized under The People's supervisorial framework which we have chosen to call the "Authority Structure." That topic, therefore, must become a foremost article in the constitution. Supporting Articles will take a considerable amount of time to formulate and implement because of the critical and fundamental nature of those decisions to be made by The People.

The elected government needs support organizations to carry out its administrative functions. Many that currently exist are competent, well-established, and provide functions generally considered by The People to be essential.

It is suggested that a set of principles be developed to guide the planning, and the following are offered to begin the process:

1. Under self-government, the services to be provided to citizens will be decided by The People. The government will not be involved in making the decisions as to services provided but will implement and administer decisions The People made.

2. A consistent naming protocol and organization hierarchy are needed so that citizens can more easily place and identify government support functions. The "Administrative State" is a misleading label that should be replaced by something more descriptive, such as "Government Support Functions."

3. **The People must control all of government**. Senior officials, elected by The People, should oversee all government support organizations, many of which, at present, are overseen by the House of Representatives. **Elected Persons should be focused solely on decision-making, and have no involvement elsewhere.**

4. Action is needed to eliminate the "swamp in Washington" effect. The units of Support Functions should be methodically spread out and relocated throughout the nation. Exposure of government employees to voters of all types will change employee attitudes and reduce concentration risk in the event of social upheaval.

5. Employees of Government Support Functions must not be permitted to become a threat to the Authority Structure. Separate standards should be applied, such as no unionization and no political party affiliation permitted. Their employment agreements should allow no allegiance other than to the nation and its constitution. Special punishment should be devised for government employees who engage in what is today called "Deep State" activities. Such actions should be designated Treasonous Activities.

6. All government decisions respecting the nation or its people must be made by the democratic vote of elected bodies, never by individuals. Government decision-making will be controlled totally by The People. Assemblies must be designed and focused solely on generating quality decisions.

7. **Government must be administered and controlled by one accountable executive. There is a clear need to restructure the President's job description and role to convert that job to the Chief Executive of Government**.

8. The democratic principle of decisions by elected bodies must be redesigned, implemented, and enforced. The totalitarian action of improper authority delegation to unelected Government Support Function units requires decisive attention. This book's proposal to align

support services units with Elected Assemblies in a Matrix organization and to ensure Assemblies make all decisions required by the units will eliminate the inadmissible totalitarian approach.

THE ADMINISTRATIVE STATE IS NOT THE MOST PRESSING CONSTITUTIONAL/GOVERNMENT PROBLEM

Aggravating and bothersome it is, but in the short run, the Administrative State is not a problem at the level of other festering constitutional sores in government. **A significant percentage of the functions within the Administrative State are not going to go away any time soon. Many were well-conceived initially and performed functions vital to good governance**. Citizens are dependent on a well-functioning Federal Reserve and Social Security Administration, for example.

Its threat to the democratic republic government comes from the impact of the Administrative State on the behavior and performance of the elected assemblies and from the political activities of individuals and factions operating within the Administrative State structure. The employees and activities symbolizing the latter threat are often referred to as "the Deep State."

CHAPTER 8

GOVERNMENT DECISION-MAKING SERIES, PART 1

CONTENT:

SECTION 1: THE HOUSE OF REPRESENTATIVES, A BRIEF EVALUATION

SECTION 2: THE MARKETPLACE BARGAINING PROCESS

SECTION 3: "MAJORITY" AND ITS RELATIONSHIP TO DECISION QUALITY

SECTION 4: PROPOSED DISMANTLING OF THE HOUSE OF REPRESENTATIVES

SECTION 5: WITH ASSEMBLY DECISION STRUCTURES IN PLACE, CORRELARY MATTERS WILL REQUIRE ATTENTION

FOREWORD

Whatever form of government the citizens select to replace our dysfunctional structure, if they intend to fulfill their ownership "plan, organize, staff, direct, and control" responsibilities, citizens must concentrate on revising the purpose, direction, and function of the elected bodies, customizing them to perform the decision process efficiently and in a manner that produces high-quality decisions. Vastly improved democratically-made decisions are our strategy for government improvement.

Human desire to control the "power to decide" gives birth to all manner of political aggression. That factor must dominate structuring the critical delegation of decision power by The People to the government. Control over the" power to decide" was the driver behind political party formation. Tight control by The People over decision processes is, therefore, the obvious (but ignored) secret to developing high-quality self-government. The resulting system must totally stifle the human desire to control the "power to decide."

Dumping the "Power to decide" on elected bodies with the cheerful direction "here, you do it! "must be the most costly of Framer errors.

Planning is the process of deciding, "What are we going to do?" The first obligation of The People is ownership planning. Its absence is a glaring weakness in our current government process. Curing that weakness is a key move in controlling the power to decide, which is the key move in creating vastly improved governance.

By defining the decision processes to be utilized and using professionals assigned by the Guardians of the Constitution to manage those processes within the nation's Authority Structure, The People's control over the critical "power to decide" is absolute. It is no longer vulnerable to the human desire to control.

In democracies, decisions are made in assemblies designed and structured solely for that purpose. This Chapter will briefly examine the manner in which today's elected assemblies work out their "voted conclusions" but will focus on the critical discussion regarding the structure of the legislative bodies and the reasoning that must be applied to their reconstitution.

SECTION 1
THE HOUSE OF REPRESENTATIVES: A BRIEF GENERAL EXAMINATION

To give readers a general background of observations and analysis concerning the operations of the nation's two elected assemblies, the following is provided.

The two presently-existing elected assemblies are where the decisions of the Nation were to be made democratically. Our proposed national goal of dramatically-improved-decision-quality, properly organized, managed, and carried out would move our self-government sharply away from its totalitarian drift and system of purchased votes toward pure and fundamental one-person-one-vote democracy.

It is not possible to achieve such a goal utilizing the existing configuration of the Legislative branches or the self-devised procedures under which the Houses operate. Given the negative opinion of Congress prevailing among our citizens, it is a reasonable guess our voters long ago arrived at that same conclusion.

The People's goal for Congress must be **"consistently produce high quality decisions."** Congress will require substantial reconfiguration to achieve that level of performance, with clear and narrow role definition the starting point. Then, **the congressional right to "self-manage" must disappear,** "gone, gone, like the landlord's smile" of Country Music fame, replaced with tight citizen-controlled decision process management.

Self-management in government means The People manage and control the government decision planning and process. *The decision process is not delegated to the Hired Management.* **The most direct route to the establishment of high-quality democratic government is by placing total control over the decision process in the hands of The People.**

It is suggested that to achieve that focus, the role of elected assemblies be narrowed dramatically to **"the democratic decision-making bodies for all government actions affecting the nation or its people."** The all-important "what we shall do" decisions should be formulated in a new strategic planning process **involving the citizens**. The "how we shall do it" decisions would then be made by the elected assemblies, and implementation carried out under the direction of the President with monitoring by Constitutional Authorities who report directly to The People.

The government exists to make the Nation's decisions democratically, and a heavy volume of voted decisions requires elected bodies configured specifically to produce that. We would venture the thought that the reason the performance of our elected bodies is so poor is their excessively-broad scope, multiple purposes, and unwieldy size, creating extreme difficulty in managing them for production.

The unwieldy House of Representatives should be disbanded and reconfigured into a series of decision bodies roughly following the current Committee pattern in place there. The House itself, which currently serves no dominant legislative purpose, would merely disappear like the bad dream it is.

This application of the "KISS" principle (keep it simple, stupid) would utilize a number of new assemblies designed solely to make decisions, which is their highest-and-best use. Incidental and non-productive functions, which currently occupy most elected assembly time, must disappear like the infamous landlord's smile.

The rules must be:
- All decisions affecting the nation or its citizens will be made by democratic vote, never by individuals.
- Decisions will not be bundled into huge "bills" but will be identified and voted individually by subject.
- Decision processes will never be designed by the decision-makers. Those will be designed and managed by expert personnel assigned by the Guardians of the Constitution, which is the designated decision control body of The People.

ASSEMBLIES DESIGNED TO FULFILL MULTIPLE DEMOCRATIC NOTIONS ARE ILL-SUITED TO DECISION-MAKING

Democratic assemblies have limited practical utility. **Our House of Representatives was created to fulfill so many democratic ideals and political notions that its real reason for existence got lost in the murk.** The House ended up being a classic political compromise, and its operating dysfunctionality is reflective of the lack of clear purpose that ruled its conception.

Our assemblies were never designed to produce quality end results, and yet all those involved in their formation understood their democratic decision purpose. They were internally organized to employ an unproductive court-room process called "contention." They derive conclusions using bargaining and vote purchasing, where accommodation of individual, factional, and constituent interests is given priority higher than the best result for the nation. They exist to somehow or other scrape together a conclusion, and finding the best solution for the nation is so remote to their purpose that it is never a consideration.

It is suggested that "selecting the best action for the nation" be the future guiding purpose of legislative assemblies.

ASSEMBLY NON-PERFORMANCE REFLECTS PARTY MANAGEMENT NON-PERFORMANCE

The organization and delegation practices of party moguls who manage our assemblies are at the heart of non-performance. "A fish stinks from the head" is an old Beverly Hills business expression. Large gatherings of loud and ambitious politicians, each pursuing a personal and party agenda, beholden to multiple interests and operating under no job description, are notoriously hard to direct and control. Our assemblies are convened only when it is necessary to pass massive multi-purpose bills or to conduct housekeeping.

The legislative bill compilation and end product, discussed further in this Chapter, speaks loudly about the extent to which democracy and good management have been compromised.

Decisions as to what issues assemblies shall address are not made democratically. Those critical decisions are made in a back room by the majority party, either by individuals or smaller groups. It is probably impossible to reorganize the existing House of Representatives in a way that would permit a true high-performance democratic decision process, certainly not as long as the Houses set the "rules of their proceedings" and political parties run the show. An entirely new approach will be required.

The most important assembly decisions of the nation are the "What to do" decisions. They are the "horse" in the decision process, and the "How to do it" legislative process that follows is the "cart."

Those "What to do" decisions are made by party leaders. That means The People have delegated to self-interest political party leaders the right to set the nation's legislative calendar and direction.

But, that's the kind of irrationality that was installed when the constitution gave the two Houses the right to manage their own proceedings. It is authoritarian decision-making, one of the reasons we label political parties "totalitarian entities."

BUYING ASSEMBLY MEMBER SUPPORT BY BURYING NON-RELATED PROPOSALS IN LEGISLATIVE PACKAGES

Legislative bill "packages" are normal procedures, often containing 2,000 to 5,000 pages and reams of specific individual initiatives not related to the legislation subject or purpose. Initiatives benefitting special interests, the party, party supporters, and trade-off inclusions to buy votes from other elected persons are the reasons for the extraneous bill content. Specific initiatives attached as riders to the legislation, or removed from it, are exchanged for voting support for the bill, achieved by bargaining and trade-offs with legislators who represent voting power or money interests. The final bill obscures pork-barrel or supports faction riders by burying them in the massive package. It places voting members in a position where, having received a benefit from the bill sponsor, they will support the package. The process prevents them from casting a rational, independent vote, thereby subverting both democracy and the nation's best interest.

Our elected assemblies exist to ratify decisions made by the majority party. The proper procedure would require that huge bills be broken down into many individual bills, each requiring separate labels, debate, and vote. But of course, submitted to that level of examination, and devoid of the trade-off pay-off factor, individual bills would probably not garner enough support to pass.

This brief discussion brings forth the realization that the procedures of democratic government must be controlled by The People; otherwise, elected persons will desecrate them to a level that is no longer democratic and productive of warped decisions. The goal of political parties is to gain power to impose their will, and if the tenets of democracy get in the way, they will be obliterated. The political party control system must be replaced by a "People Control" system.

SECTION 2
THE MARKET-PLACE BARGAINING PROCESS, THE TYRANNY OF THE MAJORITY

A simple majority-voted decisions are necessities for assemblies operating under the "contention" principle, which makes "getting together to find the best answer" a virtual impossibility. The democratic assembly bill-passage requirement, a simple majority, stands in the way of improved government decision quality. The present legislation process totally ignores the best interests of the nation and the achievement of high-quality decisions, the objective that must dominate going forward.

Assemblies of government have long recognized the weakness of the simple majority passage, and adjustments have been made, here and there, to limit or deny its use. Senate filibuster rules are an example. The simple majority standard has acquired the well-earned label "tyranny of the majority," and much has been written about its defects.

> "Tyranny of the majority" will be the label as long as assembly decisions are made by simple majority vote, which in turn will exist as long as assembly rights to set the rules of its own proceedings are in effect.
>
> Political parties are the reason "Tyranny of the majority" vote passage rules exist. High percentage passage benchmarks for all pieces of legislation, set by selected functions of the "The People's Constitutional Authorities" operating a proposed control system would eliminate the "tyranny of the majority" curse and, with it, eliminate a dominant reason for the existence of political parties.

Improvement in bill passage decision processes, critical to quality government decisions, cannot be achieved without first changing the purpose, configuration, staffing, and management of the voting assemblies. Assemblies should be configured specifically for what The People expect them to accomplish and nothing else. They should then operate within rules (including decision vote passage requirements) imposed upon them by The People. The need to achieve decisions of the highest quality over-rides all other considerations.

It is important that citizens think clearly and not be confused by practices promoted under the guise of democracy. **If The People want democratic self- government, all decisions affecting the nation or its people must be made by assembly bodies elected and organized solely for that purpose. The requirement that the elected bodies must abide by decision rules and processes, set and administered by The People, will quickly and dramatically improve decision quality.**

Riders, log-rolling, vote buying, the simple majority vote, huge bills that are not read by assembly voters, and other practices that are the nonsensical actions of huge party-managed assemblies operating under the "right to determine the rules of its Proceedings" must be banished. The rules under which assemblies operate must be set by The People. Elected assemblies will abide by them and be organized and managed solely to produce the required high-quality decisions demanded in a high-performance democracy.

THE "BUYING, BARGAINING AND TRADE-OFF" ASSEMBLY BILL PASSAGE PROCESS

In the legislative branches the ability to bargain and use trade-offs to buy vote blocks is today essential to gaining passage of party-originated bills. Readers will note the above heading defines the assembly end-product as "bill passage" rather than "decisions," because the process is not one of rational decision-making. It is a market-place process of buying votes by bargaining until a majority is reached.

Political parties exist for one purpose: to achieve assembly voting majority control. A majority party controls the required votes, but individual party members may not be politically free to support a proposed bill because of obligations to those who funded their election, attitudes in their constituency, or trades they committed in support of an unrelated bill. Each political party is today made up of two factions that require accommodation, a radical faction and a middle-of-the-road faction. Within each party, other, smaller factions exist that march to their own drummer. For any bill proposal, a party possessing a voting majority may not be able to summon enough member votes for passage.

Party leaders will use any tool at their disposal in behind-the-scene bargaining to bring into the fold those not initially aligned (including susceptible or vulnerable members of the opposition party). Trade-offs, rider inclusions and exclusions, favors, threats and promises, and other for-value vote purchase currencies are employed. Political parties use a cold, hard, self-centered business approach. **None of this is decision-making. It is market-place bargaining and vote purchasing.**

The end result, an assembly voting majority will secure passage of a proposed bill. The aforementioned activities are a process using all manner of force and wile to secure votes to pass the party-favored product. **In no way is it a focused search for the best answer for the nation.**

THE PEOPLE MUST DICTATE THE ASSEMBLY DECISION PROCESS

The voting rules and process in use were not imposed by constitutional provision, nor were they instituted by The People. They were initiated within the assemblies under a constitutional provision permitting each House to determine the "rules of its proceedings." The creation of political parties by elected assembly members played a dominant role in procedure initiation, as the voting process dove-tails with party majority rule.

Readers are reminded that, as owners of the nation, The People have the right and obligation to decide how the nation's decisions are made. If they choose to delegate decisions to the assemblies, The People will need to define and manage all important aspects of the assembly decision process.

The principle is repeated, ad nauseum, that to make self-government successful, The People must ruthlessly install and control the entire government decision process. The People, through their Constitutional Authority representatives, will not make the decisions, they will merely guide the decision process.

It is a right and duty of the owners of the nation to organize the hiring of the decision-makers, to decide what the decision-makers must accomplish, and to set and administer the rules under which the decision-makers will operate. Any other approach means The People are not fulfilling their owner duties in self-government.

The People's procedures must be designed to produce **the best decisions for the nation.** To do that, every other conflicting objective and distraction must be avoided.

SECTION 3
"MAJORITY" AND ITS RELATIONSHIP TO DECISION QUALITY

At the outset, elected persons given responsibility for implementing our Framer's government design established the "50% simple majority vote" bill passage criteria. **That benchmark is appropriate for decisions of huge voting bodies such as country**

populations but is totally inappropriate for the decisions of small bodies such as elected assemblies.

50% vote passage is called a "simple majority," and 100% vote passage is a "consensus." The strongest indication of the quality of an assembly decision is the level of voting support it received. The lower the deciding vote percentage, the lower the probability the conclusion is a quality solution. Consensus approvals generally carry a high success probability for the simple reason that the more who agree, the higher the likelihood that the decision will produce a good result.

Outlawing simple majority passage, and **setting a specific high-percentage "majority" benchmark for each assembly-voted bill passage** is a key conceptual change the nation's owners should make to improve the success prospects of voted assembly decisions. Our proposal is that the Guardians of the Constitution, designated by The People to manage decision processes within the nation's Authority Structure, would independently set a majority vote requirement specific to the passage of each and every bill and for major sub-elements of bills, imposing those benchmark requirements on the voting assembly.

The approval benchmark of a bill can be set at any level between 50% and 100% of the votes of an assembly. It is interesting to note that the Constitution, when setting assembly-required vote percentages for important matters, which it rarely did, invariably set the approval benchmark at two-thirds of the voting members present, or stated in another way, a majority vote passage requirement of 67% **The Framers exhibited no faith whatsoever in outcomes produced by simple majority vote.**

USE OF APPROVAL PERCENTAGE VOTE BENCHMARKS TO CONTROL THE DECISION QUALITY OF BILLS PASSED

For proposed bills, the higher the vote passage percentage requirement, the higher will be the expected upon-implementation success prospects for bill content.

Percentage vote passage benchmarks should logically vary widely. The following principles could be applied in determining such benchmarks:

1. Vary the approval vote requirement with "proposal impact," **an assessment of the overall benefit and risk to the nation** from implementation of the bill. Under this approach, high-impact bills might require a **90%** or greater assembly approval vote.

2. Assemblies of government have long recognized the weakness of the simple majority passage, and adjustments have been made, here and there, to limit or deny its use. Senate filibuster rules are an example. The simple majority standard

has acquired the well-earned label "tyranny of the majority," and much has been written about its defects.

3. Considerations to be taken into account in measuring "proposal impact" are the relative cost borne by the Nation for implementation, the benefits that may be derived, the overall importance of the proposition to the Nation, its level of public support, the risks of its failure, the level of disturbance, time, or other stresses implementation will impose, security demands, in-government and in-public implementation competence, its impact on the Nation's ability to meet other established goals, etc.

IMPROVE ASSEMBLY COMPREHENSION AND KNOWLEDGE LEVEL TO IMPROVE DECISION QUALITY

It has been noted that, in the design of our government, the Framer construct employed principles considered "best democratic practice" in the 1780s.

In the 1880s, a major revolution in government organization and structure began to compensate for perceived shortcomings in our Constitutionally-decreed voting assemblies. Formation of the Administrative State was initiated at that time, a process that drew to a close about one-hundred years later. Readers are referred to Chapter 6 for an examination of that huge and important disruption in government organization.

The decision to form the Administrative State was stated to be based upon a lack of respect for the performance of the Nation's Elected Representatives.

The decision of the 1880s was political rather than rational. The wrong fork in the road was chosen, obviously to protect the entrenched Monarchy Republic and its Political Elite. The ruling party's choice to engineer a costly and inappropriate bypass of the Constitution has massively increased the government's cost. The Legislative branch dysfunction, never addressed and with us still, has grown worse. The main beneficiaries of the effort were elected representatives, whom was removed much of the stress of voting law, and leaders whose preference ran toward a government more authoritarian.

CONFRONTING THE ELECTED REPRESENTATIVE QUALITY ISSUE

In pursuing the proposed goal of vastly-improved government decision-making, The People will sooner or later have to confront the elected representative quality issue that was never resolved by the massive Administrative State reorganization effort. Vastly-improved government decision-making will bring with it demands for an entirely new approach to organizing and staffing the nation's elected assemblies. Those who observe the current processes of our assemblies conclude that the elected persons staffing them do not possess capabilities optimal for the job they were elected to perform, exactly mirroring political opinions of the 1880s.

For the future, we will need decision-making assemblies of very narrow focus, and should elect people with pre-defined qualities to staff them. Popularity elections, the notion of representation, political party influences, money-bought elections, the excessive impact of political factions, and the idea that all elected persons should serve the same term are problematic practices that will have to be dealt with in revising the election process.

SECTION 4
PROPOSED DISMANTLING OF THE HOUSE OF REPRESENTATIVES

The lower house of Congress is an assembly so large and unwieldy that its leaders found it necessary to subdivide it into hundreds of committees and sub-committees. Its full-house activities have been minimized, and its legislative role largely off-loaded to the organizations of the Administrative State. Organization students will recognize that its large and unwieldy make-up birthed the huge multi-subject bills previously discussed, the absence of single-subject democratic voting, the massive committee structure, government by contention, the political party system, the formation of the Administrative State, and all of the other negative developments.

It is highly improbable that a huge Assembly can ever be utilized effectively, even with major modification and restaffing. It is a totally inappropriate size and configuration for producing the many decisions required in the governance of a nation such as ours, particularly with our proposed emphasis on decision quality.

If the nation is faced with a high volume of decisions, and believes that much better decisions is the road to great improvement in government, it must organize to make the decisions. What is needed is individual assemblies **designed to be high-quality democratic decision-making machines.**

These assemblies are the model for an organization to replace the House of Representatives, broken down into multiple smaller components, each customized to address specific segments/functions that comprise the nation.

The need is to create an assembly machine designed to produce a high volume of quality government decisions democratically.

The plan would replace the existing bargaining and trade-off system of political party majority-vote-building. **It would employ assemblies that exist solely to make decisions on a rational basis, free of politics, contention, bargaining, and outside influence.** They would be assemblies of small size to improve functionality, with member expertise matched to the Assembly's designated area of focus. Each decision would require reaching a Guardian-set majority percentage. Perhaps thirty to sixty such assemblies would result, but the actual end number is not an important consideration.

The Senate and the President would be required to ratify assembly decisions for them to become law.

Assembly members would have one focus: decision-making for a designated segment of the nation. **They would serve one master, The People**. Their work would be assigned by the President, who would develop a rolling two-year decision-and-legislation work plan emanating from The People. Political party influence is eliminated. Assembly members would have no voter representation responsibility. They would not be re-elected. All distractions and employment conflicts will have been eliminated from their job descriptions. Experts assigned by the Guardians of the Constitution, responsible for managing the nation's democratic decision process, will organize and guide each Assembly's activities, focusing explicitly on the democratic decision process.

The People's Constitutional Authorities would assume responsibility for providing "representation" to the citizens through a new citizen-involvement organization designed specifically for that purpose. The House of Representatives would be disbanded, and functions worth keeping would be transferred elsewhere.

The Senate, under this concept, would become the Nation's final democratic decision body.

SUBDIVIDE THE NATION INTO FOCUS SEGMENTS TO ORGANIZE PROPOSED ASSEMBLIES

A democratic government organized for controlled decision-making and operating under a strict rule that "all decisions affecting the nation or its people will be made by democratic vote" will generate decisions in substantial volume. Such a requirement demands an organization designed to produce that volume.

Readers should bear in mind that the current organizations of government were designed by bodies of politicians over two centuries, bodies with a notoriously poor record in that area. The probability is high that a substantial percentage of the existing units in the Administrative State are obsolete, redundant, or otherwise inappropriate. Organization experts must be deployed to assess the condition, purpose, and contribution of each. It is strongly suggested that Constitutional Authorities contain a unit specifically dedicated to rationalizing the organization of the Authority Structure, responsible for fulfilling The People's "Organize" responsibility.

The following describes the formation process for a decision-focused government assembly organization:

Divide the nation's business functions, consumers, infrastructure, and social matters into 30 to 60 segments. Create an Elected Assembly responsible for each segment. The organization principle should be intentionally fluid, as the segments will need to change as conditions change. Individual assembly size and composition will vary with the demands of its allocated segment.

Segment-focused support organizations called "Departments" already exist within the Administrative State. Those can serve as a beginning point-of-reference for configuring the decision assemblies. The fifteen existing departments would each be interfaced with an Assembly. There also exists sixty-six independent agencies, not included in any of the mentioned departments, many of them large, that must be aligned with Assemblies, an effort not attempted here.

For template comparison, the House of Representatives has 20 standing committees and 6 non-standing committees, for a total of 26. Supporting those are 108 sub-committees.

Start with the formation of an Elected Assembly complementary to each of the Executive branch Departments, which would result in fifteen new Elected Assemblies. Add assemblies, as appropriate or needed, relating to the many House organizations that are not a part of the Executive Branch and for national issues demanding focus. Those will result in a significant number of additional assemblies. The total number of Assemblies should not be a matter of concern. Providing focused assembly decision-making precisely where it is needed in an elected government of high competence is the goal.

SECTION 5
WITH ASSEMBLY DECISION STRUCTURE IN PLACE, COROLLARY MATTERS WILL REQUIRE ATTENTION

ASSEMBLY MANAGEMENT

Strategic planning for decisions and legislation should be centralized under the President, for whom the Senate will be the confirmation body. **This is a new action proposal of extreme importance.** In conjunction with this reorganization, the existing Senate should be utilized in a completely new manner, tightly integrated into the government decision process, as discussed below.

All organizations in the matrix will report to the President, and we recommend new vice-presidents be elected to manage the group, perhaps one for each fifteen assembly groups. The Vice President would be responsible for all management matters in the assigned assembly groups. **The critical People's control over the decision process within all democratic assemblies, however, would be executed independently by the Guardians.**

The assemblies will not be self-managed; the Guardians of the Constitution will assign experts to manage each. **Those experts will organize the decision input, the work flow and decision processes but will not vote in decisions.**

This arrangement will create an elected assembly decision function that is totally democratic, ensure "groupthink" does not develop, curb the factions that will attempt to form within an assembly, and eliminate any domination propensities of individual assembly members. Assembly members exist solely to participate in the decision-making and legislation process and are to do so free of any outside or inside influence, bias, or beliefs.

ELECTION OF ASSEMBLY MEMBERS

Each Assembly will be composed of twenty or more Assembly Members elected for expertise. Members whose background and knowledge are appropriate to their assembly assignment would be elected by the voters from a list of geographically pre-qualified candidates provided by the People's Election Commission. The emphasis on candidate election will match expertise to the specific requirements of a given assembly, significantly increasing election complexity.

> The effort should include a forced redistribution to eliminate from assemblies and the Senate the imbalance caused by the legal profession faction. The purpose of each assembly is to make decisions. Law-writers with legal training should be contracted as needed, not elected.

ALIGN RELATED SUPPORT FUNCTIONS USING THE MATRIX CONCEPT, STREAMLINE LAW CREATION

Form a master government organization using the "Matrix" concept, with "dotted line" relationships connecting each Assembly to its related Government Support units.

The matrix organization aligns each new Assembly with support organizations in the same field of interest. Existing bureaus, agencies and departments possess the information and knowledge needed for Assembly decision support. A primary responsibility of each will be to brief their related Assembly about existing issues, developments, and concerns and provide staff support to the decision process. Assemblies will, through this relationship, be kept current and well-informed.

The bureaus, agencies, and departments of Administrative Support will each be aligned with an elected decision body to support enforced democratic decision-making. Regulations formerly issued by Administrative Support organizations will be democratically legislated by their aligned Assembly. In this manner, all regulations and laws being imposed on the citizens will be democratically voted by elected assemblies, who will decide the process and cast the actual ballots.

No longer will departments and other non-elected organizations be authorized to issue laws or adjudicate matters. Aligned departments and other organizations will support the legislation process as required by Assembly management, and, of course, all laws created by Assemblies will require a concurring vote of the Senate and the signature of the President.

ORGANIZING THE MANNER IN WHICH INTERESTED PARTIES WILL BE HEARD

In the present system, if a person or business wants to make an impact on pending legislation, he/she would appeal to the Elected Representative for the district. He/she might also hire a lobbyist, who would solicit within the government on his/her behalf. The person or business has been totally reliant on his Representative to speak for him/her.

There are several weaknesses in that system. It involved lobbyists with extra cost to the appealing citizen. There are many possible corruption scenarios, with money changing hands. The citizen had no assurance his position was advanced before members of the House of Congress, and it probably was not. Little of this activity is "out-in-the-open."

Under the proposed Matrix Organization system, Administrative Support functions allied with an Assembly would set meetings where all parties with an interest in a matter would make their case. This process might take several days, but all Assembly members will hear the presentations, a critical aspect of their decision due diligence under self-government. The process will be far more satisfying to the appealing person or business, keeping matters "out-in-the-open" and conducted in a manner that can be observed in totality by all who have an interest. All voting assembly members will hear the same testimony.

THE SENATE: THE REMAINING GENERAL ASSEMBLY TAKES ON A BIGGER ROLE

The People should want the Senate focused on decision-making. The proposed transfer from the federal government to Constitutional Authorities of functions that should be independent of government (the judicial system, elections support, etc.) and the elimination of inter-branch check-and-balance duties will sharply reduce the non-decision workload of the Senate.

Replacing the former House of Representatives with a sequence of independent and specialty-focused Assemblies leaves the Senate as the only general Assembly. Sharply increasing its focus, and introducing special management, are the key changes.

Its two-representatives-per-state composition, totaling 100 members, makes it an ideally-sized general-purpose decision body. The proposal takes full advantage of its positive attributes, broadening its use and importance substantially, and creates the opportunity to eliminate its negative aspects.

The Framer three-branch silo structure of government, designed to facilitate internal check-and-balance, is rendered obsolete by these proposals. The door is opened to a more rational, coordinated working relationship between the President, the Senate, and the new decision/legislation assemblies by the long-overdue introduction of planning-based management. Made possible is a focused democratic assembly decision-making structure operating under close Constitutional Authority control and a co-operative, goal-oriented, and tightly controlled government led by one Chief Executive Officer.

THE SENATE WILL BE THE FINAL APPROVAL BODY, MAKING JUDGMENTS ON MATTERS PLACED BEFORE IT

The Senate's decision process and day-to-day operations would be under the management of highly skilled persons assigned by and reporting to the Guardians of the Constitution. It will be solely a decision body dedicated to making quality democratic decisions on matters placed before it. The Guardians will control its decision process and all activities, ensuring extraneous influences are strained out. They will ensure that the Senate is solely focused on matters The People want them involved in.

To become law, all proposed legislation emanating from the many Assemblies will require ratification by the Senate and the signature of the President.

The current totalitarian Presidential practice of using Executive Orders to execute major unvoted initiatives affecting the nation and its citizens will be forbidden and be replaced by a democratic process under which the Senate must vote approval or denial of all initiatives proposed by the President for implementation. That requirement alone will place a significant decision burden on the Senate.

It is proposed that laws passed by assemblies be considered by the senate in joint meetings, in which the proposing Assembly reports on and supports its legislative proposal. That process will dramatically improve information flow, eliminate duplicate efforts, and aid Senate decision-making.

THE SENATE WILL PLAY A KEY ROLE IN ORGANIZING THE NATION'S ASSEMBLY DECISION AND LEGISLATION PROCESS

All requests for decisions and legislation relative to the affairs of the nation will be routed through the Office of The President. The President will transmit to the Senate a proposed priority list for Assembly and Senate decision-making and legislation, planned two years forward. The Senate will consider and give final approval of the decision/legislation schedule, and retain those issues the Senate should itself consider. With the approval signature of the President, the schedule will be adopted and become operations orders.

The proposals, all of which emanate from within the nation, require democratic decisions that are out in the open and fully disclosed to The People, who reserve to themselves the right and capability to amend the decision process if they desire.

THE PRESIDENT WILL PROPOSE THE BUDGET, EXPENDITURES, AND TAXATION FOR SENATE APPROVAL

The Senate will play the main role in the nation's financial decisions, and the President will execute them. **Gone, with the disbanded House of Representatives, is that body's "control of the purse" authority**. A tightly controlled budgeting system will be imposed, all expenditures tied to the budget and aimed at achieving the People-generated Financial Measures, with the Senate playing the approval role. The President will plan the Budget, expenditures, and taxation, execution will be legislated by Assemblies if appropriate, but the Senate will have final approval authority.

Overall background and directional control over the financial elements of government will be established by the Well-Informed Electors through the Nation's National Imperatives and Financial Measures and monitored by the Guardians of the Constitution.

DUPLICATIVE EFFORTS IN GOVERNMENT WILL BE MINIMIZED

All duplicative activities must be strained out. No more duplicative committees. No more House of Representatives supervision of departments or Administrative State functions. With the removal of the Constitutional Authorities of activities historically called "check-and-balance," no more government approval of Presidential hires and no more impeachment trials. With no more party member elections and party politicking, much time will be freed up for focused governance.

The Senate will be focused on decision-making, with its required output from that endeavor increased dramatically. It will assign what was formerly "committee work" to an appropriate assembly. It will play a strong role in the organization and upgrading of the nation's legal code.

THE SENATE WILL RATIFY AND APPROVE THE PRESIDENT'S PLANS

The President will have responsibility, as the Chief Executive Officer, for heading up the strategic planning of the nation and instituting planning-based governance. Plans originated will require approval by the Senate, as the democratic government voting body, as well as by the Guardians.

Three main areas are involved:

1. The nation's strategic plan;

2. The National Imperatives, the Financial Measures, and the nation's budget;

3. Planning the two-year decision and legislation agenda of the nation.

NO POLITICAL ELITE, JUST FOCUSED AND PRODUCTIVE ELECTED OFFICIALS

Installation of term limits, management of the Senate by experts reporting to the Guardians of the Constitution, and putting the President in command will eliminate political parties and the political class from the nation. Upon completion of this reorganization, the Monarchy Republic creation of the Framers will have been totally dissolved, replaced by the true government of The People, by The People, and for The People. **Politics and politicians are words that should disappear from the Nation's vocabulary.**

No longer will elected members enter government service for the purpose of self-actualization and endless re-election. They will fulfill their one purpose, that of focused service to the nation under an employment contract and for a stated period of time, and then will return to private life, theoretically somewhat richer. No longer will citizens be forced to listen to the endless drivel of politics. Instead, citizens will themselves be deeply involved in the process of government.

We, The People, want the bodies of the Authority Structure to rapidly implement a dramatically improved two-way flow of information regarding the business of the nation between The People, as the owners, and The Authority Structure, as hired management. The information flow will be focused on plans and achievement status, national efforts under way, financial status and accomplishment, public debt, legislation and decision progress, and other important management information. The expectation will be that The People, after a few years, will completely understand and be current on our governance system and its performance.

CHAPTER 9

FOREWORD

Knowledgeable people observe that the quality of government decisions makes the difference between a Nation being a winner or a loser, between high or mediocre economic performance, between order and disorder, between a wealthy population and a wanting population, between happy people and a disgruntled citizenry.

Government decision-making currently, in our Democratic Republic, can only be viewed as "a disaster."

Given the importance of the subject, it is proposed that achieving vastly improved government decision-making become The People's premier strategy for achieving high-performance governance.

This Chapter will suggest how to create true democratic self-government with high-performance characteristics. It will outline, for the first time, true "self-government," with the heavy involvement of citizens in the fundamental decisions of the nation and utilizing a performance-based regimen focused on decision excellence.

SECTION 1
THE FRAMERS' "REPUBLIC"

The Framers created a form of government they called a "Republic." That fact is well known, but the Republic concept of government is not often the subject of discussion, nor is the complex "Republic" concept well understood.

History reveals important facts that underlie Framer government structure decisions and shape our understanding of why our nation is today living with the objectionable "Monarchy Republic" government form that will be discussed in Section 2.

A significant number of Framers were intensely anti-democratic. **They viewed democracy as a form of mob rule and wanted to avoid it.**[34] The Framers considered democracy very vulnerable to a drift in the direction of dictatorship. It would seem that the Framer anti-democracy position was based upon democracy's decentralization of government power because their own creation is the epitome of centralized power.

In the voting population of a democracy, as is always true, the poor voters hugely outnumber the rich voters. The democratic system gives political parties, using government as the intermediary, the power to transfer wealth from the rich to the poor, by way of a combination of taxation and welfare programs. Elected representatives, through their political parties, use the political benefits of the wealth transfer to curry re-election votes.

With that attitude prevalent among the Framers, democracy is not a word you will find in the Constitution or any other important founding document.

In early forms of democracy, citizens voted decisions on all matters. That process became too cumbersome, so in the next iteration representatives were elected to vote decisions in assembly on behalf of the citizens. Significantly, elected assemblies were typically given absolute powers, a nod toward monarchy, and a signal of serious disrespect for voters. The rule of the majority became the assembly decision standard.

Despite Framer's unwillingness to publicly use the word "democracy," it is the term citizens usually use today to describe our form of government. Many of the decision processes of our Republic, introduced within Congress over the years, are classically democratic today.

---

[34] "How Our Democracy Became Undemocratic", article Wall Street Journal by Barton Swaim, January 29, 2024.

In writing the Constitution of our Republic, applying their anti-democracy preferences, the Framers centralized all powers in the elected bodies, giving none to the citizens. Their construct emphasized individual equality and liberty and was intended to function as a limited government, restrictive in its law-making.

Creative republic voting structures were installed to improve decision-making. Two prominent examples are the Senate (membership limited to two senators per state) and the complex Electoral College voting procedure that gives a Presidential election the combined effect of a popular vote and the vote of states.

The legislative branches today employ the original Framer republic concept of government but markedly modified. The Framers were correct in their fears. Incursions of democracy into the republic have been relentless over the years, trending in the direction of authoritarianism. The add-on of the Administrative State to the original Framer construct has been a huge move toward authoritarian government, but the trend toward the "welfare" state has been equally so.

If one were today to estimate the percentage of government practice that employs the Framer "republic" plan, it would be 20%. Democracy practices that have intruded the original Republic framework are estimated at 40%. Practices introduced that are largely totalitarian would be 40%. Our present form of government is a dysfunctional hodge-podge, but it is much more accurately an authoritarian democracy than it is a republic.

What is more important is the "Republic" concept was a smokescreen for what the Framers actually installed; a form of government more properly called a "Monarchy Republic."

SECTION 2
THE DESIGN OF OUR "MONARCHY REPUBLIC" FORM OF GOVERNMENT

THE "MONARCHY REPUBLIC" CREATION OF THE FRAMERS

In the 1780s, monarchs were thoroughly detested by our citizens, and the Framers politically reflected that attitude. The nation had recently emerged from a brutal war of secession, a war colonists blamed on the English monarch King George 111. At the time, colonist's feelings about monarchs were, to be charitable, extremely negative.

Wide variations in structure and process exist in democracies worldwide, with a range of labels employed. Similar variations among totalitarian governments abound. Most utilize some amount of democratic practice, if only for "show." Readers should peruse available internet information on "liberal democracies" and consider that such governments do not usually neatly fit into the mental image implied by their label. That holds true for the government of the United States also.

Despite their dislike of monarchs, in designing their Republic, the Framers leaned heavily toward monarchy. The "Monarchy Republic" (our label) they created was masked by heavy use of the public relations façade of describing it as a Republic. "Government of the people, by the people, and for the people" was the slogan loudly proclaimed in the elections of individuals participating in it.

The heavy Monarchy feel of their republic scheme was, and is, buried so deeply and cleverly in the constitution and operating structure that few citizens have spotted its existence. It never draws a discussion! It was concealed behind the curtain of the label "republic" and the smoke screen of "government of the people, by the people, and for the people." Against that historical backdrop, consider that most citizens today call our government system simply "democratic."

COMPARING A MONARCHY WITH A DEMOCRACY

A government is a monarchy if:

Its controlling *power* is absolute and centralized. Federal government decisions are made by individuals or small groups of people, usually ratified by internally controlled assemblies for appearance's sake:

- o There is a total absence of government accountability to the people.

- o All power is vested in the government.

- o Leadership and governance are conducted by an anchored Political Elite class.

- o The government is insulated against citizen intervention, interference, or correction.

A government claims to be a "democracy" if some or all of the following are present:

- o Governing officials are elected by democratic vote.

- o Structures, processes, and practices employed within government are "democratic" and were approved by citizens.

- o The rule of law prevails. The citizenry may be granted significant freedom.

- o Governance decisions are made by the democratic vote of elected representatives.

This Chapter will delve deeply into important aspects of the Framer-created Monarchy Republic, which is heavily weighted toward the attributes of a monarchy and lightly weighted toward the attributes of a democracy. The above comparison highlights the wide range of variations that may be present in a given form of government.

HOW THE FRAMERS GUARANTEED THEIR MONARCHY REPUBLIC WOULD LIVE IN PERPETUITY

In a nod toward democratic principles, our citizens are permitted to elect or discharge officials who participate in the Monarchy Republic rule. **All other rights and powers that belong to the citizens/owners of the nation were constitutionally taken from them and placed under the control of the political elite of our Monarchy Republic.**

Each elected assembly was granted the right to "determine the rules of its proceedings" so there could be no outside interference with the critical assembly process, its control 100% vested in the hands of the Political Elite. All power to amend the Constitution and to manage government was granted to the political elite, thereby denying citizens any route by which to make changes or correct defects in their own government.

This was the nation's constitutional position at that time concerning the right to control government. The following clear statement, however, was prominent in the Declaration of Independence, the unanimous declaration of the thirteen states of America, enacted by the Second Continental Congress on July 4, 1776:

> "That whenever any Form of Government becomes destructive of these ends, **it is the Right of the People to alter or to abolish it, and to institute new Government,** laying its foundation on such principles and organizing its powers in such form as to them shall seem most likely to affect their Safety and Happiness."

That logic was consecrated by the thirteen states to justify shedding themselves of rule by the hated English Monarchy but was subsequently denied inclusion in our Constitution. It applies equally forcefully today as logic for The People to shed the abusive Monarchy Republic rule by the disrespected Political Elite.

EVERY MONARCHY DEVELOPS A PRIVILEGED CLASS

Our Monarchy Republic predictively developed a privileged class that we now refer to as the "political elite."

> The ballot box power the constitution (and its Monarchy Republic) gave to the citizens is effective only against individual candidates or elected persons. Any citizen power to make changes to government structure or operations comes through political party election, and the power is extremely limited.
>
> **The dysfunction of U.S. government cannot, therefore, be corrected by voting in elections. That has been tried repeatedly, with no success for the citizens.**
>
> Voting constitutes no threat to the Monarchy Republic's existence, **because no change to the Monarchy Republic government structure can be affected by citizen voting at the ballot box.**

Operating within rules they themselves wrote, as permitted under their constitutional authority, early elected officials in Congress adopted an in-house control scheme founded on bill passage by simple-majority-vote. That control scheme enables a political party to dominate a House with a mere 50% majority, thereby ensconcing leaders of the party as the Monarchy Republic's "political elite." **Achieving a "majority" in a House, and with it the right to direct and control, is possible if the supportive vote of about one-third of voting citizens is cast in a party's favor.** That is true because about one-third of all citizens do not vote, and the remaining two-thirds are evenly divided between the two major political parties.

Changes in political party majority control through elections merely switch the party in power but have no effect on the rules or operations of the Monarchy Republic itself. **The voter's ballot box check-and-balance against individual elected representatives has, over time, been degraded by political party influence on the election process.** Today, a 90% incumbent re-election rate is commonplace, a percentage so high that no true accountability on Congress is likely to be imposed by massive voter rejection.

90% incumbent re-election rates constitute proof of what is said in the preceding paragraphs. At high re-election rates, a ruling class of permanently-seated elite is anchored in government, a condition reminiscent of monarchies. **At those re-election rates, elected official accountability to the voters has lost 90% of its potency, since politicians not re-elected fall in the miniscule 10% range.** Despite being the designated disciplinarians of government, the voters re-elect the same representatives over and over and over again, in lockstep with the support of their preferred political party, thereby essentially discarding accountability through the ballot box.

THE CONSTITUTION IS "OFF LIMITS" TO THE PEOPLE: THEY HAVE NO WAY TO AMEND IT!

In order to maintain the Monarchy Republic intact, the text of the nation's constitution needed to be placed under the exclusive control of the Political Elite. In our nation, that guarantee of the Monarchy Republic's continued existence is firmly in place.

Article V, which contains the rules for constitutional amendment, has no provision for The People to amend their own constitution. That fact positions Article V of the Constitution in direct contradiction with Paragraph 2 of the Declaration of Independence, quoted earlier.

Had The People been constitutionally granted their inalienable right (quoting the Declaration) to change the nation's form of government, the present Article V provisions would not exist. They would long ago have been replaced by a provision stating the power to amend the constitution is vested in The People solely.

Article V specifies two groups of elected officials who may propose amendments to the constitution. **a) Congress, by two-thirds of both Houses, or b) The legislatures of two-thirds of the States.** With an approved proposal, a Convention shall be called to consider amendments. If ratified by the Legislatures (or Conventions) of three-fourths of the States, proposed amendments shall be valid. The Congress will decide which will be the route followed.

Constitutional Convention delegates were obviously knowledgeable about the Declaration of Independence, which, in their time, was a very recent event. The Framers included no constitutional language nullifying statements of the Declaration of Independence. **They obviously knew that the Constitution's Article V was a glaring contradiction to the Declaration's statement of the right of citizens to alter or amend the nation's form of government and to institute a new government "whenever it becomes destructive." Nevertheless, the Framers chose to constitutionally ignore that glaring contradiction and framed Article V to cement in place political elite control over the constitution of the Monarchy Republic being created.**

> The Article V structure was put in place purposefully. Don't delude yourself by thinking that it was a Framer mistake, or a drafting error. It wasn't. It was a willful act. It created a total absence of government accountability to the People. It was installed to put Congress in a Monarch's position, virtually impossible for The People to improve or correct. The secret was granting the political elite control over the amendment process.

The politicians who inhabit the halls of Congress are members of the same political parties as the politicians who inhabit the halls of the State legislatures. Different jurisdictions, to be sure, but the same political parties. Although both the States and Congress would be involved in Constitutional amendment, **at the end of the day it is the political parties who control the amendment process.**

ARTICLE V, COUPLED WITH FAILURE OF THE BALLOT BOX, CHECK-AND-BALANCE DENIES THE PEOPLE ANY VOTER CONTROL OVER GOVERNMENT

The Political Elite controls amendments to our governing document, the Constitution, taking that correction route away from the citizens. With the check-and-balance failure of the ballot box, brought about by the actions of the political parties, no functional voter control over the Political Elite today exists.

A primary feature of the monarchy form of government is the total absence of reigning monarch accountability to the citizens. **ACCOUNTABILITY OF GOVERNMENT TO THE PEOPLE IN THE U.S. MONARCHY REPUBLIC IS EFFECTIVELY ZERO**!

There is no question we live under a monarchy. The "monarch" is two houses of Congress and a presidency. Control of political parties over the two houses of Congress carries with it control over the fiefdom. The People of the nation are merely subjects with no aggregational power or authority. As individuals, they are allowed to vote to select who shall be a part of the ruling monarchy, but that's all.

SECTION 3
THE FUNCTIONALITY OF THE AMENDMENT PROCESS: OUR CONSTITUTIONAL AMENDMENT HISTORY

Considering the above comments, "What has been the history of the U.S. constitutional amendment process over the past 247 years?" becomes a loaded question.

DURING THAT PERIOD OF TIME, TWENTY-SEVEN AMENDMENTS HAVE BEEN RATIFIED.

We will conduct a brief analysis of amendment activity in the period since the signing of the constitution to develop a picture of the use of this vital process and to assess the overall impact of the amendment process on the nation's government.

A. THE FIRST TEN AMENDMENTS WERE RATIFIED IN 1791. THEY INSERTED CONTENT THAT HAD NOT BEEN FINISHED AT THE CONSTITUTION SIGNING.

Some Framers evidenced concern over elements of the Constitution. They signed the constitution on the condition that unresolved issues would be promptly dealt with following its signing and approval.

The first ten Amendments passed in 1791, called the Bill of Rights, fulfilled that condition.

Those ten 'Amendments" granted citizens protection against the arbitrary actions of government but were structured as "individual rights." **The rights granted to the citizens did not include the right to change government in any manner whatsoever.** The Bill of Rights was not in any way a threat to the Monarchy Republic's existence, nor to its political elite.

The first ten amendments, called the Bill of Rights, address issues that had not been resolved at the time of the Constitution signing. Thus, they were not "amendments" in the normal sense. They merely "completed the unfinished constitution."

Deducting those ten from the twenty-seven amendments ratified since the signing, seventeen true "amendments" have been approved in the elapsed 233 years.

One of those seventeen was superseded by a subsequent amendment. Plus, the amendments instituting and cancelling Prohibition offset each other.

The net true amendments to the constitution ratified since 1791 is therefore fourteen.

B. THE FOURTEEN TRUE AMENDMENTS, CLASSIFIED BY TOPIC, BREAK DOWN AS FOLLOWS:

The President and Vice President	3
Citizenship and Voting Rights, the Electoral College	6
Abolition of Slavery	1
Power to Tax Income	1
Limit to Judicial Power	1
Senator Elections	1
District of Columbia	1
Total	14

C. THE "POLITICAL ELITE" REFUSE TO USE CONSTITUTIONAL AMENDMENTS FOR GOVERNMENT IMPROVEMENT

One would logically have expected that in the 247 years since its signing, the Constitution would have been updated repeatedly. Despite the cumbersome effort entailed, given the rapid rate of change experienced by our nation in that period, hundreds or perhaps thousands of amendments truly should have been enacted just to keep our constitution current.

As the constitution stands today, that is the job of Government. Since each House of Congress was accorded the right to "determine the rules of its proceedings," there is no question about their duty. The only question is: "Why did Congress not fulfill its responsibilities?"

The conclusion one reaches is the political elite want their Monarchy Republic to remain undisturbed. Allowing amendments to the constitution to become normal operating practice would open the door to a flexible constitution, which would inevitably put at risk political elite control over their Monarchy Republic.

The no-amendment policy, in effect, is a most egregious example of the political elite placing its self-interest ahead of the welfare of the nation. For that corruption, the performance records of past and present members of both Houses should be permanently tarnished.

> Hanging over that matter is a critical piece of business only The People can resolve. Amendments must become the unquestioned bailiwick of The People, because without that right, The People cannot "alter or abolish the form of government, and institute new government."

D. DETAILED CASE STUDIES ON FAILED CONSTITUTIONAL AMENDMENTS

Understanding the Challenges of Constitutional Change Through Notable Failures

The difficulty of amending the U.S. Constitution has long been both a strength and a weakness. While its rigidity ensures stability, it also makes addressing evolving societal needs arduous. Examining major failed amendment attempts provides insight into the structural and political barriers that thwart change. Among these, the Equal Rights Amendment (ERA) and efforts to abolish the Electoral College stand out for their historical significance and the lessons they offer.

The Equal Rights Amendment (ERA)

Background:

Proposed in 1923 and gaining momentum in the 1970s, the ERA sought to enshrine gender equality in the Constitution. Its most famous clause reads:

"Equality of rights under the law shall not be denied or abridged by the United States or by any State on account of sex."

Why It Failed:

1. Political Polarization:

By the late 1970s, the ERA became a lightning rod for political and cultural battles. Conservative activists, led by figures like Phyllis Schlafly, argued that the amendment would dismantle traditional gender roles, undermine family values, and lead to unintended consequences like gender-neutral bathrooms or mandatory military drafts for women.

2. State Ratification Hurdles:

The amendment passed Congress in 1972 with bipartisan support, but ratification by three-fourths of the states (38) proved elusive. Despite initial enthusiasm, momentum stalled after 35 states ratified it. Five states even voted to rescind their ratifications, adding to the controversy.

3. Expiring Deadline:

Congress imposed a seven-year deadline for ratification, later extended to 1982. This time limit, coupled with mounting opposition, sealed the ERA's fate.

Lessons Learned:

- **Cultural Resistance:** Amendments that challenge deeply entrenched societal norms face an uphill battle. Building bipartisan, grassroots support is critical to overcoming cultural inertia.

- **Deadline Pitfalls:** Fixed ratification deadlines can be a double-edged sword, ensuring urgency but also creating artificial time constraints that limit public debate and consensus-building.

- **State-Level Opposition:** The federalist structure amplifies regional differences, making it difficult to achieve nationwide agreement on contentious issues.

Efforts to Abolish the Electoral College

Background:

Since its inception, the Electoral College has been criticized for distorting the popular vote. Critics argue that it gives disproportionate influence to smaller states and allows candidates to win the presidency without a majority of votes, as seen in the elections of 2000 and 2016. Numerous proposals have sought to abolish or reform the system, but all have failed.

Why They Failed:

1. Entrenched Interests:

Smaller states, which benefit from the Electoral College's structure, vehemently oppose its abolition. Any amendment requires their support, creating an inherent conflict of interest.

2.   Partisan Divisions:

The Electoral College often benefits one political party over another, depending on demographic trends. This dynamic makes bipartisan support for reform exceedingly rare. For example, Republicans largely opposed abolition efforts after the 2000 and 2016 elections, as their candidates won the presidency despite losing the popular vote.

3.   Complexity of Ratification:

Even when Congress has been sympathetic to reform, ratification by 38 states has been an insurmountable obstacle. The fear of unintended consequences and the difficulty of building consensus across diverse state populations further complicate the process.

Lessons Learned:

- **Overcoming Partisan Interests:** Reform efforts must be framed as benefiting democracy as a whole rather than one party. This requires exceptional leadership and public education campaigns.

- Alternative Strategies: Proposals like the National Popular Vote Interstate Compact (NPVIC), which seeks to circumvent the Electoral College without a constitutional amendment, highlight innovative approaches when traditional methods fail.

- **Institutional Inertia:** Resistance to change is often rooted in fear of disrupting longstanding systems, even when those systems are widely criticized. Incremental reforms may be more politically feasible than wholesale abolition.

Common Threads and Broader Implications

1. The Difficulty of Consensus:

Both the ERA and Electoral College reform demonstrate how the U.S. Constitution's amendment process magnifies ideological and regional divisions. Achieving the supermajority thresholds in Congress and state legislatures requires compromises that are often untenable in today's polarized political climate.

2. The Role of Grassroots Movements:

Both cases underscore the importance of grassroots advocacy in driving constitutional change. While the ERA was buoyed by the feminist movement, it ultimately fell short due to insufficient coalition-building across ideological lines. Similarly, Electoral College reform has gained traction in urban areas but has failed to connect with rural voters.

3. The Challenge of Deadlines:

Time limits for ratification, though intended to maintain focus, can stifle the natural evolution of public opinion. A more flexible approach to amendment deadlines could allow for broader engagement and reduce the impact of temporary political pressures.

4. The Importance of Framing:

Successful amendments often appeal to universal principles rather than partisan agendas. For instance, the abolition of slavery (13th Amendment) and women's suffrage (19th Amendment) succeeded because they were framed as moral imperatives rather than partisan causes.

SECTION 4
VASTLY-IMPROVED DECISION-MAKING:
THE ROUTE TO HIGH-QUALITY SELF-GOVERNMENT

The foregoing Sections discussed the ingenious locks, embedded by the Framers in the Constitution plan that ensure absolute Political Elite control over our Monarchy Republic form of government.

It is proposed The People's government improvement strategy be a *production of decisions of high quality.* Before that can be done, The People must gain control over the Constitution and establish their power to put in place the needed amendments.

The following summarizes a plan to dramatically improve decision quality.

1. DECISION-MAKING FOR THE NATION MUST BE ORGANIZED AND CONTROLLED BY THE PEOPLE.

The source of our breakdown in creating effective democratic self-government is the inability of political leaders to figure out what the necessary actions are and how to do them successfully. It is in organizing the decisions that **democracy's problems, and the problems of any form of government, are created.**

"That whenever any Form of Government becomes destructive of these ends, **it is the Right of the People to alter or abolish it, and to institute new Government**, laying its foundation on such principles and organizing its powers in such form as to them shall seem most likely to affect their Safety and Happiness."[35]

Self-government means that planning, organizing, staffing, directing and controlling the nation, through an authority structure, is carried out directly by The People. That process must be carefully designed and cast in concrete.

The definition incorporates the requirement that the Constitution, controlled by The People, must be a flexible document responsive to changing times and the nation's changing needs. **The Constitution must become the vehicle by which The People convey "direction."** The People's direction must by the decision responsibility of the citizens, be executed though the Authority Structure, may not be constrained by political structure or subdivision, and may not be strained through any middlemen, such as political parties or the media.

The Framer Republic plan donated the rights and responsibilities of The People to the elected persons and established no control or accountability over them. That plan is an outright violation of ethical principles.

"Giving total control to the politicians and letting them decide" is not self-government; it is a monarchy government. It may fit the conceptual template of a republic but does not meet the critical test for "government of the people, by the people, and for the people." In self-government, The People decide, and the hired management executes.

The Authority Rules of the Nation must grant to The People "inalienable rights" to perform their responsibilities of ownership, such as deciding the rules under which the nation will operate and ensuring that self-government is conducted as they intend. **"Check and balance" is the "Control" responsibility of the nation's owners, The People.**

If decision improvement is the primary strategy to upgrade government, dramatic changes to the assemblies and the Presidency will be required to create an advanced democratic decision machine custom-designed for tasks The People have determined must be performed. This book proposes that the Well-Informed Electors use elected Constitutional Authorities to draft, for their approval, the proposed rules and processes of the decision function and the

---

[35] Declaration of Independence, Second Paragraph

means by which they will carry out the "plan, organize, staff, direct and control" of the government decision process.

2. DIFFERENTIATE THE PEOPLE'S DECISIONS FROM THOSE MADE BY GOVERNMENT

Separating what must be Constitutional (that is to say, promulgated by The People) from what must be Governmental is the beginning point for developing a rational Authority Structure. Implemented, that action draws a clear line between the "boss" and the "hired management."

"Self Government" demands that The People be the "boss."

Constitutional decisions would be made by direct vote of the Well-Informed Electors, acting on behalf of all citizens. Governmental decisions would be made by the democratic vote of persons elected, convened, and organized in assemblies designed specifically for their purpose and acting on behalf of all citizens. Both decision processes would be controlled and directed by designated Constitutional Authorities, the execute-and-enforce arm of The People.

The most important decisions of the United States are to be made by The People. Those decisions will require a very special organization and process. The introduction of "direct democracy," to decide direction and control by The People in a nation of more than 300 million people, will not be a simple task. A constitutional guidance group will be needed to manage the decision processes of The People. Voted decisions of the People, as envisioned, will be much more complex than the simple ballot-box voting used in elections. Voting by a Well-Informed Electorate composed of millions of citizens will be frequent, perhaps sometimes several times a month. Such a system and process will require modern technology employed very intelligently.

A detailed examination of that important proposal appears elsewhere in this book.

Critical decisions will never be delegated to elected persons in government, nor will they be made by the Supreme Court. Critical decisions will be made on behalf of all citizens by the Well-Informed Elector body, always by democratic vote. They are decisions of the highest order, the nation's "what we are going to be, and what are we going to do" decisions. They are the horses in front of the cart.

"Critical decisions" include defining the nation's beliefs, its principles, its fundamental policies, the responsibilities and rights of citizens, its political and economic ideology, its form and organization of government, how government staffing shall be carried out, its delegation of authority and establishment of control over government, and decisions to define the planned forward direction of the nation.

Any matter that falls within The People's "Plan, Organize, Staff, Direct and Control" responsibility is a "Critical Decision."

The government will focus on operating the nation, one aspect being to achieve the goals and financial measures set by The People. Decisions to be made by the government will fall within its own "plan," "organize," 'staff," "direct," and "control" duties. The "How are we going to do this" aspect of the nation's decision process, employing planning-based management, will be determined and executed by the government. The following is a brief summary of the decision role of government:

- Planning, deriving, and executing solutions for the ongoing needs of the nation that require attention but do not meet the "critical" test.

- Directing and managing the day-to-day affairs of the nation. Ensuring that the nation is faithfully adhering to direction from The People.

- Ensuring that state and local government charters properly enforce accountability to The People, and that practices in those governments conform to constitutional principles.

- Ensuring the domestic tranquility of the nation, including writing the laws under which people will live.

- Managing achievement of National Imperatives, Financial Measures, the Decision and Legislation plan, Strategic Plans, and the Nation's budget.

- Managing relationships with foreign nations, assuring the nation's defense.

The Guardians of the Constitution will be designated to manage the decision process conducted within the nation's Authority Structure. The governmental decision process, covering legislative and decision proposals, will be planned by the President and executed by the Assemblies, monitored endlessly under the guidance of the Guardians, with improvements made as the learning process increases comprehension.

As full-time overseers, the Guardians will ensure that decisions are made only by those who should properly make them, are made in accordance with pre-defined democratic processes and requirements, and that all decisions are evaluated later to rate success.

These are essential controls over a self-governed Democracy "of The People" that delegates specific decision responsibility and authority to representative government and utilizes Constitutional Authority bodies to provide direction and ensure government performance. Decision-making rules and processes fall under the Planning, Organizing, Staffing, Directing, and Controlling responsibilities of The People.

3. DEFINE WHERE DECISIONS ARE TO BE MADE WITHIN GOVERNMENT

The President, the Judicial System, the Administrative State, and bodies of Congress are currently all making decisions inappropriate to their role in the nation's authority structure. In general, the following observations describe a nation swirling in self-directed confusion, unable to deal with fundamental matters essential to its welfare.

As government functionality has regressed over the years, decisions have been abdicated by some designated government bodies and assumed by others or left endlessly floating unresolved. The Supreme Court receives for resolution many decisions that have been defaulted elsewhere, most of which are "critical decisions" for which no government function wants to take responsibility. Such decisions are not made because no authority currently exists for The People to make them, and the government avoids making them. The political elite are doing nothing to resolve them using the proper vehicle, constitutional amendment, for reasons previously discussed.

Critical matters float around unresolved, such as budgeting and the national debt, abortion, censorship and speech rights, the Media problem, population control and immigration, climate policy, and the right of people to peaceably assemble, just to name a few. Those critical matters left in the party realm, and others derived from them or not mentioned, will be found swirling in time-wasting and never-ending political argument, constant unproductive litigation, infighting, and polarization. **While that is taking place, the nation wanders aimlessly, arguing all the way, with various organizations making decisions on the periphery of the critical issues but obviously unable to achieve any meaningful resolution.**

To resolve the government decision problem, two democratic structure improvements are needed:

1. A process is needed for Well-Informed Electors to make, by vote, and write into the constitution, the "critical decisions" that are The People's responsibility solely. That will first require cancellation of the existing Article V of the constitution and replacing it with new provisions authorizing Provisions and Amendments to be decided by The People only.

2. A decision-control body (the Guardians of the Constitution) located within the Constitutional Authorities would be given the responsibility to monitor and administer the entire Authority Structure decision process under voted direction from the Well-Informed Electors.

4. RE-LOCATE ALL DOMESTIC REGULATION DECISIONS TO THE ASSEMBLIES

Classify regulation as law, requiring legislation before implementation so that all actions imposed upon The People have been decided democratically. That change will eliminate the authoritarian posture of the units of the Administrative State and of individuals in government. Aligning each such unit with an assembly will convert them into true democratic government support units. Set Constitutional standards against which all regulation/legislation must be compared. Set investigation rules for all proposed legislation. Define and install interested party input rights and processes.

A high-order government process question is, "Which issues shall be placed before an elected body for consideration and vote?" The current party-based favoritism selection process is not producing results. The decision blockage of the nation is located in Congress, making it essential that The People intercede.

> We are mostly a democracy. In a democracy, decisions affecting the nation and its people are made by democratic vote, and assemblies of one kind or another perform that function.
>
> **Self-government means that The People totally control the nation's decision process.**
>
> The purpose of government is operational decision-making. and execution. Certainty is critical to people and businesses, so government decision timeliness is very important.

A formal planning process should be installed making the President the designated organizer and director of government's decision/legislation work. He/she would be responsible to The People for ensuring decision needs are methodically planned and scheduled, decisions are made timely through tightly controlled assemblies, and for the aggregate decision/legislation performance of all Assemblies. Working with the Senate, but under the direction of the President, personnel will gather all decision/legislation proposals, evaluate them, and construct a priority list. By this means, decision/legislation planning for the government will be directed and carried out at its highest level, where it properly belongs. Under a President-and-Senate-controlled structure, decision/legislation priorities would be assigned to assemblies for execution, with the list, process, and results reported regularly to The People.

The proposed plan for the government will place elected assemblies where the initial voted decisions are to be made and under the day-to-day management of professionals selected and installed by the Guardians of the Constitution. The manager of each assembly will direct the assembly work and decision process for all matters to be decided. The Guardians are The People's designated authority to monitor and supervise that decision-making, but neither they nor their assigned experts will guide decisions toward any individual solution, nor will they vote.

By these means, the nation's entire decision process will be by democratic vote and tightly controlled by instrumentalities of The People. The nation's decision-making capacity and production will be dramatically accelerated. All elected decision bodies will be designed and staffed explicitly for the role they are expected to fulfill.

5. REVISE THE ELECTED BODY VOTED DECISION PROCESS AND ELIMINATE "TYRANNY OF THE MAJORITY"

A decision faced by newly-elected representatives when our democratic government was first organized following the signing of the constitution was how assembly-voted decisions should be made. They got no direction from the Framers via the constitution, so they installed their own version of democratic voting, instituting the rule that if more than 50% of the votes were in favor, called a "simple majority," the bill was passed.

It wasn't long before the realization set in that, while a majority vote of 50%+ could be called a decision, with almost as many voters disagreeing as those who agreed, a bill so passed truly lacked support. The 50% majority decision criteria came to be known as "tyranny of the majority," subduing the minority by imposing the majority will.

The "Simple Majority" decision rule is appropriate (or acceptable) for votes of very large bodies of people, such as national populations.

It is not an appropriate decision rule for small bodies, such as elected assemblies.

The following examines voting by elected assemblies to derive democratic decisions.

a) **The best measure of the quality of a voted decision is the level of support received from the voting body.** The closer to 100% support, the higher the intellectual agreement among those voting as to the probability of a good outcome. The lower the vote support percentage, the lower the probability the decision will produce successful results.

b) The 50% majority rule is the ideal of political parties, which are factions of elected representatives whose purpose is establishing authoritarian control over an elected assembly. When a political party acquires a voting "majority" in an elected assembly, factional totalitarian control is official in that assembly, and although democratic processes may be utilized, democracy no longer exists. If a political party gains majority control over both the Houses and the Presidency, the American government is totalitarian. Political parties add multiple negatives to everything governmental, but the most destructive is their bastardization of control.

c) In our Nation's assemblies, the simple majority rule produces conclusions to proposals **but does not produce quality decisions.** Better conclusions would result from enforcing on the elected voting body a high decision majority benchmark. High levels of voting support can generally be taken as evidence that the conclusion will produce a good result. The reason we don't often see a high level of voting support for a proposal is the influence of political parties, the members of which cluster around their party's solution, splitting the voter body and making high majorities difficult to obtain.

d) The party's interest dominates all our voted assembly results. The incentive for assembly voting members runs toward support of their political party. They see no reward for seeking the best solution for an issue since their rewards flow from securing passage of the party proposal. Our nation's assemblies enforce no penalty on voting members for subordinating the nation's interest to the interest of the party because that is how political parties set the rules.

e) All assembly processes flow from the assembly's constitutional right to set the rules of proceedings. Proceedings rules should rightly originate from The People because proper rules will not be proposed by political parties whose existence is dependent on voting control. That is the reason why, to achieve high decision quality, a voting majority regimen in Congress is pre-set and administered by a Constitutional Authority acting on behalf of The People. Required voting majorities would range from 60% to 100%, varying with the proposal under consideration.

Two results would accrue from that approach: 1. Decision quality would improve dramatically, and 2. There would no longer be political parties because their existence relies upon the simple majority decision rule being in effect.

f) The bargaining carried out within legislative bodies is vote purchasing, not decision-making. Bargaining is a valid process for the marketplace but not for the decisions of democratic government. Such practices are, at a minimum, undemocratic, but vote purchasing should also be considered corrupt. Trading the interests of factions that may be damaged or enhanced by a pending decision is not decision-making; it is purchasing votes, which should not be permitted. Constituency interests, the consequence of "representation" established by elections, political faction actions, and donor obligations, leave assembly voting members burdened with performance debts that conflict with The People's "best decision" requirement. Those debts are paid off during legislative bargaining.

g) No improvement in government decision-making can be achieved as long as the Houses of Congress have the constitutional right to determine their own proceedings. That provision set the stage for the 50% majority vote, for political party control over government, for "contention" as government procedure, and for the bargain/purchase process of vote aggregating. To institute a high-quality decision process, The People must impose absolute independent control over assembly proceedings.

Readers, accustomed to observing voting in a contentious party-based assembly environment, may question this proposal's success potential. Proposals supporting it include an entirely new approach to candidate selection and elections to upgrade elected person quality, eliminating "representation" as an elected-person obligation, installing term limits to eliminate the diversionary re-election concern of elected persons, utilizing constitutional funding of all election costs to eliminate voting obligations originating therefrom, and eliminating political parties as a factor.

Couple those changes with the above decision process proposals, and an entirely new democratic decision atmosphere emerges.

6. REDESIGN AND REFOCUS THE ELECTED ASSEMBLIES TO MAKE THEM HIGHLY EFFECTIVE DEMOCRATIC DECISION BODIES

The Elected Assemblies must be refocused and redesigned to become pure decision bodies managed and directed by Constitutional representatives. Under that control, decisions will produce high-quality results. True "government by The People" will become a reality, not just a patriotic slogan.

It is proposed that the House of Representatives be replaced by a group of 30 to 60 smaller elected independent decision assemblies, each assigned responsibility for a defined segment of America and each tightly coordinated with affiliated support units of the Administrative State.

The relatively small voting bodies will be immediately subject to criticism. However, a republic permits the formation of a variety of voting bodies designed to meet a specific need. Decision quality is not determined by voting body size. It is determined by its organization and focus, the intelligence and dedication of the participating decision-makers, and the quality of management of the decision process. **The Constitution, arguably our all-time most important decision, was voted by thirty-nine Framer signers.**

The Senate would become the nation's dominant decision body, be given an entirely new set of responsibilities, and retain its confirmation vote for all proposed decisions and legislation emanating out of the Assemblies and the Presidency. The ratification by the President of legislation will also be required.

7. DUMP THE SIMPLE MAJORITY RULE IN ASSEMBLIES, DEMANDING INSTEAD A HIGH PERCENTAGE OF VOTING MEMBER AGREEMENT FOR BILL PASSAGE

50% is today's simple majority requirement for voted assembly assent, but that benchmark was not set by the Constitution. Various Articles speak about voting, but whenever the constitution discusses a majority assent concerning a given matter, **the benchmark is always two-thirds of those voting.**

The simple majority rule was established by each House to allow control by a minimal-majority political party faction. The rule meets the ease and convenience desires of voting members of the houses and lowers the arithmetic benchmark for "control" of an assembly, thereby clearing the table for political party operations. The denigrating term for the 50% majority decision, "tyranny of the majority," is an accurate label.

Each House of Congress delegated the right to manage its decision process to any political party able to command a voting majority. By that action, "tyranny of the majority" became the decision principle that dictated the management structure and process of the two houses. Control over the elected assembly decision process was taken out of the hands of the assemblies and given to the political party, achieving a majority. The 50% majority places importance on getting a decision made, eases complexity for the House membership, and attaches little importance to the effect that decisions so produced have on the nation.

Those actions in our Monarchy Republic assemblies have, predictably, brought about unintended consequences. Rather than the government of The People, by The People, and for The People, what emerged is the government of The People, by Political Parties, and for the Political Elite. **"Tyranny of the majority" converts an assembly from democracy to "largely totalitarian, employing facets of democracy."**

We state repeatedly that the route to improved government is through significantly upgrading the decision process. Decision-making is the most important function of government, its reason for existence. Why would The People support any system of government that places control over its most important function in the hands of a political party? **In self-government, that control must rest securely in the hands of The People.**

We propose replacing the large and dysfunctional House of Representatives with a significant number of small elected assemblies, each focused solely on decision-making **for an assigned segment of the nation.** The proposal disbands the large House of Representatives with its committee/sub-committee structure, its member lack of focus with built-in conflicting obligations. That structure will be replaced by a significant number of custom-designed decision units averaging perhaps only 25 elected members, each focused solely on governing a discreet jurisdiction.

In conjunction with that change, it is proposed that for each decision a pre-determined set percentage of the total assembly votes will be set and directed. **The goal is dramatic improvement in the quality of decisions, and absolute certainty that all of the nation's issues will receive prompt and well-considered solutions.**

8. DEVELOP HIGH-QUALITY PROPERLY-MANAGED GROUP DECISIONS

Foregoing discussions may suggest that decisions arrived at democratically can never be good decisions.

As operated today, approvals or rejections by our legislative bodies are not decisions for the Nation, and they are negotiated conclusions for political party business proposals. The process of arriving at a vote within assemblies is marketplace bargaining, focused on the purchase or trading of votes. The rationality and logic were bargained away before any conclusion was derived.

The trading, influencing, and pressure of "politics" employed to produce a House approval vote for a bill **is a political party business process**. Bills put up for vote are party projects that deploy public money and resources for the purpose of furthering the interests of the sponsoring party. Such influences, practices, and pressures hopelessly defile government decision-making.

Group decisions are generally vastly superior to decisions made by individuals. If the cumulative brainpower of a group is properly focused, the combined intellect will produce solutions many magnitudes more effective than those that are the product of one mind, or the product of dysfunctional huge -assembly bargaining.

But great decision-making can only be achieved if the decision group is well managed, tightly focused, unbiased, and undistracted.

CHAPTER 10

GOVERNMENT DECISION-MAKING SERIES, PART 3

CONTENT:

SECTION 1: A GENERAL DISCUSSION OF DECISION-MAKING

SECTION 2: DECISION PROCESS CONSIDERATIONS

SECTION 3: DECISION-MAKING IN DEMOCRATIC GOVERNMENT VOTING BODIES

SECTION 4: SUMMARY OF RELEVANT SUGGESTED IMPROVEMENTS

FOREWORD

Decision-making is the core function of government. Vastly-improved decisions are the proposed strategy of The People for achieving DRAMATIC improvement in the nation's governance.

It is difficult to understand and evaluate Legislative branch decision practices without some basis for comparison. For that reason, included here is academic material that would ordinarily not appear in this type of manuscript.

Probably many readers have not been exposed, in their lifetime, to the fundamentals of decision-making. The material following is extracted from the curricula of university business schools.

This Chapter delves into decision theory and practice and applies it to the processes of our two Houses of Congress. Decision principles are vital foundation information. Their purpose is to allow readers to objectively evaluate the decision practices they observe within our assemblies.

SECTION 1
A GENERAL DISCUSSION OF DECISION-MAKING

DECISION TYPES

Modern management has made significant progress in comprehending the process of decision-making. That should not be surprising since decisions determine enterprise success or failure. In current practice, decisions are classified by "type," each type requiring the use of specific techniques.

There are two basic decision types:

Programmed decisions, which are made by *comparison against similar situations available from others, or stored in memory.*

Non-programmed decisions, made by *developing solution alternatives, then selecting one of them as a course of action.*

A rational process for making a decision begins, first and foremost, with answering a critical question: "In which of the two aforementioned types does this decision fall? Is this a programmed decision, or a non-programmed decision?"

The answer to that question dictates the decision-making process to be used.

PROGRAMMED DECISIONS

People make many programmed decisions every day. The type is also called "Naturalistic Decision-making" or "Recognition-Primed Decisions," indicating that the process of making such decisions comes naturally to humans.

Recognizing a decision situation as being similar to something existing in knowledge and comparing the two reveals how the instinctive human "programmed." decision process works. Programmed decisions use information gathered through experience. An "experienced" employee is a highly desirable person whose memory contains a wealth of comparative situations that may be used in making programmed decisions.

An example of **programmed decision-making** follows:

You leave work to drive home, deeply immersed mentally in a vexing business situation. You drive the ten miles of city streets to your home, and while parking, realize that you can't remember any aspect of the drive. You made a number of decisions on the way home: what speed to drive, where to turn, whether or not to stop at the light, and how to react to the car in the next lane. How could you possibly have done all of that without being aware?

Your driving decisions were *programmed*. Your mind automatically compares each situation during the drive against similar situations in memory and determines what action to take. The driver in the car in the next lane is distracted; be careful and drop in behind him. You have to make a right turn at the next corner, put on the turn signal, get in the right lane, and stop at the stop sign. Programmed decisions are the natural human decision process!

Childhood instruction, education, training, practice, and experiences provide the memory trove we use to make programmed decisions. The memory trove is often simply called "knowledge" or "experience."

In the decision process, so much reliance is placed on comparison against memory of similar events with known outcomes that people faced with an unusual decision will even borrow comparisons from other people's memory. When they have no comparative experience on which to formulate a decision, people obtain second-hand knowledge by seeking out other persons to ask for whatever experiences they may have that would illuminate the issue in question. The memory content borrowed from others can provide a decision-maker with the required comparable situations.

Programmed decisions are, far and away, the most commonplace in our lives. They are the reason we value and emphasize "education," "training," and "experience."

NON-PROGRAMMED DECISIONS

If a decision does not fit "programmed" characteristics, it is classified as "non-programmed." People occasionally make non-programmed decisions, but far less frequently than the programmed variety. The organization and process for non-programmed decisions are not built into the human psyche. Those skills must be acquired.

Non-programmed decisions differ substantially from the programmed variety. Non-programmed decisions cannot be made by comparison against memory, experience, or knowledge. The decision-maker must create a conceptual framework to organize the decision process. Non-programmed decisions require the assimilation of information to aid in the identification of potential alternative courses of action, which are often called "options." The decision is made by selecting the best course of action from the alternatives.

Let's consider an example situation. You live in California and have to go to New York. You have never been there, and you have to arrive in one week. All expenses going there, while there, and your return trip will be paid for you when you submit an expense claim. You must decide how to travel to New York, the cost of which you will pay up-front. You have $1,000 of your own money available.

You don't travel often, so you can't compare this problem against any other experience you have had. There are a number of ways to get to New York. You could drive, fly, go by bus, go by train, hitch-hike. Each way presents different considerations.

A non-programmed decision is needed. That type of decision uses a process of developing and evaluating alternative ways to travel to New York because, finally, the decision will be made by selecting one of the ways.

One approach, after identifying the alternatives, is to immediately eliminate those that probably won't work. For example, you don't like flying so you reject that option. You also decide that hitchhiking is too risky. That leaves three acceptable ways: to drive, go by bus, or go by train.

Choosing from the three alternatives requires information on each that is one level deeper, such as cost, time required, risks, and any other considerations you think important. Using a decision tree to create a visual display of the factors guiding a non-programmed decision helps a decision-maker to comprehend and focus.

But, at the end of the day, the decision-maker will have to decide which alternative is best. All the tools on earth will not make the decision. That must be done by the decision-maker. Thinking through the factors at play in an organized manner will help in the selection of the best alternative.

DECISION TREE – NEW YORK TRIP

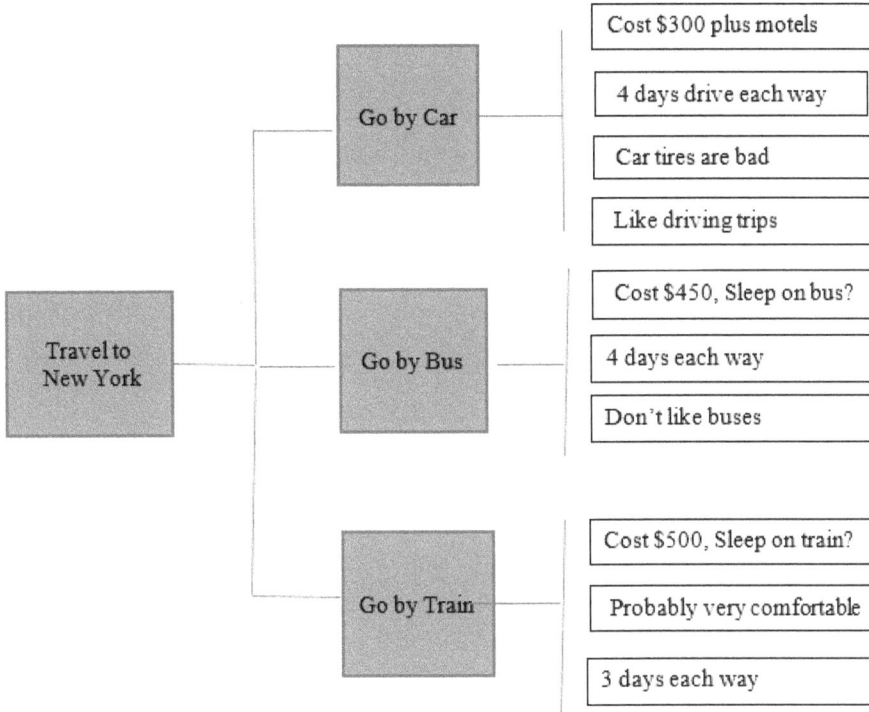

	Go by Car	Cost $300 plus motels
		4 days drive each way
		Car tires are bad
		Like driving trips
Travel to New York	Go by Bus	Cost $450, Sleep on bus?
		4 days each way
		Don't like buses
	Go by Train	Cost $500, Sleep on train?
		Probably very comfortable
		3 days each way

SECTION 2
DECISION PROCESS - CONSIDERATIONS

REASON VERSUS EMOTION

Decision-making discussions require an examination of the difference between rational decisions and emotional decisions. Decisions based on factual information and analysis are rational. Decisions based on "reactions" or "feelings" are emotional. In some life decisions, emotion plays a significant role, such as in the selection of a mate, but even in that decision, failure to employ rationality can produce less-than-satisfactory results.

Emotions are primary human motivators. Notice the emotional factors that were inserted in the "Trip to New York" decision tree!

All readers can recite the emotions: want, love, hate, fear, anger, desire, etc. Wikipedia contains a list of perhaps one hundred emotions. But interestingly, not many of us have been cautioned to treat emotions with great care when making decisions.

It is generally agreed that emotional decisions are weak decisions. Your love for that jazzy sports car can cause you to make a poor vehicle choice for your family and induce you to pay more than you can afford. Firing your best employee in a moment of anger can cost your business dearly. Better to step back and allow reason to prevail.

Consider the television ads of political parties and candidates. Most are carefully designed to provoke an emotional response from viewers, and, of course, emotional decisions are usually poor decisions. Ad content rarely focuses on factual information that will provoke a rational decision. Viewers who respond to emotion-appeal ads are, in fact, the idiots the ad was designed to reach. Perhaps that is the reason the election of our officials is referred to as "popular." Competence and performance history are better election decision standards than all the emotional components of popularity.

Interestingly, however, psychologists say that, at the very point of decision, it is emotion that takes over and propels the human action to decide. After lining up reams of logic and reason, it is still emotion that drives the "decide" action!

If a person is able.to recognize emotion at play and effectively isolate it, that person will likely experience a significant improvement in decision quality.

NON-PROGRAMMED VOTING DECISIONS ARE CHALLENGING

A citizen who has voted in an election of judges, common in many states, understands what is involved in making a true non-programmed democratic decision. Sometimes, a voter in those states will vote in one election to fill as many as two dozen vacant judicial positions.

Most judicial candidates are unknown to voters, have an obscure background, and have no party connection. The ballot provides no meaningful information. Candidates don't raise enough money to be able to purchase television advertising. Voters have a choice; they can use the "dart-board" approach, or they can do the grunt work necessary to make an informed decision. To be informed, a voter must investigate the candidates. Some newspapers provide background information, and most candidates have a website. Obtaining credible information is not easy. It is a reasonable guess that many, perhaps most, voters make seat-of-the-pants decisions to fill judicial vacancies based on less-than-ideal information.

Most citizens vote in a democracy to staff government decision-making functions. Voters typically choose from a list of three candidates or less. The decision is, therefore, the non-programmed variety ----- select from the alternatives!

Most election decisions for higher-profile positions differ from the selection of judges. **High-profile voting decisions, postured as being the non-programmed variety, are most often made in a programmed manner**. In most critical elections, one is not likely to hear of voters going through the non-programmed decision research contortions needed to make the election choice for judges. Candidates for higher-profile positions are generally well known; 90% are running for re-election, there is broad Media coverage (biased, but broad), and considerable information (but not necessarily the needed information) on which to evaluate candidates. And then, there is the political party influence!

Vital and reliable candidate information is not a strength of our election system. Our elections are conducted on information contained in candidate sales pitches.

PARTIES STEER VOTERS TOWARD EMOTIONAL CANDIDATE SELECTION

But the biggest single factor in voter decisions for most high-profile democratic positions is not the candidate; *it is the political party supporting the candidate*. We suspect that most voters do not vote to select a representative; they simply choose a political party!

In approaching the choice that way, voters have converted their candidate selection vote from the difficult and time-consuming non-programmed decision to the far easier programmed variety.

The election process makes that route more convenient for voters: "just choose your favorite political party." Candidate evaluation information comes in sales pitches that entice voters to make an emotional candidate selection decision in reaction to "grab-you" advertising.

One thing is certain; in a truly self-governed nation free of political parties, the voters would demand much more reliable information on which to base election choices. A whole new approach to presenting candidates and providing their fundamental information would be essential.

The voters might not like such a decision process, but their decision quality would dramatically improve, and with it, the quality of the nation's governance. The best-qualified candidate would be selected, not the party hack or the candidate who looks good on TV.

If we want true self-government, the quality of voter election decisions has to be dramatically upgraded. The election process we use is not producing high-quality assembly staffing. It is a significant background cause of the low voter opinion of Congress.

DECISIONS CARRY RISK!

All decisions are a search for the conclusion that provides the best mathematical chance of success. When we say, "That is clearly the best choice," we are saying, "its odds of success are the best." Every decision contains "uncertainty factors." Decisions are few that do not involve considerable uncertainty.

Even everyday programmed decisions, like deciding to stop at a stop sign, carry some small percentage risk that it may not be the best thing to do. Maybe the speeding driver behind is focused on the cell-phone and rear-ends our vehicle. Fortunately, the odds of that happening are very low. We also know that the alternative of not stopping at the sign gives maybe a 50% chance of being broadsided by a driver coming through the intersection from the side! Our programmed decision to stop is a mathematically sound choice.

The coin flip has value in explaining odds in decision-making. A coin flip produces percentages, over time, of 50% heads and 50% tails. *We have been taught that betting on the flip of a coin is not likely to produce good results.* **When betting, mathematical odds in our favor are preferred, and that is also true of decision-making in general.**

If we were able to calculate the odds of success for a given course of action, the decision would seem simpler. Unfortunately, calculation of odds for the simplest decision choice would require a special computer program, many hours of human time, and immense computing power. Think about the mental gymnastics employed by the odds-maker at the local casino, who must post the betting odds of winning for twenty golfers in a tournament and put the casino money on the line!

All that said, knowing the percentages of success will not make the decision. Have you ever tried to pick a winning golfer from casino-posted mathematical odds? The decision choice must still be made by a human.

> There is no such thing as perfection in decision-making. Even with strong favorable percentages, a decision may not turn out well. **What we can say, however, is that a decision-maker who consistently employs the highest favorable percentages will, over time, produce the most winners.** As a nation, that should be our decision-making goal, producing the most winners!

SECTION 3
DECISION-MAKING IN DEMOCRATIC GOVERNMENT VOTING BODIES

Assemblies of representatives elected by the voters are the chosen decision-making organ of democracies. Voting bodies spread the decision power so as to mitigate the possibility of one-person control, control by a few, totalitarian practices emerging, etc.

> **(a)** On complex questions, decision-making bodies, properly focused and organized, will consistently produce decisions of better quality than will an individual

decision-maker. **Democracies, generally using political parties, do not effectively utilize the decision-making potential of assembly bodies.**

(b) The capability of a decision body varies with the level of intelligence and comprehension of its members, and their ability/willingness to work together. The motivations and personal goals of members have a great bearing on group performance. Perhaps even more important is the use of decision-body leaders who are skilled in organizing and employing productive processes for decisions made by groups of people.

(c) For such bodies to function well, a carefully designed organization and decision-making process must be provided to them. Decision purity requires that voting participants be carefully screened from distractions and immunized against inside and outside influences.

(d) Many critical government decisions in a large business-based country, such as the United States, require an understanding of complex sub-systems interplaying within the larger economy. Every decision affecting industrial, financial, transportation, or other systems produces unintended consequences. Every such decision process must begin with the voting body membership gaining a high level of understanding of the sub-systems, the impact of the question or issue before them, social, competitive, and financial impacts, and a host of related matters.

(e) Because our government is democratic, the input of stakeholders and interested parties is a vital aspect of the information-gathering process.

(f) There usually exists an agency, bureau, department, or other government support function with in-depth knowledge of whatever question is under scrutiny. Use of that fund of knowledge is a tremendous advantage for decision bodies, up to the point where the support function knowledge begins to over-power the decision body mentality.

(g) **Most decisions to be made by government assemblies are of the non-programmed variety.** Factors bearing on the decision may be legislation, regulation, business practices, employment, taxation, government cost reduction, internal and international competitiveness, and a host of other matters. As non-programmed decisions, the development and evaluation of alternative solutions and the selection of the best are required. That is a decision process non-existent in our government assemblies today because of political party path pre-selection.

(h) Complex non-programmed decision-making, such as legislative proposals, should employ voting at various stages of the decision process, starting with the agreement concerning the scope and definition of the question and continuing through development and agreement on the alternatives, the decision rules to be applied, timelines, and finally, selection of the best alternative. A fundamental decision should be preliminary to most legislative initiatives: Is it better to let the market resolve, or should the power of government be applied? There is no evidence that question is ever asked today.

PRINCIPLES OF NON-PROGRAMMED DECISION-MAKING AND CURRENT CONGRESSIONAL PRACTICE

A limited comparison of the principles for non-programmed decision-making against what we observe to be the process of Congress produces the following:

1. House votes today are for approval of a pre-packaged course of action decided by the party in power. **The House process does not allow the development of, and selection from, available alternative courses of action.** The highest-importance decision in the process of selecting legislation to be brought to the floor was arrived at in the dark of their back room by the elite of the proposing party.

    That approach is not democratic. It is totalitarian. Political party elite are the decision-makers on vital matters and the selection of favored legislation. They constitute a small percentage of the proposed political party, probably less than 1% of all assembly members. **A take-it-or-leave-it vote on a legislative proposal presented by a political party does not constitute sound democratic decision-making.**

2. That process fails to take advantage of the Assembly's highest and best use as a decision body, fails to utilize voting for decisions that democracies deem must be made by vote, and denies large groups of elected representatives the ability to contribute anything to decisions of great importance. The lack of evaluation of alternative solutions, together with the above democracy shortcomings, consign the current approach to the waste-paper basket.

    Often, packaged proposals presented to a House for voted approval (3,000 to 5,000 pages) aren't read by voting members. Reading is considered decision "due diligence," but since house members understand the decision was pre-ordained by the party and their vote has been pre-committed, why bother?

3. The two legislative branches have been given the right to set their own rules. That constitutional provision was followed by **further delegation, to majority political parties,** of the ability to set the rules for decision-making. The rules that have emerged are not designed to use the Houses of Congress as problem-solving and

decision-making bodies. The rules privilege the majority party, which controls the agenda and floor time.[36]

4. **Setting the rules by which the Houses of Congress operate is the right and obligation of The People.** Those assembly bodies are populated by elected hired employees of The People, and their work is The People's work, not a political party's work. The principle is no different than the owner of a factory organizing the production line and the jobs of the workers. Trade unions (comparable to political parties) do not dictate the process by which factory production decisions are made. Congress should not set its own rules, and most certainly, a political party has no place in organizing government decision processes.

5. Voting obeys tenets generally considered "democratic." Neither House utilizes voting for the purpose of deriving the best possible decision. All legislative content is constructed by the political party in charge, with no input from the representatives of The People as a group. The political party, therefore, makes all the important process decisions, which is the reason we designate them as "totalitarian entities."

RE-LOCATE ALL REGULATION DECISIONS TO THE ASSEMBLIES

Classify regulation as law, requiring legislation before implementation so that all impositions upon The People are democratically voted. Do not allow unelected legislative support organizations to impose regulations that have the effect of law. Set Constitutional standards against which all regulation/legislation must be compared. Set investigation rules for all proposed legislation. Define interested party input rights and install necessary processes.

1. Approximately 80% of votes in Congress are for inconsequential matters, such as the appointment of government officials. In 2019, 105 laws were enacted, among the lowest number in a millennium.

2. Each House is managed by a party-selected politician whose skills are anything other than managing large numbers of people in complex decision-making processes. Leaders are selected for party pecking-order reasons.

3. Serious debate will take place only if elected persons are present. Most speeches by Elected Representatives and Senators are given to empty chambers and heard only by one or two other elected persons. Committees take up the House time of Elected Persons, but non-House time dominates. Both practices constitute legislative-body member time misdirection.

---

[36] Senator Ben Sasse, Wall Street Journal "Opinion", article Sept. 9, 2020 entitled "Make the Senate Great Again."

4. Television transmission of committee and legislative sessions has degraded the performance of individual members. Those events have become member self-promotion forums.

SUMMARY

This brief discussion (which will be pursued in much greater depth by those responsible for elected assembly re-design) leads to the conclusion that the work process and organization of the Nation's decision bodies do not meet democratic standards, management standards, decision-making standards; the People's standards, or for that matter, any standards.

Is it any wonder that the goal of improved decision-making has surfaced as critical to the Nation's future? The People rely on elected voting bodies to be the dependable source of quality democratic decisions needed in the Nation. As currently organized and managed, those bodies are incapable of fulfilling that requirement.

Other problems affecting the Legislative branch, such as the re-election fixation of office-holders, the role of political parties, the role of money in politics, and the Accountability Gap, bear on the issue. Add those to the poor internal decision processes of the Legislative branches, discussed above, and a picture emerges that is not pretty. Those are, of course, the reasons why public opinion of the two houses is so consistently low.

Various solutions to correct this are introduced elsewhere and will not be repeated here. The entire Legislative branch needs study by competent persons to produce an entirely new approach to candidate selection, election funding, legislative process, voting rules, and decision-making. It is unlikely any solution will achieve success unless the House of Representatives is completely reconstructed to create an organization specifically designed to meet the "quality decision" goal.

A simple test of The People's restructure success will be whether the created elected decision-making bodies make our citizens proud, or whether those bodies are the continuing object of citizen derision. The People's trust in government, and their opinion of it, should be the principal government performance evaluation criteria, regularly measured and reported to all.

Morals and ethics play an important role in all government actions. **Behavior of elected persons matters a great deal because of its symbolic effect on the population at large.** In the absence of Constitutional standards, anybody's standards or no standards at all will be applied. The choice of standards is a critical decision of The People.

SUGGESTIONS FOR CONSIDERATION

In self-government, if the legislative bodies are not performing, the fault rests with The People who own the Nation. Under those circumstances, The People are dysfunctional owners. They are dysfunctional owners by Constitutional misconstruction.

A number of government reorganization suggestions are presented for consideration. Following is a summary of suggestions as to how The People may perform their owner duties to correct legislative body non-performance. In parsing them, readers should keep foremost in mind that The People's task is to define and organize the work of their hired management (the office holders), give them direction as to how that work is to be carried out, and establish controls to make sure the required work is performed to The People's satisfaction.

The task of restructuring the legislative body cannot be performed by The People directly, but they (through the Well-Informed Electors) must approve and institute the actions to be taken. The restructuring tasks will be carried out by Constitutional Authorities formed to implement The People's instructions. Those Authorities may decide to create a special body (or bodies) to perform this unique project. The amount of citizen admiration for the created Government will be The People's standard for judging the performance of Constitutional Authorities challenged with the tasks.

SECTION 4
SUMMARY OF RELEVANT SUGGESTED IMPROVEMENTS

The following observations repeat information that has been provided earlier. They are included here for concept re-enforcement purposes.

FOCUS ON THE ELECTED BODIES

Set term limits for all elected persons in government. The People must control the Election system, removing all forces brought to bear that influence voted decisions. Use employment contracts to spell out the elected person's duties and terms. Focus on performance and accomplishment by using a well-designed liberal reward program.

Eliminate political parties and political factions to achieve, to the extent possible, pure one-person-one-vote self-government by The People. Heavily involve The People by organizing them to make the owner's decisions, particularly the work that is to be performed by their hired management.

Reorganize the government-elected body decision process using planning-based management, with the planning directed by the President. Make the President the Chief

Executive of all government, responsible for the performance of the Elected Assemblies, the Senate, and the support organizations. Develop Constitutional programs and instructions that give The People background direction and control over the President's activities.

Force assemblies to focus on what The People require and nothing else. Eliminate all assembly distractions and permit no self-management; instead, employ management leadership by impersonal experts. View and treat all elected persons as "Hired Management" to rid the nation of the political elite.

REORGANIZE THE ASSEMBLIES SEGMENTALLY SIZE THEM FOR MAXIMUM DECISION EFFICIENCY

Replace the House of Representatives with a relatively large group of smaller assemblies, each dedicated to the governance decisions for a pre-defined segment of the Nation. Using a matrix organization, align each assembly with relevant Support Organizations. Use the Senate as the government decision control body; its assent and that of the President are required for all voted decisions originating in the assemblies.

REORGANIZE PLANNING AND CONTROL OF DECISIONS AND LEGISLATION PROCESS

Place upon the President responsibility for producing and administering the Nation's decision and legislation plan, the plan that will set the work order for the assemblies. Establish a President-managed planning process to set the decision and legislation agenda that the legislative assemblies will execute. The decision/legislation agenda should cover a two-year forward period but be updated annually. **That proposed planning is the decision-making of the highest order.** The resultant schedule would require approval of the Senate, and the Guardians of the Constitution under their responsibility to oversee decisions of the Authority Structure of the nation.

INSTITUTE PEOPLE-BACKED CONSTITUTIONAL MANAGEMENT OF ASSEMBLY DECISION PROCESSES AND OPERATIONS

Instruct the Guardians to install supervising management to direct each Senate and the Assembly group's activities and decision-making processes. Doing so will ensure that the entire government's democratic decision structure is pure, free of totalitarian persons or processes, and totally controlled indirectly by The People.

WITHOUT POLITICAL PARTIES, A REVISED ELECTION SYSTEM WILL BE NEEDED

Separate and apart from the political party issue, it is clear that because of fundamental process flaws in candidate evaluation **the election system produces emotional rather than rational Voter choices**. That weakness is diluting the overall competence level of the assemblies, which in turn negatively impacts assembly performance and the decision processes. The entire election system should be scrutinized and reconstructed. None of The People really know what takes place within the election system, and that is certainly not a function to be run on a "trust me" basis.

Taxpayer-funded Federal elections are highly recommended to eliminate **the corrupting influence of donor money in the election process any illegal election practices, and eliminate private money influence on elections.** Citizens should view the nation's cost of taxpayer-funded elections as "hired management finder fees" to be paid by the nation's owners, so it should be funded by the application of a specific tax on the nation's owners. Prior heavy political contributors should be taxed proportionally to their former donation patterns.

Revise candidate selection and election procedures. Utilize the People's Election Commission to locate and present slates of qualified candidates to the Voters. Assure the quality and suitability of candidates by pre-defining the requirements for candidate competence, knowledge, and background and selecting only candidates meeting the criteria. Conduct election campaigns by public exposure of the candidates and their verified information to increase voter capability to judge candidates based on background, intelligence and knowledge. All election costs will be paid by the Nation, and voter decisions are made from pre-planned and thorough candidate exposure.

These proposals are designed to change the basis for voter election decisions from "Popularity" to "Expertise and Competence." Other election proposals will be welcomed.

CHAPTER 11

GOVERNMENT DECISION-MAKING SERIES, PART 4

CONTENT:

SECTION 1: FORMS OF DEMOCRACY

SECTION 2: DELEGATION, THE ACT OF GRANTING POWER

SECTION 3: IMPROVING THE AUTHORITY STRUCTURE

SECTION 4: ENHANCED INVOLVEMENT BY THE NATION'S VOTERS

SECTION 5: BY-PASSING THE "POORLY-INFORMED VOTERS"

SECTION 6: THE "WELL-INFORMED ELECTORS" PROPOSAL

FOREWORD

One of the most difficult and puzzling questions in an effort to improve our nation's self-governance is how to effectively involve the voters. If the voters do not decide matters that are their ownership responsibility, the authority structure cannot be called self-government!

Some will argue that the question was answered long ago. The Framers essentially "gave up" on the notion of self-government by creating a "monarchy republic," in which citizen involvement is limited to electing government officials. They gave total control over the nation to a self-contained and all-powerful elected group, going so far as to grant it critical rights and powers that, by any rationalization, should be exercised only by the nation's owners, The People.

To meet the definition of "self-government," those critical rights and powers must be exercised by The People. The Framers didn't see it that way. They gave all The People's obligatory rights and powers to the elected government. While railing publicly against the despotism of a single monarch, they quietly designed and installed a monarchy within our nation, differing from the common monarchy only by the fact that the monarchy management would be democratically elected. While ballyhooing their creation as "government of the people, by the people, and for the people," they methodically shut The People out of government except for electing the officials who would run it.

A Framer problem was how to give the citizens just a smidgeon of involvement in the new government……not enough to allow them to intercede in the monarchical government process, of course, but just enough to keep them interested. The Framer's answer was, "Give them a ballot box vote. Let them elect the officials. That'll keep them interested."

That Framer creation would be rated successful if the test is the creation's time-in-place. The government that frustrates our citizens today is the end result of those Framer decisions meaningfully degraded, of course, by about 240 years of entropy and the impact of intense political striving.

Along the road from then to now, the ballot box stopped performing its functions. Voter election decisions today are totally warped by the political parties that directly and indirectly run the election system. They lured The People away from exercising voting control over their hired management, instead inducing them to focus on electing political parties. The People were never granted any control over the institution called government. They can rotate people in and out of the box (the assemblies and the Presidency), but at 90% re-election rates, voter influence over the box through elected officials is obviously only 10% of what it should be.

To reverse the acknowledged gross deterioration in governance, The People must first establish their rightful ownership control position. An organized process can then be launched to take the actions necessary to create high-performance democratic self-government, a true "government by The People."

That brings us back to the opening question, "How to effectively involve the Voter in our self-government?" We will examine the puzzle from several perspectives and propose solutions.

SECTION 1
VARIOUS FORMS OF DEMOCRACY

U In true self-government, the citizens, who are the owners of the nation, would, as a group, decide which of the nation's powers they will turn over to the government and which they will retain and execute themselves.

Delegation of decision authority, from The People to their government, can range anywhere from 0% to 100% of all authority decisions. The choice percentage is the most important decision to be made in the formation of a nation's government. For U.S. citizens, this discussion has been purely academic. **Under the United States Constitution, 100% of all authority decisions were made the responsibility of the government.**

1. "REPRESENTATIVE DEMOCRACY" SELF-GOVERNMENT

In a true "representative democracy," the citizens delegate selected decision authority to assemblies, then elect the persons to staff them. Citizens of a true self-governed democracy would decide which decisions falling upon the Authority Structure will become the responsibility of government, **but under no circumstances should those ever be 100% of all decisions.**

In our "republic," **100% of all decisions** are intended to be made by assemblies elected by The People. That is not actuality, however. Most decisions are made by the political party that controls each assembly, some are made by individuals or small groups rather than by assemblies, and many by unelected management of the Administrative State government support units.

Our Federal Government is a *100% Representative Democracy*. No Direct Democracy practices exist in the U.S. Federal Government. All decisions are supposed to be made by elected representatives in assembly and employing democratic practice. In actuality, most decisions are now made by Administrative State leaders, and those decision-makers were not elected.

Federal decisions in our nation are 100% delegated to the government. **Citizen involvement in Government decisions is always remote**, limited to their decision to elect or un-elect the individuals who participate in making the decisions.

2. "DIRECT DEMOCRACY" SELF-GOVERNMENT

In a "direct democracy," the citizens/owners have decided that decision authority delegated to assemblies would be minimal or zero. 100% of all decisions would be made by the citizens. The elected government, in a direct democracy, merely executes the citizen-made decisions.

3. "HYBRID DEMOCRACY" SELF-GOVERNMENT

A "hybrid democracy" is a combination of direct democracy and representative democracy. The citizens retain decision-making responsibility over certain critical matters and delegate decision-making responsibility for other matters to an elected government.

Although the form of government in all 50 states is "Representative Democracy," "Direct Democracy" is employed in 49 of the 50 states of the Union, Delaware being the only exception. State governments that employ "direct democracy" to supplement their "representative democracy" are properly described as "Hybrid Democracies."

Most of those states, if not all, added direct democracy practices as a problem-solving mechanism to overcome decision-making deficiencies inherent in representative democracy processes. Direct democracy, an adjunct to state representative democracy, utilizes citizen-voted decisions for prescribed matters or for questions deemed better decided by direct citizen vote.

Direct democracy decisions in those states are most often by "referendums," also called "propositions" or "plebiscites," that address specific issues. Authority for citizens to petition for a referendum or invoke a "recall petition," are also common direct-democracy citizen rights among our states.

SECTION 2
DELEGATION

THE ACT OF GRANTING POWER

For nations practicing democratic self-government, delegation of authority to elected persons and bodies should always be by voted decision of the citizens/owners of the nation.

BECAUSE THE "RIGHT TO DECIDE" IS THE DEFINITION OF "POWER," THE BEST STRUCTURE OF DEMOCRATIC SELF-GOVERNMENT WILL FEATURE CITIZEN CONTROL OVER THE RIGHT TO AND PROCESS OF DECISION-MAKING WITHIN THE AUTHORITY STRUCTURE.

In a self-governed nation, all power is owned and controlled by The People, who delegate it as they see fit. Wholesale dump-delegation of that power to elected assemblies BY NO MEANS ENTITLES SUCH A NATION TO LABEL ITSELF "SELF-GOVERNED."

100% delegation of decision authority to the hired management, such as occurred in the formation of our federal government, does not produce good results. In business management, that approach is called "dump-delegation." **Dump-delegation totally unbalances the distribution of power in favor of those receiving delegated authority. Adequate control is almost never retained by the "dumper."** Typically, authority dumpers do not impose accountability.

Under our constitution, 100% of decision power was constitutionally dumped on the hired management in government, with The People retaining 0%. **When dump-delegation has taken place, owners typically retain little or no ability to correct non-performance.** That is certainly the case in our nation.

Conceived without any meaningful way for citizens to exercise their owner rights, our "Monarchy Republic," controlled by a "political elite," was granted total freedom to operate and is totally devoid of accountability, meeting all criteria for "dump-delegation." The ballot box is a very weak control mechanism, too poorly conceived, too abstract and indirect, and too far removed from the hired management to be effective. This book discusses in detail how the political parties became the ballot box candidate selection determinant, causing the re-election of incumbents to rise to the 90% level.

As that developed, the ballot box stopped functioning as intended, and incumbent accountability, such as it was, vanished…. "Gone, gone, like the landlord's smile, gone, gone away." Country/Western music does have a way of putting its finger on the pulse of the matter.

Our Monarchy Republic was designed by the Framers. The government they created was subject to minimal constitutional requirements and was given free rein to operate in whatever manner it chose. Elected Officials of our first assemblies, flinging that door open, added one more dump-delegation to compound that of the Framers. They delegated the ability to control the elected assemblies (and, under certain circumstances, the entire government) to political parties, again without imposing accountability on a political party for its actions. Some consider that losing an election functions as accountability, but that doesn't meet any rational test since election losses generate a wide range of blame. Once in a long while, voters rise up and eject an incumbent or even change the majority political party, but those events are rare and do not change assembly operations.

The Framer dump-delegation of immense power to the government, coupled with no way for The People to impose government accountability, is the root cause of U.S. government dysfunction. The Constitution neutered The People, leaving them flailing around helplessly.

To create a properly functioning democratic self-government. The People will have to totally rethink and revise the concept of powers granted to the government, place critical controls in the hands of The People, and install the methods by which The People can control the entire Authority Structure decision process. That is a much better and cleaner route than achieving dramatic performance improvement piece by piece.

> The best decisions are always made by those who have the most to lose. In democracies, the best decision-makers are always the citizens, because they are the ones who will suffer the damage from bad government.
>
> Direct-democracy decisions (those made by the citizens themselves) require the coordinated action of large numbers of people, **which presents daunting logistical problems**. That may have been a reason why 100% delegation of power to an elected representative government was the Framers' 1780s chosen path, but we don't think so. Regardless, with modern travel and electronic communication capability, logistics are not today the formidable barrier to utilization of direct democracy that they were in the horse-and-buggy days of the Framers.
>
> **Using the citizens as decision-makers is essential, when the decisions involve planning, organizing, staffing, directing, and controlling the nation's authority structure. Ensuring that the authority structure functions as required is not just the**

DELEGATION OF AUTHORITY CONVEYS SUBSTANTIAL RISK TO THE DELEGATOR

Because delegation of authority from The People to the function called "government" **is a risk of the highest order,** such delegations of authority are best decided by direct democratic vote and require the best discussion and thinking of The People. That rule was not understood at the time of the Framers, or if it was understood, it was willfully ignored. **Nobody but The People can give away their own basic rights and powers!**

It is important for readers to comprehend that our ineffective government results from powers delegated to the government in the Constitution, underlining the truth of the heading statement that "delegation of authority conveys substantial risk to the delegator**." Any owner who delegates power had best be watching closely and retain the right to take action when things do not work out as planned, because that will inevitably happen.**

Our constitution, with 100% delegation of authority to government embedded in its provisions, was written by the professional politicians of the Constitutional Convention and presented to the States for the vote. Each state convened a Convention of Delegates to consider their assent and ratification of the proposed Constitution. The constitution was approved by the vote of Conventions of a majority of the thirteen states.

Although the historical records are somewhat murky, **THE CITIZENS OF THAT ERA DID NOT APPROVE THE CONSTITUTION BY DIRECT VOTE.** Even such a high-risk decision, the approval of a new constitution for the nation, was executed by assemblies of delegates! The record is unclear as to whether the delegates were elected by citizens or appointed by state governments, but it doesn't really matter. Only the citizens can approve their own constitution. **It is their most fundamental right and obligation, the one that must not ever be delegated to representatives!**

The Framers viewed the new constitution as merely an agreement between the Federal Government and the then-existing thirteen states. Gaining the consent of those states to a new constitution was the Framer's objective. It is apparent that they viewed each of the thirteen states as the equivalent of an independent nation, each with the power to enter into a legal contract with the Government of the United States on behalf of its block of citizens.

Today, we would take the position that the nation was not owned by thirteen individual states, rather, it was owned by the approximately six million citizens who populated them at that time. *States are merely a geographical area of political construct.*

This background examines the intellectual posture of the Framers. To them, the constitution being put together was all about power, the power they determined was best placed solely with the politicians who would run the new government. The citizens were merely "the governed," subjects who needed to be kept happy, but beyond that didn't matter much. The Framers didn't respect the citizens enough to give them a vote on the constitutional deal, let alone honor their irrefutable owner's rights, which were clearly defined in the Declaration of Independence.

This discussion should serve to impress readers with a hard truth. At all times elected politicians must be kept on a tight leash by The People. In decision-making, the self-interest of the hired management consistently over-rides job performance ethics.

Giving elected politicians in each House the right to "determine the rules of its proceedings" can only be described as an absolute disaster. Elected persons so coronated then gave political parties governing rights, without even an operating agreement, accountability, and without the consent of The People, which created the situation in which we find ourselves.

To self-govern successfully, The People must continuously direct and control their hired management, defining the work they are required to perform, and setting up the controls to make sure they do it. The best way for The People to do that is by working through the Authority Structure decision protocol to dictate operating processes. This book's proposals are built on that principle. The "Here, you do it, I don't want to be bothered" delegation dump has not produced the desired results.

The nation's vaunted Framers slyly committed ugly and underhanded acts against The People and did so in a brutally self-serving manner, yet to this day, they are universally held in high esteem. **The fact that The People, over 240 years, haven't figured out what was** done to them by the Framers reverts to the question of whether The People are, in fact, capable of self-government.

THE CONSEQUENCES OF ILL-CONSIDERED DELEGATION

Our nation's government disintegration stems from provisions embedded in the constitution that gifted to the hired management rights and powers that are the sole property of The People.

Our Framers bet "all-in" on representative government, constructing it to function as the Monarchy Republic, and left The People with no process or vehicle to execute powers that are rightfully theirs alone. By giving the ballot box tool to The People to rule out underperforming legislators and senators, The People were given yes/no power over individuals in the hired management group *but power to change no aspect of the government itself.*

So much for the government of the people, by the people, and for the people!

SECTION 3
PROPOSAL TO UPGRADE THE U.S. AUTHORITY STRUCTURE

It is inaccurate to say that The People made unwise delegation decisions in the constitution. The history of its formation leaves us doubting that The People understood the provisions that ceded their ownership rights to the new Monarchy Republic and apparently did not vote as individual citizens to approve the constitution. The decisions that gave away The People's rights were elements of an agreement between the Framers, representing a weak and failing Federal government, and the thirteen powerful states that then governed the nation.

> **Control by The People over all Authority Structure decision-making is the basic requirement for "self-government." Without control over the nation's decision process, The People are not self-governing, and will inevitably become victims of the actions of those they elected. That is the nation's condition today.**
>
> **"Power corrupts, and absolute power corrupts absolutely."**
>
> Required to correct this deficiency is a new **hybrid Authority Structure** composed **partly of direct democracy,** wherein The People make decisions and exercise controls that are the sole responsibility of the nation's owners, and **partly of representative democracy,** wherein elected assemblies make governing decisions for the nation, within powers delegated to them by The People, and using rules and processes laid out for them as "direction."

Our nation's future Authority Structure has to be designed so The People exercise absolute control over the decision processes it employs.

To accomplish that, the right of the houses of Congress to manage themselves would be revoked and replaced by People-designed management of all Authority Structure decision-making. The control system will enable The People to monitor and exercise control over the entire process of decision-making, both inside and outside of the Houses of Congress.

The Framer-designed three-branch government check-and-balance system has degenerated into a political exercise that produces no accountability. Watching over government is The People's ownership "Control" responsibility, and, consistent with our understanding of audit functions, the independence of The People's "Control" is important. Given the propensities of elected politicians, their original internal watchdog activities have been totally inadequate. Watchdog duties are "control" responsibilities of The People to be conducted by The People's Constitutional Authorities and are not "watching over the work of your buddies."

SECTION 4
EVALUATING THE NATION'S VOTERS

We are a "100% representative government" at present. The sole involvement of citizens in government is to elect those who will perform government functions, a process clarified by the term "selecting the hired management."

In that environment, voter comprehension has regressed to a level barely adequate for them to perform the function of candidate election. This Chapter's introduction raised the important question of how to more effectively involve the voter in our system of government. To find an answer to that question, we will examine the voter bloc from several perspectives.

VOTER PERFORMANCE AT THE BALLOT BOX

Under the Framer plan, the vote of citizens at the ballot box was to perform two functions. The comments appended in italics are the author's evaluation of voter performance of those functions. **Readers are encouraged to do their own independent evaluation**.

a)   The ballot box is used to staff the elective positions in the Federal Government (perform the owner's "Staffing" responsibility), and to remove elected persons not performing.

> *Voters are barely competent to carry out their "Staffing" responsibility. 60% (plus or minus) of eligible citizens vote. The quality and competence of elected officials is suspect. They are held in general disrepute by citizens, who then re-elect them at a 90% rate. The culprit is political party influence over voters, political party control over the election system, and candidates made available to voters at the ballot box. The low level of voter respect for the representatives and senators they elected tells the whole story about voter performance at the ballot box.*

b)   The ballot box was to perform a check-and-balance function on government by removing from office unworthy or non-performing elected officials (performing the owners' "Control" and "Staff" responsibilities).

> *Although only 33% of respondents in the Pew Research 2018 poll declared a favorable view of Congress, citizens continue to re-elect Representatives and Senators at an amazing 80% to 90% rate. Citizens have failed miserably, through the ballot box, to correct the performance of Congress, which has long been sliding down the slippery slope.* **Given the citizen's startlingly unfavorable view of Congress, one would expect a 33% re-election rate, not 80% to 90%.**

Distilling those facts, one must conclude that voter ballot-box decisions are generally not focused on the individual candidate, **they are focused on electing a political party**. Voter decisions at the ballot box are not directed toward high-quality staffing, they are aimed at gaining and maintaining majority party control over government.

Electing political parties rather than candidates raises the question of whether our government is truly employing democratic principles.

DEMOCRACIES WORLDWIDE ARE STRUGGLING

Our nation is not alone in the democratic quagmire. Following is a circulating missive from our neighboring parliamentary democracy, Canada. For those not familiar with Canadian politics, in a spasm of nepotism and celebrity worship, the voters there elected Justin Trudeau, in his early 30s, as Prime Minister. The major factors in his election were "name recognition," as his father, Pierre Elliot Trudeau, was a popular past Prime Minister, and "the dominant Liberal party," of which Justin Trudeau was the candidate.

The following obviously biased hit piece is presented with apologies to readers. It is included only because it addresses the real question….. of whether today's citizenry in democratic countries is, in fact, capable of self-government.

"The danger to Canada is not Justin Trudeau, but a citizenry capable of entrusting a man like him with being Prime Minister. It will be far easier to limit and undo the follies of a Trudeau government than to restore the necessary common sense and good judgment to a depraved electorate willing to have such a man for their prime minister. The problem is much deeper and more serious than Trudeau, who is a mere symptom of what ails Canada. Blaming the prince of fools should not blind anyone to the vast confederacy of fools that made him their prince. The country can survive Trudeau, who is, after all, merely a fool. It is less likely to survive a multitude of fools, such as those who made him their Prime Minister."[37]

The Visual Capitalist May 13, 2022 report mapped the state of global democracy in 2022. Its summary is that "Democracy is at its lowest point since the index began in 2006.[38]

---

[37] Stated by the circulator as being an article "translated from a Prague newspaper." The author has made no attempt to validate, and suggests readers treat that with skepticism.
[38] Visual Capitalist May 13, 2022 report "Mapped: The State of Global Democracy in 2022"

There is a lot at stake. If the knowledge and comprehension of voters is low, if they are unable to vote at the intelligence level required for self-government, then self-government cannot survive.

HOW WELL INFORMED ARE OUR VOTERS?

Good articles are available on-line addressing that United States question, and readers who want to pursue it further should peruse those resources. Considerable research has been done. We will quote various sources to provide background, sufficient for preliminary general conclusions.

Readers should be warned the information that follows is not adequate for constitutional decisions about utilizing citizens to make critical national decisions. Those responsible for the evaluation of voter competence will need custom-designed research that provides reliable answers to their specific important questions.

A.   The Public is Not Well Informed

The American public is not well informed on matters relating to national economic performance and the performance of government, but not because of a lack of available information.

The Annenberg Civics Knowledge Survey[39] concluded that Americans were not well informed. It reported that more than one-half of Americans do not know which party controls the House or the Senate. A little over one-third could not name all three branches of government. A little over one-quarter know that it takes a two-thirds vote of the House and Senate to overturn a Presidential veto.

The public is exposed to huge amounts of information from television, radio, print, and the internet. Most students of the subject conclude the lack of public knowledge stems from a lack of desire to learn and absorption in other things. Many citizens are misinformed, victims of political brain-washing, uninformed adherents to factional philosophies, or from a range of other causes.

B.   Americans Vote in the Same Manner as They Do Most Things

Samuel Popkin, a professor at the University of California, San Diego,[40] suggests that Americans vote pretty much as they do most things, filtering small bits of information and using instincts. He calls it "gut rationality," which works best when choices are clear and

---

[39] The Annenberg Civics Knowledge Survey, Sept. 17, 2014
[40] Samuel L. Popkin, Political Scientist, U.C. San Diego. Exact source of quotation not available.

not complicated. Readers should bear in mind that most voter conclusions a programmed decisions made by comparison against situations retained in memory.

C.   Preconceived Notions and Biases Can Derail Judgment

Cass R. Sunstein, a professor at Harvard University, says the Electronic Media can keep minds closed, as people exhibit a tendency to go to websites and television channels that conform to their own beliefs.[41] The electronic media supplies the memory references against which programmed choices for vote-casting are made.

D.   Citizen Participation in Presidential Elections

The highest historical citizen participation rate was 81.8% in 1876, and the lowest was 49.2% in 1920. Following are the percentages for the last six Presidential elections, based on eligible voters.

2000	54.3%	2004	60.1%
2008	62.5%	2012	58.0%
2016	59.2%	2020	66.1%

Those numbers indicate a **voter apathy percentage ranging from 34% to 46%** in the most important election, for the U.S. President. Participation rates in elections of lesser significance are somewhat lower, and apathy rates are somewhat higher.

The recorded voter participation percentages are arguably adequate to elect individuals, but for citizen votes on complex national issues, they are not at a level that justifies reliance.

DO WE DARE PLACE INCREASED RESPONSIBILITY ON OUR VOTERS?

A quotation attributed to Thomas Jefferson, "When the people are well informed, they can be trusted with their own government," tells us that, from the time of the Constitution's signing, well-informed citizens were understood to be essential to self-government.

---

[41] Cass R. Sunstein, Professor, Harvard University.

Given what has been reported about the general level of knowledge possessed by our citizens, and the ambivalence of many toward the responsibilities of citizenship, do we dare to move toward Direct Democracy in our National decision process? Is it wise to place complex questions before all of our citizens for vote, if those decisions are critical to the Nation?

It is reasonable to conclude that, in the time elapsed since the signing of the Constitution, the knowledge and comprehension of citizens **has regressed to the level sufficient only to elect candidates based solely on their political party affiliation.**

The answer to the heading question, based on information available, is "NO!"

SECTION 5
BY-PASSING THE "POORLY-INFORMED VOTERS"

Given the conclusion above, a series of questions arise that must be answered.

1. Where Can the Needed Well-Informed Electors be Found?

If the nation, to improve the quality of its self-governance, requires a body of well-informed voters capable of making The People's decisions, **the required well-informed electors must be found**. The preceding data and observations were included for general information because they relate to the underlying question, "Where can the needed Well-Informed Electors be found?" The answer is "somewhere in the ranks of the people who voted." That answer is not of much help.

Of specific interest is the high incidence of voter apathy. 40%, or thereabouts, of all registered voters are just "not interested." That number is of importance when evaluating other voting influences, such as political parties, but of little value in our search for Well-Informed Electors. **We are reasonably certain that the needed Electors exist and completely certain they will not be found in the apathetic group.**

2. The Voters – What Do We Have to Work With?

The proposed government strategy for our nation is to dramatically improve National decision-making while staying within broadly accepted democratic principles. To implement that strategy, it is suggested that a voter base of Well-Informed Electors be formed and given responsibility to vote complex constitutional questions **on behalf of all of The People**. The assumption would be that, among the 60% or so who regularly vote, there exists a reasonable-sized pool of voters who are very well-informed regarding the nation and its government.

The voter base of Well-Informed Electors in a self-governed nation **should, over time, be expanded to include all citizens. That should be the national goal.** To launch direct democracy decisions, however, it will be necessary to rely upon a smaller, well-informed voter base **because the need for very well-reasoned national votes overrides all democratic activity participation considerations.**

It is not advisable that poorly informed citizens be permitted to degrade critical constitutional decision quality with their judgment. The stakes are too high. The Well-Informed Elector body formation should be accompanied by a companion effort to educate citizens, over the longer term, to the level where as many as possible qualify as "well-informed," but the nation should move ahead aggressively utilizing what is now available.

Without question, within the nation's voters, there exists a pool of well-formed voters. We just don't know how big the pool is, and we can't identify the individuals who qualify, but we know they are there. If we don't dare bet on our total voter base to make critical decisions for the nation, then how can we identify and isolate the existing Well-Informed Voters within the base?

A Well-Informed Electorate, in our view, is the exact voter body needed to make direct democratic decisions on matters that must be decided by the nation's owners. They will be located among the active voters. **The voting pool of Well-Informed Electors must be large enough to be enthusiastically accepted by all citizens as their authorized decision body, and viewed as a body of which all citizens crave to be a member.**

3. Is Education the Answer?

The need for a well-informed voter body immediately brings forth the suggestion: "Let's educate them!" That solution has been tried as far back as the early 1900s.

Critic Walter Lippmann wrote in 1922, "It was believed that if only he could be taught more facts if only he would take more interest, if only he would listen to more lectures and read more reports, he would gradually be trained to direct public affairs. The whole assumption is false."

Some will suggest that the education level of individuals will dictate their political knowledge, and the required pool of well-informed voters will be found among the well-educated. **A correlation between education level and political knowledge level is not proven and is highly disputable.** Because of the university system, political bias is more likely to be the product of that system than political knowledge. It has often been noted that the long string of initials depicting higher-education achievements, strung out behind the names of most elected persons, has not produced highly-regarded legislative bodies.

UCLA political scientist John Zollar says, "In de-emphasizing party hoopla and replacing it with stolid and solid news reporting and information, America succeeded only in boring and alienating its citizens." And, he says, "Some of the things for which the news media are criticized today, for example, covering campaigns as if they were horse races, actually lend drama and interest to a dry subject." [42]

These observations support the notion that to produce well-informed voters, a massive short-term training program is unlikely to be an answer. There is a clear hint that the manner in which citizen-critical information is presented by the nation's system of communication may determine the rate of success in achieving Voter knowledge improvement. At the outset, however, and until the political system adjusts and the media-involvement controversy is resolved, training is not an answer. **Well-Informed Electors must be located among the existing voters.**

Voter attitudes are the direct consequence of the constitutional grant of massive freedoms with no commensurate obligation on the part of citizens. If that conclusion is correct, tying voting rights to a demanding sequence of citizenship requirements, as will be the case with the formation of the Well-Informed Elector group, will reveal very important information leading to a true perspective of the issue.

4. Dumbed-down voters are the Product of the Nation's Political and Cultural Environment

The conclusion earlier was that, for its weighty and complex decisions, our nation would be unwise to bet heavily on the knowledge and insight of all of our current citizenry. Readers might interpret that conclusion to be a lack of respect for the quality and intelligence of our citizenry.

Not so!

Our citizens are not generally well-informed. Only about 60% will vote in important elections, an indication that citizen civic commitment level is low, probably the consequence of lack of accountability for Bill of Rights freedoms. Citizens are heavily influenced by political parties. They repeatedly re-elect the same people to Congress, the performance of which disgusts a high percentage of them.

However most observers believe that the citizen intellectual capability vastly exceeds the nation's utilization of it. One must ask the question, "Why is that?"

An answer is suggested. If our government decided that well-informed citizens were essential to national survival, it is a relatively safe bet we would have well-informed citizens. The government possesses that capability. **The reason we do not have well-**

---

[42] John Zollar, UCLA Political Scientist

informed citizens is the political parties who run our government prefer ignorant voters. The political environment is designed and constructed by political parties, which prefer voters who can be led by the nose. Well-informed citizens would very quickly see through the charade and become a serious threat to party welfare.

The quality of information available on candidates, the selections presented at the voting booth, the quality and manner of candidate presentation during campaigns, and the general propaganda are contrived to produce and use "dumbed-down" voters. Elections are managed by states and controlled by political activists within state government. Were our elections designed and controlled by non-party citizens and structured free of party influence, it is a reasonable bet they would be dramatically different, and the information provided on candidates would be much more meaningful than TV blather. An election system controlled by non-party citizens would morph from a "popularity" contest to a "capability" contest, and as if by magic, the performance of the voter would suddenly improve.

It is not possible to produce quality self-government if the political system creates dumbed-down voters for party purposes. That is the structure of a Monarchy Republic, not the structure of well-organized democratic self-government.

This is not an abstract discussion. Self-government does demand a well-informed electorate capable of voting high-quality decisions on complex issues.

5. Citizens Awareness is the Product of the Society that Surrounds Them.

The knowledge of the citizenry is implanted by the information environment (today, mainly televisionsion), by societal values and practices, and by the political system. Citizens are the proteges of the belief system that surrounds them. If citizens appear stupid and ignorant, that is what the information environment, societal values and practices, and the political system are producing!

The important takeaway, however, is that positive changes in the information environment in which our citizens live will produce positive changes in citizen awareness, comprehension, and behavior. **If the nation needs a well-informed citizenry, it is there for the making.** A study conducted by four professors at the University of Illinois entitled "The Political Environment and Citizen Competence"[43] provides a noteworthy summary:

---

[43] James H. Kublinski, Paul J. Quirk, Jenifer Jerit and Robert F. Rich, University of Illinois, "The Political Environment and Citizen Competence."

"Our findings offer a hopeful implication: that the much-lamented limitations of citizen competence are less inherent in the capabilities and dispositions that individuals bring to politics, **and more a consequence of deficiencies in the political environment than scholars and practitioners often suppose.**"

"Most of the responsibility for improving democratic performance lies not with the citizens themselves but with the elites who shape, and have the opportunity to alter, the political environment."

ALTERNATIVE WAYS TO DERIVE DECISIONS ON CRITICAL MATTERS OF THE NATION

This book emphasizes improved decision-making as a key strategy for making a leap forward in the performance of our Republic government. This nation has the intellectual capability to develop, install, and execute democratic self-government of startling competence. All that is needed is the development of a well-thought-out and fundamentally sound plan and national commitment to it. **Using the knowledge and judgment of The People to vote for decisions that are their unquestioned responsibility as the owners of the nation is a strategy aimed precisely at creating a self-government of high performance.**

The worst decision voted by citizens, on any matter of national concern, is likely to be magnitudes higher in quality and effectiveness than that same decision made by party-stooge elected representatives.

In the absence of high conviction that citizens are sufficiently well-informed to intelligently vote on the high-impact decisions that will set the course of the nation, The People, faced with this classic non-programmed decision, have four action alternatives from which to choose. You, as a reader, should consider these and make your own decision:

Alternative #1: Let all citizens vote on those critical decisions, regardless of their comprehension level, and just "let the chips fall where they may."

> *For pure democracy addicts, this alternative will have appeal because it conforms to rigid thinking about democratic rights and equality. **Unfortunately, this alternative has a high probability of producing low-quality decisions.** Avoidance of this route is strongly recommended because achieving quality national decisions is of far greater importance than adherence to democratic rights and equality.*

Alternative #2: Abandon the notion that voters can ever make critical directional decisions by vote because the comprehension level among the masses of voters is too low, so the decisions will be too complicated for them.

This is a decision to "do nothing." It is the "I give up, the problem is too difficult" attitude. It guarantees endless continuation of the lethal problems of our existing system. Citizens of a nation that chooses this route are not capable of self-government.

Alternative #3: Delegate to the Constitutional Convention authority to vote critical directional decisions on behalf of the nation.

An argument certain to be made will be: "You are proposing the formation of a Constitutional Convention of 50 well-informed elected persons. Why not just give them the right to make those decisions on behalf of The People? Why bother to involve millions of citizens in what will be a complex and expensive effort?"

Although this argument is more rational than allowing political parties to make the nation's directional decisions, it is a truly poor answer and a responsibility bail-out.

Utilizing the Constitutional Convention pops up because it is a simple and ready-made solution. However, it would be just another case of improper delegation by The People to an elected body of critical decisions that are The People's sole responsibility. The vital rule to bear in mind is that "some decisions must never be delegated." Constitutional decisions occupy the very top spot on that list.

Alternative #4: Identify the Well-Informed Electors in the voter mass, make certain they are possessed of full and complete quality information, and give them the responsibility to vote critical directional decisions on behalf of all citizens.

If this route is selected and successfully implemented, improvement in the nation's decision-making (and, by extension, its government) will be dramatic. Critical decisions made by the Well-Informed Electors would be of high quality and garner universal public support.

Removing from the government the right to make decisions on matters that should not be in its bailiwick will allow The People to refocus the government on the many important matters it is now avoiding.

*This alternative utilizes Direct Democracy voting principles, **but only for critical decisions**, those that ultimately decide the direction of the nation. **Those are decisions that must never be voted on by poorly-informed citizens.** It is totally appropriate to use this proposed Direct Democracy voting structure and process* *because it fits within our Framer Republic concept, wherein forms of voting should be varied to fit the decision needs.*

Representative government by elected persons will continue unabated but will be refocused solely on those matters The People determine should be the government's responsibility.

SECTION 6
THE "WELL-INFORMED ELECTORS" PROPOSAL

> Alternative #4. is essentially a bet that among our citizens there presently exists a body of very intelligent, well-informed, patriotic and dedicated people who can be relied upon to put the Nation first, and whose combined judgement is the best shot we have at making high-quality owner-generated decisions whenever they are needed.
>
> Further, the bet is that over time, proposed improvements to information quality and flow, and to actions carried out within the Authority Structure, will dramatically improve the level of The People's knowledge. The various planned changes will over time produce a citizenry that is deeply involved, and where most citizens truly qualify as "well-informed."

ARGUMENTS PRO AND CON

Those negative toward the Well-Informed Elector proposal harbor strong beliefs that the democratic principle of "equality" should dominate and should permit the involvement of all citizens, regardless of capacity, in all election processes. Yet, from the time of the Framers, that posture has been viewed as improper. James Madison stated "A well-instructed people alone can be permanently a free people."

> **The success of self-government rests on the willingness and ability of the citizens to find a way to govern themselves <u>in spite of themselves</u>. If self-government critical decisions require decision-making by well-informed voters, which it does, the above alternatives are what is available. A choice must be made. Expecting long leaps forward without expenditure of massive effort is just "blowing smoke."**

The proposition that true self-government requires The People to make decisions that direct and control their nation, decisions much more complex than merely voting for candidates on a ballot, changes the entire democratic concept our nation installed. **Such a self-**

government proposition requires a commitment by The People to place themselves in a position where they can and will carry out their five ownership responsibilities.

The proposed serious role change for The People in their self-government imposes the requirement that a well-informed citizen voter group be configured to perform The People's critical decision responsibilities. Doing that surfaces an intellectual conflict between the citizen as a dumbed-down passive ballot-box voter versus the citizen as an active elector possessing the knowledge and willingness to vote for high-impact decisions that will direct and steer the nation. **Because of differing motivations, external pressure, and vested interests, a Well-Informed Elector will be much more inclined to vote solely in the interest of The People than will any Elected Person.**

A national system that places on a body of Well-Informed Electors the responsibility for voting the difficult and knowledge-dependent Owner decisions puts voters in a position where they must exercise freedom of choice. They must decide whether to invest their time and effort to earn the designation "Well-Informed Elector" or whether they will "take a pass" on that effort and leave the vote to those who have earned the designation.

Establishing a body of Well-Informed Electors is **betting on the Nation's voter strengths, and avoiding becoming the victim of their weaknesses**.

There is no question but that in our country there exists a large number of people who now have, or are willing to acquire, the necessary knowledge. Perhaps there may be as many as 50 million. At this stage, we don't know who they are, or how many. It is also clear that a significant percentage of the voters do not have the interest, the time, or the mentality to prepare themselves for such responsibilities.

This Chapter opened by asking the question of how to more effectively involve the Voter in our system. Involving all voters is not presently a good answer, but a pragmatic solution is to qualify a special voting body called Well-Informed Electors to make critical Owner decisions on behalf of all citizens. Perhaps 30% of citizens would work to qualify as a Well-Informed Elector. Note that currently about 60% of citizens now vote.

The Constitutional Authorities would define the qualification requirements for a Well-Informed Elector, manage the group, and the information presentation and voting processes for matters placed before them. Because of the importance, those qualified to participate should meet the criteria:

1. Well-informed electors must be mature, thoughtful people. Older people are much more likely to have the time to invest and a conscientious attitude and approach. Many of the votes they will cast will be "programmed decisions," which places heavy emphasis on the experience and knowledge present in higher-age groups.

Perhaps Well-Informed Electors should be viewed as a "Council of Elders," following the ancient successful practice of our native tribes. A minimum age of 40 is recommended.

2. Background and experience are important. Verifiable employment or participation in the nation's various functions is a suggested requirement. A morals-and-ethics standard should be employed. We know from experience with elected persons in Congress that higher education guarantees neither judgment nor insight, so elector selection should be based upon testing. Well-informed electors must have been citizens for a minimum of 15 years.

Great care would be taken to avoid qualification criteria intended to "stack" the Well-Informed Elector group in one direction or another. It is necessary to secure mature-thinking voters who can be trusted to put the nation's interest first and possess essential fundamental knowledge. It is in the interest of the nation that the group be politically impartial, but obviously, a considerable percentage will have had party membership.

Thought should be given to building inducements for Well-Informed Elector qualification. The nation is asking for a significant time investment from those who will serve, and their contributions will be of great value. It is suggested that "recognition" be their reward, perhaps a qualification certificate that can be framed and displayed, a lapel pin, or perhaps special license plates or auto stickers. But, when the nature of Well-Informed Elector's time commitment is known, monetary compensation might be considered.

WELL-INFORMED ELECTOR GROUP FORMATION

The nation has not been down this road before, nor do we think it has any other democracy.

A. Because of the "new venture" risks, a "Test Approach" to the implementation of the Well-Informed Elector program is recommended. Small-scale trials should be conducted beforehand whenever possible, including on technical systems to be utilized. Perhaps the program could be introduced by starting out with simple decisions.

B. The major concern is determining the size of the Well-Informed Elector voting body. Many considerations are involved in that decision. It is recommended the Constitutional Convention be the body designated to manage the effort and make the final operational decisions because the Convention will be the ongoing administrator of the Well-Informed Elector group.

*   Acceptance by The People is an important factor. The body must be of sufficient size for its decisions to have full backing. It would be very advantageous if The People could be involved in the Well-Informed Voter body size decision.

- The larger the body, the greater the work involved in its database maintenance and in the difficulty and cost of each decision it makes.

- It is estimated the size of the body might be 5 million to 10 million on the lower side and 60 million on the upper side. Either size is large enough to meet decision credibility standards. We do not believe the quality of decisions will vary greatly if the voting body size is anywhere within the above-mentioned range.

A NATIONAL PROGRAM TO IMPROVE CITIZEN CIVICS KNOWLEDGE IS A MUST

A national education program produced by talents of the entertainment industry and utilizing national history, the National Imperatives, the Financial Measures, the Constitution, the President's Decision and Legislation Planning, the Election process, and issues of the country would be used to enlarge the well-informed elector group. The same content would become education system study material.

Scholars who have studied the voter competence issue are clear in their conclusion: "Citizen competence is less inherent in capabilities and dispositions of individuals and more a consequence of deficiencies in the political environment." The national effort to change the political and information environment, planned in this proposal, will bring huge voter competence benefits to the nation and thus is a necessary companion to a national education program.

INTEGRATING WELL-INFORMED ELECTORS INTO THE VOTING PROCESS

The proposed People's Voting Body for Constitutional matters, Well-Informed Electors, will be the vehicle by which patriotic and motivated voters are deeply involved in the nation's decision process. Under the guidance of the Constitutional Convention and utilizing direct democracy voting, the Electors would vote on the owner's decisions concerning critical matters such as:

a) **What the government of the country must accomplish**. These are longer-term goals we have chosen to call "National Imperatives." They are owner decisions regarding "direction," intended to focus the nation and its people on necessary achievements. The process of their development involves The People in the strategic planning of the nation, a new function of self-government carrying very high government improvement expectations.

b) **What debt and financial rules will the government follow.** These requirements we have chosen to call "Financial Measures." They are perhaps The People's most important "control" mechanism, and achieving them will require intense "planning," "directing," and "organizing" on the part of the President's administration. This approach, likewise, carries very high government improvement expectations.

c) **The true "Policy" questions of the nation.** Most of those are today either avoided by the government and become the subject of endless political arguments or are abdicated to the Supreme Court. Examples of true policy questions are the nation's rules regarding its financing requirements; abortion; what can, and shall, the nation provide its citizens with health care; election and voting rules and policy; updating the Bill of Rights; defining the nation's policies regarding climate change; its immigration policy, and its education policy. Those are fundamental owner "planning" matters, the firming of which will establish a solid foundation to allow the nation to move forward decisively and without argument.

d) **Defining the overriding rules, concepts, philosophies, and beliefs that shall be inscribed in the Constitution.** Those will be the economic and market system to be utilized by the nation; the rights and obligations of citizenship; rules regarding parties and factions; establishing accountability for elected persons; the morals and ethics stance of the nation, the nation's internal defense system, etc.

e) **Approval of content of the Constitution.** The Constitution contains the formal documentation of the planning, organizing, staffing, directing, and controlling decisions made by the nation's owners. It will become the "operations manual" for citizens and all involved in the Authority Structure.

f) Approving the organization, staffing, procedures, and decision processes to be employed in government.

g) The Well-Informed Electors will decide all constitutional issues and questions that may arise.

Utilizing the body of Well-Informed Electors to vote decisions on complex Constitutional matters will require national commitment, significant effort, and perseverance. No nation's process like that now exists, to the best of our knowledge. Designing, building, and conducting the needed voting processes will be a challenge of large proportion. However, it has already been said that, for a nation that could put a man on the moon, forming such a group and making it successful should be a breeze.

The nation will have put in place a special body of citizens to make its critical decisions freeing government to deal with day-to-day matters. Well-reasoned Imperatives and Financial Measures promulgated by the Well-Informed Electors will eliminate government milling and incoherence and establish a real and challenging forward-looking focus.

A cohesive nation is highly desired, and significant involvement of The People in successful self-government will be its foundation. Constructing a Well-Informed Electorate, and using that group to make highly important owner decisions by vote, would be a big step toward building cohesion and ridding ourselves of party polarization. Gone will be the endless political party contention about foundational matters of the country. Gone will be the nation's "no decision" incoherence that seems to be the major product of our current government system.

Readers should understand that, in designing and implementing a Well-Informed Elector voting body, the nation must avoid the Framer approach, "dump it on them and let's see what happens." The on-going effort to fine-tune and improve its processes will be a part of our lives for some time.

DEVISING WELL-INFORMED ELECTOR VOTING PROCEDURES FOR COMPLEX ISSUES

Voting procedures will have to be created customized to the decisions required. A national data base of all Well-Informed Electors, with secure on-line electronic communication capability and intelligently-structured vote-casting programs, will be essential. Highly effective fact presentation, issue examination, and feedback will be needed, all of which will require creative problem-solving on the part of the Constitutional Convention and The People's Election Commission.

In the voting process, pass/fail or yes/no votes would be used to the extent possible, but for complex decisions (the non-programmed variety) it will be necessary for Well-Informed Electors to choose from a range of alternatives. A number of votes may be required to resolve complex national issues, so determination to arrive at a decision for the nation will be essential.

Involvement of The People in the basic decisions of the nation and the huge national effort to create that capability creates an incredibly exciting opportunity. Success of the finished effort will be a validation of the nation's human and technical capability and ability to create a nation whose decision process is solid from top to bottom. If that fact is recognized by the citizens, national cohesion will rise dramatically, and our authority structure will be widely admired.

Successful implementation of direct democracy using Well-Informed Electors will prove that The People are, in fact, capable of self-government!

CHAPTER 12

THE PRESIDENT:
THE CHIEF EXECUTIVE OF GOVERNMENT

CONTENT:

SECTION 1: CONSTITUTIONAL STRUCTURE OF THE PRESIDENT POSITION

SECTION 2: OPERATING ADJUSTMENTS TO CONSTITUTIONAL PLAN

SECTION 3: BRIEF ANALYSIS OF THE PRESIDENCY

SECTION 4: ESTABLISH A UNITARY "GOVERNMENT BOSS"

SECTION 5: ESTABLISH THE PEOPLE'S CONTROL OVER ALL OF GOVERNMENT

FOREWORD

Those examining the government disorder of our nation should thoroughly dissect Article 11, Sections 1 through 4, which contains the Constitution's treatment of the role of the President.

The Framer allocation of duties, roles, and authority between the Legislative branch and the Executive branch has, since inception, shaped the performance of government. They set up the President as a front-man for international affairs while attempting to internally manage their Monarchy Republic using a three-silo cross-discipline system. They loaded governing authority on the elected assemblies and denied The People any ability to deal with governmental dysfunction.

That answers most of the question, "How did we end up with this dysfunctional organization?" It is helpful to review the backgrounds of Constitutional Convention participants. The dominant internal faction was lawyers. It is believed few had exposure to large organizations, or had participated in work-forces of substantial size, such as institutes of higher learning. Here and there, a military background appears. Who but a faction of lawyers would consider a contentious courtroom environment to be the best operating mode for large elected bodies?

Politics and law were the dominant skills of the Convention participants. The new government plan was a vital exercise in designing organization and process. The objective of the plan was not functional excellence, nor was it high-quality governance. It was to induce thirteen recalcitrant states to join a new-and-better U.S. federal government. The main responsibility of the proposed government, decision-making, was never highlighted, nor was the scheme ever tested, so any success after launch was purely an accident of fate.

Let us applaud the Framers for that which warrants applause. They did cobble together a government and brought together a fractured nation. Their freedom and equality principles were laudable.

Loud boos are inadequate scorn for self-serving or plainly ill-conceived Framer actions: Saddling the nation with their grossly unbalanced Monarchy Republic creation, complete with a political elite and no accountability to The People; giving the two Houses of rowdy politicians the unthinkable authority to manage themselves; denying The People their right to amend their own constitution or to correct government dysfunction; destroying government functionality with their all-powerful House of Representatives; creating a no-accountability government culture; and establishing endless dispute in government with their courtroom contention adoption..

Correction of our Framer-created dysfunction will be greatly aided by properly positioning the President in the government organization. A butt-kicker is sorely needed.

SECTION 1
CONSTITUTIONAL STRUCTURE OF THE PRESIDENT POSITION

THE CONSTITUTION WAS A BUSINESS BARGAIN

The Framer mission was to assure the nation's survival by negotiating a political solution with the thirteen-state power block. Government would be whatever that negotiation produced. The mission was clear!

Most would conclude the Framer-negotiated result was "a necessary business bargain." The Framers extolled the merits of their creation. They didn't feel any need to pre-test the operability of their concepts, opting instead to slap their solutions into place to "see what happens." Yet, in the face of that gamble, they made no provision for error-correction.

They then imbedded their solutions in concrete, encasing them in a constitution that gave the political elite sole control over constitution content. In the elapsed years, despite 33,000 amendments proposed to Congress, only 16 that were not clean-up work left over from writing the constitution have ever been approved.

The constitution documented the bargain between its parties, which were the Congress of the United States and the thirteen states. The People were not a party to the bargain, although they were continuously informed of progress. It is a classic example of what transpires when decisions flow from political negotiations, a topic explored in some depth in the Government Decision-Making Series, Chapters 8 - 11.

POLITICAL CONSIDERATIONS FASHIONED THE PRESIDENT'S JOB DESCRIPTION

The Articles of Constitutional text discussing the Legislative branch are about four times as lengthy as those discussing the President. While the Legislative branch content is pointed and contains a long list of powers and authorities, Article 11, relating to the President, is filled with what one might call "administrative garbage." At least one-half of the words dedicated to the President concern the complex Electoral College process and rules regarding impeachment!

Article 11 begins with a definitive statement, "The executive Power shall be vested in a President of the United States of America," but provides no meaningful discussion as to what Executive Power means or what its responsibilities entail, except mention of Commander–in-Chief of the Military and the President's authority to make treaties.

For a position as important as President of The United States, the Constitution's treatment can only be described as "pitiful."

One statement, "he may require the Opinion, in writing, of the principal Officer in each of the executive Departments, upon any subject relating to the Duties of their respective Offices," is particularly disturbing. It lacks contextual linkage and implies the President has no authority over subordinate "reporting" officials in his chain of command. Inserting such rubbish into Constitutional provisions for the most important job in the Nation must be viewed as gross ignorance or as an intentional effort to degrade the stature of the position.

Fear that the President would end up a "King George replica" was prevalent in the thirteen states following the rebellion against England. That state of mind, looming over all, shaped Framer political positioning.

The Framers created a figurehead President. They positioned the President to be the nation's face to the world, giving him/her command of the military and the diplomatic corps. They created a governance structure with nobody in charge. No one person or no group of people responsible to the voters is accountable for keeping government in line and functioning. The Framers opted for a three-horse troika without a driver.[44]

The Framers were very careful to state, "The executive Power shall be vested in a President of the United States of America," but did not throw any light on the concept.

The word "Executive" implies a manager who "executes." The term has undergone dramatic expansion in its use since the 1780s, but "executive power," as used in the constitution, must be interpreted as authority to execute directives or laws. That interpretation is consistent with the Framer plan of governing through elected legislative bodies, whose directives would be executed by the President. That interpretation is reinforced by the Article 11, Section 3 exhortation that "he shall take care that the Laws be faithfully executed."

THE LEGISLATIVE BRANCH WAS MADE THE "BOSS OF THE NATION"

Readers are encouraged to study the Constitution's Article 1, Section 8, which contains eighteen specific grants of power to Congress. One all-encompassing grant of power to the Legislative branch, contained in the last paragraph, reveals the true intent of the Framers:

> "To make all laws which shall be necessary and proper for carrying into execution the foregoing powers *vested in this Constitution in the Government of the United States, or in any Department or Officer thereof.*"

That provision leads to several vital conclusions:

a) **The Framers positioned the Legislative branch as the "government of the United States."** Although "equal" in the Framer three-silo structure, the Executive and Judicial branches ended up constitutionally subordinated.

b) The Framers vested the financial power of the nation in Congress, both as to the raising of money and the payment of money and gave the President a reversible veto power. The proper approach would have been to place the financial power with the President but to require legislative approval of all his/her actions. **The Framers most certainly would have been wise to avoid a situation where 435 politicians each have their fingers in the nation's money pot.** That Framer decision, coupled with 2-year re-election of members of the House of Representatives, laid the groundwork for election-support-money-spending propensities that have forever cursed the nation's budget.

c) The idea that the Legislative branch should make the decisions of the nation and the president should execute them, if that was the Framer intention, is rational

---

[44] A troika is a classy Russian sled for winter human transportation. It is drawn by three horses hitched abreast, which makes them more difficult for a driver to control.

but functionally impractical. In a democracy, decisions respecting the nation and its people are to be made by democratic vote. **The workability of the concept was damaged by excluding the President from the decision process and by performance impediments caused by the size, function, and management of the main legislative body, the House of Representatives.**

d) The Framers solved their fear of an omnipotent President by over-loading powers on the Legislative branch and proportionally reducing powers of the President. **They solved a political problem with sub-optimal organization-and-delegation processes.** Political solutions shelter the decision-makers from criticism but all too often violate management principles, resulting in subsequent operational havoc.

e) In their political solution, **the Framers created a two-assembly "boss of the nation," which may rank among the worst democratic government structure decisions ever.** When two self-managed assemblies of elected politicians can function as "the boss of the nation," with an elected President also ensconced in the government, a blue moon may well appear in the sky.

f) Rather than codifying a solid long-term government organization and process plan for a large nation, Article 1, Section 8 reads like a slapped-together "to-do" list for a new government. **That is probably exactly what it was.**

g) Section 8 can be interpreted as authority for the Legislative branch to exercise administration over the agencies and departments, even though those functions report to the President. That organizational incoherence underlies today's meandering focus of the Legislative branches and their basic and fundamental ineptness.

SECTION 2
OPERATIONAL ADJUSTMENTS TO CONSTITUTIONAL PLAN

Organizations without a leader are a rarity. If a leader is not designated, one will emerge out of the turmoil. If a leader cannot function, another, authorized or otherwise, will step into those shoes.

The two Houses of Congress obviously could not function as the "boss" of the nation in the manner envisioned by the Framers. Over the years, the houses have delegated, to Committee Chairmen, to the President, and more recently to heads of Administrative State organizations, those of their powers that are best exercised by an executive.

Presidents now execute **powers that were not constitutionally delegated to the President.** Those powers reached the hands of the President by the application of elasticity to the term "executive Power" in a variety of ways, including a President's blatant assumption of unauthorized powers. Burdened with a weird constitutional job description, Presidents have nonetheless managed to function. Four reasons they have been able to do so are worth mentioning.

THE PEOPLE'S CONSENT TO PRESIDENTIAL LEADERSHIP

Although granted limited powers under the constitution, but elected by the voters, the President has traditionally been viewed by citizens as something other than the powerless head person defined in the constitution. **He is viewed by citizens as the nation's leader.** The nation tends to follow his/her direction. Presidents do lead in varying ways and at varying competence levels.

In our nation, the President's power is what The People believe it to be, not what is written in the Constitution. That belief allows government to function, in a manner of speaking, but not to perform as it should.

1. Access to the "Bully Pulpit."

Much of the President's power comes from access to the media and use of the fog-horns of the President's office. The "Bully Pulpit" of Theodore Roosevelt's time is even more "Bully" today. Access to the Media gives the President the ability to direct attention and sway opinion, a power probably more important than any constitutionally granted.

The media is arguably the most powerful threat to democracy in the nation. The President's "bully pulpit" power and political heft is probably a factor that laid on the American people the illicit political party/media alliance threat discussed extensively in this book.

2. Access to "Party Power"

The President is usually a powerful member of a political party, its leader, even without the title. Through election rhetoric, he/she often sets and sells the party-political program. Often, the President's political party commands a majority in congress. **Although the constitution gave the President only the power to execute, wielding majority party leadership power raises him/her to the level of a totalitarian Chief Executive Officer, with full power to decide and implement.**

3. Executive Orders

Executive power is properly derived from re-delegation to the President of execution power granted by Congress. An Executive Order either falls under the President's "Execute" responsibility, or it is execution of an authoritarian decision he/she has made. In the latter case, the President is performing an action not democratically authorized.

Executive Orders are a no-man's-land. For Presidents using them, they constitute stretching or outright violation of the bounds of the republic's constitutional authority. Authority confusion always prevails among the voters, who do not seem capable of understanding who should be doing what, so no accountability is enforced by that group.

The negative effects of constitutional powers misallocation are most stark in management/administration of government, where the lack of a constitutionally-empowered and instructed Chief Executive Officer of Government results in general disorganization, and far too often, downright functional incompetence.

Nobody is responsible to manage the government. Mis-delegation of the "direct" function has granted to units of the Administrative State powers that should not be permitted to them, and has allowed Congress to meander aimlessly into the desert of non-performance. It has caused the President to become functionally despotic, always with no check-and-balance in sight, from any source.

The constitution grants the President "Executive power" and directs him/her "to see that the laws are faithfully executed." There is no constitutional authorization for the President to create law and no provision authorizing executive order issuance. The President has executive power to implement laws, which he may choose to do by issuing Executive Orders.

4. Summarizing the President's Existing Powers

It was obvious the Framer creation of a two-assembly "boss of the nation" could not work. At the outset, the two assemblies functioned by delegating to the President statute law to execute. With no effective check-and-balance and no one person responsible to manage the government, Presidents became more and more authoritarian. **After 1880, the Assemblies increased the breadth and nature of their re-delegation by creating the Administrative State and granting to its non-elected unit heads the power to write, execute, and adjudicate law in that area of jurisdiction.**

That action made the constitutionally weak role of the President more so. Presidents responded by assuming for the Executive Branch the same power delegation that Administrative State units received from the Legislative branch. The behavior of Presidents became more authoritarian, emulating Administrative State behavior and relying on Legislative Branch statutes for little.

SECTION 3
A BRIEF ANALYSIS OF THE PRESIDENCY

The five functions of management are an important analysis tool. In standard organizations, "Plan, Organize, Staff, Direct, and Control" are the responsibilities portions of which the Boards of Directors delegate to the Chief Executive Officer. Granted responsibility for those five functions, a chief executive officer has all authority needed but can utilize it only if corporate organizational units fall within his/her chain of command.

In the Government of the United States, as designed by the Framers, the two Legislative branches and the Judiciary, together with special-purpose organizations such as the Federal Reserve, lie outside of the President's chain of command. He performs certain staffing functions for them but has no operating authority over them. That situation, and others mentioned herein, produce the following assessment of the President's ability, or lack of ability, to perform the aforementioned five management functions within the nation's governance.

1. Plan:

    The fifteen autonomous and self-contained Departments of government reporting to the President plan their own affairs. A plethora of special-purpose organizations that lie outside of the president's chain-of-command also plan their own affairs.

    The President is responsible for relations with all foreign nations. Planning, little of which is visible to the public, is employed. Substantial planning is carried out in the Military.

    Such elected assembly planning as exists is performed by the political party in power. Should his/her party be in power, the President is involved, otherwise, not.

    There is no consolidated strategic plan for the nation. The President reacts to planned direction that may emanate out of the Legislature or majority political party campaign promises and conducts internal incident planning regarding matters arising within or outside of the nation.

    For the nation as a whole, our government is not "planning-based." Its overall management process would accurately be described as "reactive." That is not to say that substantial lower-level planning is not carried out in various jurisdictions, but little is disclosed concerning it.

2. Organize:

The President operates within the government organization, except as to the Executive branch under his/her direct control, which houses subject-matter personnel. As to governance, the President's organizing is focused on political and project initiatives. Administrative State units reporting to the President do their own organizing. Little is publicly disclosed concerning that.

Most "organizing" of government emanates from Congress. It is not known the extent to which professional organization guidance is utilized, but from the observed structures resulting, the probability is that such use has been low.

3. Staff:

The President has heavy constitutional responsibilities for staffing various non-elective positions in government. That activity is very party-centric and political. Staffing is a transactional activity, generally not planning-based.

Consideration should be given to making government staffing a Constitutional responsibility, and removing it totally from the Chief Executive's tasks. The entire government staffing approach, which was founded in political party activity, is extremely loyalty-based and will require re-conceptualization with the demise of political parties.

4. Direct:

The Nation's "Direct" responsibility was constitutionally given to the Legislative branch. By a sequence of events, the "Direct" function, ordinarily a companion to the "Plan" function, ended up in the hands of self-interest political parties. They do some planning to further their party goals, and whatever that party activity produces will probably become government direction. Is it any wonder that government accomplishments are extremely limited?

The President is heavily involved in political activity, the purpose of which is to direct public opinion and impose party dogma on government operations and the nation.

Although some functions appear to be planning oriented and highly skilled (the military is an example), there is no central planning and direction function for the U.S. Government as a whole, a glaring weakness. The President should be the key figure directing and managing U.S. Government planning.

5. Control:

The President job is highly *reactive*. Presidential actions are driven by legislative output, statistics, national or international events, crises and opportunities, and party direction. The job is not control-oriented. **Huge totally self-contained departments report to him/her, with a very high level of authority delegation in place, so presidential involvement in their internal affairs is limited.**

Most control activities are political, implemented by the President with an eye on public opinion.

It should be noted that control over taxation and expenditures was constitutionally vested in Congress. The President has a reversible right of veto. That control structure is totally dysfunctional, and should be one of the first priorities of government reorganization. The proposed "Financial Measures" control system is an excellent solution.

OBSERVATIONS AND CONCLUSIONS FROM THIS BRIEF EXAMINATION

The above analysis is not data-driven; it is derived from media information and some research, but mostly from observation.

It does not delve into the President's time allocation. One suspects that one-half or more of the President's time is devoted to party-related political activity. It would be very revealing to evaluate the President's time allocation, as there are indications of significant time waste in what is, arguably, the nation's most important job. In using the term "time waste," the meaning is time being devoted to matters of low importance to the nation while important matters go unaddressed.

The following are general conclusions:

a) The planning for governance that exists is performed by political parties and is totally party-centric. **The absence of centralized strategic planning for the nation is a glaring national weakness.** Heavier involvement of The People, as strongly suggested herein, demands a switch to planning-based management with serious involvement of the nation's citizens. A strong planning process would develop the important forward-looking National Imperatives and Financial Measures, the foundation for planning-based management to improve decision-making and produce an upgrade of consequence in government functional performance. Letting government set its own goals and priorities has been an absolute disaster.

b) Military and foreign affairs are the only responsibilities where all five management functions are under the President's control. Interestingly, recent high-impact decisions for military and foreign affairs appear to have been dangerously authoritarian. **If the nation doesn't want a repeat of the Afghan withdrawal of 2020, those decisions cannot be seat-of-the-pants judgments, and they must be methodically planned, and authorized by democratic vote.** Military and foreign affairs governance should be given deep separate scrutiny to construct better placement of the "direct" and "control" functions. The placement of the nation's face toward the world is not discussed in this book, which treats the President's focus as being highly internal.

c) A President with no party affiliation would be a much more effective executive. Term limits in elected positions and elimination of party politics would free immense amounts of presidential time, likely more than 50%, to devote to making government function. As a part of restructure planning, a serious study of the President's time use is needed as base-line information for critical "organize" decisions.

d) **The President's heavy involvement in government staffing decisions is a highly suspect time use.** Constitutional and political party considerations underlie that practice. Staffing, while important, is not the "highest and best use" of a president's time. Consideration should be given, with the elimination of political parties, to placing personnel selection with the Constitutional Authorities, giving the President final approval for staffing decisions within his/her span of control. That action would correct the "Staff" function time allocation imbalance, eliminate the political party influence, and ensure personnel selection is based on competence.

e) Establishing multiple Elected Assemblies, managed by Guardian-placed professionals, as the decision-and-legislation bodies of government, and with the elimination of political parties, the enforcement of a publicly-transparent President-led planning process for decision/legislation prioritization will open that entire can of worms to scrutiny by The People. Legislation "plan" and "direct" functions will rapidly introduce process and order into the decision assemblies. If properly directed by the President, the senseless bickering will disappear. It is suspected that voters will show more interest in this activity than might be expected.

f) **Getting rid of the Framer three-branch check-and-balance structure and the "contention" processes under which the Houses operate will significantly improve the government decision environment, freeing it from the trade-bargaining system of the legal profession.** Supervisorial oversight by Constitutional Authorities will be dramatically more effective. The "Direct" function of the President will then actually become powerful.

g)   The observations in a) through f) provoke the conclusion that restructure of the President's job function is equal in importance to the restructure of the functions of the Houses of Congress. Quantum-leap progress in the quality and performance of our government is totally achievable by following that path.

The job of the President cannot be considered on a stand-alone basis. The organization and operations of the Elected assemblies and support organizations must be dove-tailed with the President's supervision function.

DISORGANIZED GOVERNMENT, INCLUDING THE ROLE OF THE PRESIDENT, HAS CONSTITUTIONAL ROOTS

The President's only Constitutional authority to give direction to the Legislative branch is contained in Article 11, Section 3. Summarized, it is to "give the Congress information on the state of the Union, and recommend to their consideration such measures as he shall judge necessary and expedient." **That Article, noteworthy for its denigration of Presidential authority, relegates the President to a consultant's role.**

One would logically expect that the Constitution's treatment of the function of the President would be very specific about his/her duty, power, and authority to carry out the five management functions, but it is silent on all of that for reasons discussed earlier.

The Nation's grossly ineffective decision-making and poor-quality government operations is a recurring theme of this writing. Party self-interest over-rides the nation's needs, always and completely. That occurred as a result of constitutional delegation to the two Houses of Congress of inappropriate internal self-management power, which a large elected body is not competent to perform.

Contentious Assembly processes do not logically address the nation's decision needs, and when they do, produce negotiated political solutions of low quality and largely devoid of public support. Avoidance by the Legislature of fundamental and essential issues tells us plainly that the Nation's needs are not receiving attention.

The cost of poor decisions (*and, most critically, no decisions*) remains undiscussed and untallied despite being considered by many as sufficient to threaten the survival of our self-government. Poor assembly decision processes and the endless contention, symptomatic of serious dysfunction within the decision bodies, are believed to be the root source of The People's lack of trust and faith in their own government.

WHY SEPARATION OF POWERS AND INTERNAL "CHECK-AND-BALANCE?"

The Framer Plan was to insulate its "Monarchy Republic" creation against outside corrective efforts **by making it self-contained. Fenced off against interference, particularly by The People, it totally controls its own destiny**.

The plan produced a government that shut out The People, which, of course, is a *MONARCHY*. The three-branch check-and-balance structure, with separation of powers and interbranch monitoring, was a wheel of the Monarchy Republic wagon rotating to keep all critical scrutiny in-house. It required persons in the three branches to check each other, which was intended to allow the Monarchy Republic to totally self-manage.

In implementing their design, the Framers loaded multiple executive-type powers on the Legislative branch, denuding the President and unbalancing the government powers equation, most importantly supervision of the government itself.

SECTION 4
ESTABLISH A UNITARY "GOVERNMENT BOSS"

We are a nation without a government boss. There is no one person responsible to manage government operations in their totality. The People have no management rights and no functioning control representative. No person is "watching the store." Among the world's large organizations, few operate without a strong executive manager in charge. The Government of the United States is one of the few!

Our government was structured as three independent branches pursuing their own agendas, operating totally without supervision in an atmosphere devoid of accountability to The People. **Government is a no-whip three-horse "troika" without a driver.** Two of the three branches are under political party direction; the third is a non-elected organization. Ours is a government without focus, mired in contention, poorly designed and managed, overly influenced by the legal profession, and totally undermined by rampant factional self-interest. Our authority structure is not focused, laser-like, on producing top-quality national government. It is an authority structure focused on piecing together actions that will keep the majority party happy. Somehow, in our government "troika," the sled ended up in front of the horses.

That, of course, means that the responsibilities of the President must be re-prioritized. We recommend eliminating all the President's political activities replacing that time with Plan, Organize, Staff, Direct, and Control activities. We also recommend that little of his/her job be discretionary that several critical new activities be constitutionally established as "job requirements."

The proposed new job function of the President as the Chief Executive Officer of Government does not envision him/her being the nation's face to the world, responsible for international affairs and relationships. For time and space reasons, that puzzle is not addressed in these chapters. An entirely new organization with its own leader should be created to manage the nation's face to the world. That approach requires a separate study and planning effort.

Our government requires, above all else, a strong and competent administrator! Putting a strong elected executive in charge of government performance is a readily-available route by which The People can quickly turn the nation toward high quality government. It should probably be a first step in government reorganization.

Federalist Paper #70 stated the Framer political opinion that guided the President's job structure: **"A vigorous Chief Executive is inconsistent with the genius of republican government."**

That statement probably was a political smoke-screen, to dampen the era's public fear of the President becoming an autocratic King George look-alike. The President's diminished job structure was, however, a key move of the new republic government scheme. The decision to go that route was political, neither rational nor organizational.

A more accurate statement would have been: "An energetic butt-kicking Chief Executive Officer is what it takes to make our government function as it must."

What is needed is an executive accountable to execute the five functions of management. To achieve that, we propose the President be designated "THE CHIEF EXECUTIVE OFFICER OF GOVERNMENT."

THE CHIEF EXECUTIVE OFFICER'S JOB MUST FLOW FROM THE PEOPLE'S DELEGATION OF POWER TO GOVERNMENT

Clear thinking about delegation and roles is best achieved by utilizing the oft-mentioned five functions. They apply to management of every organization.

The People of our nation are a massive population. For such a huge group to practice self-government, an organization and process must be conceived by which that mass of people can make and control implementation of the key decisions demanded by their five owner responsibilities. If the required organization and process cannot be constructed, then self-government is likely not possible. The People, in that case, should consider other forms of government.

Only one group may decide what type of government the nation will have and how it shall function. **"The People" is that group. They must decide, in a process free from political taint.**

They must decide how much of their own responsibilities they are willing to turn over to government, and what duties they will retain unto themselves.

They must set the critical direction of the nation by defining its goals and its restraints.

They must plan and implement a control structure by which they will know for certain that government is doing exactly what they have requested. The key controls must run through the decision process.

By those means, and those means only, can true self-government be achieved.

Upon execution of those requirements by The People, government will have received from them a delegation of powers that define its function, an authorized organization structure, and clear direction. Within the boundaries of those People-delegated directions, government then also must plan, organize, staff, direct, and control.

It is proposed that, **insofar as the government of our nation is concerned**, responsibility and authority for the execution of those five functions be placed on the President. That way, The People will know whose butt is to kicked for non-performance, and The People should have absolutely no compunctions about doing that. The President would be given a set of specific required actions to ensure basic pre-set processes are followed.

The Framer mis-delegation to the Legislative branch, with a very weak "Plan" and "Direct" function, is the source of much of our governmental pain. The Plan and Direct functions of our government need significant upgrading, but that cannot take place until they are removed from Congress. Execution is governments, the responsibility of a strong elected Chief Executive Officer of Government, endlessly monitored by the Authority Structure of The People.

SECTION 5
ESTABLISHING CONTROL OVER ALL OF GOVERNMENT

CONTROLLING AND DIRECTING THE ADMINISTRATIVE STATE

The massive bureaucracy called the Administrative State is a big-league organization and control problem. Some if its components report to the President, some are independent units monitored by the Legislative branch, and a number are self-managed, floating in an unclear status. Administrative State costs are huge, supervision of its functions is suspect, and the potential is high that very nasty activities will surface from it. Until they know otherwise, The People must view that situation as a disaster-in-waiting.

What is most disturbing is The People have no direct control over that huge segment of government, in which signs of inappropriate muscle-flexing are rampant. **Excessive power-delegation to units of the Administrative State has created a state-of-mind wherein some units are attempting to influence national outcomes, which should not ever be their role**. The FBI, the Justice Department, and the CIA are engaging in activities of that nature, and there are others.

One person, the President, cannot personally oversee such a massive number of individual units; his/her span-of-control would be enormous. **Present oversight of Administrative State functions by the legislative branch, which is controlled by politicians, is certainly not the route to follow**. The Legislative branch should supervise the nation, not other organizations. The legislative branch has no effective accountability to The People (please refer to "The Accountability Gap") so the mass of Administrative State units it supervises have no accountability to The People either.

The organizational no-man's land called the Administrative State is discussed in detail in Chapter 8. It is worthwhile, however, to provide some summary thinking:

1. It is not wise for The People to delegate supervision of huge powerful blocks of government to in-government factions. The best solution is to position the President as the Chief Executive Officer of Government, *and to enhance his span-of-control capability with elected supervising subordinates.*

2. The old notion that The People's control should be limited to the currently-existing elected Executive and Legislative branches is obsolete. *Huge and powerful elements of government, established by political parties and positioned outside of the People-controlled elected branches, have long ago made it so.*

3. Self-government demands that **The People establish direct elected supervision and control over all non-elected functions now dominating our government**.

   It is suggested that the organizations of the Administrative State be congregated into cohesive groups and an elected Vice President placed in charge of each group. Term-limited, a Vice President's accountability to The People would be established by two-year performance evaluations during contract term. The Vice Presidents report to the President, who can order a replacement election in the event of non-performance.

Having to make the Vice President election decisions at the ballot box will dramatically enhance citizen curiosity, comprehension, and involvement in presently-opaque government functions. **Self-government demands that The People be watching all aspects of government, and possess the ability to understand when change is needed.**

4. We have proposed, in The People's Direction and Control Series, removing from government a number of functions that are more appropriately instruments of The People and designating them "constitutional bodies."

That moves to Constitutional Authorities vital infrastructure such as the Elections Commission, the Judiciary, Media control, and others. The purpose is to free them from political interference **and to give The People direct control over** the **vital elements that are an anchor of our Authority Structure.**

5. Chapter 9 of the Government Decision-Making Series proposes reorganization of the House of Representatives and implementing new decision processes there. A matrix organization is suggested correlating each of the new Elected Assemblies with existing units of the Administrative State under supervision of elected Vice Presidents. The purpose is to provide the new assemblies with support functions to aid their decision process and to move field decisions affecting the nation and its citizens into the new democratic assemblies. **Those decisions are now being made on an undemocratic basis by unelected Administrative State managers**.

This organization proposal should open up The People's view, install controls, and put in place the ability to move forward with added improvement.

6. The Administrative State contains many functions that were created for political purposes. The plan work must include identification, evaluation, and elimination of those where appropriate, with the intent of reducing government cost and complexity.

To help picture the change that would take place in government process if the President's job is correctly structured, the following clarifying observations are offered.

1. Government Will Function Best as an Integrated Body under Unified Management, with Contention Eliminated

Government cannot function well if composed of independent islands. Each organization of government must integrate with the whole. Organizations exist solely to meet the requirements of The People and must be under management dedicated to that ideal. The performance of the whole is what matters.

Government based on "contention" is built on a foundation of sand. Faulty principles, such as "contention," will reflect through all operational processes. Of the alternative operational modes available, "contention" is probably the worst. Contention within the legislative branch affects the behavior of all of government. Why would "contention" be the chosen operating atmosphere of a nation that prides itself in cohesive self-government?

Contentious government behavior needs to be replaced by planning-based unitary government behavior, directed by the President, utilizing management principles already well established in the major businesses of the Nation. Policing of elected government performance will be carried out by the Constitutional Authorities, who are responsible only to The People.

Government exists to make the decisions delegated to it by The People. It may perform other delegated functions. It is proposed throughout this book that under self-government, The People dictate and control **all democratic decision processes** through their designated constitutional body, the Guardians of the Constitution. Constitutional Authority structure and management is established to monitor government performance, ensuring that The People can hold the President and Vice Presidents totally accountable for providing efficient, high-performance government.

2. It Is Proposed that "Achieving Quality Democratic Decisions" be the Principle Guiding the Design of Government Structure and Process

The make-up and structure of government components must be designed against an over-riding principle. **We suggest the principle be "generation of the best democratic decisions possible on matters affecting the nation and its citizens."** To do that, the People, through Constitutional bodies, must tightly control wherever and however such decisions are made.

We propose that great attention be paid to making certain all decisions that affect the nation or its people are made by democratic vote, never by individuals. That focus will, if properly applied, produce true democratic government by The People and provide protection against authoritarian individuals who will inevitably infiltrate and attempt to take control of decision bodies.

The President will be fundamentally a planner, director, and executor of The People's decisions and of government decisions made democratically. There will be fifty or sixty elected assemblies making decisions, which, if ratified by the Senate, the President must ensure are implemented. Decisions he/she does make will concern the planning, staffing, and organization of the work processes of government.

3. Government, Like All Organizations, Needs a Highly Competent Chief Executive

We propose that the quality and effectiveness of government operations be assured through the day-to-day management of the President, the Chief Executive Officer of Government.

The People, in their self-government, need an accountable Chief Executive they can send packing if government does not perform. In his/her role, the President will be responsible to make certain that all government organization components are performing as The People expect and that the work flow processes are functioning properly and within budget.

To be successful in such an operating environment, the President of the United States will have to possess high executive competence. No celebrity is likely to survive. That realization should put an end to "popularity-based" presidential elections and introduce "competence-based" selection.

4. Convert Government to Planning-Based Management

Government decision-making for the nation suffers acutely from the absence of integrated strategic planning of its direction and aspirations and inadequate involvement of the various segments and people of the nation.

Planning should develop the back-bone for the Nation's governance activities and decisions. Planning is a forward-looking process starting with The People, and involving all in-government units that have an interest. The plans so produced would be approved by appropriate democratic vote of the Well-Informed Electors and given to government for execution. Elective person incentive payments should be heavily influenced by achievement of planned actions.

Four major planning processes should be featured:

a) Plans to identify and prioritize the important direction and control efforts of the Nation, called **the National Imperatives and the Financial Measures,** will be developed by The People and voted by the Well-Informed Electors under work guidance from the Constitutional Convention.

b) The **Decision and Legislation Plan, developed under the President,** identifies and schedules the decision work of the elected bodies of government. It is suggested a two-year horizon, updated annually, be employed. The planning process directed by the President will involve gathering decision and legislation requests from the People, states, and government, then sorting and prioritizing them. The output will be a two-year plan, requiring Senate approval and management of all decisions and legislation to be carried out by the Assemblies and Senate. Those plans will develop and dictate tight directional operations of the nation.

c) A **Strategic Plan for the Nation** is needed. The Strategic Plan, focusing on the nation's needs, problems, and affairs, will incorporate the aforementioned plans and will require significant input from The People. It is suggested a five-year or ten-year planning horizon be utilized. This plan will integrate segments of government not covered above, such as external affairs, international relationships, and the Military.

d) **The Financial Plan of Government** is critical. It is suggested that a five-year horizon be utilized, compiled by year. This document will quantify the costs and revenues resulting from the three aforementioned plans and existing operations, and requires significant financial decision-making on how to best achieve the Financial Measures. It is obvious the excessive spending that has marked recent history will have to be reversed. The completed Financial Plan ultimately becomes The People's direction and the control document for ensuring government performance.

5. Manage the Decision and Legislation Process

Chapter 9, in the "Government Decision-Making" Series, proposes a major reorganization of the House of Representatives into 50 to 60 independent decision-making assemblies, each focused on a specific segment of the nation. The assemblies would be aligned in a matrix organization with related organizations of the Administrative State.

The decision processes of each assembly would be under daily management of professionals assigned by the Guardians of the Constitution, who will manage the process, quality and integrity of democratic decision-making but not participate in it. The unproductive and distasteful performance characteristics of the present system will promptly disappear. The aggregated production requirements of the elected bodies would be better managed if the matrix organization reports to elected Vice Presidents under direction of the President.

Such a change would unify the production of all legislative functions within the span of control of the Chief Executive Officer of Government, as outlined in 4.c. above.

7. President's Proposed Job Function and Broadened Span of Control Suggests a Reorganization of the Executive Branch

The Chief Executive Officer of Government, under this proposal, will direct a large and diverse work-force. The organization structure of the Executive branch needs to be completely re-thought, an action long over-due from most every perspective. The Framer's ancient President job structure, modified piece by piece by various incumbents over the centuries, today consists too heavily of political activities that The People must insist be replaced by high-quality and productive government management.

There are a range of organization approaches that could be applied, but attempting to examine those in detail takes the content of this book well beyond its physical boundaries.

One principle rises to the fore. Given the President's huge span of control, the number of administrative officials elected by The People should be expanded, **so that all activities of government are overseen by voter-elected officials.** That process will expose The People to parts of government now obscure to them, an action designed to apply true government by The People. It will also provide the spade by which the dark activities of the Deep State will be rooted out.

By focusing the President on management of government, his/her ability to invest time in foreign affairs will be very limited. Consideration should be given to creating a completely separate organization that would assume responsibility for all aspects of the Nation's relationship with foreign nations, and covering such matters as trade, military alliances, debt and finance, and others. The Chief Executive Officer heading this international organization would need a set of skills completely different from the Chief Executive of Government. In addition to the Consular and Ambassadorial functions, probably the Military, the Space Agency, the CIA and other related organizations should be incorporated into it. Oversight by the People's organization, the Constitutional Authorities, makes the proposed two-unit government structure well worth considering.

Massive longer-term projects such as these will require a special planning commission under the Guardians of the Constitution, with approval oversight by the Well-informed Electors.

CHAPTER 13

THE JUDICIAL BRANCH

CONTENT:

SECTION 1: FRAMER DECISIONS RESPECTING THE JUDICIARY

SECTION 2: POLITICS AND THE JUDICIARY

SECTION 3: THE OBSOLETE CONSTITUTION PROBLEM

SECTION 4: A BRIEF ASSESSMENT OF THE JUDICIARY

SECTION 5: SUMMARY AND ACTION PROPOSALS

FOREWORD

When designing our constitution, the Framers were absorbed in the critical task of installing a new federal government that could resolve the nation's threatening financial problems and bind the thirteen independent states into one Union. But, even when faced with such a challenge, it is always possible to slip goodies for the legal profession into the deal.

Inclusion of the Judiciary in the three-branch Framer structure might strike the reader as a strange comment after that introduction, and properly so. No Judicial officials are elected, a democratic imperative for organizations accorded a dominant role, but the Judiciary performs functions most people might consider "governmental." Of the "Plan, Organize, Staff, Direct and Control" imperatives," Direct" and "Control" are the only two that might qualify as governmental contributions from the Judiciary.

The conclusion we draw is that the Framers needed broad public acceptance of their three-branch internal check-and-balance system to head off demands by The People for closer oversight of government, a risk their Monarchy Republic creation couldn't tolerate. To keep all oversight activities within the confines of government, they needed participation from a third branch of government to sell the public on the efficacy of their in-government check-and-balance concept. The unelected Judiciary, the blood-brother of the huge lawyer faction, included in the three-branch check-and-balance structure would never be a threat to the two elected branches, Congress and the Executive branch. The Judiciary was well regarded by citizens, lending credence to the plan. The Judiciary fit, albeit less than perfectly, into their "monarchy republic" scheme.

The bulk of elected persons in the Legislative branch were lawyers. By elevating the unelected and lawyer-populated Judicial branch into the nation's check-and-balance structure, they made sure that the friendly lawyer faction would dominate government. Ability to structure legislation in a manner that conveyed long-term benefit to the legal profession was no small self-serving matter. Even in an egalitarian society, some are always more equal than others.

SECTION 1
FRAMER DECISIONS RESPECTING THE JUDICIARY

IINFLUENCES THAT AFFECTED DECISIONS

The Framers were not far removed in time from the early democracies that had replaced and assumed power from their monarchy predecessors. The Framers were keenly aware of strong citizen resentment of monarchical abuses. Memories were raw about the tyranny to which they, as colonists under English rule, had been subjected.

It is worth harkening back to previous discussions concerning the Framers' 1780s-era perception about the "right kind" of government. **They created a "Monarchy Republic," which they called simply a "republic." It was a label that describes a democratically-elected and internally managed ruling assembly system possessing monarchical power and granted virtual immunity from accountability.** They dump-delegated power and authority over everything in sight on to the new Monarchy Republic, even going so far as giving it power to manufacture the rules under which its elected assemblies would operate. They purloined from The People and gave to their Monarchy Republic all the ownership rights and powers that inherently belong to the citizen/owners of a nation, *even going so far as denying The People the right to amend their own constitution.*

The citizens were given one pitiful sop …. the right to elect or discharge politicians via the ballot box.

Lord Acton, a 19th century British politician, is credited with coining the famous credo "Power corrupts, and absolute power corrupts absolutely." Many interpret that to be a statement about poor democratic leader morals and ethics, but "even the most moral leader will succumb to corruption if that course is open before him."

But Acton's observation is, in fact, a fundamental principle to be taken into account in the choice of form of government. It pinpoints the reason totalitarianism is to be avoided. Monarchy Republics are democratic government structures that utilize principles we would now label "totalitarian." Applying Lord Acton's credo, approval of such structures carries an engraved invitation for The People to experience the abusive power of absolute authority.

The government system created by the Framers did expose elected officials to the vagaries of elections. So, yes, there was a ballot box re-election sword placed in the hands of the voters. **However, the political party quickly became the focus of elections, not the candidates themselves**. By giving political parties wide power in government and prominence in elections, the ballot box sword that threatened elected officials shriveled to the size of a small pocket knife.

The heart and soul of the Framer Monarchy Republic was the power of its Houses of Congress to "set the rules of their proceeding." Out of that power flowed rules befitting a Monarchy Republic. The Nation's titular leader, the President, was granted extremely limited authority, reflecting the Framer fear of an elected leader powerful enough to throw a monkey wrench into the gearbox of their Monarchy Republic creation.

The Framer internal check-and-balance scheme, of each branch of government second-guessing the actions of two other branches, requiring that one branch be an independent judicial system that interpreted the laws written by the elected representatives while acting as a "justice system" that The People would regard as an ethical element.

To facilitate their three-branch internal check-and-balance concept, **The Framers elevated the non-elected Judicial System to the level of the two elected branches, crowning it the third branch of government**. The Judiciary is an official government service system that adjudicates legal messes flowing out of human activity within government's less-than-perfect framework of laws**. It** has no direct accountability to The People. It is not a democratic governing body and, therefore, is no domination threat to the political elite who run the Monarchy Republic.

Lawyers dominated the Framer group. The Judiciary is staffed by lawyers. The nation's elected assemblies are dominated by lawyers. That could not have had anything to do with the decision to include the Judiciary in this weird three-branch internal check-and-balance concept, could it?

Nah, not likely! The Framers wouldn't do a thing like that, would they?

STRUCTURE OF THE AMERICAN JUDICIAL SYSTEM

Article 111 of the Constitution, and Amendments 1V, V, V1, V11, V111, and X1, contain provisions concerning the Judicial System. The system is referred to as Federal to distinguish it from those of the various States.

This Framer construct granted to Congress the power to designate and instigate inferior courts, both District Courts and U.S. Courts of Appeal. Congress oversees selection and appointment of justices through a Senate confirmation process.

The Federal Judiciary today consists of 94 district-level trial courts, 13 courts of appeal, two specialized courts, and finally, the Supreme Court. Various States of the Union maintain their own court system, which operates separate and apart from the Federal system. Many State judges are elected rather than being appointed.

Courts are given the sole power to interpret the law and apply it. Inferior courts are constrained by rulings of higher courts and the Supreme Court, with which they are required to comply.

The Supreme Court is an appellate court, the final arbiter of the meaning of law.

JUDICIAL BRANCH STAFFING

Nothing is said in the Constitution about the number of Justices that comprise the Supreme Court, an endless political controversy in this Nation. Early Supreme Courts were lower in the number of Justices, but since 1869 the number has been nine, **set by Congress**. The number of Justices is properly a policy decision of The People, a rule that should be enshrined in the constitution. There is nothing rational about it being a subject of frequent political controversy and attempted political manipulation.

As stated earlier, the Judiciary is the only government branch in the three-branch check-and-balance system where seated members are not elected. Judges have no fixed term of employment, a concept intended to give them "insulation against public passion." They can be removed by impeachment in a Senate process identical to that used against Presidents. Death or retirement are the only other termination routes. Federal judges, at their own discretion, may serve for life.

HOW WELL DID THE FRAMERS DO WHEN DELEGATING POWERS TO THE JUDICIARY?

Framer delegation-of-authority mis-steps are often discussion topics in various Chapters. Those missteps set in place in the House of Representatives the Accountability Gap that undergirds its dismal performance. The missteps are repeated in Constitutional delegation of powers to the Judiciary.

However, there are significant differences between the Legislative and Judicial branches, both in role and function, differences that have dampened down the negative impact on Judicial branch performance of those conceptual improprieties. The single accountability to The People by an elected Legislative branch is through the ballot box, but the unelected Judicial branch is accountable to no one. The limited public exposure of its players and the narrow role of the Judiciary work to shield it from scrutiny. **In violation of every known rule of organization or management, or of democracy, the judicial branch is under no obligation to report to The People or to any government institution.**

The Framers set no standards of performance for the Judiciary and did not require any other branch of government to do so. A prominent feature of Framer "dump-delegation" is the absence of performance standards, which are, of course, the basis for establishing accountability. The Judicial branch, like the elected assemblies, is totally self-managed. While we know that many decisions are made in its various courts, including the Supreme Court, we don't know how efficient court operations are, how promptly decisions are rendered, and have no means by which to evaluate the quality of those decisions. Thinking citizens suspect that this branch of government is no different from the others and fear that if the curtains of secrecy are drawn back, ugly truths will be revealed.

It was in their effort to shield members of the Judiciary from public retribution for unpopular decisions, viewed by many as an essential shield, that the Framers created a singular problem for The People. Guaranteed life-time employment "during good behavior," with never a pay reduction, is not warranted for any government employee, but judges were granted that. "For every complex problem, there exists an obvious and simple solution, and it's dead wrong!" Judges are important, but not that important.

We do know that the Supreme Court annually selects for review 150 cases out of 7,500 that apply for writ of certiorari, which calculates mathematically to 2% of submissions. The decision as to which cases will be heard is made by vote of Supreme Court members without public disclosure. Citizens **have no idea whether the Court selects the cases most important to the nation. There is no check-and-balance, no visibility, and no secondary review of this critical, highest-level decision process.**

SECTION 2
POLITICS AND THE JUDICIARY

INDEPENDENCE IS A CORNERSTONE OF CITIZEN TRUST IN THE JUDICIARY

In a democracy that fosters immense political party involvement in government, designating the Judiciary an arm of government is totally inappropriate, an arrangement guaranteed to generate controversy. That Framer action, when constructing their three-branch check-and-balance system, probably was contrived to advantageously align the judiciary more closely with the lawyer-heavy Congress, for the long-term benefit of the legal profession.

Court officials are appointed, not elected. Courts are an official service-and-control mechanism that serves The People by adjudicating legal messes stemming from human activity under government's less-than-perfect framework of laws.

The Judiciary is more a function of The People than it is a functional companion to government. Instead of being postured as part of government, it should be another watchdog over government, assigned the additional duty of exercising quality control over government's huge jumble of laws.

Above all other considerations, its independence from the political system is a "must."

There is general agreement that trustworthy and unbiased courts are essential to a successful democracy.

For courts to be respected by the citizenry, they must be viewed as independent in their judgments. The mental picture conjured up by the old motto "Justice is Blind" is one of a judicial system representative of our ethical and moral values of fairness, truthfulness, and honesty. To meet that test, members of the judiciary cannot be encumbered by political bias. Chapter 2 discusses the importance of "trust" in holding together a self-government democracy and highlights the problems degradation of the "trust" factor is causing today. An independent Judiciary is an important element of public trust.

But, in a democracy where the selection of judges falls under the jurisdiction of elected Senators, all of whom are hard-core party faithful and many of whom are lawyers, striving for political advantage always over-rides reason, judgment, and the needs of the nation. The recent Barret confirmation hearings evidenced the truth of that statement. In our vaunted democratic republic, where the judicial system is the likely final arbiter of policy questions that have been defaulted by the Legislative branch, history is replete with parables of politicians seeking to warp the judiciary to achieve party goals.

The political party view, that judges are an important political asset, leads to endless controversy and battles in the Media about the appointment and approval of Federal judges, but also about the rulings of judges before whom important disputes have been placed. The impact of those public arguments on citizen trust has apparently never been measured.

To summarize, the judiciary is expected to be independent, unbiased and non-political, yet the selection of judges is a matter of extreme political importance. Seating of sympathetic judges is the goal of every political party.

The People's interest, which is the only interest that counts, is best served by a non-political judiciary staffed with judges who will render unbiased decisions. Nonetheless, judicial rulings continue to reflect the political bias of the region in which the judge or jury is located, making it a prominent factor in venue selection for important trials.

Political party actions, related to the Judiciary, run contrary to the best interests of The People.

Granting political parties, a place in government is a virtual guaranty of a biased judiciary.

This book proposes that judges be geographically relocated every few years. However, if the justice system is made a component of the Constitutional Authorities, and if political parties are outlawed, relocation may no longer be necessary.

POLARIZED POLITICAL BEHAVIOR HAS BROADENED THE ROLE OF THE JUDICIARY

Extension of the judicial role to prosecution of "political crimes" in many democracies (Egypt, Brazil, Ukraine, and more recently, the U.S.) emanates from extreme and frequently emotional polarized political aggression. Our Republic, in the past decade, has seen more than its share of that behavior.

Polarization degrades the functioning of democracy. One observable side-effect is the judiciary's growing prominence in disputes, as judges extend their decision-making into areas that, under our organization of government, are clearly the responsibility of the non-performing and abdicative Legislative branches. As the contribution of the Legislative branches to governance has receded, the prominence of the Judiciary is rulings that "write law" has grown proportionally. Abstention or mis-behavior of one branch of government is inevitably the cause of immense pressure on another, producing unintended reactional consequences.

> "As the courts ascended and Congress descended, the American people responded. They began to do the logical thing. They concentrated their efforts on the seats of real power in the U.S., the federal court-houses. They turned to litigation over legislation because they know that the law requires the courts to respond."

The above quotes author Walter Russell Mead, who wrote a Wall Street Journal article of June 30, 2020, entitled "The Global Political Pandemic." Further quoting that article, "Once political polarization leads to the politicization, real or perceived, of judicial and police institutions, democratic decline can become acute and life-threatening." There are strong indications our Nation has reached that critical departure point.

The constitutional confrontation between the political party system and our Nation's need for an independent judiciary reaches its zenith whenever the opportunity to place a new Justice on the Supreme Court presents itself. **For a political party, a Supreme Court with a majority of Justices sympathetic to its point of view is the ultimate advantage**. Another way of saying that is "The goal of every political party is a Supreme Court politically biased in its favor."

A POLITICALLY-BIASED SUPREME COURT IS OBVIOUSLY NOT BIASED IN FAVOR OF THE PEOPLE

We will not here, repeat the endless history of political activity relating to the Supreme Court. Interested readers can readily access that on-line, perhaps the most interesting tidbits being accounts of threats or efforts to "pack the Supreme Court" by expanding the number of Justices. That is relevant history because, in the wake of a November 2020 seating of a new Justice, political party threats of just such an effort have again blared their ugly rhetoric over the airwaves. That our justice system should be vulnerable to political party manipulation for political purposes, proof of both an ineffective Constitution and the endless degradation of the nation by political parties. A revised constitution will contain rules eliminating that risk, as manufactured controversies are senseless and destructive.

Those accounts highlight the requirement that a critical foundation of our democracy, Justice, be positioned totally outside the scope of political party influence. Justice is a fundamental requirement of The People. Dedicated to The People, it cannot at the same time be an instrument of governance or the play-pen of political parties.

Alexander Hamilton, in The Federalist Papers #78, made several cogent observations concerning the Judicial System. Political interference in the judiciary was a concern, even back in the 1780s:

> "There is no liberty if the power of judging be not separated from the legislative and executive powers."

> "The Judiciary, by the nature of its functions, will always be the least dangerous to the political rights of the Constitution."

> "Complete independence of the Courts of Justice is particularly essential in a limited Constitution."

SECTION 3
THE PROBLEM OF AN OBSOLETE CONSTITUTION

SHOULD CONSTITUTIONAL INTERPRETATION BE BASED UPON CURRENT MEANING?

There is argument today concerning the question of how the Supreme Court should interpret the Constitution. Should interpretations be based on the original Framer intent, or should they be based on current meaning?

The oft-quoted Pew Research Center Survey[45] reports that a 55% majority of Americans now say rulings should be based on what the constitution means in current times, while 41% say the rulings should be based on the constitution as originally written. That statistic can be interpreted to mean that a majority of Americans consider our Constitution obsolete.

For deep thinkers, the controversy raises the real question: "Why are we discussing this at all?" This is silly!! The real issue is, "Why is our constitution not current?" **Obviously, if the constitution was current, its rules would provide the answer, discussion finished!**

Trying to govern the most active country on earth using an obsolete constitution is comparable to trying to win the Indianapolis 500 driving a 1903 Model T.

Primary efforts of The People need to be focused on bringing the Constitution current. Upon achieving that, most of the controversies of our day (including the above interpretation question) will be "gone, gone, like the landlord's smile" of country/western music fame. What an improvement that would be!

---

[45] Pew Research Center, April 2018, The Public, the Political System, and American Democracy., P. 84

WHY ARE WE FACING AN ABSTRACT ARGUMENT OF THAT NATURE?

Baseline materials for this book, referred to frequently, are the five duties of ownership and rules about delegation of authority. "Direct" is one of the five responsibilities of ownership. The People's direction is contained in the Constitution, the purpose of which is to establish the rules under which government and citizens operate. If the Constitution is unclear or obsolete, the nation's sense of direction and cohesion disappears, and argument becomes the order of the day. The People's obligation to provide The People with clear fundamental instructions falls under their "direct" duty, a responsibility of immense importance.

The lack of a current constitution is the source of the intense political activity surrounding the Supreme Court, its membership and make-up. **Supreme Court rulings often provide fundamental direction to the nation that is not contained in the Constitution, and concerning which the legislative branches are unwilling to promote Amendment.** The Supreme Court tries, but as they say on the farm, "That's all a steer can do."

The People have no direct means to amend the Constitution, so they are constitutionally denied any ability to clear up controversy by clarifying provisions or providing fundamental direction. The political elite, who control the means to amend, argue loudly about how to interpret it and work to pack the Supreme Court, **BUT MAKE NO MOVE TO UPDATE OUR CRITICAL DOCUMENT, THE CONSTITUTION**.

WHY DO THE POLITICAL ELITE NOT FULFILL THEIR MORAL AND ETHICAL RESPONSIBILITY?

The political elite want to continue operating in the murk of an obsolete Constitution because it affords them great latitude and provides them with a shield. The political elite do not want the Constitution amended. We know that because if they did, a great number of amendments to update would long ago have been completed. **Not to bring the constitution current is a self-serving decision by the political elite to assure their undisturbed retention of Monarchy Republic.**

Updating the constitution would put the Monarchy Republic at risk. If the long list of pressing constitutional issues is ever formally addressed, pointed questions are likely to be raised about the lack of government contribution and its chronic dysfunction. That would open for public discussion the role and function of political parties, the notion of the Monarchy Republic itself, and a range of other questions that would make political stomachs squirm. Such a threat causes politicians to shout, "Leave the Constitution alone, fellow Party Member!"

Given political elite unwillingness and citizen inability to deal with anything constitutional, questions of a constitutional nature are automatically relegated to endless argument in Government. As has been discussed, no party or elected persons will accept the risk of doing what is necessary to amend the Constitution, so any such constitutional question is automatically once more delegated down the chain of command, this time to the Judicial System, then elevated uphill to the Supreme Court.

The buck-passing charade ultimately lands the constitutional question on the table of the Supreme Court, a place where no party can control the outcome. **That explains the intense political effort to pre-pack the Supreme Court with Justices who will make decisions sympathetic to the party point of view.**

By this convoluted process, the political elite have managed to anchor their position, protect the party system and their Monarchy Republic, and avoid voting risky decisions which may invoke accountability to the voters. They have diverted the public's focus by arguing abstract questions, in which futile exercise brilliant Media pundits and outspoken voters loudly and willingly participate. The nation, while this is going on, continues speeding down the road in its 1903 Ford.

In this complex world, for the political elite that's not a bad outcome!

SECTION 4
A BRIEF ASSESSMENT OF THE JUDICIARY

WHAT IS THE PUBLIC'S OPINION OF THE SUPREME COURT?

The American public, in the 2018 Pew survey, viewed the Supreme Court favorably 62% versus 38% unfavorably[46]. The survey makes the observation that party members change their view based on whether or not an important recent Court decision has gone their way. Even in evaluating the Supreme Court, political party considerations warp ethical judgment and public responsibility.

The 2018 citizen favorable and unfavorable opinion of the Supreme Court percentages are roughly similar to those of 1985, so it is probable that the 62% favorable percentage is a reliable public opinion measure. The measure is both good news and bad news. The good news is that it is somewhat reassuring to know the Supreme Court is, on balance, viewed favorably. The bad news is **that a 62% favorable rating has all the allure of a cold cup of coffee. 100% favorable would make the coffee hot!**

---

[46] Pew Research Center April 2018, "The Public, the Political System, and American Democracy"

In the order of things, the Judicial System is not the most pressing matter in our turmoil of governance. It is far from perfect, but quality of justice is not at the top of the Nation's current pressing problem list. The likelihood of a catastrophe in the Judiciary appears low. Its performance shortfalls are the consequence of management dysfunction in the court system, which would evaporate with establishment of accountability. **That the Judicial System requires a rigorous independent evaluation and changes made, is obvious.** However, it will not be possible to fairly evaluate the Judicial System until it is severed from political influence, so that it can be rigorously examined on a stand-alone basis.

That Supreme Court decisions are influenced by politics is another "good-news/bad-news" story. The bad news is Supreme Court decisions are influenced by politics; the good news is at least decisions were made because without the Supreme Court there would have been no decisions of consequence made at all.

> An important question is "Does our judicial system need renovation, or is the problem the political parties?" The clear answer is "Although the judicial system needs renovation, the real problem is the political parties."

CONCLUSIONS AND THOUGHTS

This book focuses relentlessly on the need to make improved decision-making the strategy for upgrading our government. It suggests a variety of new approaches, introducing total control by The People over the nation's decision process, identifying decision-making processes and organizations that are not functioning, and suggesting relocation of decision points. The Judicial System holds a prominent place on the nation's list of decision-makers.

It exists to make the legal decisions required by the citizens. The proposed Constitutional Authorities (of which the Justice System will be a part) will have the responsibility over court operations and will upgrade activities that produce decisions. They must undertake the broad and thorough evaluation and upgrading effort. The first required action is to get Constitutional Authorities anchored in place.

WHAT ISSUES ARISE CONCERNING THE JUDICIAL SYSTEM?

The flow of justice through the system is very slow, which would seem reflective of a lack of performance accountability, a fatal defect imbedded in all Framer-conceived governance structures. Legal decisions often demand repeated outside information research and submissions, so there is probably some justification for the slow pace of justice. More likely, however, slow legal decisions are the rule because there is no sense of urgency within the system, nobody to enforce accountability. It lacks a system butt-kicker.

a) The judicial system should not be permitted to set its own verdict timing standards. Those should be set either constitutionally or controlled by Constitutional Authorities and become one of the first bases for establishing accountability at the court level.

b) Judges should be geographically relocated on a rotating basis to relieve them from local political pressures, to which few are immune. See earlier comments on this topic.

c) A Constitutional plan should be devised for monitoring and overseeing the work of the courts. The activities and performance of every judge should receive the same independent evaluation.

d) An after-the-fact feedback system from citizens who utilize the court system, focused on identifying unacceptable practices, is needed.

e) A number of courts have a reputation for cozy, club-like relationships with the legal profession, maintained at the cost of good public service. The relationship of the legal profession to the Judicial System should be ruthlessly scoured.

f) As long as political parties exist., evaluation for political bias in decisions should be a most important basis for judicial accountability

g) The first judgment concerning every matter placed before the Supreme Court must be answering the question, "Is this the proper body to make this decision?" Many issues placed before the Supreme Court for adjudication are national policy matters, which, in a self-governed democracy, should be decided by The People. To improve Government decision-making, ensuring that decisions are made in the proper jurisdiction is a matter of utmost importance, one that affords an opportunity for great improvement.

h) This author takes the position that the Supreme Court should not decide what cases it will adjudicate out of the 7500 cases offered annually for writ of certiorari. That practice is cut out of the same bolt of cloth as the one giving each Legislative branch the right to "determine the rules of its proceedings."

Our recommendation, discussed in various parts of this book, is that the Guardians of the Constitution be given responsibility to rule who shall make required decisions, whether the decisions be in government or in the Judiciary. Each decision under consideration by the Supreme Court should be screened by the Guardians and, if necessary, re-routed to the decision body most appropriate to decide the matter in question.

Requests for writ of certiorari probably is the most consequential list of potential problems in the nation. The fact that only 2% are responded to by the Supreme

Court is troubling, in that 98% go unanswered. What is more troubling, however, is the realization that most of the requests stem from skipped decisions in the Legislative branch.

It is suspected that a very large percentage of the unanswered requests stem from grossly inadequate legal codes, which indicates that orders to correct the law should be issued to the Assemblies as a part of the President's Decision and Legislation planning. **The list of requests for Writ of Certiorari should be the first document reviewed by the planners who compile the two-year Decision and Legislation plan.**

i)   The Supreme Court should be the appointed guardian of the Nation's legal code, responsible to see that it is in first-class, up-to-date condition. The Court should be given authority to require that Assemblies repair legal codes found incomplete, conflicting, difficult to interpret, or out-of-date.

The trove of legislated code and case law must be organized for the convenience of The People and made readily available to them. People believe the legal code is currently organized to generate work for the legal profession. Citizens should be able to research (and understand) current law on any topic without having to hire a lawyer to research case law for comprehension.

The useability and accessibility of the Nation's legal codes should be the third basis for Supreme Court accountability.

j)   The number of Justices on the Supreme Court should be permanently set by the Constitution at nine or some other number. Let's decide it, put it to rest, and never again have to listen to politicians arguing that matter.

k)   Lifetime employment for jurists is an extremely suspect policy. A mandatory retirement age of 75 (or whatever other number is voted appropriate) should be established. Screening judges from retaliation has produced the unintended consequence of screening them from accountability, never a good thing. Regular rotation and creating openings for more talented people, is a better policy.

n)   **Justices and judges should be retained solely on the basis of competence.**

To guaranty high quality jurists, a Constitutional program of rating all judges annually and mandatory termination of the bottom 1% (or some other selected number) at stated intervals is one way to produce a very beneficial scouring effect. Such a proposal would be the fourth basis for establishing accountability.

Those are but a few of the more-obvious areas needing resolution. That they exist at all speaks to Constitutional entropy and tells us why the public gives the Judicial branch a luke-warm 62% favorable rating.

Pressure on the court system signals non-performance elsewhere in governance. Government confusion, avoidance of decision responsibilities, lack of pinpointed accountability, political party antagonistic activities, internal management problems, and a host of others end up affecting the Judicial system.

Efficiency in government can be dramatically improved by focusing on identifying those and rooting out their causes. Huge reductions in government turmoil and expense are available if The People are willing to tackle this high-priority challenge.

The People must eliminate obvious problem areas before performing a comprehensive evaluation of the court system. A substantial reduction in Judicial System case-load is possible.

Unlike the Legislative branch, the Judicial System is not a totally failed system.

SECTION 5
SUMMARY AND ACTION PROPOSALS

IMPROVING JUDICIAL BRANCH PERFORMANCE

As long as political parties are granted unwarranted deference, elimination of political interference with the judiciary will not be possible. Political interference with the judiciary is a standard self-serving political party activity.

There are three ways to resolve the conflict, a) Eliminate political parties, or b) Move the Judicial branch outside of the sphere and influence of government, or c) Combine both actions.

This book proposes that political parties be outlawed in our Nation or that a to-be-formed Constitutional Authority, the Guardians of the Constitution, be granted Constitutional power to regulate political parties out of existence. Enactment of either of those solutions is not by any means assured. Government today is controlled by politicians who are members of political parties, which is their primary allegiance. The media is in alliance with both political parties. About two-thirds of voters of our nation are members of a political party, and seem generally willing to let political parties guide their thinking. Recent studies indicate that 62% of citizens favor changes in the fundamental design and structure of American government, but we don't know what percentage of them understand the political party threat or would support their control or elimination.

MOVE THE JUDICIAL BRANCH AWAY FROM GOVERNMENT, INSTALL IT IN THE CONSTITUTIONAL AUTHORITIES

Placing the Judicial system within Constitutional Authorities, and designating it an element of Constitutional Vital Infrastructure, will place it where corrective action can begin immediately. No longer would government or politicians be involved in anything concerning the Judicial System. Administrative oversight responsibilities associated with the change will be minimal for the Guardians of the Constitution, well within their capability.

This placement will enhance the ability of the Guardians to monitor and manage the decision process within the nation's Authority Structure, actions vital to improving decision quality. The Supreme Court has inappropriately but necessarily made policy decisions, and removing from its jurisdiction a plethora of matters of that nature will free up its time for important matters it has foregone in the past. Further, all litigation regarding elections will be removed from judicial calendars and placed under the jurisdiction of the People's Election Commission.

The launch of control by The People, by development of a new Constitution, and creation of the Guardians of the Constitution and other Constitutional Authorities to execute on behalf of The People are likely to receive the support of The People, who lack trust in government, and because of a large negative percentage change in the People's support of government.

The Constitutional Authorities made up of Infrastructure bodies free of political influence and instituted solely to be control organizations, is the ideal location for the Judicial system and more reflective of its mission. It is an instrument of The People, an organization that exists for their protection. The Judiciary will be an excellent companion to another basic control instrument, the planned People's Election Commission, also a vital activity that will function properly if isolated from political exposure.

Transferring The People's Judicial System from government to Constitutional Authorities will leave a gap in the three-branch system of government designed by the Framers, **rendering that Framer check-and-balance concept obsolete.**

THE LEGAL PROFESSION

It isn't possible to discuss the Judicial System without venturing into the no-man's-land of the legal profession, just as it is not possible to discuss Congress without examining the effects of the legal profession's extreme influence.

The legal profession has an incestuous influence on the creation of law because the workings of the law is the source of that profession's revenue. **It has an outsized influence in the two Houses of Congress, which were granted power to set their own procedures and operations. The legal profession, therefore should receive the blame for that institution's non-performance and bad reputation.** It has an incestuous influence on the Judiciary because it provides the people who become judges, and that is where it conducts its business.

Law is the predominant profession in Congress. In the 117th Congress, 32% of House members and 33% of Senators had JD degrees.[47] Participating in legislative decisions does not require a law degree, it demands intelligence, broad knowledge, and excellent judgment. The legal assistance needed to fashion and construct law to implement legislative decisions can be secured by contract with outside firms.

It is fair to guess that the legal profession may be the most influential profession in America. Little is undertaken without a lawyer being involved. Business practice has most if its foundation in law. That is not to say that the profession's influence has been all positive. The profession's guiding hand lies behind much of what is done in government, but its contribution to the history of our legislative heritage is marred by poor management practices and poor organization. The influence of this dominant political faction on the procedures utilized in Congress and its introduction of the "contention" process of the Houses are examples.

Which brings us to considering the effects created by the over-balance of lawyers in Congress. What is right about permitting legal profession dominance there? It is a "faction" with self-interest predominating. Why is "affirmative action" not being enforced? Is the legal profession imbalance a major cause of our current legislative non-performance, and the horrendously negative view of Congress present among The People? One way of looking at it is, if Congress is failing, then how can the legal profession avoid blame? It factionally dominates Congress!

And then, there is the profession's control over the Judicial System where virtually all participants are lawyers. If there ever were system elements plagued by inbreeding, the judiciary and government are prominent

---

[47] American Bar Association, Governmental Affairs Office Publication

Our interest is focused on government, where talent distribution staffing decisions will be needed for the make-up of government decision bodies, including the Judiciary and the assemblies. It is suggested that lawyer count should be limited to 3% of a government assembly.

The rules must be: Don't allow factions in assemblies because intellectual justification favors equitable distribution. Use legal talents for those things where such talents can strongly contribute, but do not become the victim of its negative propensities. Steer them away from organization and process decisions.

CHAPTER 14

THE PEOPLE'S DIRECTION AND CONTROL: PART 1

CONTENT:

SECTION 1: THE PEOPLE AND THEIR GOVERNMENT: A VITAL RESTRUCTURE OF THAT RELATIONSHIP

SECTION 2: SELF-GOVERNMENT DEMANDS THAT THE PEOPLE PERFORM THEIR RESPONSIBILITIES

SECTION 3: PUTTING THE PEOPLE IN CONTROL OF THE CONSTITUTION

SECTION 4: REVISING THE NATION'S "AUTHORITY STRUCTURE"

SECTION 5: THE WELL-INFORMED ELECTORS

SECTION 6: COMPONENTS OF THE CONSTITUTIONAL AUTHORITIES

FOREWORD

*The duties and obligations of owners, to Plan, Organize, Staff, Direct and Control, are responsibilities The People must fulfill if they intend to conduct democratic self-government. **The assumption underlying this Book is that The People do so intend.** That being the case, The People would be wise to make the substantial effort to ensure their self-government is the very best they can achieve. Success isn't going to come easy, but the success rewards will be mind-boggling.*

In self-government, The People decide the important issues. Being a huge body for decision-making, The People of our nation will need an electronic voting channel and will then vote only on carefully constructed questions. As we intend to be a self-governed democracy, no matter how difficult or complex, and methods will have to be developed that allow The People to fulfill their owner responsibilities. Voting is the way of a democracy.

"Direct Democracy," a form of government in which critical and fundamental decisions are made by The People and not by elected representatives, is a vastly superior democratic authority process. It is difficult to carry out operationally, revealing why early democracies turned to utilizing problem some representatives instead. Since that time, technology has dramatically broadened the capabilities that make direct democracy possible, however.

Tasks and requirements that are complex or unwieldy for a large group of citizens will require the assistance of special purpose elected bodies we call "Constitutional Authorities." Decisions will be made by The People. The Constitutional Authorities will be the managers of the processes by which that takes place, and the implementers of The Peoples' decisions.

Some owner responsibilities, such as Organizing and Controlling, can't be carried out by a huge body of citizens. Those responsibilities require smaller groups to do what the huge mass of The People cannot, but the nation's critical decisions must still be voted by The People.

The Framers arranged government into three branches and set them up to check-and-balance each other. This book strongly recommends the utilization of Constitutional Authorities for vastly-improved People-directed check-and-balance. The Government of the United States, streamlined, upgraded and tightly controlled, will continue its function, albeit modified substantially to eliminate dysfunctional attributes.

When Constitutional Authorities have been formed to carry out The People's will, true "government of the People, by the People and for the People" will finally exist in this nation.

The People will have installed the vital authority functions that are their responsibility. They will also have re-located, for better placement within The People's Constitutional Authorities, certain vital operations that should not be a part of government.

Remember the oft-stated planner's credo: "For every complex problem, there exists an obvious and simple solution, and it is dead wrong!" Constitutional Authorities are not a simple organization solution, that is certain. They are designed solely to assist The People in carrying out self-government, and to ensure that the nation's overall Authority Structure functions exactly as The People intend.

If the organization needed to accomplish that is complex, the complexity is the price of a well-conceived democratic self-government.

SECTION 1
THE PEOPLE AND THEIR GOVERNMENT: A VITAL RESTRUCTURE OF THAT RELATIONSHIP

Our Republic is "owned" by The People. That isn't often the subject of public discussion, muted and directed as our nation is by its Political Elite, aided by its Media. With a little thought, readers can divine the reasons why that is so.

The ownership of the Nation by The People is a truth that has been in place from the very beginning. It was formally stated in the second paragraph of the Declaration of Independence. Following is the relevant text:

"That to secure these rights governments are instituted among Men, deriving their just powers from the consent of the governed, and that whenever any Form of Government becomes destructive of these ends, it is the Right of the People to alter or to abolish it."

Understanding that The People have the right to alter or abolish government is necessarily followed by an examination of the implications of ownership. The second paragraph of the Declaration of Independence quoted above states that, as owners, The People have the right to make changes to the form of government they have established if they find it no longer functions as required. That brilliant insight from long ago has astonishing application today. What The People must do as owners is as clear as a bell!

In the years elapsed since the Declaration, the principles of authority that govern working relationships within human organizations of the business and civic community have been defined and refined. The changes to our form of government suggested herein will methodically employ those established principles.

OWNERS POSSESS ALL FUNDAMENTAL RIGHTS AND OBLIGATIONS

Modern management/ownership utilizes generally-accepted truths concerning organizations.[48] "Plan, Organize, Staff, Direct, and Control" are the terms used in management texts to define the responsibilities of ownership. In self-government, to assure government functionality the owners of the nation have the obligation to fulfill those responsibilities. **If they do not do so, they are not practicing self-government. Furthermore, if the owners do not correct government dysfunctionality, it is unlikely it will be corrected!**

If owners decide to hire managers to carry out functions on their behalf, they must decide what owner rights and obligations and/or how much of them they will delegate to their hired management. To fulfill their "control" obligation, the owners must also decide how to harness their hired management, to hold them accountable for the performance of their responsibilities.

---

[48] Principles of Management, Koonts and O'Donnell

WE HAVE BEEN TAUGHT THAT THE PEOPLE, IN THEIR RELATIONSHIP WITH GOVERNMENT, FILL TWO SEPARATE AND DISTINCT ROLES

Clarity of thought is critical for owner/citizens of a self-governing nation. Please consider the implications of the following:

The People (as a group) are the owners of our nation. In a self-governed nation, the citizens as a group will conduct themselves as owners and perform the ownership functions.

The People (as individuals) are the citizens of our nation. They have been taught as citizens to subjugate themselves to the government they created. The "consent of the governed" rule is very real. **However, our Constitution-created government is not self-government by The People.** Described by our Framers as a "republic," it is more accurately called ''a Monarchy Republic." As citizens of a Monarchy, The People are given no way or means to conduct themselves as owners. Accordingly, they resignedly subjugate themselves to the ministrations of the political elite.

It is interesting that the topic of "equality" is never a part of discussions about the relationship between The People and the Elected Persons in government. In our nation, equality between The People and the Elected Persons does not exist. Citizens are treated as, and taught to behave as, "subjects." Elected Persons behave as "political elite" and view The People as subjects. **One prominent politician famously used the term "deplorables" to describe The People!**

Being "subjects" is a totally inappropriate posture, if that posture is assumed by the owners of our nation. Since elected persons are "hired management," treating them as political elite is also totally inappropriate.

One might assume a considerable amount of re-education will be required to alter this behavior, but in actuality, installing this book's suggested roles, functions, and organization will promptly clear up that confusion. Changes in behavior will be instantaneous and very noticeable.

SECTION 2
SELF-GOVERNMENT DEMANDS THE PEOPLE PERFORM THEIR RESPONSIBILITIES

Elected Persons who collectively perform governance in our nation are The People's "hired management." The role of The People as owners and the role of elected persons as hired management, is the topic of discussion here. If The People decide to hire management to conduct functions of governance on their behalf, the power they delegate to that hired management must be clearly defined and balanced with performance accountability **That is a fundamental principle of authority delegation, as practiced in our nation's organizations today.**

CERTAIN RESPONSIBILITIES of the owners of our nation **MAY NOT BE DELEGATED to the hired management.**

Following are authorities and responsibilities The People **may never delegate**, must always retain unto themselves, and are obligated to perform:

Defining the beliefs, values and fundamental rules of the Nation.

Defining the rights, duties, responsibilities, and obligated involvement of citizens.

Defining the nation's Authority Structure; its form of government, its political process, its election system, its judicial system, and others.

Defining the authorities and responsibilities delegated to Government.

Designing, monitoring and controlling the Authority Structure decision process.

Defining the nation's Forms of Economic and Civic Organization.

Determining the goals of the nation, and establishing its controls, particularly those that are financial.

Identifying threats to the nation and its selected form of government, and constructing defenses against those threats.

Planning and instituting the Constitutional Authorities needed to implement The People's wishes, and to ensure the Nation and its government function as The People intend.

Writing the Constitution that documents the owner decisions, and keeping it current. Ensuring that document clearly instructs The People's lives and the Nation's self-governance.

By our Constitution, most or all of the fundamental rights and responsibilities of The People, who are the owners of the Nation (specifically those identified above as "May Not Be Delegated") were improperly granted to government by the Framers and were placed under the sole control of the hired management.

We laud the Framers for the many positive things they contributed in constructing our constitution. We curse them for the self-serving, underhanded, and devious actions they undertook to deny The People control over their own government. **Readers should not** forget that the Framers did that while publicly extolling their creation as "Government of the people, by the people, and for the people!" That duplicity exemplifies a serious lack of ethics, always commonplace among elected persons, that was also present among our Framers.

The delegation document, our constitution, was written by the Framers. They, of course, were the premier politicians of their era and, as such, logically expected to be elected to dominant positions in the new government. **Predictably, in framing the Constitution, they made it virtually impossible for The People to hold them accountable for performance in their government role. The worst thing that could happen is some might lose an election!**

They accomplished that by granting to government rights and responsibilities that belong solely to The People, a gross self-interest action. They then took away from The People all routes to correct erroneous provisions of the Constitution by corruptly placing The People's Constitutional Amendment alternatives solely under the control of the "hired management."

TO JUSTIFY THEIR ACTIONS, THE FRAMERS USED AN ARGUMENT THAT CONTRADICTS THE DECLARATION OF INDEPENDENCE

Alexander Hamilton, in Federalist #59, describes a principle applied by the Framers in writing the Constitution: **"Every government ought to contain in itself the means of its own preservation."**

This principle is fundamentally sound, and is a strongly supported feature of Constitution 2. The People's difficulty with it flows from who is given the right to exercise the principle. It is a principle that should be exercised by the nation's owners, The People, only.

The principle was used in the construction framework of the Monarchy Republic, which "contained in itself the means of its own preservation." That was accomplished via the convoluted Article. V., which corruptively placed all amendment power in the hands of the political elite.

That construct completely ignores the fact that our government is the creation of The People, who, as the Nation's owners, must make the "preservation decisions." **A monarchy republic government staffed and run by "hired management" must have no inherent right of self-preservation.** The notion that elected officials should hold such a right is ludicrous. The sole owner of that non-delegable right is, and must always be, The People.

The Framer's Article V construction flies directly in the face of the Declaration of Independence statement, "That whenever any Form of Government becomes destructive of these ends, it is the right of the People to alter or to abolish it."

The constitution's grossly excessive delegation of powers to the political elite, a delegation devoid of any personal or institutional accountability, and generally referred to in management as "dump-delegation," is the root cause of today's dysfunctional government. This book, in various chapters, describes dump-delegation in brutal detail and proposes a number of changes to correct that corruption.

> In applying the principle "Every government ought to contain in itself the means of its own preservation," the Framers clearly stated their self-serving purpose, that government should be totally under the control of the political elite, not under the control of The People, and that the political elite should the group to dictate "the means of its own preservation."
>
> **Rather than being a principle of a democratic republic, that is the guiding principle of an authoritarian monarchy.**

SECTION 3
PUTTING THE PEOPLE IN CONTROL OF THE CONSTITUTION

To take control of the Constitution, The People must first establish their right to amend it. Its Article V, which puts forth the routes to amend the constitution, installs the political elite self-preservation principle described by Hamilton. It provides various routes for the hired management to make constitutional amendments, but no route whatsoever for the owners of the nation to do that.

The right to amend the constitution belongs inherently and solely to The People, otherwise they are slaves to their own hired management, a slave condition inherent in monarchies. Hired management possesses no inherent right to amend anything constitutional! No document constructed by elected persons can over-ride the inherent and irrefutable rights of owners unless the owners, by inaction, allow it to be so.

The owners of this nation must document their position that the constitution is the written direction of The People, **not of the political elite.**

THAT BRINGS US TO THE QUESTION OF THE AGES: ARE THE PEOPLE OF THIS NATION CAPABLE OF ESTABLISHING GOOD GOVERNMENT FROM REFLECTION AND CHOICE?

Alexander Hamilton's introductory paragraph to Federalist Paper #1 is worth reviewing. The question Hamilton raised two hundred and forty-odd years ago is still relevant, still unanswered. It is the heart of this book's gut-wrenching discussions, conclusions, and the nation's pressing unmade decisions:

> *"It has been frequently remarked, that it seems to have been reserved to the people of this country, by their conduct and example, to decide the important question, whether societies of men are really capable or not, of establishing good government from reflection and choice, or whether they are forever destined to depend, for their political constitutions, on accident and force."* (Alexander Hamilton)

That question hangs menacingly over our nation and is at the heart of this Book's proposals. Whether it forever remains a question only The People of this nation can resolve, and the sooner they resolve it the better. The People today face making a critical choice, a classic non-programmed choice, from the following alternatives:

1. The People can "Take the Easy Way Out:"

They can continue to muddle along, led by the political parties, searching for a messiah President who might keep their entropy-deteriorated and incoherent government functioning at some minimum level, and hoping that the party system does not first bankrupt the nation or the nation does not first collapse into anarchy.

2. Or, they can "Tackle the Dysfunctional Government Problem, Which Will Probably Involve Pain:"

The People can address the need for Constitutional change head-on, with "reflection and choice," and proceed to create high-performance democratic self-government by remodeling our current dysfunctional system. That route will inevitably bring The People into direct confrontation with the Political Elite, comfortably ensconced as they are in their boxed-in and heavily-guarded Monarchy Republic.

The following examination may be of assistance to readers as they consider the two alternatives.

If The People fail to take charge of the governance of their country by addressing the foundational errors, entropy, and political party abuse that have degraded the Framer-designed system and fail to remove the political-establishment-consecrated activities that are destroying it, The People will have defaulted their ownership responsibilities. **They will have proven that societies of men "are not capable of establishing good government from reflection and choice."**

If The People default on their responsibility, the nation will be "forever destined, for its political constitutions, to depend on accident and force."

This is a challenge probably not many citizens want to face or have the stomach to tackle. Most are accustomed to laying back comfortably, watching the senseless political theatre play out on the television screen, and voting whenever election day comes around, but otherwise, not getting all worked up over the obvious turmoil and incompetence in Washington. They know there's a problem in government but have been trained to look to their favorite political party for a solution. If someone suggests, "We need to restructure the entire government," that person is likely to be met with a blank stare. Citizens don't really understand their government, have never seen organization restructure, and have no idea what needs to be done or where to begin.

Ultimately, how intelligently The People divide responsibility between themselves and their hired management and how intelligently they make necessary changes, give clear direction, and establish the controls to be sure the hired management executes their will determines whether or not they are, in fact, capable of self-government.

HOW LIKELY IS IT THE PEOPLE WILL PERFORM THEIR OWNERSHIP FUNCTIONS?

It is this books conclusion that the People CAN perform the functions of ownership. The larger question, however, is whether they WILL.

A respected non-partisan think-tank called Pew Research Center completed a survey that provides insight. Its 2018 report entitled "The Public, the Political System, and American Democracy[49]" opens with a summary view paragraph worth quoting:

> "Most Americans say democracy is working well in the United States – though relatively few say it is working very well. **At the same time, there is broad support for making sweeping changes to the government system. 61% say "significant changes" are needed in the fundamental "design and structure" of American government to make it work for current times."**

The Pew research supports a conclusion that most Americans are capable of forming an opinion about the performance of government. It suggests also that The People WILL

---

[49] Pew Research Center April 2018, report "The Public, the Political System, and American Democracy

SUPPORT[50] changes to the Constitution that relate to the design and structure of American government.

The People do understand their system of government badly needs significant changes. **There is little reason to believe, however, that The People are sufficiently motivated to undertake such an effort on their own volition. There is also no way of knowing whether they are capable of grasping the complexity of the situation or of evaluating solutions proposed.**

WHAT MIGHT INDUCE THE PEOPLE TO PERFORM THEIR OWNERSHIP RESPONSIBILITIES?

There are two ways by which needed changes to the design and structure of American government might come about:

1. The People undertake change in response to crisis.

Our dumbed-down citizenry is poorly informed and lethargic, extremely vulnerable to the exhortations of their favored political party, and prone to react only to crisis situations. If it is true that they will undertake change only in response to crisis, that is proof "they are forever destined to depend, for their political constitutions, on accident and force."

2. Leadership emerges that convinces The People that change must be undertaken.

Our dumbed-down and lethargic citizenry tends, as they have been trained, to respond to leadership. Unfortunately, available leadership is likely to emanate from the party system, and that kind of leadership will not produce the changes the nation must make. *If the citizenry were to find strong, unbiased leadership, and were able to ignore political parties in their constitutional thinking*, that would signal "they are capable of establishing good government from reflection or choice."

The Pew Research Center survey states 61% of Americans say "significant changes" are needed in the fundamental "design and structure" of American government to make it work for current times. There is, unfortunately, little assurance the change will not result from "accident and force."

A major purpose of this book is to intellectually stimulate "reflection and choice" among citizen/readers. It will use proven management principles to dissect and explain the dysfunction in our democracy. It applies those principles to suggest ways for The People to execute correction. And, it proposes real solutions for consideration.

---

[50] Emphasis by Author

Because self-government is complex, any worth-while solution will also be complex. A great deal of doubt exists as to whether The People are willing to expend the effort needed to comprehend a complex solution. It is apparent that special leadership will be needed to energize The People, leadership that cannot come out of the political party system. It is highly likely that extremely creative use of the Media will be a part of the solution, whether in a positive or negative manner.

Alexander Hamilton is probably floating around in the ether of another dimension, agonizingly awaiting an answer to the question he posed. **It remains the premiere question of our nation and of our time. One way or another, it is going to be answered.**

SECTION 4
THE "NATION'S AUTHORITY STRUCTURE"

We propose for the nation an Authority Structure made up of two components:

1) A group of direction and control functions called "Constitutional Authorities." **They are the implementation and control arm of The People, established to carry out ownership rights and obligations.**

2.) A Federal government that governs the nation, restructured, refocused, scoured of inappropriate activities, and operating under the watchful eye of the implementation arm of The People, the Constitutional Authorities.

With the establishment of Constitutional Authorities as proposed, it would not be appropriate to refer to the proposed new authority configuration as "government." It, with government, are together more accurately described as "The Nation's Authority Structure."

The People's responsibility to Plan, Organize, Staff, Direct and Control obviously cannot be easily carried out by three hundred and thirty million citizens acting together. Yet to self-govern, The People must make the critical decisions, institute the required components, and make them perform! If The People cannot do that, what they are doing is not "self-government."

The People will find it necessary to create and staff constitutional bodies that execute their five ownership functions. Those constitutional bodies will be "process managers" for the actions developed and directed by The People. The People will be the decision-makers by vote, the constitutional bodies will design the decision processes to be employed and will carry out The People's direction.

For a nation possessing the capability of putting a man on the moon, constructing a system that will permit The People to make and install their owner decisions should be child's play!

ESTABLISHING AND UTILIZING CONSTITUTIONAL AUTHORITIES

On the assumption that The People have the will and capability of "establishing good government from reflection and choice," a plan for The People to carry out their ownership responsibilities in that challenge is proposed.

The Constitutional Authorities so proposed will not govern. They will help The People by constructing and implementing the decision process, then will carry out The People's voted decisions. **Administrative decisions the Constitutional bodies make will be only those needed to implement the "Plan, Organize, Staff, Direct and Control" edicts of The People.**

We propose those People-Assistant bodies be called 'Constitutional Authorities."

The organizational proposal is to congregate the Constitutional Authority bodies under administration of a small group called the Guardians of the Constitution, thereby putting in place strong elected on-deck administration guarding against the powerful influence on government and The People of the potent activity called "politics."

This proposal converts the Nation's Authority Structure from pure "representative democracy" to a "hybrid mixture of direct democracy and representative democracy." In the proposed Authority structure, a clear line of demarcation will be drawn, between the all-powerful directional duties and responsibilities of The People, and the duties and responsibilities assigned to Elected Persons who are The People's hired management in government.

- Under the plan, all matters deemed to be the sole responsibility of The People will be administered by Constitutional Authorities, with decisions made by vote of the Well-Informed Electors, **in a *direct democracy* process**.

- All matters delegated to Government by The People will be decided by assembly vote **in a *representative democracy* process**. Government will be redesigned and reorganized **to produce quality decisions**, to eliminate totalitarian practices that have crept into it. All assembly decision processes will be conducted under the direction and supervision of the Constitutional Authority function called The Guardians of the Constitution.

Existing functions essential to democracy but which should not be controlled by government or by political parties (which we call Vital Infrastructure) will be transferred from government to the Constitutional Authorities, **where they will operate. Readers should view the Constitutional Authorities as an organizational boundary that clearly marks the distinction between The People's responsibilities and those of Government.**

The Framers divided government into three branches and required each to act as check-and-balance on the other two. That system relied on organizations of government watching over each other, a woefully weak control system riddled with interest conflicts and gross imbalance. The Constitutional Authorities, as powerful non-conflicted superiors to government, will take over all check-and-balance duties. This change is guaranteed to produce improved quality control and with it, improved government performance. "Hard-headed and demanding owners" will be watching!

The following rough organization proposal is what may be referred to as a "plan framework." It is highly conceptual, and there are no assurances that the proposals will necessarily meet the test when subjected to intense scrutiny. Nothing proposed has been tested. Concepts may be dramatically changed or even abandoned, responsibilities and tasks may be switched, and other changes made by the final decision-makers.

The intent is to reason, and using the product of reasoning, to put forth a proposal for reader consideration that addresses true problem resolution.

THE CONSTITUTIONAL AUTHORITY ORGANIZATION

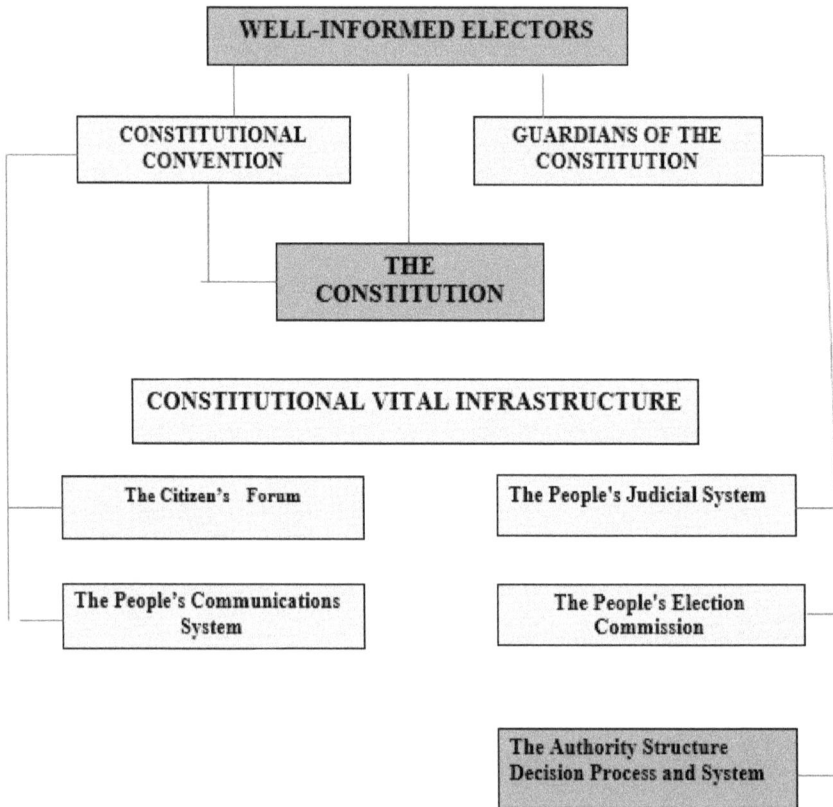

WELL-INFORMED ELECTORS

CONSTITUTIONAL CONVENTION

GUARDIANS OF THE CONSTITUTION

THE CONSTITUTION

CONSTITUTIONAL VITAL INFRASTRUCTURE

The Citizen's Forum

The People's Judicial System

The People's Communications System

The People's Election Commission

The Authority Structure Decision Process and System

SECTION 5
THE WELL-INFORMED ELECTORS

In Chapter 11, entitled "The Voters," available information about the characteristics of the Nation's voter population was examined to determine whether that population could be utilized to make the complex direct democracy decisions that, with implementation of the proposed Constitutional Authority Structure, will become the designated responsibility of The People.

> The conclusion was that the existing voter population IS NOT COMPETENT TO MAKE CRITICAL DIRECT DEMOCRACY DECISIONS, **and that a body of Well-Informed Electors should be selected from among them to vote such decisions on behalf of all The People.**

Citizens who do not qualify as "Well-Informed" will, of course, continue to vote the election of hired management who serve in the Authority Structure and in Government, and to participate in various involvement activities provided, **Knowledge of civic affairs, lack of political bias, and study dedication that are needed to cast "well-informed" votes are believed to be absent in a significant segment of our citizen population.**

A decision to implement such a plan will involve a national choice between two conflicting perspectives: The first the view that Democracy demands all voters participate in national decisions, even though a large voter percentage will degrade decision quality because they are not capable of casting an "informed ballot." The second the view that the importance to the Nation, of decisions on matters that must be decided by The People, is so great that those who vote must have the knowledge needed to cast an "informed ballot."

> For National decisions of this importance level, in order to achieve decisions of high-quality, the sacrifice of generally-accepted notions about democratic equality is not only justified**, it is essential**. In our Democratic Republic, the demand for decision quality is so high that it dominates considerations such as who may vote, and how to construct the voting body.

The long-term goal of the Nation must be to raise the civic knowledge level of the total voter population so that as many citizens as possible will qualify as Well-Informed. Self-governed democracies require a well-informed citizenry. **Uninformed citizens are today voluntarily leaving the ranks of active citizenship and do not vote in elections, so their exclusion from the Well-Informed Electors will deprive them of nothing.** If they decide to participate in the future, they may do so by personal commitment expended toward qualifying as a Well-Informed Elector.

The formation of the Well-Informed Electorate fits precisely into the Framer voting concept of a "democratic republic." The Well-Informed Electors are a voting body custom-designed for a specific democratic decision purpose. Well-Informed Electors will stand beside the Electoral College and the state-apportioned Senate as examples of specialized voting bodies formed under our nation's republic concept.

The introduction of citizen-voted decisions **to replace the vote of elected representatives on matters deemed the sole responsibility of The People** will be a quantum leap forward in our nation's decision process. Readers should bear in mind that elected representatives are avoiding decisions of that level of consequence, and are not promoting consideration of Constitutional Amendments envisioned under the provisions of Section V of the Constitution.

Creating and operating a Well-Informed Elector group of citizens will demand substantial administrative capability, a responsibility to be assumed by the Constitutional Convention, assisted by the units of Constitutional Vital Infrastructure. The People's Communications System will maintain television communication channels and the capability of sophisticated on-line two-way communication with the large voter body. As has been stated previously, assembling a Well-Informed Electorate and developing the custom-designed techniques and communication capability needed for that body to vote the nation's complex direction and policy decisions should be child's play for a nation capable of putting a man on the moon.

One final thought. The Well-Informed Electors will become The People's policing body, watching over the actions of individuals and groups that comprise the Constitutional Authorities. A check-and-balance on Constitutional Authorities is as important as on any other function in our self-governed democracy.

SECTION 6
COMPONENTS OF THE CONSTITUTIONAL AUTHORITIES

The division of responsibilities between The People and their hired management will mark the dividing line between those two organizational components. This Section will outline the organization proposed for the Constitutional Authorities, which will assist The People in formulating and implementing their intent.

Within the Constitutional Authorities will be located a subgroup of organizations that have long existed in government, plus some new to be formed, that fall under a common umbrella.

This group will be labelled "Vital Infrastructure." They are essential service components in the nation's Authority Structure but separated for the purpose of visibility and control.

1. THE GUARDIANS OF THE CONSTITUTION

The primary body of The People, responsible for watching over the efforts of all Constitutional Authorities, will be the Guardians of the Constitution. This small elected body will additionally have the challenging duty of directing and upgrading the decision processes of the Nation, whether they be decisions by Constitutional bodies or of the Elected Assemblies of Government.

This body will not govern. It is the direction and control arm of The People and the "operations head" for the Constitutional Authorities. It ranks superior to all branches of government and other constitutional bodies, except the Well-Informed Electors. It will direct the Constitutional Authorities and the units of Vital Infrastructure. It will guide and police government activities as the "check-and-balance" for the nation. It will ensure the President is carrying out his/her responsibilities as the Chief Executive of Government.

The Guardians of the Constitution will launch a series of steps to write a new Constitution, establish the Constitutional Authorities, import functions from government, and take a range of other actions, including a never-ending focus on epitomizing the quality of government decisions.

The principal duty of the Guardians will be directing and overseeing the Authority Structure of the Nation on behalf of The People, focusing on developing an exemplary decision process. The Guardians will install the functions by which The People will direct and support the Authority Structure to assure that the required improvements in decision quality and government process are achieved.

a) The Guardians Shall be a Tribunal

No action may be undertaken by the Guardians without a vote, and all decisions require consensus agreement. Guardians will have no individual authority insofar as the nation is concerned but may individually supervise functions of the Guardian mission.

b) Selection/Election of Guardians

It is suggested that the Guardians be ten individuals selected in special election to serve for one term of six years. One Guardian would be elected from each of ten regions, each region composed of five states but balanced for population parity. The People's Election Commission will set regional boundaries, locate candidates, and five candidates from each region for the Guardian position will be offered to the region's citizens for election. Individual Guardians will not, in any way, represent the region in which he/she was elected.

The purpose of utilizing ten regions is to ensure all citizens have a direct vote in these important selections.

Guardian candidates must be free of political background and taint. The group may (but is not required to) include one lawyer. A strong legal wall is required to separate Constitutional Authorities from domestic politics and government. Past members of government may be Well-Informed Electors, but shall be otherwise barred from participation in Constitutional matters and from serving in any constitutional position. Each Guardian will stand for re-election after three years, with total service of six years and no re-election thereafter.

Good candidates will be selected from various occupations, with the goal of establishing diversity of background. Strong management and decision-making expertise are fundamental requirements, a dominant consideration in candidate selection, and candidates must be qualified as Well-Informed Electors. Continuity in the group will be vital, so the election of members will be rotated.

2. THE CONSTITUTIONAL CONVENTION

The Constitutional Convention will be the deliberation body in the Constitutional Authorities. It is designed to be an assembly of mature and well-informed citizens. An important focus will be steering the derivation of major decisions of The People of the nation, including the National Imperatives and the Financial Measures, decisions that will be authorized by vote of the Well-Informed Electors. It will be the guiding philosophical, management, and instructional body for the Well-Informed Electors, the constitution, and all related matters.

A great deal of thought and attention will be needed to carefully allocate Constitutional duties between the Guardians of the Constitution and the Constitutional Convention.

The revised and upgraded constitution will serve as the source of civic material for the education system and the Authority Structure, so most decisions of the Well-Informed Electors will become content, and of highest importance level in the nation.

a) Duties of the Constitutional Convention

The Constitutional Convention exists to develop and maintain current the Constitution of the United States. It must develop content and manage the decision process of the Well-Informed Electors who will debate and approve content, which means it must direct the systems and processes required to accomplish that. It will be the body that establishes and administers the relationship between the Constitutional Authorities and The People, ensuring that it is functioning at a high level.

A major responsibility of the Constitutional Convention will be guiding The People's development of the National Imperatives and Financial Measures. Those decisions will set the nation's forward direction. Further, it will oversee the activities of the units of the Constitutional Vital Infrastructure.

It will be assigned additional important Constitutional duties, and at the discretion of the Guardians of the Constitution may function as the decider of specific important questions deemed not to require a vote of the Well-Informed Electors.

It will conduct trials of impeachment, and its 65% vote shall constitute an impeachment decision. A member of the Supreme Court selected by the Convention will act as the judge to conduct an impeachment trial.

b) Selection and Election of Deputies

The following general rules should govern the assembly of the Constitutional Convention:

One (1) Constitutional Deputy will be elected from a candidate list of five from each State by special election under direction of the Election Commission. Successful candidates would be accorded the title of "Constitutional Deputy" and be elected for one term of six (6) years, with one-third of the group replaced every two (2) years.

Constitutional Deputies would be paid an annual salary equal to that paid to a Senator.

Any person who has been a citizen for twenty-five or more years and whose age lies between forty years and seventy can be elected a Constitutional Deputy, provided his/her credentials and background meet the requirements. Candidate testing would be conducted to ensure qualification, and specific knowledge maintenance requirements would be established to ascertain that Constitutional Deputies meet the "well-informed" criteria.

Great care will be exercised by the People's Election Commission to ensure Constitutional Deputy candidates are free of political bias, have not been members of a political party, are not lawyers, and have not engaged in government or politics. No person from a business, profession, or activity in any way dependent on government funding may be a candidate. Election support from a politician or political party, any political faction, or function or employee of the government, directly or indirectly, shall be a treasonous offense. Provision should be made for the removal of any elected Deputy found to be behaving or voting in a politically biased fashion.

3. THE PEOPLE'S COMMUNICATIONS

Chapter 17 launches a lengthy and detailed four-chapter examination of the Rights and Freedoms provisions of Amendment 1 to the Constitution. A considerable amount of space is allocated there to the nation's communications media.

PROPOSED VITAL INFRASTRUCTURE:

THE PEOPLE'S COMMUNICATIONS

- NATIONAL NEWS CHANNEL

-WELL-INFORMED ELECTORS CHANNEL

-CIVIC EDUCATION CHANNEL

-SELF-GOVERNMENT CHANNEL

The proposed People's Communication Commission will assume responsibility for "the Media" to eliminate it as a threat to the survival of our democracy and ensure that its operations fully support the requirements of our Constitution, The People, and our form of government. The operations of the Federal Communications Commission will be melded into it.

The Commission will separate the News Service Providers from the mainstream media and will establish them as a Constitutional Vital Infrastructure entity dedicated to dramatic improvement in the flow of information between The People and the Authority Structure and the development of the well-informed citizenry essential to a self-governed democracy that features heavy citizen involvement.

It is proposed several Authority-owned television channels be established, each dedicated to a specific communication purpose, and utilizing high-quality professionals for content and delivery. It will develop and communicate to citizens news concerning national affairs and government action, training material that meets the factual and accuracy level required to classify the owners of a self-governed democracy as "well-informed," and a vastly improved two-way flow of information on the process of the Authority Structure.

It is proposed that a chairman and seven Commissioners be elected for a one-time service of six years to serve as the managing group for The People's Communications Commission. The election process should stagger the periods each Commissioner serves, with elections every two years. The election process would be conducted in the same fashion as the following Election Commission proposal.

4. THE PEOPLE'S ELECTION COMMISSION

The 2020 Presidential Election exposed major weaknesses in the Nation's system for electing government officials. Public trust in the system has diminished substantially.

It is proposed an organization be created within the Constitutional Authorities called The People's Election Commission. All Federal Government and Constitutional elections would be conducted under its direction and control.

The People's intent is to totally replace political party involvement in election functions, eliminate any government involvement in the elections that produce its members, and totally remove the taint of private money from the election process.

Our political system has demonstrated no ability or willingness to re-establish confidence in national elections and continues to give political parties priority. The federal government's attitude (reinforced by the media) is "Move right along. There's nothing to see here," but meaningful segments of the voting population aren't buying that answer. Elections, along with everything else, have evolved into polarization.

1. This book proposes that the Federal election system be totally removed from Government jurisdiction, and the role of State Governments in Federal elections be eliminated. Insulation from politics is essential, as is the confidence of The People in the election system.

2. An elected Constitutional Authority, called The People's Election Commission, consisting of one Chairman and six Commissioners, is proposed to manage the election system.

3. An entirely new concept, its duties would be broadened to candidate selection and approval, election cost funding, management of candidate exposure to voters, and management of voting.

4. All election costs would be paid by the taxpayer, eliminating the corrupting influence of private money. As an equality principle, no wealthy or influential persons or entities would have power over or involvement in elections. Election funds would be generated through the income tax system from an annual tax levy on corporate and personal income.

5. The People's Election Commission will have responsibility for managing the controls on Political Parties and Political Factions, with the intent of eliminating Political Parties and nullifying the influence of Political Factions.

6. An important function of the Commission will be to maintain the Well-Informed Elector group, qualify its members, record its activities, and conduct all voting by that group.

5. THE PEOPLE'S JUDICIAL SYSTEM

Chapter 9 examined The People's Judicial System. A politically-untainted and broadly supported judiciary is an important function of our Nation's Vital Infrastructure and its decision-making process. The conclusion reached was that The People's Judicial System should be transferred out of government and be designated a Constitutional Authority, removing it from the political realm and placing it under the control of The People.

The goal must be to end political influence on the Judicial System, and eliminate the excessive influence of the legal profession on the Judiciary, exercised inside and outside of government. The proposal places it under administrative direction from the Guardians of the Constitution. The Guardians will monitor the flow of decisions within government and the Constitutional Authorities, including the multitude flowing through the Judicial System. The Guardians will re-direct decisions to the organization that properly should make them, when in their judgment that is necessary.

The Supreme Court has been the recipient of a multitude of undecided issues that were defaulted by the government organization primarily responsible for dealing with them in the first instance (usually the Legislative branch), political abuse of the decision process that needs to be halted and reversed. Vital improvement can be achieved only if an organization with authority is directing and controlling the decision process, a power, and responsibility to be vested in the Guardians.

Ensuring that all the nation's decisions are made within a tightly controlled and purely democratic process is critical to improving Authority Structure decision quality, which is the strategy proposed for vastly improving government. To that end, this book strongly advocates that The People exercise control over all of the nation's authority decisions.

At issue here are some fundamental questions: Does the law exist to generate income for the legal profession, or does it exist to serve the nation and its citizens? The answer, we propose, is to serve the nation and its citizens. Who is responsible for making sure we have the highest quality legal code on earth, the Legislature or the Supreme Court? We propose the Supreme Court. We propose that the role of elected assemblies be to produce the required law and the role of the Supreme Court be to ensure that it is current and meets high standards for citizen use.

It is proposed the Judicial System be made responsible for management of the Nation's statute law, and be given responsibility to direct Legislative revisions to remove duplication, extreme complexity and redundancy, and eliminate conflict.

The goal must be to make the law understandable to the ordinary citizen, pinpoint gaps to be corrected, and achieve whatever other improvements are needed.

If a citizen has to hire a lawyer to root through endless uncodified legal decisions to finally determine what is relevant law, the legal code fails to meet suggested simple standards.

The proposal is a large undertaking, probably requiring a decade or more to complete. It should be started promptly.

After a short period has elapsed following establishment of the Judicial System as a Constitutional Authority, an in-depth study by the Constitutional Convention will be undertaken to determine what further actions are needed to improve the timeliness and quality of Judicial decisions and to measure and evaluate progress in upgrading the legal code. At the same time, a separate Commission should be launched to evaluate the prison system, sentencing guidelines, criminal law and the death penalty, the role of prison guard unions, and the role of the legal profession.

There is a huge amount of effort that must be expended in upgrading the judicial system.

6. THE CITIZEN'S FORUM

A range of proposals having to do with citizenship are presented to upgrade the ability of citizens to fulfill their responsibilities in the recommended self-government Authority Structure. The proposed increased involvement of citizens in the process of self-government will demand national investment in education, records, testing, information and feedback gathering, and the like.

A small body of seven elected Forum Managers would manage and execute The People's plan concerning citizenship and organize the interface of citizenship with the work of Constitutional Authorities. Formation of the Forum provides the means to broaden the involvement of citizens in governance well beyond complaints and requests for help.

Constitutional proposals that would change the functions and obligations of citizenship make it necessary that a special Vital Infrastructure body, which we have labelled "The Citizen's Forum," be convened to put in place and administer planned activities. Any that currently exist in government would be transferred to the Citizen's Forum.

The Forum would be challenged to create a citizenry with an upgraded understanding of the responsibilities of citizens in self-government, and significant participate in advanced decision-making. The Morals and Ethics aspect will be a substantial challenge for the Forum.

1. It is intended that Citizen's Forum facilities and services totally replace the "right of the people to peaceably assemble," conveyed in the First Amendment. The Forum will provide an organized, civilized, formal, and highly effective way for citizens to accomplish the same free expression with much greater impact and results and free the nation of risks associated with large gatherings of emotional people. It has also been proposed elsewhere that if assemblies continue to be permitted, a new set of very pointed constitutional provisions should establish accountability for the behavior of local government and police who approve and oversee them, and of the individual citizens who participate in them.

The two approaches demonstrate that the peaceable assembly issue has two obvious solutions available for The People to use for selection purposes. There are probably others. The message is that the self-serving and destructive no-action path being followed by our political parties is a political desecration that inflicts a variety of high costs on the nation.

2. The Citizen's Forum will assume responsibility for citizen representation, which was the duty that put "Representative" into the job title of those elected to the House of Representatives. With the proposed government revision proposal and formation of Constitutional Authorities, citizen action paths, including the function called "representation," should logically be located within the Authorities. **The sole purpose of changing citizen representation is the achievement of dramatically improved performance from assembly Persons by eliminating work conflicts and creating intense job focus. (See The Elected Assembly Series)**

3. A national effort to establish reliable and vastly improved two-way communication between The People and their Authority Structure for significantly improved self-government will be the responsibility of the People's Communications. Two critical components of the effort are constitutional isolation and control over News Service Providers, guaranteeing citizens and the Authority Structure a steady stream of relevant and reliable information concerning the nation and its affairs. (See Chapters 17 to 20 for a detailed discussion of this issue). **Removal of political parties and the News provider activities of the Media, which are severe communications blockages between The People and the Authority Structure, is the second critical reason for the effort.**

4. To meet the requirement of Trust among citizens, which is fundamental for successful self-government, establishing the focus on the morals and ethics of Americans is the starting point. **Moral and ethical behavior must become a national standard and a citizenship obligation.** This effort will produce a wide range of unexpected benefits to the nation.

To address the citizen Trust deficiency, a clear constitutional statement of moral and ethical standards is needed to provide constitutional Direction to The People. A "Morals and Ethics Score System," patterned after Credit Scoring, would provide the public with information on individual citizen behavior as depicted by morals and ethics blemishes. Introducing "shame" into the equation, by posting publicly the morals and ethics failings of individuals, it is believed will dramatically alter behavior. It could be far more effective in establishing personal accountability than expensive prison time.

The" trust" issue is important. Its correction isn't rocket science. It simply requires a good plan and the People's determination. Freedom, without counter-balancing accountability, will never generate trust.

Designing accountability measures is not fun, but it is very necessary. Remember the saying, "Doing the same thing over and over again, and expecting different results, is the definition of insanity." Our nation needs to significantly upgrade its approach to accountability.

---

5. Our regression of interpersonal trust flows from the absence of citizen accountability, ineffective youth education, and an ineffective criminal law and penalty system. If we want successful self-government, investment in strong morals and ethics among the citizens is the starting point. The effort is necessary if the nation wishes to improve safety, reduce crime levels, reduce prison populations (See Chapter II, entitled "Trust"), and the pressure on policing. Its expected contribution to prospects for successful self-government is a highly important reason.

The People pay for the misbehavior of miscreants.

The proposed dramatic changes to the duties and responsibilities of citizenship, such as the requirement of citizen voting, establishment of the Well-Informed Elector group, and implementation of the Morals and Ethics Score System, lead to the idea that it may be appropriate to consider creating several citizenship and non-citizenship classes. Doing that might be effective if we implement it with a citizen identification card with enforced usage.

6. The Citizen's Forum would provide offices throughout the Nation where citizens may interface and communicate directly with the Constitutional Authorities. In this self-government proposal, the flow of information between The People and their execution team,

the Constitutional Authorities, must be at a level and quality never previously envisioned, considered, or achieved.

The Forum should provide special service to citizens, giving them a venue where they can formally request consideration of new laws, elimination or amendment of existing law, or address any matter citizens think important. The information flow should be formal, with complete documentation. A summary of citizen requests and feedback would be directly channeled into the President's proposed 2-year Decision and Legislation plan. (See Chapter 12, The President)

7. Public opinion surveys (and their publication) on the performance of various government and constitutional operations should be a primary responsibility of the Forum. Those surveys are an important statistical evaluation that should be regularly tallied, charted, and communicated to The People.

Surveys provide foundation information for the President, to be built into the administration of the Hired Management. The People must jettison the endless re-election system currently in place, instituting public discredit and firing of public service personnel for a range of misbehavior and poor performance matters.

SUMMARY OF THE CITIZEN'S FORUM

Define the responsibilities of citizenship, incorporating updated obligations

Implement a Morals and Ethics program for the nation

Eliminate the Right to Peaceably Assemble, replace it with citizen communication rights through the Forum

Establish a Citizenship Personal Accountability program interfaced with the Freedoms

Represent citizens before the Authority Structure, replacing representation by elected persons

Prepare and publish surveys of Authority Structure and Government performance

Accumulate, and forward to the President, citizen suggested new laws

Foster increased citizen participation in government

Establish, update and control citizenship instruction in Educational Institutions.

CHAPTER 15

THE PEOPLE'S DIRECTION AND CONTROL SERIES: PART 2

CONTENT:

SECTION 1: THE PEOPLE ARE THE OWNERS OF THE NATION

SECTION 2: THE PEOPLE'S PERFORMANCE OF THEIR OWNERSHIP RESPONSIBILITIES

SECTION 3: OUR FRAMERS CREATED A "MONARCHY REPUBLIC"

SECTION 4: CLEAR NATIONAL DIRECTION WILL ELIMINATE UNCERTAINTY FOR CITIZENS AND THE NATION

FOREWORD

As Pogo, a comic strip swamp character of years gone by, once famously proclaimed: "We has found the enemy, and they are the US!"

The Legislative branch, that democracy love-object of our Framers, is now our source of national discomfort because of its poor performance. The ballot boxes endlessly re-elect the same people, making voting places an abject democratic failure since they are the only existing check and balance on Legislative branch performance.

The two Houses of Congress are insulated against actions of The People, except actions through the ballot box exercised against elected persons as individuals. Congressional accountability to The People has either slipped away, has been purposefully removed, or was never there in the first place.

The Constitution granted the Legislative houses full authority to manage their own proceedings, a fatal Framer error that allowed the Elected Persons to selfishly bastardize our unique concept of democratic republic government. They did so by (among other things) creating political parties. If a party achieved a voting majority, it was given the absolute right to rule its House.

Summarizing, with the failure of the ballot box as a check-and-balance, no vehicle now exists by which The People can give the Legislative branch direction or enforce performance accountability. Despite our ballyhooed "government of the people, by the people, and for the people," The People can do absolutely nothing to correct the Legislative branch's non-performance. They have been reduced to party electors displaying herd behavior.

That states the problem. Here, we will sort out the players in the game, discuss responsibilities, evaluate performance, and engage in the reasoning that generates solutions.

SECTION 1
THE PEOPLE ARE THE OWNERS OF THE NATION

THE RESPONSIBILITIES OF OWNERSHIP

For intellectual reinforcement, the Section title statement is repeated frequently in this book. It is not at all clear that The People have an understanding of what ownership implies or have ever even discussed the subject!

The formative concept for the Democratic Republic called The United States of America was a *government of the People, by the People, and for the People.* That statement became our slogan.

> **In self-government, "Ownership by The People" is the principle that governs all reasoning concerning who should control the distribution of powers and responsibilities within the nation's Authority Structure.**

The People are explicitly the owners of the nation. Formative language in the Declaration of Independence states that the owners determine what government shall be and have the right to make changes deemed necessary. **That statement is rarely challenged. It is generally ignored.**

Today, in our nation, "Government of the People, by the People, and for the People" is nothing more than a political slogan recited at ceremonies.

OWNERSHIP IS NOT AN ABSTRACT CONCEPT; IT CARRIES MONUMENTAL RIGHTS AND RESPONSIBILITIES.

The People have ownership rights and ownership obligations. For self-government to function The People, as a group, must effectively perform their role. **Dumping**

responsibilities onto self-managed assemblies of elected persons IS NOT GOVERNMENT BY THE PEOPLE. It constitutes a total abdication by The People of their responsibilities. Not fulfilling their responsibilities, The People have violated the rules of delegation of authority and acceptance of responsibility, and in the process, created a range of problems.

There are two sides to the ownership equation. On one side of the equation, The People will ultimately bear the consequences of government failure, often called "existential risks.". The other side of the equation, balancing it, is the five powers granted to the owners that allow them to execute the actions needed to avoid government failure.

THE OWNERSHIP RESPONSIBILITY EQUATION

EXISTENTIAL RISKS   =   THE OWNER'S FIVE POWERS

Management texts inform us that there are five ownership/management functions: **Plan, Organize, Staff, Direct, and Control.**[51] If the People intend to conduct self-government, they must shoulder the burden of ownership, gird their loins, and march forth to carry out those five functions. If they do not do that, they are not conducting "self-government" and not taking the actions necessary to defend the nation against its existential risks.

Our Nation exists in a world of great uncertainty and danger. Do you have a hankering to learn the Chinese language with a gun at your head? The existential threat is real. **Avoiding such an outcome demands, in our nation, the creation of dramatically better self-government. To achieve that, The People must perform their five owner/manager functions.**

ELECTED PERSONS ARE HIRED MANAGEMENT

Important issues can be rationalized only if one confronts reality. Reality may be something completely different from what one has been taught and usually is not something a person wants to confront face-to-face.

If The People are the owners of the Nation, what terms accurately describe those who now conduct government?

---

[51] Principles of Management, Koontz and O'Donnell

> In business terminology the persons elected to represent the owners in the conduct of government *are HIRED MANAGEMENT*.
>
> Owners tell the hired management what must be accomplished. Hired management carries out the owner's instructions. That is reality! No other arrangement will succeed.
>
> **If their position is threatened, hired management will go to great lengths to make sure that REALITY IS HIDDEN, OUT OF REACH, OR OBSCURED.**

The concept that government is carried out by "hired management" may be difficult for citizens to grasp and accept. The citizens of this "self-governed nation" (employing widely-used terminology) are accustomed to thinking of themselves as "Subjects" and of government as "the Ruler." **Citizens are taught to subjugate themselves to governmental authority, and most placidly, our citizens accept that requirement. In that mental posture, it is all right to sit back and wait for the government to tell us what we will do. The political elite who run our Monarchy Republic have trained us well!**

Self-government reality requires that the Hired Management, who conduct the functions of government, carry them out **following specific rules established by the owners**, utilizing processes and procedures given to them as "direction." **The power to manage their internal affairs, granted to our Houses of Congress, violates the requirement of owner-specific rules**. The reality is there are some functions the Hired Management will be given broad authority to carry out, and for others, they will be held to tight rules defining what they can do and what must be done.

SECTION 2
THE PEOPLE'S PERFORMANCE OF THEIR OWNERSHIP RESPONSIBILITIES

The best tool for evaluating owner performance is the five Owner/Manager Responsibilities. Readers must bear in mind that the five responsibilities are textbook and current-best-practice obligations. The constitution does not mention those responsibilities in any fashion. In the year 1776 the responsibilities had not yet been identified in studies of the ownership/management process.

Following is the author's evaluation of The People's performance in carrying out their ownership responsibilities. Readers should make their own evaluations.

a) The "Plan" Responsibility of The People

There is no Constitutionally-established process by which The People can plan our Nation's governance or set its forward path. **Approval of new Constitutional Amendments, which would implement owner planning, is totally controlled by the hired management, using the processes defined in Section V of the Constitution.**

Floating a party program proposal in an election dance does not qualify as "Planning." It is an election tactic. Strategic Planning for the nation does not exist. Certain individual organizations, such as the Military, conduct strategy and organization-level planning that is believed to be of good quality, but for the nation as a whole, **strategic planning does not exist**. The nation staggers along, reacting to occurrences, operating without any agreed-upon national decisions as to where it wants to go.

As The People are excluded from planning the affairs of the Nation, the rating of their performance is "Non-Existent."

b) The "Organize" Responsibility of The People

The "Organize" function designs and establishes the organization and process that shall be employed within the Authority Structure. Limited structure and process rules are contained in the Constitution. Today's framework of Government is the basic Framer concept but has been modified significantly by elected persons political party activity. **Elected Assembly rules and procedures were not specified in the Constitution. They were designed by the first-elected "hired management" group immediately following the signing.**

A major organizational change to government, accomplished without amending the constitution, was the imposition of the massive Administrative State onto the Framer government plan. **It was planned by a political party and implemented under the authority of the Government. It was not planned, organized, or approved by The People. Under the "mandate" concept, The People supposedly approved it in general elections.**

No government organization planning has been carried out by citizens; all was carried out by the hired management. Voting for a program proposed by a political party may be described as "approving" but does not qualify as "Organizing." Such decisions have been made by the party in power.

The People's performance of their "Organize" responsibility is rated "non-existent."

c) The "Staff" Responsibility of The People

The "Staff" function is the election process by which persons who conduct government are hired and fired by The People. It includes selection and approval, by government leaders, of executives who manage major support functions of government.

In our democratic republic, citizen involvement in the election "Staffing" process consists of voting at the ballot box. Because of political party influence and other factors, the ballot box is highly suspect as a "hiring" mechanism and, evidenced by the high re-election rate, has become dysfunctional as a "firing" mechanism. The Federal election system, **controlled by State governments and always under party direction,** has lost credibility because of questionable practices and persistent claims of voting fraud.

Citizen voting involvement in elections is weak (50% to 60% of citizens vote in the most important Federal elections) and the aggregate effect of those citizen votes on the organization concept of government is minimal. **The election system and its candidates are controlled by political parties. The influence of private money on elections is a very powerful factor.**

The election system must be rated "Barely Adequate." The People's performance of their "Staff" responsibility would be rated "Weak," and that rating is charitable.

d) The "Direct" Responsibility of The People

The "Direct" function is the process by which the hired management, and the boss communicate about the government's work. The work of government, which today elected assemblies and managers of government support organizations carry out under the direction of political parties, is to a limited and fragmented extent specified in the Constitution.

In a self-governed democracy, direction from The People is composed of two components: The first is the "Plan" process, which identifies what shall be done. The second is the "Direct" process that converts those decisions into implementation.

In a self-governed democracy, communications between The People and the hired management are sacrosanct because they guide and direct the nation. Errors and misstatements cannot be permitted. Third parties cannot be allowed into the communications chain.

There are two key groups that must be seamlessly melded, the boss (which is The People) and the hired management (the elected persons) who must carry out the direction. The most difficult aspect of the seamless melding is creating the needed two-way communication between Government and The People.

Under the government self-management process that evolved in our Nation, the Houses of Congress delegated the Nation's direction-setting to political parties. **Candidates offer party direction proposals to voters during elections.** Political parties claim that the voter election of a party candidate constitutes voter approval of any direction proposed by that party and candidate, the so-called "mandate" claim.

Voting on the "direction" offerings of political parties constitutes the only "direction" decision voters are able to make. Direction proposals are made by individual candidates representing political parties, and voters vote in the election of those candidates. They do not vote specifically on direction proposals. There are a range of reasons a candidate may win the election, direction proposals being only one. Because of that nuance, it is impossible to evaluate the direction selection acumen of our voters.

Within the elected assemblies, direction issues are decided by parties that have established majority control. Thus, whatever direction the nation has is the direction of a majority political party, which obtained the "majority" designation by the supporting vote of roughly one-third of the nation's citizens. Direction, under those conditions, certainly cannot be considered direction by The People.

The "Direct" performance of The People, under the current system, is limited to selecting from political party candidate choices. The Nation's method of determining its "Direction" is "Very Poor."

e) The "Control" Responsibility of The People

The "Control" function is the means by which the owners determine whether the work was performed as required and decide what is to be done in the event of hired management non-performance. The People's sole means of "Control" is carried out in elections by voting incumbents in and out. The current 90% incumbent re-election rate indicates the "Control" function is "Inoperative."

A conceptually weak system at the outset, the ballot box "Control" responsibility of The People has degraded to the point where it is now rated "Failed."

WHY IS THE PEOPLE'S EXECUTION OF THEIR FIVE RESPONSIBILITIES OF OWNERSHIP SO POOR?

Of the five citizen ownership performance obligations concerning their government, two are today rated "Non-existent," two are rated "Failed," and one is rated "Weak."

The Constitution provided The People, as owners of the Nation, with the means to perform only the "Staff," responsibility, by voting the hiring and firing of Elected Persons through the ballot box mechanism. Performance of that duty is rated "Weak."

The Government, as structured and operated, does not provide any means for The People to fulfill their other ownership obligations. There is no open discussion of this major issue.

The ballot box, the only "control" tool of The People, is weakly effective in performing the "Hire" function and, at a 90% re-election rate, is totally ineffective in performing the "Fire" function.

Since Staffing decisions made by voters at the ballot box generate hired management for the two Houses of Congress, the poor performance of those Houses is connected directly to voters inability to use the ballot box mechanism to enforce accountability. What little accountability the ballot box originally imposed on the hired management has long since evaporated, "gone, gone, like the landlord's smile" of country music fame.

Political party influence at the voting booth ensured that. But the fact of the matter is the ballot box system was, from its very beginning, a woefully weak system and process by which to involve The People in government. **The voting system was never intended to assist The People in carrying out their Plan, Organize, Staff, Direct, and Control responsibilities. Its sole purpose is, and has always been, to elect the officials of government.**

ELECTION SYSTEMS ASSOCIATED WITH THE BALLOT BOX ARE OBSOLETE

The ballot box and the election systems associated with it are a "simple solution to a complex problem." They became the key tools of democracy in an era of paper-based technology and horse-and-buggy transportation. They have seen no improvement since then; instead, the contribution of the function has regressed.

The Framers constitutionally delegated performance into the hands of the hired management elected to conduct government, who in turn delegated it to the political parties. Political parties have paid attention to the voting process only when an election advantage was believed to be available.

Ballots have been adapted to accommodate voting "yes or no" on complex referendum questions by states that employ "direct democracy" voting. Given the government's view of the capability of today's average citizen, the practical use of the ballot in national elections is limited to voters making "staffing" choices.

The ballot box works to elect officials for representative government or, using management lingo, to "staff" government-elected positions. Technology has replaced paper ballots here and there and is used to tabulate results, but the ballot box does the same things it did at the outset. Most human involvement in elections is the activity of political parties, which culminates in the election. Voting systems and the rules relating to them are generally state-controlled.

This book proposes a major overhaul of the election system, to be accomplished by transferring responsibility for all Federal election processes to a new Constitutional body (The People's Election Commission), thereby eliminating political party involvement. The Election System is designated, in this book, as a Vital Infrastructure component.

A major reconstruction is proposed to eliminate the influence of private money to fund campaigns, dramatically improve selection of candidates and management of the entire election process, institute fixed-term one-time service for elected persons, create a significant incentive pay program, and institute a complete revision of the duties and responsibilities of assembly elected persons to eliminate their substantial work conflicts.

SECTION 3
OUR FRAMERS CREATED A "MONARCHY REPUBLIC"

Democratic organization principles in use by our early state governments and those employed in other democratic nations were the models imported into the constitutional design of our federal government. Democracies had then not long been in existence.

Nations in the immediate post-monarchy era functioned as **direct democracies, where all decisions were made by a vote of the citizens.** The government's role was to implement the decisions made in that fashion. For various reasons, direct democracy was rather rapidly replaced by **representative democracy**. Under that organization form, citizens elected representatives to make the nation's decisions, and delegated authority to them to execute.

The crude and simplistic thinking in the early democracy era was, "having elected representatives, the citizens ought to step aside and allow the government to do its job." If dissatisfied, citizens should vote out Elected Representatives and elect new ones.

Early representative governments were a democratic adaptation of the "monarch" system they replaced. To elect representatives, democratic voting was employed. Once in place, elected assemblies would "rule" as had the deposed monarch but were required to make their decisions democratically.

Elected Representatives in our nation's assemblies of government were constitutionally granted blanket authority to manage themselves while governing the nation. The People were allowed to elect the persons who would participate in the government, but to do nothing else. That model of government is fundamentally Monarchical, differing only because it employed democratic elections.

THE BREAKDOWN OF THE BALLOT BOX FUNCTION DESTROYED ASSEMBLY ACCOUNTABILITY

Inter-relationship complexity emerged, and unexpected consequences negatively affected the performance of our democratic republic.

a) The ability of voters to hold their Elected Person accountable via the ballot box *does not translate into establishing accountability to the voters by the Elected Person's assembly.* The term "Legislative Branch Accountability Gap" describes virtually zero accountability to voters by the House of Representatives and the Senate.

b) **Voter rejection of a political party does not constitute voter enforcement of accountability in an Assembly**. Voter rejection of a political party is only that, voter rejection of one political party. That party will simultaneously be replaced in the assembly by another, but the Assembly continues "business as usual."

c) With Representative re-election rates running at nearly 90% in the House of Representatives**, elected representative accountability by voter rejection is being enforced at the 10% margin, with 90% of incumbents retaining their seats through continued voter acceptance.** There is no accountability being enforced against the Houses of Congress, although the party in power may be switched as a consequence of an election. Basic rules and activities of the legislative branch change little with a change in the party in power. **Holding a political party accountable does not translate into enforcing accountability on the involved House of Congress.**

The "Legislative branch Accountability Gap" allows Congress to ignore its responsibilities, play the political party game, avoid controversial legislation, pursue political enemies, and focus on trivia. The citizens have no way to tell Houses of Congress not to do those things, which are carried out regardless of the political party in power. **With no House accountability to The People there is nothing to stop it, and no penalty!**

LEGISLATIVE BRANCH DECISION ABDICATIONS MOVE THE NATION TOWARD AUTHORITARIAN GOVERNMENT

Elected assemblies exist to make decisions democratically. Lack of accountability to The People allows assemblies to consciously avoid making democratic decisions on issues that carry re-election risk. For that reason, very few important issues are currently being addressed in those assemblies.

Because nature abhors a vacuum, recent Presidents Obama, Trump, and Biden have stepped into the breach and used the powers of the Presidency to replace decision abdication in the legislative branch. Those Presidents, reacting to need but burdened with legislative malaise, have resorted to the use of Executive Orders.

If their purpose is not the implementation of the law, Executive Orders are raw totalitarianism, critical government decisions made and executed by one person rather than by a democratic vote of an elected assembly. Executive Orders inevitably are brought into use by Presidents when the Assembly legislative process breaks down. They are used to launch initiatives, with implementation carried out by units of the Administrative State. Performance breakdown in legislative assemblies is a principal cause of totalitarian encroachment.

The democratic process of our Republic is severely damaged. The damage has caused a noticeable drift toward authoritarian government, the evidence of which is an ever-increasing barrage of Executive Orders. Other signals of the slide toward totalitarianism are steadily- increasing levels of unchecked censorship in the media, increasing lawlessness and social unrest among The People, decisions of great importance being made by Departments or by the President rather than by elected assemblies, and the on-going mind-control propaganda of political parties with the aid of their media partners.

Do not expect political parties and the political elite to halt the drift toward totalitarianism and away from democracy. **They are the root cause of the drift.**

The drift will not be halted until The People perform their owner duties.

SECTION 4
CLEAR DIRECTION WOULD ELIMINATE UNCERTAINTY FOR CITIZENS AND THE NATION

It was mentioned elsewhere that China should be admired for its clear sense of direction produced by its organized determination of and pursuit of defined national objectives. One may not admire the Chinese political or value systems or agree with their thrust or intentions, but the clear sense of direction and the understanding of its importance are outstanding attributes of China's government.

Forward planning, now under discussion in their Party Summit, is focused on the 14th Five Year Plan, which establishes the broad guidelines for Chinese growth over the next decade and a half. In a Wall Street Journal article on March 5, 2021, writer Chun Han Wong stated:

"China's legislative assembly and other political pageantry this year will be showcasing the party's leadership as a successful governance model, one that is resilient and capable of delivering on the promises it makes, in contrast with apparent chaos in the West. Quoting Nils Grunberg, a senior analyst at the Mercator Institute for China Studies in Berlin, **"in the eyes of the Chinese leadership, the competition with the West has been won."**[52]

Unfortunately, that Chinese assessment is accurate. The United States is endlessly mired in a muddle of argument, indecisiveness and contention, focused on trivia, riddled by in-fighting and retribution, and flipping every election cycle from one direction to another as a different political party gains control. Every change in administration produces a many-month reversal as the party assuming power figures out how to undo the actions of the previous administration and implement new policies of its own making. **The United States endlessly pursues political party agendas, as contrasted to agreed-upon nation agendas, thereby creating an environment of contentious uncertainty in which businesses and citizens must operate.**

The dramatic difference in the sense of direction is not a comparison of Chinese communism and U.S. democracy as political systems. **It is, instead, a comparison of planning built into the Government processes of those two systems.** The Chinese system is organized and focused, utilizing proven strategic planning principles. The U.S. system is devoid of planning, disorganized, contentious, bifurcated, short-sighted, and, as political parties change control, subjected to repeated flip-flops from one muddled sense of direction to another.

A clear and enduring sense of direction for a nation establishes stability and confidence**, allowing the business and private segments to make plans and decisions in an atmosphere of certainty**. As all who have planning and decision-making experience know, minimizing uncertainty is fundamental. Uncertainty confounds decision-making because it dramatically increases risk.

One of the greatest improvements that could be made for the benefit of our Nation's Free Market and Free Enterprise environment is establishing certainty about the country's direction and the actions it intends to take.

PEOPLE-GENERATED DIRECTION: THE NATION'S OWNERS DETERMINE WHAT IS NEEDED AND PROVIDE FOR IT

The introductory material of this Chapter outlined the job of The People as owners of the Nation, using the time-honored "Plan, Organize, Staff, Direct, and Control" list of responsibilities. The People's performance of those responsibilities was found to be lacking in our analysis because Constitutional provisions for the involvement of The People do not

---

[52] "Xi Thinks Big as Party Summit Starts", article by Chun Han Wong in The Wall Street Journal, March 5, 2021.

exist and because the one existing fragile vehicle for voter involvement, the ballot box, is no longer adequately performing its function.

But The People must carry out their five responsibilities. The question becomes: "How can 330 million citizens possibly do that?"

The answer is two-fold: **"The People must first legally position themselves to carry out their responsibilities. Then, they must design, construct, and implement the processes and technical communications systems required."**

For a nation possessing the ingenuity to put men on the moon, doing those things should be a breeze. Given our nation's political condition, however, overcoming the lethargy, ignorance, and vested interests, and mustering national will and cohesion is quite another matter.

"DECISIONS BY THE PEOPLE" IS CALLED "DIRECT DEMOCRACY"

Our republic, designed by the Framers, is a 100% Representative Democracy. All of the Nation's decisions, under our Monarchy Republic structure, are intended to be made by vote of assemblies of elected persons.

Ignoring the Federal 100% representative democracy design, almost all of our states (49 out of 50) have amended their constitutions to incorporate *"direct democracy,"* a calculated move to utilize voter involvement in the decision process.[53] Referendums are initiated by state legislatures to derive citizen decisions on difficult or controversial issues that they feel will expose their members to re-election risk. "Citizen-launched" referendums are constitutionally authorized and utilized in many states.

The emergence of direct democracy practices in our states acknowledge that the many imperfections in representative democracy voted decision processes too often result in decision avoidance.

Process flaws in representative democracy are the reason the Framers selected our form of Federal government, that of a Republic. That form authorizes the use of modified voting structures and processes to circumvent the gross imperfections of pure representative democracy voting.

The "direct democracy" referendum systems employed by various States by-pass legislative inaction that is the by-product of their own Legislative Accountability Gaps. Although not at the Federal level, our nation does have Direct Democracy history and experience!

---

[53] Trans-Atlantic Democracy is Torn in Two. William A. Galston, The Wall Street Journal Op Ed September 11, 2019.

DECISION-MAKING: THE HORSE COMES BEFORE THE CART!

There is a critical difference between deciding *"what has to be done"* and deciding *"how to do it."* In the order of things, the decision of *"what has to be* done" always comes first. Deciding *"what has to be done"* is derived from planning. **Such decisions involve a commitment of resources and the assumption of substantial risk.**

"What has to be done" decisions are THE REALLY IMPORTANT DECISIONS. **Those decisions are the responsibility of the owners of the nation.**

When *"what has to be done"* has been determined, the *"how to do it"* decisions follow. Owners transmit their *"what has to be done"* decisions to their hired management as "direction." In the ordinary sequence of events, the hired management's *"how to do it"* decisions follow.

In any decision and execution process, the horse must be in its proper place in front of the cart. **In properly organized democratic self-government, the People's "what has to be done" decisions are the horse, government's "how to do it" decisions are the cart.**

PEOPLE-GENERATED DECISIONS FIT OUR REPUBLIC'S GOVERNANCE PLAN

Our Framers conceived and ballyhooed their Republic concept of government in which customized voting improvements were employed. Interestingly, they did not ballyhoo the Monarchy replication on which their Republic creation was based.

Two examples of customized voting are state-based representation in the Senate and the Electoral College system used in the election of the President. The purpose of those is to induce equity in voting by states whose populations vary widely in size.

The Framers, oftentimes criticized, must be given credit for working improvements into their "Republic" decision-making. Those were political compromises negotiated in the process of luring the thirteen states into the new Constitution but ended up being voting process improvements of considerable functionality.

The Nation desperately needs new voting process improvements for citizen decision-making, and that introduces a citizen-generated forward strategic planning process. **Short-term partisan government flip-flopping and direction-changing simply must be scuttled in favor of rational, longer-term national goals determined by The People.** That change would be a gigantic leap forward on our road toward superior decision-making and creating a government of high functionality. The improvement in the quality of governance could be startling and bring with it badly-needed corollary benefits in national cohesion and trust.

Strategic planning, employing a longer-term planning horizon, would be the custom-designed voting process, a badly needed addition to the Framer-created voting flexibility models already in place. This action will be a significant step by The People toward the performance of their five ownership responsibilities.

> **"Direction" decisions made by The People** will convert our "representative government" model into a hybrid system combining direct democracy with representative democracy. **Directional decisions made by The People will put the decision horse where it must be, firmly in front of the cart.**

THOSE "WHAT HAS TO BE DONE" DECISIONS!

In the evolution of our political process and government, respect for the logical order of things dropped by the wayside. The People, who should decide the planned direction of the nation, are given only the opportunity to choose at the polls from a slate of party-sponsored candidates, each ballyhooing party agendas and initiatives. *Our convoluted election approach does not feature the determination of an agreed-upon national direction, choosing instead to focus attention on the agendas of self-centered political parties.*

Candidates for office shouting, "If I am elected, I will ....!!!" is a totally irrational way for a large and important democratic nation to set its long-term objectives. Candidate exhortations of that nature are nothing more than attention-getters, raw promotional activities designed to drum up votes.

What a nonsensical way for a great nation to set its direction! A strategic planning-based system, where The People determine what the nation must do to improve itself over the longer term, is the only rational approach. It is unlikely to be found in any democratic nation that permits political parties to engage in governance.

> George Washington thought policy and important directional decisions should be developed by citizens, not by government or political parties.
>
> He obviously understood that the best decisions are made by those who have the most at risk, which is always The People.
>
> Allowing political parties set the goals of our Nation is about as intelligent as General Motors allowing its trade unions to set the company's business direction!

National Imperatives, decisions of "What are we going to do," and Financial Measures, decisions of "What financial controls are needed," are The People' decisions about "How we are going to make certain our nation has a clear sense of direction and purpose." **Those decisions must not ever be delegated to hired management; they are solely the duty of The People. The job of hired management is to achieve the goals, not to set them.**

Setting such goals certainly is not the business of trade-union-like political parties. Properly developed and implemented, a well-planned owner process of determining the nation's imperatives and financial measures would eliminate much of the party-created faux activity with which we are endlessly bombarded.

True national direction decisions made by The People will rank miles higher in importance than the self-serving initiatives of political parties or the promotions of their candidates. Our nation will derive incredible stability and support from People-generated direction and the certainty that flows from rational decision-making. Achievement of chosen directions will vastly improve our nation's self-confidence, wealth, and well-being!

The process of establishing National Imperatives and Financial Measures cannot be focused on trivia. It must be zeroed in on the "Big Picture" to identify the critical actions that will further the welfare of the Nation; it must accurately define and directly confront the Nation's problems and opportunities. **THERE IS NOTHING MORE IMPORTANT!**

For a nation possessing enough intellectual talent to land the Rover on Mars, creating a process by which The People determine "What has to be done" should be child's play. Unless, of course, citizens decide to dump it on the politicians!

THE PEOPLE'S DIRECTION, SUMMARIZED

Deciding which major opportunities and problems to address and what is needed as financial controls on the Government are high-risk and high-value decisions. If The People decide, a national consensus is established, which includes *The People shouldering the risk associated with their decisions.*

Provided with People-generated decisions, the Executive and Legislative branches will receive clear and unambiguous direction from the owners, coupled with relief from major decision risks. The job of those branches then becomes simply deciding "how to get it done." And that is how The People should want their elected persons focused. Get rid of the endless arguments and put them to work on productive goals set by The People.

Congress will ultimately decide "how to get it done" and enact the necessary law. When National Imperatives and Financial Measures have been set by The People, the elected assemblies will be challenged by the President to accomplish their allocation of tasks. It is critical that the order of events and purity of roles be religiously observed, otherwise system disorganization sets in.

We, The People, cannot say "It's too difficult, it's too complicated," and we cannot allow those we elect to use that excuse. This is our country, and if we don't make it function it is absolutely certain that nobody else will. As President Kennedy said regarding his proposal to put a man on the moon, itself a true national imperative, "We choose to do it not because it is easy, but because it is difficult."

And if we, as a nation, were competent to put a man on the moon we certainly are competent to figure out how to organize The People to democratically set national goals and financial controls. Difficult and complicated perhaps, it also is incredibly important, because it is the rational way to set the Nation's direction, without which the nation wanders in a fog. It will convert the Nation's decision process from random political party pot-shotting to proven planning-based decision-making, **and undertaken by those who have the only real stake in the outcome, The People.**

Fortunately, the necessary techniques are well developed within our country's business community. Most major corporations have, in place, Strategic Planning personnel who are highly skilled in those processes.

National goals and financial controls will eliminate the brutal costs of inaction, dysfunctionality, argument, and misdirection. They, coupled with other suggested Legislative branch organization changes, will correct a major breakdown in our system of government and close the "Legislative Branch Accountability Gap." **Direction and control by The People are one giant step toward rationalizing the Nation's decision process and, at the same time, involving all citizens in vital common efforts.**

The President and Congress would be executing The People's program, instead of a political party program supported only by a minor percentage of all citizens.

The President and Congress will find no escape, they will come face-to-face with accountability. To create a functioning and respected Congress, direction and control by The People is essential, just as a government competent performance is essential to the Nation's success.

Watch the Legislative process begin to function! And watch the polarization evaporate!

CHAPTER 16

THE PEOPLE'S DIRECTION AND CONTROL
SERIES: PART 3

CONTENT:

SECTION 1: SETTING THE NATION'S DIRECTION AND CONTROL
OVER GOVERNMENT

SECTION 2: THE NATIONAL IMPERATIVES, THE PEOPLE'S
FORWARD-LOOKING GOALS

SECTION 3: FINANCIAL MEASURES, THE PEOPLE'S CONTROL OVER
THE NATION'S FINANCIAL CONDITION

SECTION 4: PRO FORMA ILLUSTRATION OF PROPOSED FINANCIAL
MEASURES

SECTION 5: ROLE COMMENTARY AND SUMMARY

SECTION 6: USE OF PERFORMANCE INCENTIVES

FOREWORD

Identifying and defining the direction of the nation is classic Strategic Planning, by which The People will fulfill three owner responsibilities: "Planning" the Nation's direction, "Directing" its hired management, and establishing "Control" over accomplishment.

Three strategic processes are needed: the first, to determine and set the National Imperatives that define what The People intend to accomplish over time; the second, to establish Financial Measures that set the objectives and risk tolerances within which the Government must manage the nation's financial condition. The third is the President's two-year Legislation and Decision planning that will direct Assembly work on matters that require decision and/or legislation but that are not included in National Imperatives and Financial Measures.

Citizen involvement in and comprehension of all initiatives is vital. This Chapter finalizes The People's Direction and Control, a three-part series discussing how The People can set and launch the Nation's move forward and ensure the outcome. It dives one level deeper than previous discussions, outlining how to carry out planning by The People. Solid longer-term planning is missing in our governance, and putting it in place will be a giant step toward high-quality self-government decision-making.

SECTION 1
SETTING THE NATION'S DIRECTION AND ESTABLISHING FINANCIAL CONTROL OVER GOVERNMENT

The question "What actions must the Nation take to assure a highly prosperous and successful future?" requires a strategically- planned answer from The People.

We envision accomplishing the People's responsibility by two separate and distinct initiatives:

a) "National Imperatives" is a label selected to describe the longer-term goals and objectives that The People determine the nation must accomplish. **Developing National Imperatives is a formal act of strategic planning, a critical act fulfilling The People's "Plan" responsibility.**

b) "Financial Measures" is a label selected to describe a number of specific financial limitations and targets The People determine must be achieved by government. **These also will be developed in a formal strategic planning process.** They will be "goals" until achieved, after which they will remain in force as "controls," to be maintained by government at the required condition or level.

THESE INITIATIVES, CRITICALLY IMPORTANT FOR SUPERIOR GOVERNMENT, BECOME THE SOURCE OF PATRIOTISM, COHESION, AND NATIONAL PRIDE

National Imperatives and Financial Measures will become The People's "Direction" to the nation's Authority Structure. The individual initiatives that make up these critical directional goals ultimately become a principal measure of government performance, thereby making them The People's government accountability "Control" tools.

National Imperatives and Financial Measures will be developed and proposed by The People, with the final selection decisions made by the Well-Informed Electors.

> **This work will be a most important patriotism and cohesion-building effort that draws our citizens together in a manner that has seldom (perhaps never) before been experienced. By participating, citizens will learn more about their country and its government than is possible by other means.**
>
> **The process will give citizens a true stake in the nation's future welfare, and assure them that they are truly self-governing. The effort provides answers to the "What are we going to do" question.**

The planning process will require:

a) A. Constitutional guidance group (the Constitutional Convention) to organize and manage the planning effort and oversee accomplishment.

b) An organized approach to developing proposals from all interested parties. It is proposed two groups be involved: the citizens, and the employees of the Authority group.

c) A process by which the guidance group will synthesize the many proposals into a communication framework for purposes of debate and decision, and;

d) A knowledgeable and competent citizen body, the Well-Informed Electors, to vote for the final selections.

Delivery of National Imperatives and Financial Measures to the Government will complete this part of The People's "Plan" and "Direct" responsibility. Then, The People must fulfill their "Control" responsibility by making sure the Imperatives and Measures are achieved.

SECTION 2
THE NATIONAL IMPERATIVES

Imperatives are specific major objectives of the nation that are completed to drive the nation forward in an agreed-upon direction. Imperatives will identify the nation's aspirations, which may concern any aspect of the nation, such as systems of government, critical national functions such as the medical system or the educational system, major policy revisions, infrastructure needs or actions, etc. Imperatives will constitute the best judgment of citizens as to major efforts needed for the nation to move forward successfully.

Imperatives will vary widely in cost, complexity, importance, time to accomplish, and other factors. Imperatives cannot be compared one against another, they will be very individual. Some Imperatives may be completed in less than one year, and others may require several years, even a decade or more.

Scheduling and time to completion would be studiously developed for each after the imperative has been Constitutionally approved. Project Management, an admired planning and execution control tool utilized in Aerospace companies, should be used to manage the accomplishment of each Imperative. Those systems utilize detailed work schedules and achievement milestones to plan and track progress toward project completion.

The introduction of projects initiated by The People will require that plans be developed to utilize the operating organizations of government, including the Elected Assemblies, to carry them through to completion:

a) Financial Measures (which to a considerable degree will be constraints on day-by-day government operations) would be achieved partially through the planning and daily execution of the President. Some will require major project treatment and result in significant altering of government operations.

b) National Imperatives would be projected to significantly improve the nation. Each Imperative would be under the direction of an experienced Project Manager. Involvement in the various functions of government would be planned during the development process.

THE NATIONAL IMPERATIVES DEVELOPMENT PROCESS

National Imperatives is the planning system that will develop answers to The People's question: "What do we need to get done in this nation of ours?" The effort demands the involvement of The People and will utilize forward-looking quality planning, organized and led by experts. A rudimentary view of the effort involved is offered here.

The Constitutional Convention will mastermind the effort to identify potential Imperatives. The Convention will develop and corral the creative input of two groups: the Citizens (including businesses and institutions) and the employees of the Authority Structure. The Convention will be responsible for gathering a list of potential imperatives from the Authority Structure, and the Citizen's Forum will be responsible for gathering a list from the citizens of the nation.

While the Constitutional Convention is working with the units of the Authority Structure, the Citizen's Forum will be pursuing citizen input, hearing presentations, and absorbing data from expert groups, businesses, State and Local Government, etc. It is not possible to know how much time will be expended in those aspects of the planning effort, but it will be measured in months.

When the lists from the two main sources have been compiled, the Convention will place them before the Well-Informed Electors, who will consider them and approve, on behalf of all The People, the prioritized final list.

In order to effectively prepare the Well-Informed Electors for their decisions, Convention members must develop a strong grasp of the nation's affairs and understand what is working and what is not, what is critical and what is not. They must become very familiar with the financial condition of the Nation its ability to fund, and understand what must be done to ensure the Nation's financial stability and security. The Constitutional Convention will develop the information used by the Well-Informed Electors in their decision process.

Recognizing the great importance to the nation of National Imperatives and Financial Measures during their development process, the emphasis must be on thoroughness and involvement rather than on the speed of the process. We suggest the Convention allocate one year for Imperatives and Financial Measures development, with the goal of having the final lists approved by the Well-Informed Electors available by the end of the allocated calendar year. The public, the President, Elected Members, and those running for political office…. all concerned will know the thoughts and intent of the nation.

DETERMINING THE NUMBER OF IMPERATIVES APPROPRIATE FOR A CYCLE

A major planning issue will be how to synchronize a group of Imperatives and Financial Measures, with widely divergent completion dates, to the proposed six-year service period of elected persons. That synchronization would be helpful for incentive compensation purposes. The Convention will oversee Imperative planning and development and may go so far as to specify the time allotted to the Government for the completion of each specific Imperative and Measure and may wish to set specific incentive pay to Elected Members for each. Units of the Support Services group will unquestionably be heavily involved in the planning and execution of actions that must be intelligently conceptualized.

The planning and development of National Imperatives would be a process involving many people. Because it is a process, in which every action is generated out of other interactions, it is not possible to define here the specific order of activities. The Constitutional Convention must instruct the steps of the process as they are taking place, and they may vary significantly from what is described above.

APPROVAL BY THE WELL-INFORMED ELECTORS

The Constitutional Convention would submit the two lists of proposed National Imperatives (one from citizens, one from government employees) to all citizens and to the Well-Informed

Electors. It will be a most important communication event, involving citizens first-hand in the true process of self-government.

Well-informed electors will be asked to do their evaluation and cast a vote on each Imperative to rank those selected in priority order. The Electors may cast a number of votes during that process. Aside from the importance of the Well-Informed Elector decision, information valuable to elected bodies can be derived from feedback and from the vote tallies.

The Well-Informed Electors will have wide decision authority to modify proposals or to add or delete proposals and to set the total number.

Imperatives affirmed by a pre-defined majority vote of the Electors will be presented to the President as The People's direction and the required work of all within the nation's Authority Structure. The President will present them to The People and to the elected assemblies of government, and following those events, will lead the implementation planning.

SECTION 3
FINANCIAL MEASURES: THE PEOPLE'S CONTROL OVER THE NATION'S FINANCIAL CONDITION

In our loose, political-party-infested government system, huge current deficits are created with the wave of a political party wand because of a total lack of any control whatsoever by The People over the financial structure of the nation. Debt has risen year after year, its level provoking a reduction in the Nation's credit rating in 2013 and 2023. Government spending in response to the Covid crisis in 2020 and 2021 will have increased the already-ballooned debt by perhaps 30%.

Most disturbing is the lack of public uproar about the ballooning debt, which raises questions of whether the media is complicitly round-filing this issue. It certainly raises questions about how much voters truly comprehend.

Business owners who fail to control finances often wake up to find disaster on their doorstep. Although such owners may be the victims of their own financial folly, the most common cause of disaster is their failure to properly delegate and control the financial actions of employees. **Survival of a nation, like business survival, is dependent on the right financial controls being in place to constrain and direct the hired management.**

Many decisions will be needed. An important decision will be whether or not to develop Financial Measures in the same effort as for the National Imperatives.

REPLACING THE FRAMER CHECK-AND-BALANCE PLAN

With the installation of Constitutional Authorities, The People will replace the dysfunctional Framer check-and-balance scheme, installing in its place authority-based oversight by The People. Financial Measures will become dominant oversight tools, putting control in the hands of those who are at risk (The People) rather than placing it with the political elite. Assuming Financial Measures are intelligently set, they will bring an abrupt halt to poor income-expenditure management, massive political party spending to promote re-election, and uncontrolled growth of the national debt.

The assemblies of government, on whom the constitution placed financial faith, have not proven worthy. Re-election and political parties have become of greater importance to Elected Members than good government and the financial condition of the nation. The nation's governance structure and process are devoid of any means for The People to change directions or to enforce elected body accountability.

The broad subject of how the elected organizations of government should be re-positioned to bring greater rationality to financial activities is discussed elsewhere in this book.

THE PEOPLE'S CONTROLS: THE FINANCIAL MEASURES

It is proposed The People place a clamp on the nation's financial activities and conditions by establishing Financial Measures that the government must accomplish. The Measures, self-government at its finest, are both "Direction" and "Control" by The People.

Financial Measures tell the Government specifically the direction it is to pursue. A proposal is included to give the initiative "wallop" by providing significant elected member bonus compensation for achievement of the various Financial Measures and providing for the removal of elected persons who cannot produce what is required.

A worthy companion to the National Imperatives, Financial Measures will be developed under the direction of the Constitutional Convention in a broad-based planning process similar to that employed in the formation of the National Imperatives but custom-designed for the uniqueness of the Financial Measures system. It is a program of The People, but the extent to which they can comprehend and contribute is not known at this time. The Convention will work closely with the Well-Informed Electors, the ultimate decision-makers, but in the first pass, the Convention will find it necessary to utilize the Treasury, the Federal Reserve, and other experts for information and for training themselves and the Well-Informed Electors.

The Constitutional Convention would have responsibility for all administrative interfaces with the Government. **Financial Measures become "Imperatives" to the Government, requirements that must be achieved. It is highly recommended that a special expertise** group be established to identify and evaluate the potential consequences these controls could have on the nation's economy. Its findings would be input to the decision process of the Well-Informed Electors.

Readers should note that because Financial Measures are critical decisions of the nation, the Well-Informed Electors will be the final decision body. Financial budgeting and achievement of budget, however, will be the responsibility of the President, so his input and that of the Treasurer will be important. The budget must, of course, meet the Financial Measure requirements.

It is proposed that the Constitutional Convention be authorized to approve temporary breaches of individual Financial Measures, but any permanent breach would require a directional vote of the Well-Informed Electors.

The following table is a display of what the finally-voted Financial Measures might look like. These are suggestions only. The final Measures may be different from these in many respects. It is important that the end result be simple, understandable by citizens, and identify the nation's important financial controls.

When finalized, the Financial Measures would be communicated to the Nation, the subject of wide and in-depth discussion. Thereafter, tabulations of the nation's performance of the Measures would be regularly reported and discussed.

SECTION 4
PRO FORMA ILLUSTRATION OF PROPOSED FINANCIAL MEASURES

THE PEOPLE'S DIRECTION AND CONTROL
FINANCIAL MEASURES FOR THE NATION

Growth of Gross Domestic Product	4% Minimum Annually
Maximum Direct National Debt	75% of Annual GDP
Maximum Indirect National Debt	200% of Annual GDP
Maximum Annual Budget Expenditures	15% of Annual GDP
Maximum Allowable Annual Deficit	2% of Annual GDP, Zero Over 5 Years
Maximum Allowable Trade Deficit	Zero in 5 years
Federal Reserve Balance Sheet	Max 20% of Annual GDP
Maximum Inflation	3% Rate
Maximum Unemployment	4% Rate

THE PURPOSE AND FUNCTION OF EACH FINANCIAL MEASURE

1. ANNUAL GROSS DOMESTIC PRODUCT (GDP)

The Gross Domestic Product Growth measure is the most important "Direction" for Government. It is suggested the nation set a growth path rate higher than what has been produced in recent history. In order to achieve the higher growth goal, a brake must be applied to government actions that weigh down business efficiency, hinder national production, or misallocate resources, with new growth-oriented programs initiated to replace them.

GDP generates the wealth of the Nation and, of course, provides the funds employed by the government. Without GDP growth, The People will not see improved wages or a better living standard, nor can the national debt be paid down. In choosing a more rapid growth rate, The People would be directing the Government to place the highest importance on GDP growth in all of its decisions. If a slower growth rate is chosen, The People would have the capability to achieve other goals.

GDP growth is the best measure of national performance, the nation's productivity, worldwide competitiveness, the efficacy of taxation and spending policies, financial control, and management of resources, all of which influence national economic health.

It is suggested that an annual GDP growth of at least 4% be achieved in our Republic. That measure, or another set by the Well-Informed Electors, will be the primary financial goal of the Nation, a decision of the highest importance.

The People may decide to continue the Nation's current path, which is sacrificing Gross Domestic Product growth at the altar of other goals. The decision as to which route the Nation will take is to be made by Well-Informed Electors, by vote, with the welfare of the Nation in mind.

This writer suggests that a firm relationship between the growth of GDP and the paydown of the nation's intolerably high debt ratio be established as a national policy and worked into the Financial Measures.

2. DEBT MANAGEMENT OF THE NATION

The current debt level of the United States is high enough that it must be considered a significant threat to the nation's stability. By establishing Debt Management Measures, the Federal Government would be directed to develop and implement plans to reach designated debt levels by a pre-determined future date. The accomplishment plan would be produced under the direction of the President and require the affirmation of the Well-Informed Electors.

In this direction, The People would be stating that the Nation's creditworthiness and financial capability are the second most important Financial Measures. Achievement may require deferral or cancellation of desirable or popular programs, implementation of new taxation, or other financial action. Debt control is tied closely to the achievement of the GDP goal and control of government expenses, so it will be an important statement of direction and an equally important measurement.

It is proposed, to open the discussion, that the maximum national debt (defined as the direct borrowings of the nation) be set at 75% of annual GDP, about $20 trillion in current dollars, a level to be reached within a defined time period. Another way to approach that would be to decide the aggregate national debt must be reduced by $1 trillion (or some other number) every year. Another approach would be to set the annual required reduction to national debt based on the growth of GDP over an annual average.

The approach imposes short-term expectations, upon which accountability can be assessed or incentive paid. The final control percentage and defined time period would be set by the Well-Informed Electors, with counsel from the nation's financial experts.

Indirect debt (Medicare, Housing, Student Loans, etc.) would be tabulated with the tolerance levels set by the Well-Informed Electors by vote in the same action.

Some will say, "This proposal will ham-string government!" Another view might be "Elimination of party-promotion government largess spending will provide the money needed for the Nation's debt reduction." The nation's view will have to be determined in the government budgeting process, under the direction of Constitutional Authorities, with final directional decisions made by the Well-Informed Electors.

Readers must be aware that the nation's huge national debt is a problem of great significance. It has been easy for out-of-control political parties to balloon the debt over the years, absent any accountability. Our current form of government has proven itself incapable of disciplined financial management. Getting the national debt under control will be a massive undertaking, requiring highly intelligent problem-solving, national fortitude, and a considerable amount of time.

3. THE GOVERNMENT BUDGET: INCOME AND EXPENSE MANAGEMENT OF THE NATION

The accepted methodology employs a "budget" for planning, deciding, and tallying expected financial outcomes. A completed budget becomes "direction" for those having execution responsibilities and a "control" mechanism for those who evaluate performance.

A government budgeting process is in place but it is noteworthily ineffective. The causes of ineffectiveness are a) undisciplined self-management by the Legislative branches, b) Constitutional mis-delegation of financial responsibilities among the elected branches, c) absence of accountability to The People, allowing assemblies to avoid performance penalties, d) lack of steady and high-quality disclosure to voters concerning the budget and financial condition of the nation, and e) party political interests and goals are given priority higher than the financial condition of the Nation.

A clear budget Financial Measure establishes The People's demand and government accountability for professional budgeting and financial achievement. Critical financial planning considerations will involve tying the level of possible improvement to the constraints of the economy. This Measure will generate immense pressure to eliminate mismanagement by the government and the economy. Government system and structure deficiency causes described above will require correction in order for the desired quality of financial management to be installed.

1. The President shall, before the commencement of each fiscal year, compile a Federal budget for the forthcoming year's activities and for one additional year. Budget planning will be the responsibility of the Treasury, under the direction of the President, but each line item and the final budget will require approval by the Senate.

2. Managing the Nation's income and expenditures to conform to the budget will be the responsibility of the President, supported by all units of government.

3. The target for budgeted annual expenditures could be up to 15% of that year's GDP. (The selected control number would be proposed by the Guardians and approved by the Well-Informed Electors).

4. Except when the Nation is engaged in a declared war or is in crisis, the budget should be balanced or produce an operating surplus. The maximum permitted annual deficit could be set at 3% of annual GDP. In the event a deficit is incurred in any year, the aggregate deficit over that and the succeeding three years could be set not to exceed zero percent of GDP. Debt reduction should be a required budget item. Any such control would be a proposal approved by the Well-Informed Electors.

5. On completion of each fiscal quarter, the Senate and the President will review The People's performance against budgeted income and expense and enact corrective actions.

6. The finalized budget and quarterly performance must be thoroughly communicated to The People via constitutionally controlled media, allowing discussions, questions, and feedback.

7. The President will maintain, through the IRS and under the direction of an assigned Elected Assembly, an ongoing review of the Internal Revenue Code and quarterly propose changes to the Senate for their consideration. The Code shall at all times be

current and appropriate to conditions. It must support the income requirements of the Nation, debt reduction, and the balanced budget requirement.

8. The President and the Senate shall monitor performance and, in the event of failure to meet the budget requirement for either revenue or expense, shall direct necessary adjustments.

9. The Guardians of the Constitution shall approve each Budget and may direct action they deem necessary for performance correction.

Responsibility for achieving the components of a balanced budget will fall on the President, the Chief Executive of the Government. In his/her proposed expanded role and possessed of a new planning process, he/she will be able to respond to the demand for dramatically improved government operations.

4. ADDITIONAL MEASURES

Four (or more) Financial Measures, in addition to those mentioned, shall be developed by the Constitutional Convention. The numerical measures in the above display are for discussion proposals only, as the final Financial Measures to be utilized will be decided by the Electors. Those displayed are suggestions, and the following discussion is solely for edification.

Unemployment 4% - Having a national goal relating to employment is very important. The goal set by the Well-Informed Electors will drive many critical governance decisions. A Measure establishing a low rate of unemployment would initiate a wide range of government policy changes covering unemployment benefits, off-shore labor policies, immigration, student graduation, and other factors affecting the labor pool.

Federal Reserve Balance Sheet – The proposed aggregate shall not exceed 20% of the Nation's annual GDP. This control is necessary to prevent the Fed from funding, on its balance sheet, excessive financing costs of the nation or engaging in unwarranted financial programs by authoritarian direction.

Inflation, 3% - Maintaining a properly-valued currency is dependent on inflation control. The actual percentage number would be set by the Well-Informed Electors. The current measure is 2%.

Trade Surplus/Deficit – Manage to a surplus within four years, then maintain a surplus. The policy position would be set by the Well-Informed Electors, with the assistance of the Treasury and the Constitutional Convention.

THE CYCLE FOR FINANCIAL MEASURE DECISIONS

Administrative responsibility for the development of Financial Measures and their achievement will fall on the Constitutional Convention. It will lead their development, in concert with the National Imperatives, on behalf of the Well-Informed Electors, who will have final decision authority.

The most desirable approach would be to re-evaluate Financial Measures on the same cycle as the employment terms of the Elected Members and Senators. If the term selected is six years, the Financial Measures cycle could be set to match. Financial Measures cannot be achieved by the government in short time frames, so performance evaluation of Elected Persons may have to encompass the entire span of their service and likely will have to utilize "progress toward achievement" assessments.

The Constitutional Convention and Well-Informed Electors need latitude to review and institute a reset of individual Measures at any time based on their assessment of functionality and impact on national conditions. This will not be a simple assessment, as achievement of an individual Financial Measure is certain to produce unintended consequences elsewhere in the economy.

Setting and achieving Financial Measures may turn out to be the most important decision process of the Nation, because it focuses on correcting a serious threat to its future by putting the hired management under performance pressure. Managing the Financial Measures process and achievement will be an intellectual challenge for all involved.

SECTION 5
ROLE COMMENTARY AND SUMMARY

Events of recent decades have exposed, for all to see, the Constitution-enshrined imbalance of power between the Legislative and Executive Branches. The authors of the Federalist Papers worried about the rabid political nature of the Legislative Branch, the extreme weight of its numbers, the cumulative volume of its discourse, and the disproportionate weakness of the role of the President.

The existing Constitution gives the power of the purse to the Legislative Branch. It also vests in that branch the power of impeachment of the President. It vests, in the President, no counter-balance powers. The authors of the Federalist Papers must have been prescient when they pinpointed those risks, which have surfaced as an underlying cause of the extreme constitutional stress our nation is suffering.

Under the present Constitution, the President has only his "bully pulpit" to induce any activity whatsoever in the Legislative Branch. Legislation completed, of course, requires his signature to become law, but that is only after the fact. Congress, in recent decades, has been avoiding the nation's problems, is mismanaging the country's finances and debt, and has spent its time trying to use its constitutional impeachment authority to dislodge a disliked but legally elected President.[54] The President has had no effective check-and-balance on the actions of the elected assemblies.

> Establishment of the Financial Measures and National Imperatives is one major step toward controlling government, by forcing it to follow The People's direction. The Measures and Imperatives are intended to focus assembly attention on the nation's key opportunities and problems, a badly-needed discipline now absent in government. An important allied action is vesting, in the President, control over the government process.

National Imperatives and Financial Measures **are directions from The People to the government** concerning what must be accomplished. An elected official of consequence in government must be assigned responsibility for accomplishing the People's National Imperatives and Financial Measures, and that elected official must be the President, the Chief Executive Officer of Government.

The job of the President is today arguably the most misdirected and improperly utilized position in the Nation. His/her required performance relative to National Imperatives and Financial Measures, plus duties executing the Decision and Legislation Plan, will dramatically shift his/her attention away from political trivia toward governing fundamentals.

SETTING NATIONAL IMPERATIVES AND FINANCIAL MEASURES IS NO GUARANTY OF ACCOMPLISHMENT

The People will demand that National Imperatives and Financial Measures receive priority attention and direct the Executive branch and government assemblies to fulfill them. The People do not dictate how implementation is to be carried out. It is expected that the elected assemblies will create and construct the actions necessary for achievement.

Their decisions will, no doubt, be the subject of considerable public discussion. Knowing their actions will be under intense scrutiny and that incentive compensation and service continuation are on the line for each elected person, there is little doubt the elected branches

---

[54] This text was first composed in 2019, but reflects conditions over successive years.

of government will perform National Imperative and Financial Measure duties with great care. That is what The People expect of them and what is needed to achieve success.

The People, watching the assembly progress toward achieving Imperatives and Financial Measures that they have determined to be necessary, may experience a delightful new sensation, an unexpected (and never-before-experienced) jolt of pride in their government.

THE FINAL STEP IN ESTABLISHING LEGISLATIVE BRANCH ACCOUNTABILITY

The President, having accepted the National Imperatives and the Financial Measures from the Convention, will present them to the nation and to Elected Assemblies and direct their accomplishment. The President will schedule the study, debate, planning, and legislation for each. He/she will monitor activity and progress and consult to discuss issues, ensuring the end product will meet his/her approval and that of The People.

SUMMARY

Term Limits and assembly restructure will wipe away the re-election fixation of Elected Members and Senators. By initiating financial rewards for achieving what The People expect of them, eliminating political party involvement, and establishing focus in the assemblies by eliminating their right to "set the rules of their proceeding," the nation will, after almost 250 years, finally witness the performance of professional government. With the government decision process directed by professional outside management controlled by the Guardians of the Constitution, the character and performance of our representative democracy will make a remarkable U-turn.

The most important step toward improved National decision-making is placing The People in a position to make the decisions they alone must make. The National Imperatives and Financial Measures will be among the most important decisions of The People because of the clear sense of direction and control they will impart to the government and to the citizenry and the uncertainty they will remove from private and business decisions.

The People will see a dramatic change in the tone and discourse of the nation as a result of these initiatives.

SECTION 6
USE OF PERFORMANCE INCENTIVE

Accountability requires specific measurements against which performance can be evaluated.

Financial Measures will give brutally clear Direction to the government. Evaluation of government performance toward their achievement provides the means for The People to exercise Control and establish government accountability. For the first time, it will allow The People to fulfill their ownership responsibilities, thereby engendering a strong sense of national cohesion and pride.

Although derived somewhat differently, National Imperatives provide the same clear Direction and an equally important Control mechanism. National Imperatives and Financial Measures, acting together, will be systems by which to evaluate the performance of government and, therefore, the performance of elected persons.

Finally, in our nation, the installation of these measures allows The People to escape the constitutional shackles of the Framer Monarchy Republic by establishing organized and pure self-government.

Implementing improved decision-making, the principal strategy of The People will require upgrading how decisions are made, one example of which is implementing the National Imperatives and Financial Measures. They demand a reward plan for elected persons based on delivery by the hired management of what The People have decided must be accomplished.

The Performance Reward Plan proposed here violates the concepts upon which every known existing compensation practice for elected persons in democratic governments is based. In the private sector, Performance Reward Plans allow owners to direct hired management like conductors direct an orchestra, playing beautiful music from a score. Existing employment practices for elected persons are charitably described as an invitation to an "off-key" scrum.

In our government, elected persons are hired by management. They are contracted to execute what The People have decided to do and, within their assemblies, to make decisions that The People have directed them to make. Modern personnel practices require that they be given clear direction, be compensated well for achievement, and be replaced if performance does not meet requirements.

Some will say incentive compensation is an expensive tool. But if Financial Measures are met and National Imperatives are achieved, think of the immense financial contribution to the Nation that will have been produced! The cost of the Performance Reward Plan will be minuscule compared to the financial benefit derived.

INTRODUCTION

This book suggests that The People of the United States convert their government from a Framer-era barely-functioning horse-and-buggy vehicle to customized modern high-performance self-government.

We envision taking one giant step toward that goal with the introduction of two classic self-government initiatives designed to anchor in the nation a strong sense of direction and control. Those are designed to give the government clear and unmistakable operating direction, communicating where The People wish to take the nation, thereby fulfilling a significant aspect of The People's ownership responsibility.

Introducing those proposals successfully requires penetrating the psyches of multitudes of citizens who are sloshing about in a swirling pool of political-party-and-media delusion, desperately clutching their life-vests. The leaking horse-and-buggy contraption is littered with mistaken party beliefs, tribal behavior, contention and mistrust, political striving, misinformation, and ancient-origin authority misplacement, all sloshing and gurgling.

Instead of searching outside the container for safety, terrified citizens launch a frantic search for a phantom messiah president to rescue us all. The odds of finding such a person are roughly comparable to the odds of winning a lottery.

---

a) "National Imperatives" is a label selected to describe the longer-term goals and objectives that The People determine must be accomplished. **Developing National Imperatives is a formal act of strategic planning and execution of The People's "Plan" responsibility.**

b) "Financial Measures" is the label that describes a list of quantified government financial limitations and achievement goals selected by The People under their "Plan" responsibility. **These will be developed in a formal strategic planning process. They will be "goals" until achieved, and then they will remain in force as "controls" to be maintained at the specified level.**

Self-government, an interesting democracy adaptation, is broadly agreed to be the most desirable form of national authority. There are few written principles for self-government, and for that reason and others, not many democracies practice it. The practices and systems embedded in the U.S. Constitution emerged from grass-roots problem-solving or were imported from other governments. Democratic government in our nation is not a cohesive, rationally planned system but, instead, is a conglomeration of individual practices believed to conform to democratic principles, with interfaces between the practices functioning accidentally rather than by design.

This book proposes injecting into that concoction a group of system solutions based upon proven business principles, which to the average citizen will probably seem mind-bogglingly complex. Elimination of political parties in favor of clear decision control by The People, changes designed to produce decisions of high quality and a fundamental reorganization of government are proposed. The revised system will be designed to allow The People to make the nation's critical directional decisions, and to totally control government behavior.

Planning-based management is introduced, to define the conclusions of the citizens and convert them into statements of direction. These are but a few of the proposed changes. Not mentioned is the suggested change of converting our government-elected persons to "hired management," complete with employment contracts, enforced term limits, and incentive compensation.

We will delve, following, into those startling human management change proposals.

THE HUMAN RELATIONS CHALLENGE SUMMARIZED

Achieving true self-government requires that The People dramatically improve the employment arrangement with their hired management. The following summarizes proposals from various chapters:

1. Our assemblies could benefit markedly from a completely different type of candidate. The sourcing and selection of hired management persons requires that the right talent be located and placed before the voters for a democratic election. **It is proposed that the election process and all candidate selection be managed by Constitutional Authorities and all election expenses be paid by the taxpayer.**

2. Elected persons currently have no defined employment agreement. Time, compensation, permitted activities, behavior, and other terms of employment must be defined contractually, and required performance must be properly documented.

3. **Current elected assembly self-management is a failure. Embedded distractions, poor processes, conflicts, and contradictions must be removed**

from the work environment. The Constitutional Authorities will establish professional management control over each of the assemblies, and of the decision processes used in them.

4. The compensation and rewards system directs the hired management to do what The People want to be accomplished and at a high level of achievement. Elimination of the work conflicts present in assembly-elected positions and achievement of true employee focus are the key changes needed.

5. It is strongly recommended that all elected persons be contracted as hired management for a term-limit period. Their proposed six-year term and compensation package should feature no pension benefits but high incentive compensation for performance and two-year retention reviews.

"HIRED MANAGEMENT" PERFORMANCE REWARD PLAN

Government will receive "What must be done" direction from The People in the form of National Imperatives and Financial Measures and from the President in a two-year Decision and Legislation plan. Those are intended to be the drivers for all organizations of government. From the President down to the assemblies with their coordinated support organizations, all will focus on "How to do it" and "Getting it done."

Government cannot achieve the nation's Imperatives and Measures in a short period of time. They are longer-term undertakings involving much research and planning before execution begins. Achieving the GDP growth benchmark or converting the trade deficit to a surplus could take any number of years. For example, one potential Imperative, eliminating the wide swings in the economy caused by the use of interest rates to correct economic and government decision mistakes, might take perhaps ten years. With national determination and focus, other Measures could be achieved in a short time span but then must be maintained at a required level.

Establishing and communicating the goals of the three initiatives and reporting progress will embed them in the national psyche. That is their purpose!

The challenge of granting incentive compensation to individual elected persons based on contribution to a huge undertaking that may not be completed during the elected person's time of service is totally possible within available knowledge levels.

INCENTIVE COMPENSATION, TERM LIMITS, AND DEDICATED FOCUS

This book proposes that term limits be imposed on all elected persons whose service should not be side-tracked by efforts to establish themselves in perpetuity as The Anointed of the Nation. One long trip down that road should have been enough for our citizens.

Elected persons must be focused, laser-like, on achieving what The People have decided is needed, evidenced by the Imperatives and Measures and the President's Decisions and Legislation plan. The secret to superior national performance is an unrelenting focus on identifying and accomplishing goals that The People have decided "truly matter."

It is proposed that one-time six-year service terms would be the norm for elected persons. Every two years, one-third of each assembly would terminate service and be replaced by the newly elected. To achieve performance under such an arrangement, The People need to replace the self-actualization motivations currently driving elected persons (endless re-election, huge pensions, party power, fame or recognition, a place in leadership) with a new set of motivators that support only the nation's achievement. **Properly employed, a performance compensation plan with substantial monetary rewards for an elected person's accomplishment could be a powerful motivator.**

A performance reward plan is only one action, among many, that would improve the performance of our elected bodies. The People must also upgrade assembly internal operating processes, to complete installation of their "direction" and "control."

The People must terminate the current senseless milling and unproductive contentious misdirection of the legislative bodies, and achieve instead intense focus through day-to-day management of activities. Those actions were discussed in Chapters 6 through 9.

PROPOSED ELECTED PERSON EMPLOYMENT MUST BE UNDERSTOOD BY CITIZENS

The Performance Reward Plan outlined here is a conceptual framework to assist readers in evaluating a complex proposal. **It is not possible, in this brief treatment, to present any depth of detail. The detail will ultimately be the job of compensation specialists, and their final product may differ substantially.**

As a citizen, you should understand the proposal and how it would function to direct assembly performance and drive the improvement you would want in that branch of government. **A superior plan will not be difficult for competent specialists to create.**

True self-government requires that the achievement of Financial Measures, National Imperatives, and the President's Decision and Legislation plan be regularly reported to The People, including rewards allocated. Those reports would become a central post for constitutional communication to keep The People totally involved in the process. **The positive impact on national cohesion and trust could be quite remarkable.**

PERFORMANCE REWARDS AND FAILURE PENALTIES

Performance rewards speak for themselves, but without penalties for failure, the motivational process will be meaningless, the equation unbalanced. Those administering cannot excuse non-performance. The clearest direction achievable is needed.

> Individual incentives must be reconciled with the fact that elected persons are participating in democracy, where decisions are made by assembly vote. In that environment, performance of an individual is largely determined by the performance of the group. Incentive payments may be the same for all assembly members, to encourage group problem-solving. But some participants will contribute more than others, and some less, an evaluation to be made by the professional assembly management for reward consideration purposes. Individual performance defects would be dealt with separate from the incentive system.

Those penalized for group non-performance will be ineligible for incentive compensation and may suffer other penalties. If failure to meet Imperative or Financial Measures completion is persistent, the plan administrators should consider whether elected persons should be replaced. In that upgrading process, non-performing assembly bodies will be flushed out, and newly elected persons will be given the opportunity to achieve what is required.

Utilizing this approach, the People will have given brutally clear direction to the Government through Financial Measures, National Imperatives, and the President's Decision and Legislation Plan, assuring the pursuit of their direction through effective administration. The benefits to the nation will vary with the consistency of the rewards and punishments selected but will be substantial.

CHAPTER 17

THE RIGHTS AND FREEDOMS SERIES: PART 1

CONTENT:

SECTION 1: THE BILL OF RIGHTS, AN UNBALANCED EQUATION

SECTION 2: APPLYING THE RULES OF AUTHORITY DELEGATION TO FRAMER DECISIONS

SECTION 3: THE CONSEQUENCES OF GRANTING BROAD FREEDOM WITHOUT IMPOSING ACCOUNTABILITY

SECTION 4: CONSTITUTIONALLY ESTABLISH PERSONAL ACCOUNTABILITY

SECTION 5: FREEDOM OF SPEECH (FREEDOM OF EXPRESSION)

SECTION 6: SUMMARY OF RIGHTS ACTION PROPOSALS

FOREWORD

The first ten amendments to the Constitution, commonly referred to as the Bill of Rights, were ratified on December 15, 1791.

They seem to have been positioned as protection for The People against the new form of government implemented earlier. The clear message was, "We have given massive powers to the government, but its behavior regarding these rights granted to The People must be hands-off."

The First Amendment's 1791 provisions are seriously affecting today's daily life. Space limitations do not permit discussion of all Rights, even though there is much worthy of examination among them. This Chapter will focus on the implications of the Bill of Rights, and future chapters will examine selected Freedoms considered problemsome.

The First Amendment was an awesome gift to The People as individuals, requiring absolutely no accountability on their part for anything! American people are proud of that Framer gift. They should be! Arguably, it ranks as the most momentous "free lunch" in history, and they were the lucky recipients.

We wonder if they ever stop to ponder the question, "Why were we so lucky?" This Chapter will examine what are believed to be the political reasons behind this magnanimous act of benevolence.

And yes, there is no such thing as a free lunch!

SECTION 1
THE BILL OF RIGHTS, AN UNBALANCED EQUATION

The notion of "People's Rights" emanated in the year 1215 from the Magna Carta, the English rights declaration drawn up following a successful revolution against their monarchy.

The first Amendments to our Constitution passed in 1791, four years after its signing, were the result of a Framer's promise to complete the unfinished work of the Constitutional Convention. Amendment 1, which contains what is generally called "the Bill of Rights," and Amendment 2, establishing the "Right to Bear Arms," are those most familiar to our citizens.

Given the limitations of time and space, the focus of this Series will be on Amendment 1, specifically Freedom of Speech, Freedom of the Press, and the Right Peaceably to Assemble. We will discuss matters arising from them that are considered important to the design of an advanced high-performance democratic self-government for our nation.

This book's organizational analysis of the division of power and obligation between the owners of the Nation and their government applies Principles of Management, first defined in 1950 and broadly accepted since that time. Most of the important Principles of Management emanated from the Military, where direction and control of huge "people organizations" is the managerial challenge.

As the owners of our nation, The People **as a group** decide whether or not they are willing to delegate powers or rights to citizens **as individuals**, and if so, on what terms.

When writing our constitution, the Framers ignored the rights and obligations of The People that stem from their ownership of the Nation. The People's rights were, without constitutional discussion, taken from them and gifted to the new government. That misappropriation of ownership rights is a principal cause underlying today's Federal government dysfunctional condition, because through it government's accountability to The People was eliminated.

The fact that the Constitution failed to acknowledge and accommodate the rights of The People was apparently on the list of matters the Framers were not able to resolve before the Constitution was signed.[55] Several Framers signed the new Constitution on the condition that uncompleted issues would receive prompt resolution. After the Signing an effort was begun, led by Framers George Mason and Thomas Jefferson, to decide the uncompleted issues and write the necessary provisions. Finalized about four years later, out of nineteen original proposals, Amendments 1 through 10 were approved.

HEAVY DELEGATION OF RIGHTS TO THE PEOPLE WITH NO COMMENSURATE ACCOUNTABILITY

Amendment I, called the "Bill of Rights," is a delegation to citizens and inhabitants of the United States of defined unfettered rights and privileges, without limitation and with no accountability imposed on the recipients.

Readers will recall text about bargaining as the decision process within our government. They should view the Bill of Rights as the end product of a Framer "bargaining" mind-set because doing so provides a way to perhaps explain those otherwise murky decisions. There were several potential trade-offs when the Bill of Rights largess was under consideration. One view is because the Framers created a government with no accountability to the citizens, they were loath to enforce Bill of Rights accountability upon the citizens. Another view is that the Bill of Rights was a repayment to the citizens for the Framers' constitutional action of seizing citizen's fundamental rights and gifting them to the government.

The Bill of Rights largess, by either view, was delayed compensation to American citizens for highly questionable Framer constitutional decisions.

This author posits that the convention's scheme of granting to government massive power with no compensation to The People, the template for establishing the Framer "Monarchy Republic," generated second thoughts among delegates. We suspect they feared the new constitution too heavily favored the political class at the expense of The People. The fears were not strong enough to provoke a reconsideration of the constitution's well-disguised grant of monarchical powers to the newly elected government, plus the gift to the government of fundamental ownership rights taken from The People, but we suspect it did produce a concern among a number of Framers, and provoked thoughts that the whole deal needed to be made more attractive to the citizenry.

---

[55] The Constitutional Convention included a committee called "The Committee on Postponed Matters."

For whatever reason, the Bill of Rights was postured as a huge gift. Grateful citizens apparently never asked, "Why were we so lucky? Why this great act of benevolence?" The price paid by the nation has probably never entered the minds of citizens, then or since.

SECTION 2
APPLYING RULES OF AUTHORITY DELEGATION TO FIRST AMENDMENT DECISIONS

Because the First Amendment was a delegation of rights (authority) to The People as individuals, it is appropriate to consider it from the perspective of the management rules of delegation. Those rules originated in the Military and have been widely adopted since the Framer time:

"Every delegation of authority[56] must be balanced by imposition of a commensurate level of accountability."

Management people sometimes also quote an allied doctrine: "For every action, there is an equal and opposite reaction." We will consider here the unidentified "equal and opposite reactions" involved in the massive unbalanced gift to citizens by the Bill of Rights.

The Bill of Rights was remarkable. It was a no-strings-attached gift to the citizens of powerful personal rights and freedoms, then widely trumpeted as a "great application of the freedom principle." One suspects that the unfettered gift was instead designed to insure the Monarchy Republic creation against retribution from irate citizens who might take issue with its deeply corruptive favoring of elected politicians over the citizens.

Viewed from that perspective, the First Amendment was a brilliant political move by the Framers. **The Bill of Rights gift to the citizens bought, for the political elite, insurance that their Monarchy Republic government creation was not likely to be attacked by unfairly treated citizens.**

Imposition of no accountability on citizen recipients for questionable behavior under the Bill of Rights provisions, was a perfect bargain trade-off for citizen acceptance of a government devoid of any accountability to The People.

Amendment 1, a classic "simple solution to a complex problem," makes no mention of political bargain considerations. Each grant in Amendment 1, such as the establishment of religion or freedom of speech, is immensely complex within itself. The simple solution of grants of freedoms without limitation, detailed definition, or defined accountability created

---

[56] Rights are Authority

the appearance of an act of great benevolence. **In actuality, there is every reason to believe it was merely a calculated Framer political strategy.**

Readers will observe that the unbalanced Freedoms of the Bill of Rights, conceived by our nation's Political Elite, are a problem of Constitutional origin. Such problems can't be resolved by citizen actions, such as electing a new President. The Constitution provides The People with no route to make necessary Amendment revisions.

MORALS AND ETHICS HAVE REGRESSED

The Framer view of 1780s citizen ethics and morals must have been the direct opposite of what we view those qualities to be among today's population.

People of the 1700s lived largely under puritan standards. Morals and ethical rules in the early history of our Nation were derived from religious teaching. Designed for a society of high morals and ethics, the Amendment 1 grant of unfettered rights, liberties, and freedoms must not have been viewed as "high risk." The grants were not too liberal, considering the level of morals and ethics then prevalent in the population.

Entropy inevitably applied its rasp. As the years rolled by, our Nation's population swung away from religion toward secular values, our government from democracy toward totalitarianism, and the social environment from simplicity to complexity. Society's moral and ethical behavior loosened in lockstep. Society today is acknowledged as being far more tolerant of moral and ethical lapse than was the society of Framer time. Dramatically-improved communication has played a strong hand in the loosening of standards, but other factors have been influential.

The magnanimous grants contained in the Bill of Rights, devoid as they were of citizen personal accountability of any type or nature, are the probable background cause of our nation's long history of ethical and moral decline. Morals and ethics regression in our nation is a silent cause of the very threatening loss of that democratic self-government essential called "TRUST."

What an ugly "unintended consequence" that is, emanating as it has from the complete absence of individual accountability in the much-lauded Bill of Rights!

If you were a Framer voting to make those same Bill of Rights delegation decisions today, given what you know about the character, ethics, and behavior of our Nation's population, **would you vote to grant blanket rights and liberties with zero accountability attached?**

Some would, but thinking latter-day Framers would more likely mutter, "No, I don't think so!" and cast a ballot reflective of that conclusion.

There are those who will argue that the legal system imposes accountability on individuals for their actions, and it does. But, the legal system captures only a small portion of actions that most would regard as "unethical" or "immoral." The terms "illegal," "unethical and "immoral" have different meanings. Available statistics concerning morals and ethics are those captured by our legal net, but the nation's untallied problems from citizen moral and ethical behavior would make up a much larger statistical tally.

SECTION 3
THE CONSEQUENCES OF FREEDOM GRANTS WITHOUT IMPOSED ACCOUNTABILITY

It is a fair guess that few citizens make the connection between the unbalanced Bill of Rights and a number of troubling negative societal behavioral characteristics with which all are very familiar.

To name a few: a desire (and the right) to self-protect with firearms; a built-up large prison population; a high-and-increasing crime and violence rate; overburdened courts; a deeply troubled education system; and a general degradation of human behavior.

"For every action, there is an equal and opposite reaction," says an ancient doctrine. In algebra, "An equation consists of two expressions that equal each other." In accounting, "The debits must equal the credits." With its far-reaching impact, that classic unbalanced equation, the Bill of Rights, heavily influences the behavior of citizens. That being the case, the unintended consequences flowing from the lack of Bill of Rights accountability will not automatically reverse themselves.

The United States has one of the largest prison populations (expressed as a percentage of the total population) among the nations on Earth. Do you think there is not a cause-effect connection between our nation's First Amendment freedom grants without accountability and our high prison population? And if the prison statistics report only the moral and ethical lapses resolved within the judicial system, what does that tell us about the impact the unbalanced Bill of Rights has had on the behavior of the population as a whole?

Given the regression in society's morals and ethics since the formulation of the Bill of Rights and the negative effects of that regression, an unfettered delegation of rights and liberties to the population today cannot be intellectually justified. There are two broad solutions (or combinations of them) that could be applied, using the hammer of authority, to correct: a proportional reduction of freedom rights and liberties or, alternatively, imposition of penalties for violations.

The prospect of building more prisons to house an enlarged population of violators isn't very attractive, is it? Betting on correction through our prison system is generally viewed as a losing wager. **The national goal should be to decrease the inmate count, not increase it.** There is only one intellectually supportable course of action, that of attacking the morals and ethics problem the way it has historically been attacked by broadcasting miscreant negative actions within the community.

A solution is to implement a national morals and ethics improvement plan based on collection and planned publication of individual citizen morals and ethics violations. Public shaming, denigration, and negative community reaction to unacceptable behavior, is the way society has historically imposed personal accountability on individuals. It was done without increasing the prison population.

THE BILL OF RIGHTS HAS AFFECTED CITIZENS ATTITUDES

Our Rights and Freedoms, patriotically celebrated at every opportunity by grateful citizens, have created another unintended consequence of note. They have fostered an "entitlement" attitude within our population.

Because there was no stated personal accountability in the Bill of Rights, a citizen reasonably concludes that citizenship imposes no obligation. The citizen is not obligated to be well-informed about what is happening in the Nation or to participate in elections by voting.

"Just stay out of trouble and enjoy the privileges of citizenship" is a common personal attitude statement. **That is not a bad attitude; it is just not appropriate for a democratic nation that is behaviorally trending negatively but still intends to self-govern.**

A person has "the right to speak your mind out" as long as it is not slander. Misdirection and misrepresentation are the moral and ethical foundations of our political system, and citizens understand that. Persons feel entitled to engage in massive public disturbances under the blanket protection of the "right peaceably to assemble." A person can promote anti-democracy under the umbrella of "freedom of speech" or "religious freedom." If a person is a member of the news Media, he/she can blather political bias and censorship with no fear of recrimination.

Most of the rights and freedoms granted in the First Amendment today negatively affect the nation by cumulatively undermining the behavior of society and the performance of government. **There is, unfortunately, a willingness on the part of many citizens to accept any level of objectionable behavior as a cheap price to pay for "freedom."** Whether that trade-off should be the constitutional bargain of the nation is a matter for The People, as a group, to decide.

SICKNESS ELSEWHERE IN THE REPUBLIC PUTS PRESSURE ON "RIGHTS AND FREEDOMS"

All four freedoms relate to expression. Freedom of expression is considered a foundational essential in democratic self-government.

Stress is evident whenever democratic government becomes dysfunctional. As dysfunction deepens, the need for people to communicate magnifies. Polar bifurcation in this stressful time drives public displays of vindictiveness, particularly through social media channels. Vindictiveness is a commentator's morals and ethics deficiency. In such circumstances, political factions and individuals in politics, government, and private life multiply their efforts to use the vehicles of expression advantageously.

Events in recent history of the abuse of "Rights and Freedoms" that are producing symptoms of stress in the nation are: media behavior (from the media alliance with political parties) of warping and distorting messaging (Freedom of the Press and Speech); splitting of the citizenry into two political camps (Freedom of the Press and Speech); political censorship by Facebook, Twitter, and other social media platforms (Freedom of Speech); outright lying by elected officials and other government leaders (freedom of speech); censorship in institutions of higher learning (Freedom of Speech, and the right peaceably to assemble); an excessive number of gatherings turned riotous with severe injury and property damage (Right of the People Peaceably to Assemble). Those abuses are increasing the intensity of polarization and decreasing citizen trust in government.

The government has advanced no solutions. It is regarded by many as the cause of the problem. Political personnel in government have exerted pressure on social media conduits, inducing them to censor and to make control-oriented computer-programmed censorial decisions that aid or foster political communication. Rights and Freedoms problems receive an occasional political comment or argument, but no concrete action from our Political Elite.

SECTION 4
CONSTITUTIONALLY ESTABLISH PERSONAL ACCOUNTABILITY

Personal accountability, assessed against citizens for moral and ethical lapses, is the best correction route among a limited number of choices. The proposals herein, of creating a morals and ethics reporting system, suggest a vehicle to establish personal accountability without using prisons. Changing the behavior of individuals who are presently unaccountable is the direction problem-solvers must go for correction.

Control over freedom of speech should be attempted only by Constitutional Authorities, never placed in private hands, and never placed in the hands of political party-driven government.

As a general overriding statement, the Freedoms granted in the Bill of Rights are not properly structured for today's social, political, government, and communications environment. Entropy has had its way.

GENERAL OBSERVATIONS ABOUT THE BILL OF RIGHTS

1. The delegations are fundamental rights **owned by The People as a group.** That is documented in the Declaration of Independence. The Framers, through the Bill of Rights, gave the rights **to The People as individuals.**

2. Amendment 1 provisions are not properly structured for our current circumstances. Broad guidance statements are not adequate today, given the massive and rapid communications, society's complexity, the need for public education, and the nature of the abuses being observed. The proposed use of the Constitution as a training instrument for citizen civics knowledge adds importance. Greater provision detail is needed to more closely align provisions with circumstances. The need for detailed, thorough, and understandable constitutional guidance is very high.

3. To provide the needed expanded Amendment 1 provisions, our proposal is that Constitutional revisions to the Rights and Freedoms be made by the Well-Informed Electors, the citizen voting body for constitutional matters. Developing such provisions should not be the responsibility of the government, nor should changes to Amendment I be addressed using the existing politician-controlled amendment process defined in Article V, for reasons discussed herein.

4. The overriding weakness in Amendment 1 is the lack of personal accountability to balance the auspicious grants of rights and freedoms to individuals in the Republic. The establishment of accountability for misbehavior utilizing the Rights and Freedoms is unlikely to be accomplished by one simple, all-encompassing action. **But, the constitutional establishment of personal accountability is the action route the nation must take.**

5. Chapter 2, entitled "Trust," observes that significant regression has occurred in the morals and ethics of the population since the time of the Framers, magnifying the effects caused by lack of citizen accountability for abuse of the nation's Rights and Freedoms. **This book recommends that our Constitution contain provisions declaring strong morals and ethics among The People as an essential foundation for self-government and supplementing them with a national program to improve those characteristics within the population by establishing personal accountability. The purpose is to create the societal environment needed for public retention of Rights and Freedoms and, of course, broadening citizen involvement in self-government.**

   Without a successful effort, the nation may be ultimately driven to substantially shrink the Bill of Rights freedom grants or to adopt a fully authoritative form of government.

6. Enforcing personal accountability for morals and ethics requires that a public tabulation and reporting system be devised. Event or occurrence information describing negative personal performance (to include activities outside of the scope of rights and freedoms abuses) would be reported to collection centers by various existing sources, tabulated, and then made accessible to the general public online. **The anticipated citizen behavior changes resulting from well-publicizing adverse personal behavior, coupled with focused training to upgrade the population to largely Well-Informed Citizens based on a revised Constitution, should, over time, secure the level of morals and ethics needed for high-quality democratic self-government.**

7. In a democratic nation, grants of full rights and freedoms are conceptually possible. In order to justify a **high level of rights and freedoms, our Nation would require a variety of improvements. It must first recognize that it cannot achieve a well-designed, focused, people-controlled, high-performance democratic self-government utilizing a citizen population of low morals and ethics.** The number of rights and freedoms granted should be based on a solid statistical tabulation of national citizens moral and ethical behavior, which should be frequently reported to and examined by both the Authorities and The People.

8. **Acceptance of personal accountability by individuals and frequent discussion of the issue is essential. One must conclude that our nation is, at this time, in no condition to justify full grants of freedom.**

9. Reducing the rights and freedoms delegated to The People is a very real choice. Citizens should be made aware of another alternative, that a nation of poor morals and ethics should perhaps abandon democratic self-government. Such a nation may be better off switching to an authoritarian government as a system more in synch with the poor moral and ethical characteristics of the population.

SECTION 5
FREEDOM OF SPEECH (FREEDOM OF EXPRESSION)

Freedom of Speech is a problem of such magnitude that the author has elected to give it a special position in this Chapter.

There is general agreement that the word "speech" is too narrow to adequately describe the scope of public discourse. The word "expression" is in common use, broadening the meaning to include verbal, non-verbal, visual, or symbolic communication.

The media threat is caused by a tight media linkage with an ineffective political system and government. Together, they have failed to guaranty The People the quality and dependable distributed information necessary for self-government. The challenge of rationalizing the media and its destructive effect on democratic governance is daunting, but competent Authority Structure organizations can devise solutions for such challenges. Our government, as it exists today, is generally considered incapable of performing such a task.

Of all the "freedoms," Freedom of Speech is the most difficult to reconceptualize. Only with the establishment of Constitutional Authorities reporting directly to The People is the following proposal possible.

PROPOSAL

We begin with the principle that the nation must ensure the quality of all communication necessary to its self-government, most specifically two-way communication between the authority structure and The People concerning people/authority business. Those communications must be pure, factual, highly informative, and vulnerable to no third-party doctoring.

News is the heart of self-government communications because it has been the historical source of information flow relating to governance. Perhaps "news" is an inappropriate label today.

Without quality-controlled and highly planned two-way communication between The People and their Authority structure, heavy involvement of citizens in government is not feasible. The required communication quality can only be achieved if all impediments to communication, standing between The People and their Authority Structure, are removed.

PEOPLE/AUTHORITY COMMUNICATIONS FLOW THROUGH IS NOW THROUGH NON-GOVERNMENT BUSINESSES AND CONTROLLED BY THEM

Two-way communication between The People and their Authority Structure is Vital Infrastructure, although it has never been defined as such. What exists has evolved over the years, but not by direct government action. All were installed and controlled by non-government entities or groups of hired management under arrangements put in place by The Framers.

If The People intend to conduct self-government, direct and controlled communications between them and the Authority Structure is a fundamental necessity. Those communications must be pure and reliable, not filtered through non-government functions, and under the complete control of The People. The information passed through the communications channels is essential to well-informed decisions by both parties to self-government as they manage the nation's business.

Currently postured organizationally between The People and their Authority Structure are two non-government (third party) groups through which all communication is being channeled:

1. The News Media, whose reporters search out and acquire politics-based information on the activities of Government and of The People. That information is processed and reported to the public via various communications. Decisions as to what will be reported and how it will be reported are made by news media, which totally controls the information flow.

   No other meaningful communication channels exist between the two critical groups, The People and the Authority Structure.

2. The Political Parties, third-party participants in government and controlled by groups of elected persons, are positioned between The People and Government. They control the flow of information between the elected persons and the

citizens but also control the news. In that role, they make many decisions concerning the content and structure of communications.

These two groups are "tweeners" that have no right to the control positions they occupy, and their positions are huge impediments to the efficient functioning of The People and their Authority structure. They must be eliminated from their preferential position as a high-priority action in any government improvement effort.

ESTABLISHING "THE PEOPLE'S COMMUNICATIONS" STRUCTURE

To meet the elevated requirements of high-performance democratic self-governance, a proposed Constitutional Authority, called "The People's Communications," would be given responsibility for designing and executing business-of-the-nation communication both ways between The People and the Authority Structure. Today's communications regarding the business of the nation meet perhaps 10% of the conceptual need.

The People's civics knowledge can be dramatically improved by the establishment of sophisticated online news, information, and training channels providing an improved way for discussion and decision-making. In the effort, The People would be provided with a wide scope of required reported information concerning Authority business and general Government performance. Today's reported information meets an estimated 5% of the conceptual need. It is party-directed and self-serving, protective of the political elite, and in no way meets the needs of true self-government.

Citizen inter-personal or group discussion of governance matters, not permitted in the public Media, would be conducted in a fourth channel.

Isolated discussion of the aforementioned topics in designated controlled channels, totally excluded from the Public Media, would eliminate the need for public media speech control, a truly important factor in the solution.

Effective government is a priority higher than any other. **"Open but controlled" two-way communication between the authority structure and The People is an essential ingredient for high-performance democratic self-government.**

Those communications must guaranty accuracy, truthfulness, and thoroughness, to ensure The People and the Authority Structure receive unadulterated and factual information.

Permitting such critical information to be distributed through non-Authority private media is an absolute guaranty the interests of The People and their self-government will be subverted. The information distributed to citizens will inevitably be manipulated for private third-party purposes.

The proposal imposes tight control over critical communications. All communication between the Authority and The People, including two-way, would be pre-structured for transmission under the direction and control of The People's Communications, using rules approved by the Well-Informed Electors. Transmission would occur through designated controlled electronic communication channels. Existing media would be totally excluded from participation.

CENSORSHIP HAS BECOME RAMPANT

"Censorship" is generally defined as "suppressing or removing subject matter deemed objectionable." **All censorship is based on someone's opinion as to what is objectionable**.

> Despite the Bill of Rights edict "Congress shall make no law abridging," Congress has passed laws denying speech freedoms such as defamation, hate speech, breech of peace, incitement to crime, sedition and obscenity. It is noteworthy that Congress chose not to amend the relevant Constitutional provision, instead enacting constitution-defying legislation.
>
> But apparently because of the "Congress shall make no law" prohibition, it has proceeded no further down the law-making path, essentially abandoning speech censorship to civil society. Government does not ever acknowledge the threat represented by the media.

Authoritarian governments make censorship a vital component of their people-control system. Democratic governments, on the other hand, view free speech as a basic and fundamental requirement for a successful social and governance climate. But, lo and behold, as our Monarchy Republic hurtles toward totalitarianism, censorship is appearing here, there, and in another place. Surprise, surprise!

There is, of course, no such thing as "free speech." Censorship, informal or otherwise, is always present. In our civil society, informal common understandings of "acceptable conversation" are firmly anchored and obeyed. True, those understandings are not law and exist by common agreement, but they are *an agreement to invoke censorship*.

Authority structures of nations exist, among other reasons, to adapt formative idealistic concepts such as "freedom of speech" to the realities of everyday life. Freedom of speech may be the broad ideal, but for the welfare of all, detailed rules are necessary. Absolute Freedom of Speech placed our nation in the communication atmosphere of the old "Wild West." Some curtailment was inevitable, and the question is always how it should be carried out.

Our proposed approach of isolating self-government communications from the mainstream media is intended to establish a constrictor that will allow continued free speech in the general media. Removal of the "tweeners" who have established untenable positions between The People and their Authority Structure is a fundamentally required action to achieve that.

ELIMINATING THE CENSORSHIP THREAT

"Nature abhors a vacuum," as the saying goes, so speech censors who have entered the game are now organizations and intermediaries that exist for business, educational, political, or other purposes. Universities censor the speech of people whose views are not internally popular. Social Media dominators Facebook, Twitter, and others censor individual speech on their platforms, including the speech of the President. Politicians and media pundits use derisive labels like "racist, misogynistic," and "radical" to denigrate individuals who take advantage of free speech rights.

Private industry censorship, broadly practiced today, is arguably the worst of all possible solutions. "Free Speech" is not a reality. Censorship is very much in effect. It is not, however, governed or regulated. It is a tool utilized by the media/political party alliance to control citizen thought and behavior. Censorship is one of the reasons we label our media "the most dangerous threat to our democratic self-government."

Censorship has become a "freedom" to be used advantageously by persons and entities that have no right to practice it but have acquired a position that allows them to do so. In the process, self-appointed censors willfully modify or curtail the free flow of information that does not support their beliefs or goals.

Censorship is usually political in nature, supporting a political party or its position, dogma, or aims. It is generally the by-product of inter-party competition or actions of party supporters or factions. **Political parties are the driving force behind most censorship**, as political parties are the source of the "contention" on which the political process is based. Interference with constitutional rights and everyday life by the political parties is woefully apparent, as evidenced by the inability of our "superior form of government" to organize and execute a resolution to the censorship problem.

It is a reasonable conclusion that the practice of censorship would disappear with the elimination of the party system, but citizens, viewing the puzzle from a "country" perspective must inevitably confront reality. Pure Freedom of Speech, the Framer ideal, never has been and never will be achievable. Better the nation should accept a diluted form of Freedom of Speech, define the lesser freedom reality, and intelligently manage it.

WHAT SHOULD BE THE PEOPLE'S POSITION REGARDING CENSORSHIP?

A revised constitutional position on censorship, difficult as it is to promulgate, is needed. Violations of acceptable discourse and the background forces causing them must be correctly isolated and managed. If the underlying stresses and forces are not identified and intelligently dealt with, the authoritarian alternative of controls laid on speech and expression will not produce results.

Censorship is, in itself, an unintended consequence of stresses and forces in play elsewhere. It distorts the flow of valid information essential to democratic self-government. Since censorship has political roots, the stresses causing it to flow from the human process of politics. That is where censorship must be attacked.

We submit that the competition and contention of party-based politics, as conducted within our nation, are what generate the demand for censorship. Eliminate the party-based contention and the citizen/authority structure communication distortion from "tweener" activities, and the desire for tight controls on expression will regress and might disappear. Along with it a long list of other undesirable stress symptoms appearing in our communications will also evaporate.

> We suggest that the political party problem be dealt with promptly, and the censorship problem be deferred. After a reasonable period of time, when party removal has shaken out, a review of freedom of expression and of censorship would be conducted. It will reveal the impediments and the best course of action to address the remaining critical freedom of expression distortions.

a) Acts of censorship are a threat to the government of The People, so permission to engage in any and all such acts should be centralized in the Constitutional Authorities, acting under guidance.

b) Freedom of Speech requires that constitutionally-prescribed penalties be imposed on those who violate it by censorship. Violations committed by elected persons, in general, should be deemed treasonous acts against The People. Violations by ordinary citizens should be morals and ethics violations, a part of their permanent misbehavior tally.

c) Protected communications, where censorship is necessary and totally appropriate, are two-way between the nation's Authority Structure and The People. **Those communications must meet the strict information flow requirements of democratic self-government that features heavy involvement of The People.**

d) Enterprises in the Media or in Education should be denied the right to censor. **Censoring would be the sole province of the Authority Structure of The People.** Private enterprises in the Media or in Education do not set or impose standards, nor do they govern.

e) The Education System, for censorship purposes, should be held to the same communication standards as the nation's media. Schools and universities operate as "communication mediums" between sources of information (books, knowledge, expertise) and receivers of education (students). What is taught relating to the nation's governance system must be controlled by The People and cannot be left to the personal judgment or discretion of educators.

SECTION 6
SUMMARY OF RIGHTS ACTION PROPOSALS

RESOLVING THE MEDIA THREAT ISSUE

"Direction" and "Control" are two of the five responsibilities of ownership. Self-government decisions regarding the delegation of rights to the Media fall under the direction and control responsibility of The People.

The Media Threat is a "direct" and "control" issue. The question is, "Why should the Media be permitted a position that allows it to control the thinking of the nation's citizens?" The answer is, "It should not, of course."

The next question is, "Who should ensure the veracity and quality of communication between The People and the Authority Structure that represents them?" The answer is "The Constitutional Authorities. Their function is to carry out The People's Plan, Organize, Staff, Direct, and Control instructions."

Most of the Nation's difficulties with the Freedoms delegated to The People under Amendment I result from political parties or personal activity related to politics. Elimination of political parties and installation of pure democratic self-government, devoid of factional interference, will clear the field, allowing the evaluation of the Freedoms in a non-contentious environment. That approach is strongly recommended.

1. The single most important goal must be the elimination of the Media threat to the nation's system of government. The Media must be positioned <u>outside of the nation's authority structure messaging system</u> so it cannot influence content.

In tandem with that vital action, firm Authority steps are needed to ensure that The People are sufficiently prepared to carry out their citizen duties in self-government. With the establishment of the Constitutional Authority called The People's Communications, the resulting controlled information flow can become "a strong contributor to the achievement of the high-quality democratic self-government intent of The People."

2. Stepping back to look at the media dispassionately, it becomes clear that it is one huge, uncontrolled "blob." Through media corporations' vertical integration to expand capability and competitive power, the influence of huge corporations has become too intense, making governing them very difficult. Inter-company competition and regulation by the FCC have not adequately constrained the industry's practices, pursuing their purpose of conglomerating the media into one huge intellectual monopoly, marching to one drumbeat of political beliefs and values supported by perhaps only one-third of the voters. Regulation has not addressed that issue.

Communication about our nation's business is vital transmission of information. **The Media should not set policy, determine societal values, set direction, fashion political thinking, opinionate, or sell to the public. Those are governance choices of The People's Authority Structure, not choices of the media. The People's self-government communication must not, therefore, be filtered through a conglomerated single-drumbeat media nor influenced by the actions of totalitarian political parties in alliance with that media.**

3. Our Media is not concentrated through corporate ownership but is intellectually concentrated by the commonality of political and social beliefs expounded under the direction of mainstream media management. It will be necessary to break up that drumbeat. The drumbeat is focused on integrating, into the minds of the citizenry, beliefs that have not been decided by The People to be the guiding principles of the nation and are not universally shared.

4. Placing the segment called the News Media under tight Constitutional control should provide the necessary isolation to purify the information flow. Additional actions could be deferred to a later time when the progress gained by repositioning the News Media can be assessed.

5. A factual and accurate two-way flow of information about the nation's business is essential to true self-government. It is a proposal deeply linked to the significantly increased involvement of The People in the nation's governance business. Media News must be detached from the mainstream media, transferred to Constitutional Authorities, and repurposed to purify and expand the information flow and develop the needed well-informed citizenry.

> The totalitarian rule "Control the Message!" must be adopted by Constitutional Media News, and employed within strict democratic standards. To that rule must be added "make sure discussions of authority structure business are truthful, complete, unbiased, unfiltered and dead accurate, and make sure the communication is two-way."

6. Media News is of such importance to the nation's proposed broadly upgraded self-government model that it should be accorded high ranking within the Constitutional Authorities. A Constitutional organization would be formed in which all news is researched, produced, and transmitted to The People. Private expertise would be employed contractually. Forums for government business discussion, removed from the Social Media Platforms and controlled separately, would replace similar unregulated functions today provided by Facebook, Twitter, and others.

7. Social Media censorship is a free-speech deterrent of totalitarian derivation.

Censorship is currently imposed by private companies of the media segment called "Social Media Platforms" that facilitate interpersonal communication. You will recognize the major players of the segment; Facebook, Twitter, Google, etc. **Since none of the nation's governance business communication would flow through those conduits, censorship in the private media sector would disappear under the proposed arrangement.** The Social Media Platforms, in their new role, as required by constitutional provision, would be denied the right to conduct or transmit any governmental or political discussion but would otherwise enjoy freedom of speech.

8. Although the Social Media platforms would be limited to non-political non-governmental discussion, they would otherwise be given wide free speech latitude. Should The People later find it necessary, they can, by constitutional decision, impose constraints at any future time.

It is strongly recommended that accountability for public speech be enforced against speakers who violate established rules. Individual misbehavior would be morals and ethics violations, incidents of which would be reported into the Morals and Ethics tabulation system. Through that means, accountability for inappropriate citizen behavior on social media would be enforced.

SUMMARY OF ACTION PROPOSALS

The Bill of Rights needs a complete revision to bring it current. It must become a set of fundamental provisions decided and maintained current by The People and broadened dramatically to make them well understood by the public.

Rules for elected body oversight and functions should never be promulgated by the bodies, but always imposed from above as "direction and control."

Proposals for correction can be distilled into the following key actions:

1. Revision should begin with the definition and enforcement of accountability against all beneficiaries of Rights. The People, through Constitutional Authorities, must assume responsibility for the functionality of overall Rights and accountabilities to ensure a balanced program that meets the goals of the nation.

   The citizens have to look to the top of the organization pyramid, which in a democracy is an elected body, to establish responsibility for making the individual Rights dictums functional. Revisions should focus on the responsibilities of key officials and elected bodies because most of them are non-swimmers in the river of effective administration. Then, the focus must be on how an elected person's non-performance can be evaluated by citizens who must decisively remove the non-performing. Written elected person employment agreements are a key element of any such system.

2. The role of police departments and individual police officers must be rethought and revised. It is recommended nationwide rules be imposed constitutionally. Here again, accountability must start at the top of that authority pyramid. Elected bodies have to dramatically improve effectiveness, so performance requirements and penalties must be applied to responsible elected bodies and department administration. **Lawsuits by citizens for perceived abuses should be permitted only against the responsible elected body, never against the foot soldiers. Punishment of foot soldiers is the job of the function departmental hierarchy, not the courts.**

3. In composing a new Constitution, focus on **personal accountability** for citizen and elected person actions. The Morals and Ethics discussions contained in this book make several proposals that are significant to the subject of Personal Accountability. The proposed morals and ethics reporting system should be established to publicize adverse citizen performance under the Bill of Rights, including violations that are Freedom of Speech related.

4. Establishing accountability for participants in the nation's authority structure requires regular performance reporting to The People of information on a range of related national conditions, problems, and initiatives. The purpose is to evaluate the state of "Trust" in the nation, with a specific focus on trust in government, the national status of morals and ethics, performance under various initiatives such as civic knowledge of the citizens, etc. Such reporting will never be proposed under the existing political party system, but in self-government, that is the kind of information the citizens require. The People must then hold the authority structure accountable.

5. Special attention is needed to control and purify People/Authority communication on government business. That will require organization revisions to the Media and to the Constitutional Authorities, who must assume responsibility.

CHAPTER 18

THE RIGHTS AND FREEDOMS SERIES; PART 3

CONTENT:

SECTION 1: HOW FRAMER TREATMENT OF THE PRESS CREATED THE MEDIA THREAT

SECTION 2: SUMMARY OF DEVELOPMENT OF THE MEDIA

SECTION 3: THE MEDIA MONOPOLY

SECTION 4: PLAN TO ELIMINATE THE MEDIA THREAT

FOREWORD

In a high-performance, self-governed democracy, for an issue of great importance (such as the Media), the intentions of the nation must be absolutely clear so that no one will suffer confusion. The People should not require the services of a law firm and a psychic to understand the nation's principles and intent.

To dissect the huge nebulous blob called "the media," one must wade through a slew of putrid water. Perhaps the wader will emerge with some grasp of the terminology pollution in which the Media has immersed itself, the built-up constitutional and Supreme Court legal muck, and the political and operational undergrowth that makes the pond visually impenetrable. But then again, perhaps the wader will not.

This Book focuses on the U.S. Constitution and government. The Media threat, crying for attention, towers above those two subjects as a dominating landscape feature. Yet it would be a fairly safe bet that, in the large group of elected politicians in our government, it would not be possible to find a half dozen capable of intelligently discussing fundamental questions concerning the Media.

The Media discussion starts with Amendment 1, the so-called "Bill of Rights," which contains our ancient and entropy-ravished freedom provisions. You, as a citizen, will be challenged as you try to unwind that conceptual, historic, organizational, linguistic, and legal entanglement.

Readers are warned that they are unlikely to come away from this discussion with a sense of deep satisfaction because it is not possible to do justice to such a huge and complex topic here. With that caution, we begin a discussion of one of the greatest threats to the survival of our democratic republic: the Media.

SECTION 1
HOW FRAMER TREATMENT OF THE PRESS CREATED THE MEDIA THREAT

WHAT IS THE DEFINITION OF "THE PRESS?"

The First Amendment does not define "the press." In the Framer time, the "press" meant businesses that composed and printed newspapers, located primarily in the larger population centers. Today, that mode of communication is called "print publications." Those businesses were what the Framers meant when they wrote "the press" into the First Amendment.

Persons employed in "the media" have since given "The Press" a new meaning. "The Press" now describes those who produce news content or work in that space, whatever the source or distribution vehicle. Perhaps that description is an attempt to insulate those who perform the news function by associating them with the First Amendment and cloaking them in a constitutional aura. The White House Press Secretary conducts a "press conference" with a group of reporters called "the Press." The conference is communicated electronically, but some of the products probably do reach the "Press."

The "news" is still communicated via print publications, most of which originate in the Mainstream Media, the main player of which is the New York Times, a print publication. The Mainstream electronic media leader that generates the "news," CNN, also provides entertainment, information, advertising and product sales, and a broad range of other content and services. News is the exclusive focus of but a few Media members, albeit important to those comprising what is called the "mainstream media."

Today, print publications are a small and shrinking segment of a conglomeration of news communication vehicles, so small that the two major political parties disagree on whether failing print businesses should be given financial assistance or merely be allowed to pass away.[57] One would think the word "Press" would have long ago been abandoned, and

---

[57] "Parties Split on Aiding Survival of News Outlets, by David Bauder, The Associated Press, Nov. 16, 2019

suspects it is in use because the Press remains prominent in Amendment 1 of the Constitution, the important Bill of Rights, and connection to it conveys prestige.

WHY WAS THE PRESS INCLUDED IN THE FIRST AMENDMENT?

The Framers shielded the watchdog press from retribution by politicians and the government, stating in the First Amendment, "Congress shall make no law respecting an establishment of religion, or prohibiting the free exercise thereof, or abridging the freedom of speech, or of the press........."

Even in those days, the press freely supported or denigrated politicians and political positions. If the Framers observed abuse from that practice, they ignored it.

The press was accorded Constitutional status **because the Framers intended it to be the main watch-dog over politicians and government**, expecting information concerning their activities would be faithfully reported to the Voters. **That Framer check-and-balance structure was intended to ensure that voters had access to information so they could make well-informed decisions at the ballot box.**

The "well-informed voter" is a concept fundamental to democratic government. It is foundational to any plan that imposes elected person accountability. Voters are the politically active among the nation's owners, The People.

Any connection between news services provided today and the original check-and-balance structure of the Framers is unrecognizable, except in the smaller cities of the American heartland. Local newspapers there continue to monitor state and local governments. Mainstream media is evident everywhere. **Heartland newspapers may be the only functioning check-and-balance on political malfeasance existing today. Their presence is, however, local and spotty.**

PROBLEMS WITH APPLYING "THE PRESS" LABEL TO "THE MEDIA"

The "media" label, as universally used, encapsulates a diverse mixture of national and local enterprises engaged in the many facets of communication, together with their employees and physical capabilities. It includes businesses that have always been considered "the press," as well as many whose relationship to the press is from distant to non-existent. An increasing number of media businesses use electronic information transmission capabilities to provide services for profit. The media label includes content and service providers who conduct business via its transmission capabilities, such as the "News" Media, entertainment, multiway communication, and much more. Such an all-encompassing label has influenced the following Encarta Dictionary North American definition of "media":

"The various means of mass communication considered as a whole, including internet, television, radio, magazines, and newspapers, together with the people involved in their production."

The word "medium," of which "media" is the plural, has many uses, one of which is to describe a state of cooked meat. The most applicable definitions of a medium are "a state between extremes," "a substance through which something is carried or transmitted," and "a means of mass communication, e.g., television, radio, or newspapers."[58]

The many interpretations of "media" make it a confusing term. Because a medium is an in-between condition or function, "media" correctly describes the *physical means by which mass communication is transmitted*. Television, the Internet, telephone service, satellite service, printed publications, and other physical transmitters of mass communication are accurately described as "media**." Media is the connectivity between an information source and an audience.** Services and content made available are not "media." They are merely services and content.

That said, it is unfortunately necessary that the prevailing popular interpretation of "Media" be used here.

"THE MEDIA" HAS NO SPECIAL PRIVILEGES OR INDEMNITIES

Legal authorities and ordinary citizens have struggled to understand whether Amendment 1 prohibition, "Congress shall make no law abridging the freedom of speech, or of the press," differentiates those two freedoms or whether they are one and the same. The Supreme Court concluded that freedom of speech is the dominant delegation and that freedom of the press is a derivative of freedom of speech, thereby according to the press, no special privilege.

The right to claim Freedom of the Press protection was narrowed in the Supreme Court's 2010 Citizen's United decision. The court majority in that case concluded that extending Freedom of the Press protection to media corporations but not to other corporations, presented a host of problems, and so all corporations should be equally protected.

That decision concedes that Media's responsibility for developing a well-informed citizenry, the reason Bill of Rights protections were granted to the Press, no longer exists.

---

[58] Encarta Dictionary: English (North America)

The law of this critical matter is complex, requiring citizens to "impute" and "distill" to arrive at useable conclusions because, although totally changed by the 2010 Citizen's United decision, the relevant Constitution clauses have not been amended. **A high-performance democracy would long ago have rewritten its Constitution and supporting text to include specific provisions necessary to make the constitutional position current and clear to all readers**.

"FREEDOM OF THE PRESS" PROTECTION IS LEGALLY CLOUDED BUT STILL INCLUDED IN AMENDMENT 1

The changing use of words is normal as language evolves. Over time, the meaning of the narrow term "press" expanded to include the communication businesses and everything involved in it, becoming that big catch-all collective noun, "media."

The question today is why the Media, considering the Supreme Court rulings, in the minds of most, is still treated as though it retains its original First Amendment protections. Citizens are confused as to what Freedom of the Press protection now covers because Amendment 1 remains in the Constitution as originally written, despite judicial repudiation of its reason for existence.

In our "Old Stone Age" Constitution, the language and structure of the First Amendment is obsolete. It does not provide clear direction. It is very difficult to respect or admire a constitution in that condition. Amendment 1 irrevocably ties "the press" to "freedom of speech" by including them in the same sentence, "abridging freedom of speech, or of the press."

For The People to have to research Supreme Court decisions to derive the correct reading of such a critical provision substantially benefits the legal profession but is an absolute desecration of self-government democracy. What is more damaging to public comprehension, perhaps, is that the sentence also ties the press to the word "freedom," implying it is a component of the nation's foundational, highly-regarded "freedom" principle.

Businesses using communication media today are purveyors. Selling or distributing products has nothing whatsoever to do with elected representative performance or government. Its relationship to Freedom of the Press and the nation's need for a "well-informed electorate" is non-existent. However, those two issues are true People/Authority Structure matters imbedded in the Media functions that deeply affect our governance, so they demand attention.

> Any constitutional right of the Media to act as middlemen, by composing and distributing governance information between the nation's Authority Structure and the nation's citizens, has long since disappeared. Removing the media as a threat to the existence of our nation depends upon the intelligence of The People correcting that monumental flaw in the nation's system of governance. The key action that must be taken is to secure vital business communications between the two main groups comprising our Authority Structure, by eliminating outside interference positions within the information flow.

SECTION 2
SUMMARY OF DEVELOPMENT OF THE MEDIA

The rapidity of developments in electronic communications brings forth one pervasive line of thought.

If the nation is encountering problems because of communications media performance today, those problems will be magnified going forward. The rate of future technological change cannot be expected to slow down if the current hype surrounding the launch of Artificial Intelligence is any indication.

In their drive to achieve high-performance democratic self-government, The People must ensure the media is brought into alignment with the information flow requirements of constitutional authority governance utilizing heavy citizen involvement. **The flow of vital information between those two all-important groups (The People, the owners of the nation, and their Authority Structure of hired management) must be constructed in a manner that guarantees immunity to third-party manipulation.**

The past thirty years have introduced improvements to the one-way communication of the staid old newspaper-based "press" and to the one-way electronic media that evolved from it. Recently, technology has introduced incredibly popular two-way or many-way communication capabilities, dramatically broadening the use of electronic media. The "media" existing twenty years ago has added a more convenient distribution system for news, two-way or many-way communication for people and businesses, entertainment, and information on virtually everything, available at the flick of a finger. With the introduction of the cell phone a decade or so ago, all of that can be accessed everywhere, immediately!

Added to those technological leaps is the substantially broadened use of the Internet as a major alternative communication medium. The media revolution has swung power far away from print publications, the emblematic old "press" of constitutional distinction, toward businesses and services available on electronic platforms. The power shift is best measured by the redistribution of advertising revenue. Google's advertising revenue rose from $4 billion in 2004 to $54 billion in 2018. During that same period, the advertising revenue of U.S. print publications dropped from $42 billion to $16 billion[59].

A media monster has resulted, very powerful, complex and difficult to comprehend, allied with political parties, holding immense and very threatening control over public opinion, and concerning which there is no corrective or control effort by our ineffective Government. Supreme Court rulings state that electronic media businesses have no privileges or indemnities that are not available to ordinary citizens, so the Bill of Rights provisions are no longer a functional advantage for them, nor a barrier to enacting controlling legislation.

Could government inertia be because the media "influences a large number of people, and reflects and shapes prevailing currents of thought?" Or, could it be that the political parties, comfortable in their incestuous relationship with the media monster, don't want change?

The media controls the message. In doing so it controls government direction. The monstrous threat to the nation and The People that it constitutes is not an isolated and abstract complication, it is a foundational issue in our system of governance.

Self-government means that The People intend to drive the nation in directions they have determined to be necessary or appropriate. It means they assume responsibility for and have decided to perform the critical owner tasks involved in Authority Structure activities.

Credible, true, factual, and unbiased information flow between The People and the nation's Authority Structure is a basic and fundamental requirement of democratic self-government. That flow is necessary to create and maintain a Well-Informed Citizenry capable of fulfilling their involvement in the nation's affairs, and to provide governing bodies with critical information upon which to base the nation's directional decisions. **No non-authority organization should be permitted to occupy space and perform functions between the citizens and the Authority Structure where it can in any way influence the flow of vital information.**

"News," the information citizens use in assessing the business of governance, is our focal point of concern. The term "news" is inadequate to describe the needed information flow. A better term would be "Authority/People Governance Information." The word "News" has never been separated formally into its components, one of which is information essential to the conduct of the nation's governance. This book takes the position that the information

---

[59] Testimony before the House judiciary Subcommittee on Antitrust, Commercial and Administrative Law, July 3, 2019

component is not news at all. Although current events may be prominent, its purpose is reliable and untarnished information flow and discussion regarding the nation's authority structure and governance business.

MEDIA IS ASSEMBLED INTO A HUGE MONOPOLY

The vast majority of broadcast and basic cable networks (over 100 in all) are controlled by six corporations. Most of those six are vertically integrated, owning or controlling all functions from production to product delivery, as well as multiple communication-related activities.

- News Corp./Fox Corp.
- The Walt Disney Company
- National Amusements (owns Paramount Global)
- Comcast (owns NBC and Universal)
- Warner Bros. (Owns Discovery)
- SW Scripps Co. (Cablevision), known as Altice U.S.A.

At first glance, readers could conclude that the broadcast and network media has been carefully segregated, and no monopoly concentration could possibly exist. Nothing is farther from the truth! The media operating environment has evolved to a place where the boundaries of corporate ownership are overridden by the monopolistic aggregational functioning of the media as a whole.

Seamlessly interfaced within its power-structure environment of corporations, higher education, and government (which are so interlinked with corporate power it is difficult to distinguish them) *the Mainstream Media performs a totally inappropriate function of leading the national thought process.*

The mainstream media leaders (CBS, the New York Times) are directing the mass audience by setting the intellectual framework within which the entire Media operates, telling others what they are supposed to care about. Articles of prominent writers generated in the mainstream media are sold nationwide to other media participants, saving them the cost of having to write the news themselves and ensuring that a common perspective is presented. **To guarantee the commonality of beliefs, media employees with non-conforming ideas are ruthlessly weeded out.**

CHOMSKY'S VIEW OF MEDIA ATTITUDES

Rather than attempting to explore here the relationships that make the media's diverse functions monopolistic, it is suggested that readers conduct their own examination of this structure that we define as the greatest threat to our nation's democratic survival. A prolific American writer on this topic (among many others) is Noam Chomsky, whose observations outline the concerns of this chapter. For a short and revealing overview of the Media, Chomsky's Article "What Makes Mainstream Media Mainstream," "Z" Magazine, October 1997, is recommended reading.

GOVERNANCE ISSUES

The pace of development and its effect on the government is shocking and scary. A very visible symptom of stress caused by the activities of those who communicate via Electronic Media is the continuing acrimony between President Trump (now ex-President) and the Press Corps. The Press Corps, a collection of news-gathering mainstream media personnel mainly aligned with the opposition party, has been bitterly hostile to the elected President while at the same time attempting to steer the politics of the nation in a direction different from his.

In a recent CNN discussion, Gerry Levin, CEO of AOL-Time Warner, made this startling statement: **"Global Media will become the dominant industry of this century, more powerful than governments." Michael J. Wolf, advisor to media moguls, made another statement, equally startling: "Entertainment – not autos, steel, not financial services – is fast becoming the driving wheel of the new world economy."** It should come as no surprise to hear that corporate media executives have infiltrated the World Trade Organization, which is a heavy proponent of globalization to be accomplished by diminishing the role of nation governments.

Statements such as those from Media insiders must be taken as a clear warning. Similar developments, added to our own observations concerning occurrences within our nation, are the reason this book labels the communications media as the Number One Threat to the survival of democratic government in the United States.

The Bill of Rights Amendment 1 opening prohibition "Congress shall make no law respecting" is, given Supreme Court rulings, in some key issues, no longer a constitutional excuse for government inaction.

The House of Representatives, late in the game, is conducting bi-partisan hearings intended to produce legislation addressing the monopoly issues, but given the recent legislation record of Congress, that would be too much to expect. The Association of State Attorneys General announced they were beginning an investigation into the anti-trust implications.

A brief review of history will lead readers to the inevitable conclusion that the government, left to its own devices, will do nothing to resolve the media threat.

WHAT GIVES THE MEDIA A POSITION THAT MAKES IT SO THREATENING?

Placing the Press (and, by extension, the Media) in a position to dominate government/citizen communications was an unintended consequence of a well-intentioned Framer action examined in Section 1 of this chapter.

By setting up the Press as the key communicator in their check-and-balance ballot box scheme and charging it with informing voters of politician-and-government non-performance, the Framers established the Press as the dominant communications intermediary between government and The People. They accorded the Press special mention in the Bill of Rights and by Bill of Rights wording, irrevocably associated the Press with Freedom of Speech and freedom in general. Those actions elevated the Press, in the minds of citizens, to an unwarranted anointed position.

In the Framer time, print publications were one-way communication to The People of information regarding government happenings and performance. The other half of that equation, communication from The People to the government, relied on public gatherings, guaranteed by the Bill of Rights provision "right of the people peaceably to assemble." The People's Assembly consequences, reported by the Press, informed elected persons and citizens in general of the concerns and attitudes of The People.

From the time of the Framers, whether intended or not, the Press has been the constitutionally-anointed communication intermediary between the government central authority and The People. No other intermediary existed in that space until the last few decades. For most of that time the Press remained true to its constitutional mission, and complaints about it mainly concerned political reporting bias.

From the 1980s, as electronic communication began to dominate **and with media companies changing their newsrooms to profit centers,** the media, and political parties joined hands, and the whole news process that informs the public mind changed wrenchingly. Media communications grew rapidly, the Press shrank, newsroom profitability became a focus, the entire business structure coming to be known as the "Media" exploded in size, and the assembly of a media monopoly was under way.

What is threatening now is the media occupies space and conducts itself in a way that intolerably degrades the functioning of our democratic system. Because of the unique position it was accorded constitutionally, the media is the sole communication vehicle between the two major components of our democracy: the governmental authority structure and the citizenry. When we say "communication vehicle," we are not only

describing channels of communication. We are describing those who actually compose the communications and transmit them.

A label that has worked its way into our lexicon is "mainstream media." Wikipedia defines it as **"A term and abbreviation used to refer collectively to the various large mass news media that** *influence a large number of people, and reflect and shape prevailing currents of thought."*

The definition is eye-popping. It clearly defines the power and influence of the mainstream media, so pervasive that it has become the term by which the segment is now defined. Readers will also note that mainstream media power centers in the "large mass news media."

The analysis of the Media threat is as follows:

1. The Mainstream Media controls the News Service Providers. It decides what news shall be transmitted to the nation, and how that news shall be slanted.

2. The media is positioned between the Citizens and the Authority Structure. It decides the flow of news, which is the information utilized in the process of government by those two dominant authority functions. "He who controls the message controls the outcome."

3. The media's reason for existence is profit, not democratic self-government.

4. Because of its unique position it sets national direction and shapes prevailing thought. **In a self-governed democracy those may not be private party functions or privileges. <u>Setting national direction and shaping prevailing thought is the duty and responsibility of the self-governing People.</u>**

THE CONTENT PURVEYORS

In a self-governed democracy, communications between the Authority Structure and The People must be segregated and totally controlled so those two functions can make their decisions based on thorough, pristine, and validated information. Communications of such vital importance must never be entrusted to private enterprise or to political parties.

The past twenty years have seen the emergence of a highly influential and rapidly growing group of media service providers that use, in creative and meaningful ways, the new many-way communication capabilities of electronic media. Apple, Google, Twitter, Amazon, and Facebook and their brethren are companies using that electronic vehicle to bring together buyers and sellers, keepers of information and users of information, producers of entertainment and viewers thereof, gamesters, people and their friends, and much more.

They are content purveyors and service providers **who use the media to sell and distribute their products.** They employ custom-designed platforms and the electronic media transmission capabilities of networks and the Internet to sell and deliver their services. The magnitude and dominance of their position allow them even to dictate the percentage of revenue advertisers must pay. The dominance of their positions in governance, communication and commerce has become a national issue because they are the center of the communications media information problem.

The preceding paragraph is vitally important. Its message is: Do not be confused. Media are *physical vehicles (mainly electronic) that facilitate mass communication.* The businesses that use the electronic media are simply that: Businesses that use the electronic Media.

The businesses are what The People must control, not the electronic communication vehicles.

Media service providers should have no role in monitoring politicians and government, but a number of them facilitate interpersonal discussion, and users of that capability inevitably engage in political discussion. That involvement requires the media providers to make judgments concerning acceptable discourse, which generates the opportunity to censor speech. Media providers are entitled to "freedom of speech" protections but not the right to censor.

The concern The People must confront regarding Media activities is its ability and propensity to set the direction of the nation by audience control, monopolistic behavior and theme commonality.

Setting the nation's direction, which is critical to good governance, is the responsibility of The People, via their Constitutional Authority Structure. In a self-governed democracy that function is certainly not the right nor the privilege of the businesses that make up the Media.

Varying concerns about the Media include business monopoly practices, personal privacy, censorship, and sponsoring the messaging of political parties for public thought influencing.

SECTION 3
PLAN TO ELIMINATE THE MEDIA THREAT

The media threat to our Authority Structure must be resolved by The People if they intend to develop and maintain a self-governed democracy of high quality and performance. It will not be possible to build the necessary national cohesion for that kind of government if the information flow between the Authority Structure and The People is controlled by political parties and their cohorts in the media structure. The flow of such corrupted information is totally inappropriate for self-government decision-making.

The Framers made the Press the communications vehicle of their time. In Amendment 1, they gave the Press a preferred position within the Bill of Rights, "freedoms," thereby making it an element of the freedom concept. From that well-intentioned beginning, a gigantic media threat exploded.

The People must now separate the Media into two components: one that delivers the nation's electronically-provided commercial services in a free speech environment, and the second designated to perform essential communication between the Citizens and the Authority Structure, ensuring the sanctity of the Nation's business. The second component must necessarily be contained within an Authority Structure tightly controlled communications body performing prescribed information flow control functions in a manner meeting the authority requirements of The People.

This Section will further define the broad issues of the Media Threat and develop an approach to a planned solution. It is a complex and many-faceted puzzle. Readers are reminded that strategic planning such as this requires the involvement of many people and a very organized approach. Our kitchen table proposal may not survive such an examination. Hopefully, it will have served its purpose of clarifying reasoning, stimulating concern and interest, and maybe even pointing the way.

This is a broad plan framework that will identify components of the Media Threat and propose remedies. Where known or highly probable solutions exist, their conceptual application will be noted. It will not be possible to delve deeply into the details of solutions. Where no potential solutions have been identified, that will be noted, and perhaps a discovery approach will be suggested.

Readers will understand that this plan and supporting information is highly conceptual.

CREATE AND DEFINE THE NATION'S CONSTITUTIONAL POSITION

The first step by The People should be to create the nation's constitutional position regarding the threat to democratic self-government the media represents. It becomes the foundational reason for developing a highly functional new Constitutional Authority and communication of the preliminary plan to the citizens.

A complete restructure of the nation's communications system, presently referred to as "the media," is not only warranted, it is essential. To do that requires that the nation's authority structure be directed to delve, in-depth, into "the media" to identify the specific threats and concerns involved, define the nation's interests, and suggest the rules to be applied in deriving solutions.

ESTABLISH THE CONSTITUTIONAL CONTROL BODY

Elect The People's Communication Commission governing body. It will produce two plans:

The first is an operating plan for the aforementioned Authority Structure and Citizen communication organization and operations. A previous chapter discusses an overall Constitutional Authority proposal to which readers may wish to refer.

The second will be a dissection of the existing public Media structure into components to provide the foundation for splitting it up for control purposes.

PLACE UNDER CONSTITUTIONAL CONTROL THE NEWS MEDIA AND OTHER COMMUNICATION CHANNELS POSITIONED BETWEEN THE AUTHORITY STRUCTURE AND THE PEOPLE

Transfer the existing Federal regulatory body, the Federal Communications Commission (the "FCC"), to the People's Communications Commission. Purge dysfunctional political appointees. The new Commission will have authority over the development and regulation of all communication systems and activities, which will be designated "vital infrastructure."

Remove from the Media corporations the units of News Media communication between The People and their Authority Structure. Insert those into the People's Communications Commission as Vital Infrastructure components. Plan all companion organizations and management requirements such as a Current Events Channel, Well-Informed Elector Channel, Civic Education Channel, and Self-Government Channel.

Reason: To establish constitutional control over two-way communication between The People and the Authority Structure to ensure all information flows against outside manipulation. The controlled structure is needed, over time, to produce a high percentage of Well-Informed Electors in the voter population, foster greater involvement of The People in the functions of the Authority Structure, and facilitate other Authority Structure/citizen activities.

DESTROY EXISTING MEDIA/POLITICAL PARTY ALLIANCES

Eliminate Political Parties and their role in government, so none exist to ally with the media. Review all Political Factions and take similar necessary actions.

Reason: With political parties eliminated and political factions controlled, there will be no purpose for such alliances. Implement and enforce the "one person, one vote" rule.

ESTABLISH PERSONAL ACCOUNTABILITY FOR UNPATRIOTIC OR UNDEMOCRATIC SPEECH OR ACTIVITIES

Implement the proposed Morals and Ethics Violation tabulation system to record and publicize personal accountability violations. Significantly broaden the Treason definitions to include a wide range of activities destructive to the nation and The People's selected form of government. Increase penalties for a violation to the level of "extremely meaningful" and base their severity on the miscreant's public stature.

Reason: These are actions to establish personal accountability. Use personal accountability rules to influence the behavior of citizens, as well as media personnel and other spokesmen. Measure and publish national progress.

DISSEMBLE THE "MAINSTREAM MEDIA"

The Mainstream Media exists to influence and control the public through opinions for the ultimate purpose of assisting political parties to direct the course of government. The major actions that will destroy the Mainstream Media are the outlawing of political parties and the removal of the news media from private ownership. With those gone, the basis and reason for the Mainstream Media is dramatically reduced and changed. Establish a Communications Commission policing operation to monitor and regulate prominent personalities within the media.

Reason: The Mainstream Media is the operating foundation of the Media threat. It directs the course of government and influences The People, which it must not be permitted to do.

ELIMINATE THE MEDIA MONOPOLY

The actions proposed above will go a long way toward deconstructing the media monopoly. Unfortunately, its remaining components, five to seven huge corporations, each controlling vital segments of the communications delivery structure, are too large and too powerful to be left intact. In their present form, they are a threat, as those corporations acting together (and in some circumstances individually) could cripple the nation.

There is no simple or pretty solution. For the nation to freely move forward it must eliminate the media threat. Media corporations will have to be broken up into component parts so that they will lose the power to do what they have been doing. The only question is how to do that.

It is suggested that the five to seven media corporations that dominate be forced to divest everything except one main business. Divestiture would be accomplished by spinning off businesses, privatizing them, or consolidating them with similar businesses owned by others. The purpose would be facilitating national control and regulation, increasing the ease of handling by congregating all media businesses of similar purpose. Perhaps the nation would end up with ten or so such segments, their content commonality making them much easier to understand and regulate.

Since the People's Communications Commission will be regulating all public media components, it is suggested that each component be matched to a specialized regulatory organization. There are many matters to be considered in the final decisions, but the following examples of the segmentation approach are provided to open the discussion:

a) Data Centers and Bulk Processors. Many are huge subsidiaries of the six media corporations listed in Section 3. They have a unique set of issues, such as national location and distribution risk, the risk of intense concentration of data storage, electricity consumption and availability, and vulnerability to third-party intrusion.

Reason: National risk control and the facilitation of regulation for a large component of vital infrastructure.

b) Service Delivery Businesses. Already a huge component of the media, Facebook (Meta), X (Twitter), Google, and others have captured large followings and are generating heavy public discussion because of control and censorship concerns. Personal accountability for inappropriate speech behavior may be a necessary element of the new structure.

Reason: Solve censorship problem, reduce threat represented by media conglomerates, improve the capability of The People to regulate.

c) Using the concepts utilized in a) and b) above, segment all of the remaining businesses of the conglomerated media corporations. There are many decisions that will be made in structuring the list. The following may result:

- Data Centers and Bulk Data Processors

- Service Delivery Businesses

- Interpersonal Communication Businesses

367

- Transmission Services: Space and Satellite, Land-based Electronic Communications (Land lines, Towers, etc.)

- Printed Publications

- Entertainment and sports production and broadcasting

- Transmission of Financial Information and Transactions

- Information System Programming, Equipment and Manufacturing

- Etc.

Reason: The five to seven media giants are the dominant Media threat. Their components are probably not threatening individually, so those would remain independent businesses.

All components of the huge media structure would be placed under Constitutional Authority regulation, structured in a way that will eliminate the conglomerate threat and facilitate Authority control.

Readers are encouraged to remember that the break-up of the threatening media is a challenge that has been confronted by authorities in our nation many times over the past century. It has taken courage to undertake those massive actions affecting big businesses and significant segments, but the undertakings have generally been broadly accepted. The breakup challenge that confronts the nation today must be regarded as just another major step in the on-going management of the nation but also understood to be of critical importance.

CHAPTER 19

FOREWORD

The previous chapters provided background, some history, and a brief mention of national issues relating to what is called "the media." There is a reason those chapters constrained discussion. The "media" is a topic so complex and voluminous that doing it justice would require not one book but several.

We are focused on the Constitution and our breakdown in governance. This book discusses the "media" not only because of confusion concerning its constitutional role but also because of its greatly-feared position and sway over the conduct of governance.

The media (at the time of the Framers, "the press") was accorded a special place in the Constitution. Instead of repaying the nation for the special consideration it received, the Media has made decisions and engaged in practices that establish it as the major threat to the nation's democratic, self-governed existence.

SECTION 1
INTRODUCTION AND HISTORICAL BACKGROUND

Amendment 1 to the Constitution contains the following: "Congress *shall make no law* abridging the freedom of speech or of the press."[60] There was a reason the press was given special consideration. It was designated by the Framers to be the critical check-and-balance against Government malfeasance by ensuring the electorate was well-informed. That was to educate the citizens to make sound voting judgments.

The media (that massive "extended family" of the early press) has stationed itself (or was stationed by The People) under the protection umbrella constitutionally accorded "the press," assuming it could continue to pursue its ends without fear of governmental control. *Laws that have been enacted to control political activities typically exempt media.*

Readers may have garnered the impression that the media has been exempted from government regulation. Nothing could be farther from the truth. **But, the broad and intensive regulation to which media has been subjected generally by-passes the Constitutional issues discussed in this Series.**

In the early 1900s regulation of the telephone and radio was established. In 1934, the Federal Communications Commission, a newly-instituted independent agency of the U.S. Government, assumed responsibility for the regulation of radio broadcasting from the Federal Radio Commission and of telephones from the Interstate Commerce Commission. In the ensuing decades, that Agency, commonly referred to by its initials, "the FCC," has added regulation of television, satellite and cable, bandwidths, frequencies, and ancillary matters.

The long tenure of this Agency, coupled with Federal legislation prompting many of its activities, has heavily influenced business segments of the Media. The history of the FCC contains noteworthy battles, from the 1940s breakup of companies controlling radio, the broadcast-time controversies of that era, the 1950s controversies over TV station spacing and subsequent battles over TV channels, the 1960s activities relative to VHF and UHF channels, the 1980s anti-trust breakup of the giant A T & T monopoly, and modern-era matters of bandwidth, broadcast towers and the like.

The focus of the FCC has been on maintaining competitiveness and eliminating monopolies. The legislation established its right to regulate content such as indecency and obscenity, ignoring the Amendment 1 Freedom of Speech "Congress shall make no law" provisions but within constraints.

It is not known whether the FCC has considered the insidious political party/media relationship that produces the political propaganda that has split our country into two antagonistic groups. An FCC opinion states, "the public interest is best served by permitting free expression of views." There is no question that the Agency possesses the knowledge and talent to implement changes to Media content rules, were it given direction and authority to do so.

---

[60] Contraction and italics by Author

THE "THREAT OF THE PRESS," A MAJOR ISSUE OF THE 1940s REMAINS BUT WITH DIFFERENT PLAYERS.

The Hutchins Commission of 1942 examined the role of the press. Its report contains the following commentary:

"The modern press itself is a new phenomenon. Its typical unit is the great agency of mass communication. These agencies can facilitate thought and discussion. They can stifle it. They can debase and vulgarize mankind. They can endanger the peace of the world; they can do so accidentally, in a fit of absence of mind. They can play up or down the news and its significance, foster and feed emotions, create complacent fictions and blind spots, misuse the great words, and uphold empty slogans. Their scope and power are increasing every day as new instruments become available to them. Those instruments can spread lies faster and farther than our forefathers dreamed when they enshrined the freedom of the press in the First Amendment to our Constitution."

Alignment of the press with political parties, politicians, and causes is not a product of the electronic age. That curse has been with us since the early time of the Constitution and has often produced as much division and ferocity as we now experience. History is riddled with stories of Presidents and parties using the press in an abusive manner. But the Press of those times, mainly a periodic newspaper, was a mere shadow of the noisy, intrusive electronic monster that dominates our lives today.

Think deeply about the quoted content of the Hutchins report, which was the political professional's view of the print media during the 1940s WW2 era. That was a time before television, computers and the internet, cellphones, satellites, and all the modern devices that now bring us news. But its threat was obvious, even then, and interestingly, the descriptions of its ploys have changed little in the intervening time.

The threat described is not the media that transmits the messages. It is the messages themselves, what is now called *"content."* The nation's threat from the Media was not brought about by technological change, as dramatic as it has been. **The threat emanates from the actions of those who use and control the mediums of communication.**

CONVERTING NEWSROOMS TO PROFIT CENTERS

The decision of major broadcast network executives to convert their newsrooms into corporate profit centers launched destructive internal behavior changes. Viewership and ratings, the underpinnings of broadcast profit, were built up by hyping the presentation of news content. In the process, patriotism and ethics were thrown out the back door.

As the insidious relationship between the news media and political parties solidified, they jointly and unobtrusively implemented a totalitarian-type mind control strategy. Was the Hutchins Commission, quoted earlier, gifted with foresight? With a relentless stream of commentary positioned to support party dogma and by posturing content so as to exalt their party of choice, the news media captured viewers and listeners, building as an audience a zombie-like cult of party faithful. Party faithful are not only mind-controlled; they are markedly close-minded, methodically discarding information that does not agree with what they have been led to believe.

It would be difficult to conjure up a more ingenious formula. It was a home run for political parties and the news media. Unfortunately, there were unintended consequences. **It was not a home run for the nation.**

The formula produced political polarization and a marked reduction in The People's trust in the government. Of course, with the change in newsroom direction and mission, mainstream media also ceased to be a check-and-balance on politicians and government. Media members lost their independence by unabashedly aligning with their party of choice. To criticize any malfeasance of that party would be intolerable behavior. With the zeal and focus of hit-men, however, they attack the politicians, politics, and activities of the opposing party.

AUTHORITY STRUCTURE "CONTROL OF THE MESSAGE"

In devising the Constitution, our nation invited privately-owned companies to be the unaccountable communication middlemen between the nation's authority structure and its citizenry. That gave private businesses a vital in-between position, controlling the flow of information about authority structure business.

In doing so, the nation also gave away the ability to execute self-government "Direct" and "Control" functions, ceding those to the Press (now the Media). Muddled and corrupted thinking about the organization of our Authority Structure has been present forever. It is probable that a "free press" was mistakenly viewed simply as a component of our vaunted "freedom" package. "If the nation is going to have "freedom of speech, then the press has to be equally free," was the thinking.

But, without The People's "Direct and Control" over the flow of information between the nation's two critical bodies (the citizens being one, and their authority structure being the other) private business misdirection of that information flow was put in place. Confusion and argument reign. A poorly-informed citizenry is the end result, causing a serious downgrade of the quality of our democratic government.

In our nation, government "control over the message" has always been denigrated, sneered at by politicians as a "totalitarian strategy." The thought that "control over the message" could possibly be a component of democratic Vital Infrastructure is alien to most citizens.

Few understand that control over "the message" is essential <u>to all forms of government.</u> In democratic self-government, control of government by The People is a "must." "Control over the message" is the fundamental function of people involvement in self-government.

A nation would never grant control over "the message" to a government run by political parties. Focused authority structure and control, so that the message does not end up becoming a threat, is critical.

Regardless of the nature or form of government, the reality is that "He who controls the message controls the outcome."

Turning the message over to private enterprise control is a serious strategic error, one of putting control of the outcome in the hands of third parties. Our nation is today paying a deadly price for ending up in that condition.

The People have lost the Framer-planned constitutional watchdog on the Federal Government because, one way or another, virtually all mainstream media participants have aligned with a political party and now focus on promoting that party's values. **The content and slant of broadcast news are determined by commercial enterprises and are light years removed from meeting the citizen/authority communication requirements of advanced democratic self-government.**

SECTION 2

HOW DO WE KNOW THE BALLOT BOX FUNCTION IS FAILING?

THE REPUBLIC'S NEED FOR INFORMED VOTERS: WHOSE RESPONSIBILITY?

Ours is the government of The People, by The People, and for The People. **At least, that is what we have been told.**

From the time of the Framers, it has been acknowledged by prominent politicians that our self-government plan requires a voter base possessed of reliable and accurate information, so that well-informed and rational decisions can be made by The People at the ballot box.

That demand is magnified when The People have been granted only one vehicle with which to influence government: the ballot box.

The lack of a well-informed voter base is, of course, at the heart of the nation's critical problem of a non-performing Legislative branch (see Chapters 7 to 9). The denizens of Congress are running wild, chasing non-productive party goals and re-election, showing little interest in either their Constitutional mandate or the needs of the nation. The People cannot enforce accountability on Congress, even though they totally disrespect it. The People are not well informed, but the dominant self-government sin is that they possess no workable check-and-balance capability.

Chapters 6 and 7 discussed the "accountability gap" in the Legislative branch. In this Series, we examine "Freedom of the Press" as an important factor in the creation of that condition. The "accountability gap" in the Legislative branch stems from the absence of a well-informed voter base, *coupled with extremely heavy political party influence on voter behavior*. Those, in turn, result from the media deciding not to perform the function that justified its original Bill of Rights freedom umbrella and from its subsequent alignment with political parties for the purpose of achieving common business objectives through nation-wide mind-control.

Political parties are the chief influencer. Voters focus on electing the party, not the candidate. Most voters don't understand that, and they continue their focus on supporting their party of choice. As long as that persists, the ballot box will swing no accountability weight.

Given The People's generally dismal performance ratings of Congress, and their continuing disgust with the two Houses, the 70% to 90% re-election rate of its members should reflect The People's positive performance ratings of Congress, which is only 10% to 30%. That mathematical contradiction stares the nation squarely in the face.

If, in the opinion of voters, the Legislative branch is not fulfilling its Constitutional role, that is proof that the ballot box check-and-balance is not working. The ballot is the only tool available for voters to impose government accountability. The voter decision process is the culprit.

Voters do not see the persons they elected as being the cause of the non-performance of the two Houses. Most do not see political parties as being the cause, they see the Congress institutions as the cause. None-the-less, when all the "Yeah, but" arguments are scraped away, political parties are the reason government is not performing.

WHY IS THE VOTER BASE NOT WELL INFORMED?

The mainstream media is not a reliable source of factual information. It is a purveyor of politics, opinion, bias, and political party propaganda. *Compromised by their political affiliations and their monopolistic commonality of belief with the people who populate the broad media structure, instead of producing well-informed voters, the media is producing biased and polarized voters.*

> In January 2018, Knight Foundation-Gallup published a survey of 19,000 U.S. adults. **It found that "Eighty four percent of Americans believe the news media have a critical or very important role to play in democracy, particularly in terms of informing the public – yet they don't see that role being fulfilled, and less than half (44%) can name an objective news source."**

There are, of course, those among the political elite and the media who view voters as a deplorable lot and who do not believe that any amount of education will improve voter judgment, change voter behavior, or produce a well-informed electorate. The belief goes further to the notion that government should be carried out by professionals who know what is best and will do the right thing, thereby mitigating the bad effects of inept elected politicians and lessening the need for well-informed voters. To the factions holding those undemocratic views, any effort expended to create well-informed voters is a waste of time.

Summarizing, three forces in our republic combine to create a poorly-informed voter pool:

1. The communication and behavior of political parties, which are designed to produce "dumbed-down" voters receptive to propaganda.

2. The News Media which promotes political party agendas by broadcasting and reinforcing party propaganda.

3. The absence of Authority Structure direction stating that well-informed voters are essential and the absence of a companion national effort to produce them.

Although the point of view that "voters are a deplorable lot" is commonplace among the political elite, that view runs contrary to the beliefs upon which the Constitution was based. Readers, in considering that, should bear in mind that they may not ever have witnessed the performance behavior of a well-informed and unbiased voter group.

WHAT IS THE BEST PATH FOR THE PEOPLE?

We, The People, must decide how much faith we should place in ourselves. Unless we choose to abandon our nation's formative beliefs, there is only one answer:

Place your bet on a well-informed electorate and believe that, possessed of reliable factual information and properly positioned systemically, such voters will make the best choices. **Rejecting that bet is abandoning belief in democracy as a form of government, and self-government as an advanced form of democracy.**

A bet on today's U.S. citizen population is not a bet on a well-informed electorate. A relatively small proportion of today's citizens are well-informed.

The People's best strategy, playing the cards they are dealt, is to identify and place our bet on that block of citizens in the population that are well-informed, then committing ourselves to increasing the size of the block.

Constitutionally, the "Well-Informed Voter" shortage is an inextricable by-product of the media threat issue. They should be dealt with concurrently, which is the strategy of this book's proposals.

SECTION 3
THE MEDIA PROBLEM CANNOT BE IGNORED. IT THREATENS THE EXISTENCE OF OUR DEMOCRACY.

Concluding the discussion of the news media's failure to perform its democratically-important functions, we should examine the risks associated with allowing the media to continue on its current path.

Government-monitoring activities by the bulk of the Media have eroded to a charade level, and the original Framer rationale for granting Freedom of the Press is no longer relevant. Given its size and power and the threat to the Republic that it is, the Media of today is more in need of a Constitutional check-and-balance than is the government on which it was originally intended to perform that function.

The Media is a force of immense and still-expanding power. It dominates the thoughts and discussions of The People and, because of its position and conduct, **has become *the major threat* to our democratic republic form of government.**

The influence of media/party alliances has reached a height where "the message is controlled," and those alliances will "determine the outcome." Our Republic would be wise not to remain exposed to such a prospect. **Controlling the outcome is the Authority Structures' reason for existence.**

The question The People must address is: "Do we want our nation to be self-governed and set its own course, or do we want its direction to be set by an unaccountable third-party Media?" That choice has to be confronted.

We are postured to lose our democratic form of government. When a political party has majority control of government, and is aligned with a dominant media, totalitarianism is in place.

In a recent Opinion article in the Wall Street Journal, David B. Rivkin and Lee A. Casey states the following:

> Media institutions, like the prerevolutionary French aristocracy, enjoy legal privileges whose rationale expired long ago. As a result, their exemption from campaign-finance law is vulnerable to constitutional challenge. "We have consistently rejected the proposition that the institutional press has any constitutional privilege beyond that of other speakers," the Citizens United court verdict declared.[61]

It can be reasonably concluded that our government today possesses the power, within existing law, to do what is necessary to direct the Media to function as it must. It has done so several times in the past. However, it is a safe bet that our government will not exercise that power.

COMMUNICATION BETWEEN THE AUTHORITY STRUCTURE AND THE PEOPLE MUST MEET THE PURITY DEMANDS OF HIGH-PERFORMANCE SELF-GOVERNMENT

A form of government that cannot bring itself to address a national threat of the magnitude under discussion is not acceptable for a nation such as ours. *Our first and foremost concern must always be survival.*

---

[61] "End the Media's Campaign Privilege" by David B. Rivkin and Lee A Casey, Wall Street Journal September 4, 2019. The Citizens United case was ruled upon by the Supreme Court.

There are few topics that illicit deeper concern about the functioning of our government than the communications media. The unwillingness of the government to address the blossoming and extreme threat the media represents is a testament to the government's corrupted ineffectiveness. That unwillingness is caused by structure, process, interest conflicts, misdirection under political party control, and elected officials propensity to place self-interest ahead of the interests of the nation.

EXPECT DRAMATIC PROGRESS IN CRIME REDUCTION, PRISON POPULATION DECREASE, AND POSITIVE CHANGE IN SOCIAL BEHAVIOR

It has not been sufficiently emphasized that the constitutional actions proposed will produce a broad range of behavioral side-benefits that reduce anxiety and fear among the population. The positive social consequences of pursuing the proposed courses of action would be dramatic.

SECTION 4
ACTION PROPOSAL

A. NEEDED "MEDIA CONTROL" CONSTITUTIONAL AMENDMENT

Alignment of the mainstream media with political parties for the purpose of mind-control, leading ultimately to totalitarian political control, is the addressed threat.

The media thinks it has the right to implant in the population what it has decided is the proper national sense of direction. The warning signal of what the future might hold for us, a signal that we ignore at our own peril, is the severe political polarization we observe today, which is traceable directly to party/media alignment. Added to the polarization, more recently, we have seen enhanced political censorship and political party efforts to control acceptable speech and thought, and witnessed strong increases in the number of assemblies that have turned riotous. We should consider those to be intermediate phases on the road to crisis.

Because the privileges enjoyed by the Media are viewed by most as imbedded in the Constitution under the First Amendment lead-in "Congress shall make no law," there is only one guarantied route by which media activities can be brought under control to allay its huge risk to the Republic. **An amendment to the Constitution is required**. A legislative solution is possible, but the motivation in the two Houses of Congress does not run in that direction due to political party affiliation with the media, so that route is unlikely to produce results.

Under Section V of our Constitution, all routes to the Constitutional Amendment are vested in the political class. That is the same group of politicians who partner with the Media in the illicit alliance discussed here. **The likelihood of the political class fostering a Constitutional amendment to reign in the Media is zero.**

It is crystal clear that any amendment to reign in the Media will have to be initiated by The People. Any such effort by The People will be fought, tooth and nail, by the media and the entrenched political elite, both of whose interests would be at risk.

The following describes needed Authority Structure actions directly and indirectly related to the Media, and the reasons for doing so. **This is not a complete list.**

B. PLACE THE NEWS SERVICES UNDER CONTROL OF THE PEOPLE

> For direction and control purity, two-way information flow regarding the nation's business (between The People and the Authority Structure) must be enshrined under control of The People, as Constitutional Vital Infrastructure, governed by new provisions to the Constitution, and placed under total control of constitutional authorities.

The information flow in focus here has historically been provided and controlled by what is now called "the media." The specific information is generally referred to by the descriptor "news."

1. All News Service Provider information flow relating to the nation's Authority Structure and Government Affairs (perhaps more simply called "the nation's business") would be removed from Media companies, consolidated, and placed under Constitutional control. News topics and commentary concerning them would no longer be permitted transmissions of the national Media.

2. If taken while leaving political parties in place, this action would produce dramatic improvement, but simultaneously disbanding political party operations would add assurance of positive results. Political parties are the background cause of most of the nation's governance information distress.

3. The Communications Vital Infrastructure would be broadened to include essential activities that establish a Well-Informed Electorate. **On all matters that are the designated responsibility of The People, the Well-Informed Electorate would, on behalf of all citizens and employing direct democracy, vote to decide the required new constitutional provisions.**

C. REVISE THE BILL OF RIGHTS TO INGRAIN COMMENSURATE PERSONAL ACCOUNTABILITY

1. Revise the stand-alone concept of "Rights" by including defined "Personal Accountability" tied to the utilization of those rights. Balance the grant of rights and privileges with equal accountability and meld those into the concept of citizenship.

2. The broadened and revised Bill of Rights constitutional provisions would become a basic citizenship training document for all who pass through the education system, for residents, citizens and prospective citizens, and be written in a manner that facilitates those uses. The provisions would become citizenship principles, emphasizing personal behavior and accountability.

3. An important aspect of the revised Bill of Rights would be the correlation of citizen behavior to personal rights and privileges. The relationship of morals and ethics to personal conduct, trust, and the nation's self-governance would be melded together, setting the rules that are to be obeyed. Tied to that provision would be the initiation of Morals and Ethics Tabulation and Reporting, developing a public record of citizen violations, to introduce public shaming as punishment for morals and ethics misbehavior.

4. It is suggested the concept and rules of Treason be revised and broadened to include treason crimes against the Nation and its Constitution, violation of citizenship obligations, and excessive aggregate morals and ethics abuses by individuals.

5. A citizen's obligation to participate in self-government, to be well-informed by closely following the News and developments, to vote in elections, to serve the nation in times of need, and to participate in national efforts of all kinds would be clearly established, with appropriate disrespect penalties.

6. If The People want to enhance meaningfulness of the program, they might consider establishing several classes of citizenship measuring the performance of individuals as citizens under personal accountability, augmenting the program with identification cards signifying the assigned citizenship class of the bearer.

D. UPDATE AMENDMENT 1, THE BILL OF RIGHTS

1. All rights listed in current Amendment 1 should be subjected to thorough review and update. It is suggested that each Right include within itself the explanations required by ordinary citizens to understand without needing legal research or interpretation.

2. A complete revision of the "Right of the people peaceably to assemble, and to petition the Government for a redress of grievances" should be undertaken. A discussion of that issue, with a proposed plan solution, is included in a forthcoming Chapter.

3. The most pressing revision relates to "abridging the freedom of speech, or of the press," which will bring The People into confrontation with the media problem of our nation.

4. The "establishment of religion" provision needs reconsideration to address the inherent conflict of Muslim religion dogma with the concepts of democracy.

5. "Ownership of Personal Data," the subject of a forthcoming Chapter, should become a new "rights" provision.

6. The "right to Abortion" is a festering Constitutional issue in our nation, the subject of much debate and raw feelings. Many consider it a "personal rights" issue. That must be resolved, and the resolution included in a new Bill of Rights provision. It is time The People decide how our nation will handle this polarizing disagreement. It will not disappear of its own accord, will not be solved by delegation to the States, and will not be resolved within the party system.

7. Another festering constitutional issue is "Equality," which was never consecrated as a "right," even though it is a well-entrenched concept. Racism, homophobia, mistreatment claims going back centuries, destruction of national monuments, the royalty-level homage accorded persons of wealth and fame, and a host of related issues require national examination and constitutional decision.

E. RESTRUCTURE THE MEDIA

1. National direction, from The People to the Nation, must be provided through the Constitution. Media cannot be permitted to set the nation's political or governmental discussion, policy, or direction. **That role belongs solely to The People.**

2. The Media's responsibility to the nation is its highest responsibility. **Alignment of political parties and factions or branches of government, with Media elements must be designated as "Treasonous."**

3. Transfer of the News Service Providers from the Mainstream Media to the Constitutional Authorities will eliminate a large part of the Media risk to our nation's governance, but other actions of large impact will be necessary. The Media must be designated "Vital Infrastructure" and placed under control of Constitutional Authorities. **Those actions may necessitate the breakup of the large vertically-integrated corporations that dominate the industry.**

a. The first part of the process must be the development of principles by the Well-Informed Electors, under the guidance of the Constitutional Convention and with the aid of the F.C.C., declaring what aspects of the media constitute the greatest risk and what major actions must be undertaken. From those principles a long-term plan would be developed. This is a large undertaking.

b. The probability is that ownership of channels of communication should be separated from all content ownership. The channels are the nation's physical communication capability, a strategically critical infrastructure element of the nation with heavy national security implications, equivalent in importance to the rail, highway, and air transportation systems.

c. Vertical integration of media businesses should probably be forbidden.

4. **The main objective of The People must be to break up the intellectual and political thought monopoly imbedded in the Mainstream Media**.

Any attempt by Media Owners or groups to direct thought through the control or distribution of content material must be forbidden. With the exception of third-party controlled sporting events and general entertainment, no content material may be sold to or otherwise shared with other media participants.

The Media may not attempt to influence the opinions of listeners. The People cannot allow themselves or their government to be led intellectually by media talking heads.

CHAPTER 20

THE RIGHTS AND FREEDOMS SERIES: PART 4

CONTENT:

SECTION 1: THE MOST POWERFUL FORCE IN THE NATION

SECTION 2: SATISFYING THE "WELL-INFORMED ELECTOR" NEED

SECTION 3: RESPONSIBILITIES OF THE PEOPLE

FOREWORD

"America will never be destroyed from the outside. If we falter and lose our freedoms, it will be because we destroyed ourselves." (Abraham Lincoln)

We point fingers of scorn at dictators who impose tight control over their media, but we should instead be learning from them. Regardless of the form of government, totalitarian or democratic, the dominant rule is:

"He who controls the message controls the outcome."

"Who controls the message in our nation?" The answer is clear. The Media controls the message!

Communication is more vital to a self-governed democracy than to any other form of government. It determines what citizens know about their self-government, and what they do depends on what they know. The failure of our nation's political elite to structure and guaranty vital communication between its citizens and the government is at the heart of our regression in governance quality.

"Destroying ourselves" is what we are doing. Destruction will be the end result if The People fail to take purposeful corrective action.

This is a matter of survival of our form of government, more important than all other considerations. *Our media cannot be allowed to be the destructor of government. Instead, it must be made a strong contributor to government's success. Whether or not that happens is The People's choice.*

This chapter discusses the issues involved and proposes elements of a plan to eliminate the Media as a threat to our governance and to create the information flow essential to self-government.

SECTION 1
THE MOST POWERFUL FORCE IN THE NATION

THE MEDIA MONSTER, MAINLY ELECTRONIC, IS THE MOST POWERFUL FORCE IN OUR NATION

It is more powerful than the Military because it can dissuade us from using that capability. The government would be inert and ineffective without it but may be inert and ineffective because of it. It can twist, slant, misinterpret, and otherwise distort any message. **Its practice of selecting topics that may be publicly distributed and refusing others is gross anti-self-government.**

Throughout most of this discussion we shall use the term "media" the way those involved in it use the term. Everything is lumped into one huge ball, the electronic and paper media, content, people, communications systems such as the internet, the providers of services who utilize the media, news, entertainment, etc. To media people, and probably to a significant segment of our population, "the media is that huge ball." Fortunately, the content and make-up of the "ball" is never defined.

The media continues to mushroom in size. It dominates the lives of our citizens. It has the power to control the thoughts of The People and, through that, The People themselves.

Thinking persons will understand that the forceful pace of media growth is probably driven by the Media's untenable "tweener" controlling position between The People and the nation's Authority Structure. The business advantage of that position is mind-boggling.

In democratic self-governance, such power cannot be placed in private hands, allowing misuse by those who do not have the nation's best interest at heart. For such power to be in the hands of business interests that collectively abide by monopolistic common political alignment and beliefs is "democratic self-government survival insanity."

Our communications are controlled by private interests for whom the welfare of the nation is not the principal consideration. The influence of citizens is minuscule by comparison. In what is supposed to be a self-governed nation, the influence power of government is seriously eroded by Media activities.

REVISITING "THE PRESS"

The media's ancient forefathers are still present among us. The print publication was thought by the Framers to be the vital means by which citizens could monitor politicians and the functioning of government. They gave it a very special "tweener" place by way of the First Amendment: "Congress shall make no law respecting an establishment of religion, or prohibiting the free exercise thereof: *or abridging the freedom of speech, or of the press...........*"[62]

Media participants wrap themselves in the mantle of that almost-holy First Amendment provision by conducting themselves as though the conveyed rights exist and belong to all media players. Foregoing chapters have explored the media in considerable depth, and have noted Supreme Court judgments that nullify that perspective.

Added to that is the realization that much of the public has difficulty separating Freedom of the Press from Freedom of Speech because of our obsolete constitution and because of the very poor communication of Supreme Court verdicts that change meaning. Confusion reigns regarding those fundamental constitutional provisions, and confusion is a severe negative factor.

THE EXISTENTIAL THREAT THE MEDIA REPRESENTS

In the order of things, actions to defend our government's survival **against internal threats** must have the highest priority. Ensuring that our form of government is not at risk to undemocratic internal forces is at the very top of the priority list. Such forces are the most difficult to control and eliminate because of Freedom beliefs and other confusion.

Communication critical to the nation's business should certainly not ever be placed in a position where it can be subjected to interference by private interests or political parties. The guiding principle must be that self-government communication, between The People and their Authority Structure, *is vital communication. As such, must be under the sole control of the Constitutional Authorities, which represent The People only.*

Purity, accuracy, thoroughness and relevance are demanded in such communications. **They must be absolutely reliable.** All information flow between The People and their Authority Structure, including People-to-People social communication respecting the authority structure and The People, must be isolated and controlled by Constitutional Authorities. This is not function where public media should be permitted to intercede.

---

[62] Italics by the Author

The above position statement comes into eye-ball to-eye-ball confrontation with general beliefs about "freedom," such as freedom of speech, freedom of the press, and freedom to pursue business interests without government interference.

The media survival threat is a constitutional issue that lies outside the bounds of and is superior to all general "freedom" considerations.

Today, information The People receive regarding politics, government, and the affairs of the Nation **is whatever the media decides to give them**. Regardless of the form of government, **no private entity can be permitted that position in the communications system.**

If the nation's value system and beliefs, information concerning events, and information concerning government affairs is to be communicated between the citizens and their authority structure, **the obligation to control and ensure purity in that communication belongs solely to The People.**

Giving the privately-owned Media the right and opportunity to decide, posture, and control government/People communications is about as rational as giving Political Parties the right to control elected assemblies if they corral a majority of seats. In both cases, the conduct of The People's vital government is placed in third-party hands. At that point, it is out of the control of the nation's owners, The People, putting the nation at great risk.

For those reasons, we rate Media activities controlling the flow of critical information about governance as **AN EXISTENTIAL THREAT TO THE NATION.**

The government cannot be trusted to make critical decisions concerning such vital information flow because the government is today marching solely to the drum-beat of political parties that are locked in a partnership with the media. That is the threat. Left with an open field, political parties and their allied interests will inevitably make the media their control tool, as has happened in our nation.

IN SELF-GOVERNMENT, COMMUNICATION IS VITAL

It is proposed that no discussion of self-government or its business be permitted in the existing Media. Any use of the Media to communicate to the public regarding the business of the Authority Structure would be treasonous.

Vital two-way communication between The People and their Authority Structure must be as tight as communications respecting national security between the Government and the Department of Defense. Other public communication presently conducted through the Media would continue. Because no political discussion would be permitted in that segment of the

Media, pressure for censorship should disappear. If it does not, additional actions can be taken.

"HE WHO CONTROLS THE MESSAGE CONTROLS THE OUTCOME"

The most threatening actions of the Media are:

1. **Aligning with political parties to control the message, media strategy for gaining mind control over the citizens.**

2. **Formation by the Media of an industry-wide conformance monopoly for message consistency.**

Those two strategies are mutually supportive, and are utilized simultaneously.

The end result of the threatening alliance between media and political parties, the political polarization we experience every day and the zombie-like behavior of party faithful, are clear demonstrations of what happens when "the message" is being controlled by independent players operating outside of the authority structure.

The danger is there for all to see. *He who controls the message controls the outcome!*

SECTION 2
SATISFYING THE "WELL-INFORMED ELECTOR" NEED

The lack of a "Well-Informed Electorate" is the result of Media's "control of the message."

By aligning with political parties and conducting itself as described, the media has made clear it accepts no responsibility for the government that results from its information distribution policies. It does, however, intend to create a society whose thought patterns follow media principles and beliefs. **The media is not the nation's designated policy formulation body. That is a role reserved for The People solely.**

The obligation of the media, of producing well-informed voters has long ago been abandoned at the altar of the profit motive utilizing its supporting mind control strategy, political party propaganda. The Media sees its role as championing a favored political perspective, not producing a well-informed public. The newsroom must produce a profit!

The People's self-government is left with a critical unsatisfied need, that of a well-informed electorate. Self-government cannot leave that outcome to chance. Authority

Structure control over the flow of vital information that produces a well-informed electorate is a fundamental requirement.

Congress, handcuffed by the First Amendment, has indeed made no recent laws "abridging freedom of the press." Of course, Congress is run by the political parties that are in unholy alliance with the media, a conflict-of-interest ensuring that neither of those has incentive to go down that road.

And, sure enough, they haven't! **So, as always, it will be up to The People**.

WHAT ABOUT FREEDOM OF SPEECH?

SEPARATING "FREEDOM OF THE PRESS" FROM "FREEDOM OF "SPEECH"

THE INTELLECTUAL CONFLICT BETWEEN "FREEDOM OF SPEECH" AND "CONTROL OVER THE MESSAGE"

The first concern that surfaces whenever there is a suggestion that information flow be brought under control is the invasion of the Freedom of Speech provision of the First Amendment. If you institute "control of the message," are you not controlling Freedom of Speech in violation of that highly-favored Constitutional right?

Under properly-structured advanced democratic self-government, The People, owners of the nation, would make all decisions regarding acceptable public speech. They will decide the extent to which expression rights may be utilized, how, and by whom. In such circumstances, The People may limit Freedom of Speech in the Media, **if they conclude the blanket delegation of that Freedom is threatening to the self-government Authority Structure.**

The People may decide to re-organize the Media, dividing it up for better control over the behavior of its individual components, which history records as having already been done several times. A wide range of potential actions are the right of The People if they are truly practicing self-government and intend to ensure the survival of self-government through the unobstructed flow of vital information.

This book proposes only that the sanctified two-way communications of the Republic, **between the Authorities and The People, and discussion among The People themselves regarding the business of governance**, be isolated and purified. Companion to that action, our democracy's public general Freedom of Speech should remain in place.

SECTION 3
RESPONSIBILITIES OF THE PEOPLE

MEETING CONSTITUTIONAL AUTHORITY REQUIREMENTS WHILE PROVIDING FREEDOM OF SPEECH

Following is a summary plan to neutralize the Media as a threat to our Democratic form of government by making "Control of the Message" a strong positive contributor to our democratic self-government. Most elements of the following list have already been discussed.

- **Constitutional Authority News Content (a new title is needed) must be constructed so that communications considered "constitutionally vital" are carefully isolated for The People's message control purposes.** All public discussion of government business would be channeled through that constitutionally-controlled media.

- The proposed enhanced role of The People in the nation's highest-level decisions, deemed necessary for high-performance democratic self-government, means that the development of a 'well-informed electorate" is a pressing priority.

- The statement "Congress shall make no law abridging freedom of the press" must be removed from the Constitution and replaced with a new provision showing how the above-defined communications will operate and setting forth the rules.

- Designing and transmitting news regarding Authority business will be the responsibility of The People, and a significant broadening will be necessary to meet the requirements of advanced democratic self-government. All actions taken within the Authority Structure would be reported, which should produce a significant improvement in government accountability, quite the opposite of the current situation.

- **Content provided through The People's Communications is a feature element of The People's plan for developing and enhancing the Well-Informed Electorate.** News Providers, contained in a new vital infrastructure body of the Constitutional Authority called The People's Communications, would be equivalent in stature to the People's Election Commission and the Justice System. It will design and disseminate the factual information needed for democratic self-government and Constitutional Authority decision-making.

- News shall be transmitted to and from the public through designated and labeled communication channels that may be used for no other content. News providers will be politically neutral, report facts and explanations only, favor no position, and express no opinions. The type and nature of Authority and Government information transmitted will be enhanced, including providing an array of authority-performance information that is currently being suppressed. All news must be reported in such a way as to either neutralize opinions that have political implications or to address strong political opinions by presenting equally strong opposing views.

- All news respecting government business would be the Constitutional responsibility of The People's Communications, including news concerning the Authority Structure's actions, including those of the government. The success of this operating concept will require measuring the extent to which the electorate is well-informed. Regular testing and public reporting of measurement results, as a part of the nation's business discussion, will be needed.

- The People's Communications will perform a variety of related functions. It will provide education for citizenship and for Well-Informed Elector qualification. It will manage the secure communications between the Constitutional Authorities and the Well-Informed Electors concerning the topics of their decision process. It will publish vital performance data.

- Many questions arise about prospective relationships between the News Service and the revised functions of government. With no political parties, and all elected assemblies under Constitutional management, the process of government should be free of bias to a large extent. Our nation's recent experiences generate fear of abuse, so tight control is needed. Because of the importance to a functioning democracy of highly informative and factual news reporting, "doctored" news should be treated as treasonous activity against the nation.

- Political news, public opinion statements, and other material normally categorized as "political" but not deemed "vital" will be transmitted only in Constitutional, carefully licensed, and isolated channels of communication called Political Discussion. Political discussion would not be mixed with any other content. Channels providing such information will prominently display warnings that are the equivalent of those required on tobacco, liquor, cannabis products, and drugs.

CHAPTER 21

FOREWORD

"Information is Money" is the topic of this Chapter, as is the Golden Rule: "He who has the gold makes the rule."

This Chapter will focus on one topic, "User Data Ownership." In the overall governance of the United States of America it is a minor matter, though its effects touch all citizens.

Readers, however, will quickly realize that the overriding issue, the poor governance that hangs over our nation, is what brings this subject to the forefront. Ineffective government allows nagging messes like User Data Ownership to float inert in the kettle, uncooked.

SECTION 1
PROPOSED CONSTITUTIONAL PROVISION FOR DATA OWNERSHIP

INTRODUCTION

There is a substantial amount of concern among American citizens about what Media companies do with the personal data they collect when interacting with individuals, on-line and otherwise. Currently, gatherers of personal data claiming ownership are custodians and sellers of personal data, usually without hassle or limitation and with no concern whatsoever for the rights of data subjects. They are able to do that because this country's laws on the subject are incohesive. **Citizens are denied ownership rights to their own personal and private data!**

The user data privacy and ownership issue is relatively new, an outgrowth of modern technology that makes possible improved data accumulation and storage by service providers operating via the electronic media. Such businesses electronically gather and store huge amounts of personal data on their users, including behavioral habits and like/dislike propensities. The old saying, "information is money," defines the activity.

The gathered data is sold to a product marketer who will isolate targets meeting his pre-determined buyer characteristics. The product marketer designs sales programs for delivery to those data subject targets by mail, telephone, or electronic platforms. Such sales programs usually produce high rates of return for the product marketer, and because of that characteristic, generate huge profits for data gatherers who are able to sell packages of data at high prices.

BACKGROUND INFORMATION

In this Chapter we will use the terms "Data Person" and "Data Subjects" to describe the individuals whose data is gathered. Custodians of personal data will be termed "Data Gatherers" or "Data Custodians."

In the quarter ending June 30, 2019, Facebook's (now called "Meta") revenue was approximately $17 billion, an annual run-rate of $68 billion, virtually all derived from sales of user data or targeted advertising similar to that described in the foregoing paragraph. Facebook gathered personal information on its users to help advertisers efficiently present proposals to those users and benefitted handsomely in the process. Facebook users whose personal data was gathered, 1.59 billion worldwide, received Facebook services but nothing else[63] and may have been barraged with a wide variety of sales intrusions. For the June 2019 quarter, Facebook's average revenue per user was $7.05, an annual run-rate of $28.20. Facebook's efforts to monetize user data, while viewed by many as unfair, are a major and on-going part of the company's business.

If you are an elderly person and have received at your home a personally-addressed letter offering mortuary services, you can reasonably conclude that a Media Service Provider has gathered your personal data, determined your age, and sold a list of age-group persons fitting the specifications of the mortuary's advertising firm. There are many avenues and approaches

---

.

for businesses to capitalize on personal data, but vastly more efficient ways of isolating and identifying potential buyers of a company's product are dominant among those.

Concerns arise about the safety of gathered user data as hackers, for nefarious purposes, have gained access to reams of it in recent years. Hacker sales of purloined user data affect the safety of millions of ordinary people whose personal information ends up in the wrong hands. At a minimum, upon being informed of such data breaches, data subjects must change passwords and take other security steps to attempt to protect themselves from theft by electronic invasion. In the worst cases, data subjects have a major financial catastrophe on their hands.

THE DEPTH OF DATA PERSON COMPREHENSION OF THE MATTER

A Journal Reports/Artificial Intelligence article in the Wall Street Journal on October 14, 2019, quoted a 2018 global survey by Ipsos: "Roughly two-thirds of those surveyed said they knew little or nothing about how much data companies held about them or what companies did with that data. And only about a third of respondents on average said they had at least a fair amount of trust that a variety of corporate and government organizations would use the information they had about them in the right way."[64]

> The data subjects, who are citizens and other residents, have no control over the activities of the gatherers. Their reasonable claims to ownership of their own data are being ignored by the gatherers, while data subjects are at substantial risk and inconvenience because their personal information is being sold into the hands of third parties.

Data gatherers are the recipients of huge payments from the sale of personal data. Personal data is an informed, direct path to the data subjects and a gold -mine for sales strategies that produce high rates of return, thus of immense value to merchandisers and marketers.

THE U.S. LEGAL APPROACH IS CATASTROPHIC

> The European Union has made enlightened progress in dealing with Personal Data, as a result of having to tie together, in key legal areas, the many nations making up their Union. *In the European Union, ownership of personal data is vested in the data subject.* The Union's laws on the subject are clear and concise, covering all important aspects.

---

[64] Wall Street Journal article "Should Consumers be Able to Sell Their Own Personal Data" October 14, 2019

In the United States, on the other hand, no single data protection legislation exists. Instead, there is a jumble of hundreds of laws at the Federal and State levels. No law specifically defines ownership of the data or rules for transfer, and those that exist tend to be loose and non-specific. The Federal Trade Commission is the Agency responsible.

The laws of the various States range widely but in general, do not define ownership. Such Federal legislation as exists is often sector-specific, for example, the Gram-Leach-Bliley Act defines the personal data rules for financial institutions.

For an issue as critical to our people as the definition of ownership of personal data, clarity of law, the protection of the individual and his privacy, and most everything else about the issue, it is an absolute mess. There is no centrally-planned approach, another by-product of our "legislative branch accountability gap." What governance exists on this matter must be rated "grossly inept."

SECTION 2
ARGUMENTS CONCERNING OWNERSHIP OF USER DATA

The Wall Street Journal contained a good article "Should Consumers be Able to Sell Their Own Personal Data?" arguing the two sides of the issue.[65] The following is a condensation of the major points of the article:

Arguments supporting the affirmative are:

- Data doesn't diminish with time; it is indefinitely re-useable. Ownership is valuable.

- Control over personal data **is a fundamental privacy issue**.

- If it was owned by the data subject, personal data could be sold to trusted buyers and not sold to untrusted buyers.

- Firms assembling the data may not be willing to distribute it to buyers who would use it for the benefit of society or to competitors. Sales by the data subjects were they permitted to do so, could dramatically stimulate competition.

- Sale decisions that generate financial incentives but sacrifice privacy, should be made by the data subjects. Personal data is, after all, their own information.

---

[65] "Should Consumers Be Able to Sell Their Own Personal Data?" Christopher Tonetti for the affirmative, Cameron Kerry for the negative. Wall Street Journal, Journal Reports, October 14, 2019.

Arguments supporting the negative are:

- Consumer ownership of personal data will do little to help privacy and may well leave consumers worse off.

- Today, consumers give up all rights to data ownership in return for convenience, free services, connection, etc. A small amount of money may induce them to give up even more rights.

- Consumers lack information regarding data value and the market and, therefore, are unlikely to negotiate well.

- How can the rights of the data-collecting business be reasonably accommodated?

- There would be enormous technical and logistical costs of engineering a system to manage ownership by the data subjects.

- Our digital society and economy operate through broad ecosystems of data sharing. Those systems would be undermined.

- Giving data subjects ownership rights may encourage even less privacy, because of consumer willingness to disclose for money.

- The answer is Federal regulation of data gathering while giving consumers the right to access, correct, and delete information.

The arguments supporting the negative show little respect for consumers and their ability to make decisions, leading to a preference for Federal regulation over consumer choice.

It is generally conceded that conversion to a system of ownership of personal data *by the data person* would necessitate considerable capital expenditure on the part of data gatherers. However, because the data-collecting organizations involved are already heavily immersed in data management, they are eminently capable of creating the system add-ons needed. They managed and funded the system development to accumulate the personal data in the first instance, so the cost and inconvenience of having to revise their system should not be a consideration.

Giving individual consumers (the data subjects) the right and power to sell personal data housed and controlled by a corporate gatherer is a seriously suspect solution for all of the reasons mentioned in the arguments. Theoretically, it is possible, but from a practical perspective, it is not.

SECTION 3
PERSONAL DATA AS A CONSTITUTIONAL QUESTION

The focus of this Book is on matters more critical to the welfare and survival of the Republic, having to do with the bigger issues of governance and the Media. Despite the importance of the Personal Data issue, it is not at the level of the major issues that form the basis of our Constitutional crises. For a large self-governed nation, it falls into the category of "everyday business." A decision must be made, and implementation must take place. It is, however, an issue with Constitutional ramifications.

The Personal Data issue must be viewed as an example of the lack of competence prevalent in our system of government. It is a demonstration of its unwillingness or inability to deal with fundamental governance issues of the nation that are screaming for attention.

Why, then, is the topic of Personal Data discussed here? The following are the reasons:

1. Protecting The People from rapacious commercial enterprises, those that take advantage of a superior technical position to extract ill-gotten gains is a primary responsibility of the government. That is a matter of ethics. Our government has failed to protect its citizens and is not being held accountable for its failure.

2. Personal data is owned by the data subjects, not by data gatherers. Arriving at any other conclusion is irrational. The European Union approach is the correct path. Rights of data ownership is a fundamental issue of equity, as well as of individual security and privacy, and therefore must be a "Constitutional rights" subject.

3. If The People do not take control over the issue, their rights will end up being dealt away in a congressional compromise, or, more likely, no action will be taken by the government at all. Either way, the outcome will assuredly not be in the interest of The People. For political reasons discussed several times in this book, the political elite will not undertake a Constitutional Amendment.

4. It is not possible to consider the Constitutional issues concerning the Bill of Rights without confronting the personal data ownership question, which stems directly from the business activities of dominant Media Service Providers. **The media is identified as a major threat to our democratic form of government. The data ownership question highlights the negative behavior of media service providers, of taking advantage of favorable positions to exert an unfair financial advantage.**

5. A major aim of this Book is to prompt The People to take control over their governing document, the constitution, and having gained control, to drive the quality

of government dramatically upward. Ownership of personal data is a good example of the important interests of The People that their elected persons are ignoring. The government avoids addressing any issue of importance, including those that are constitutional. Elected persons have not addressed this issue because they know that The People have no way to hold them accountable.

6. The ineffectiveness of the Legislative branch, discussed extensively in previous chapters, is highlighted by comparing European Union law regarding personal data against the patchwork law jungle that exists in the U.S. The People, denied a meaningful policy solution by the Government, are being harmed individually and financially. Government, led by political parties, must cater to a range of interests but too often ends up ignoring the interests of The People.

SECTION 4
USER DATA OWNERSHIP AND SALES ISSUES

Sales of user data are being consummated regularly without the express permission of the data subjects. User data, in our nation, is assumed to be owned by the Media business that gathered it.

It is suggested that the European Union's definition of Personal Data, recorded earlier, be the definition adopted in the United States Constitution.

Information gathered and stored by governments requires treatment different from data gathered by businesses. Governments gather information from a wide range of activities, and that which has historically been public information should remain so. Examples are births, deaths, and marriages. Real estate ownership and taxation records, education records, licensing records, legal records of the court system, citizenship, and records of military service. Such records have historically been the essential records of government. Ownership and control over such data should remain vested in the government that collects it. Other personal information maintained by governments that should be owned by the data subject are Social Security records, Income Taxation records, Medicare and medical records, for example.

The right of a non-government organization to collect data from its own customers is not questioned. **But ownership of personal data collected should be constitutionally protected, and defined as owned by the data subject, not by the gatherer or custodian.** *It is, after all, the subject person in a different form.* That rule should hold true for all manner of personal data, such as medical history, DNA, credit and financial histories, internet, telephone and e-mail information, elements of a list that may be considerably longer.

Further, non-government data collectors should be held constitutionally to a high standard for the security of data in their custody, and subject to substantial constitutionally-defined monetary liability to data persons for data loss, misuse, or sale without the permission of the data person.

RIGHTS AND RULES FOR SELLING USER DATA

It was stated that the gathering organization has a stake in the ownership of personal data collected and stored. The stake arises from the effort and investment expended to gather and store the data. No sale of the data can be accomplished without effort on the part of the data gatherer/custodian. The rights and obligations of the custodian to manage and control the sale of the data's use and to participate in the sale proceeds stem from those considerations.

Attempting to convey selling rights down to the level of individual data subjects, as some suggest, would create an impossible administrative mess. The control of the gatherer would be seriously degraded, a factor intrinsic to the data's market value. The gatherer, selling in bulk, is positioned to derive the highest value, which is important to all involved. For gatherers, the cost of handling data sales would balloon if each data subject were to sell individually. Conveying selling rights to data subjects would result in a multitude of individual sales, increasing costs and making bulk sales of the unsold remainder unattractive to purchasers. It appears that conveying selling rights down to the level of individual data subjects would make data, in general, much less attractive to buyers.

The best solution is to give the data gatherer the right to sell in bulk, and grant the data subjects the right to decline participation in the sale. Consenting data owners would participate in sale proceeds, but declining owners would receive nothing. The interest of all parties is best assured by that approach.

Sale concurrence should be by a specific agreement between the data gatherer and the data subject, and not bundled into a general operating agreement. The European Union has solved that problem by permitting simplistic on-line sale approval mechanisms. Assuming a data subject consents to the sale, proceeds should be split 50/50 between the gatherer and the data subject, reflecting the equality of their individual stakes. The split price is high enough that, presumably, most data persons would agree to sell. Without permission, the gatherer could not sell data relating to a data owner but would be free to sell that of all who consent to the sale.

There are those who say that the sale of personal data should not convey rights to a buyer that infringe on the data subject's privacy, such as contacting a data person or placing advertising before that person. Under that theory, such rights would be held separate and also saleable by the data person. To attempt to separate those rights from those of raw data ownership, however, creates transactional complexity. Better to not separate such rights but to define them merely as elements of data ownership. Data owners not wishing to be contacted, under that approach, should not consent to a sale.

GROSS VIOLATIONS OF INDIVIDUAL PRIVACY

Transfer of personal data affects the data person, of course, because the sale of such information to third parties inevitably results in bombardment by telephone or a range of other gross privacy invasions. Until the change is enacted, the data subject receives no compensation but is still subjected to that harassment. The fact those privacy invasions have not been addressed legislatively is to be expected, given our ineffective Congress.

SECTION 5
CONCLUSIONS

In the Constitution should be inserted an addition to the Bill of Rights, of which the following is a draft proposal:

PROPOSED CONSTITUTIONAL PROVISION

OWNERSHIP OF PERSONAL DATA

"A data subject is an identified or identifiable individual. Personal data is any information that relates to that individual. Different pieces of information that, collected together, can lead to the identification of a particular person and also constitute personal data.

Personal data, if gathered and stored by data gatherers, is owned by the data subject. It may not be sold by data gatherers, distributed, or otherwise released without express permission from the owner and upon payment to the data subject of not less than one-half of sale proceeds. Personal data accumulated by governments that has historically been public information is exempt from this data ownership sale provision."

CHAPTER 22

THE RIGHT "PEACEABLY TO ASSEMBLE"

CONTENT:

SECTION 1: CURRENT EVENTS INVOLVING THE RIGHT PEACEABLY TO ASSEMBLE

SECTION 2: CITY COUNCILS AND POLICE BRASS CANNOT ESCAPE ACCOUNTABILITY

SECTION 3: CONSTITUTIONAL PROVISION PROPOSAL

FOREWORD

Nowhere is the lack of elected official accountability more evident than in their observed behavior when acts of groups taking advantage of "The Right Peaceably to Assemble" turn anarchist and/or riotous. Most such assemblies are local in nature and set in a specific location for a reason.

This is a local government performance matter. At issue is broad ignorance of the well-established rules of delegation of authority and imposition of accountability, as applied within the organization structure of local elected governing bodies and their police departments.

The apparent absence of fundamental knowledge is resulting in poor governance, poor delegation practices, and poor personnel administration. But worst of all, the lowest officers in the police organization are blamed and legally attacked for actions taken under the duress of riots, while the true miscreants escape Scott-free. That is an egregious violation of basic concepts of "right and wrong."

"If the worker didn't work, the manager didn't manage," goes an age-old management rule. Also worth quoting is the old Beverly Hills business observation, "The fish stinks from the head."

There are few situations where a new constitutional provision is more needed. Given the people who must apply them and the people who engage in assemblies, the rules and penalties under which Peaceable Assembly may be conducted must be detailed and explicit. For activities as incendiary as assemblies, the rules must be meaningful, tough, and applied universally.

SECTION 1
CURRENT EVENTS INVOLVING THE RIGHT PEACEABLY TO ASSEMBLE

Nothing granted by Amendment 1 has provoked more dissidence among The People this year than the "right peaceably to assemble." In city after city, under the banner of Black Lives Matter and other banners, and provoked by a group called Antifa, peaceable assemblies have degenerated to anarchy. It has been reported that protesters were hired by internet advertising and fees were paid to those who participated. Demonstrations thus staffed can hardly be described as "a spontaneous assembly of citizens seeking justice."

The activities generating the anarchy are part of a massive effort by totalitarian factions to create division among the citizens, under a general strategy designed to weaken support for democratic government.

Peaceable Assembly activity has evidenced its usual earmarks: degeneration to riot, extensive damage to businesses, confrontations between rioters and law enforcement, and death and injury to bystanders and to others involved. The riots were unusual in several respects: their duration, in some cities continuing nightly for weeks; the degree to which law enforcement was attacked for its activities, the attacks sometimes affected by local government efforts to disband law enforcement; the gross ineffectiveness of city governments carrying out their responsibilities for law and order; the support of political parties for "right of assembly" activities that are riotous, and their overall inability to propose or advance a solution; and, finally, the apparent ambivalence of The People to the destructive activities being reported on television.

SECTION 2
CITY COUNCILS AND POLICE BRASS CANNOT ESCAPE ACCOUNTABILITY

The immediate reaction of readers to the above set of facts will be to question the "right peaceably to assemble" provision of the Bill of Rights. That certainly is a legitimate reaction, as the provision rightfully should be questioned given the nation's recent experiences with it. But in the larger context, what is transpiring is a complete breakdown of our government authority structure because no effort to correct it has been launched through the existing self-government system. And, The People have not joined together to demand action. Apparently, confusion reigns!

The peaceable assembly that degenerates into riot has various causes:

The first, discussed at some length in the opening section of this Chapter, is the failure of the Framers to establish accountability for the actions of those taking advantage of the Rights and Freedoms of the First Amendment. Thus, rioters can apparently burn, loot, and vandalize without personal liability and, for many, perhaps most, no criminal liability. Accountability cannot be enforced because rioters can disguise themselves to avoid recognition. Organizers can abuse the Right Peaceably to Assemble by hiring protesters with no connection to the stated cause and by hiding the real reasons behind a so-called "protest" for anarchist purposes.

The second is the lack of accountability of State and Local Government in locations experiencing riotous activity for failure to "ensure domestic tranquility." By exposing their citizens to the peril of riotous behavior and their businesses to vandalism, those governments have failed to execute their fundamental responsibility. Lack of state and local government accountability has a constitutional source. It mirrors the accountability-free status of the Federal government. The absence of accountability may be built into the chartering documents of local governments or may result from the failure of the ballot box to act as a check-and-balance against ineffective local government, but in its essence is the product of political party influence on citizen voting decisions. There are many in our nation who strongly believe that corruption and malfeasance in state and local governments is the biggest untold story in the nation's advancing breakdown of democracy.

The third is the involvement of political parties, associating with and supporting the objectives of riotous protesters for party advantage. Involvement of political parties in such anarchist activities should engender public revolt, but because of the unholy alliance of political parties with the Media, news reporting does not expose their roles. It is yet another demonstration of the destructive effect of political parties on democracy, their alliance with the media, and their apparent ability to establish immunity from true blame.

The fourth cause is the successful efforts of local governments to escape responsibility for police action. Local governments blame their police departments rather than take responsibility for police department actions. Under the rules of delegation stated in the first Section of this Chapter, city governments can delegate authority to, and establish accountability of their police departments, **but in doing so, cannot eliminate their own responsibility, which remains unchanged and in place.** Local governments possess all needed authority to administer their police departments: the right to guide the hiring of all personnel, starting with the Chief; their right to establish or approve standards for hiring, training, performance, and discipline. Their right and responsibility to approve operating procedures, etc. With that authority must come commensurate responsibility for the performance of law enforcement.

That delegation rule establishes the clear obligation of the Mayor and Local Government to ensure that the police department performs as required. **Local government is to blame if the police department does not meet standards. Unfortunately, the politician's natural tendency to "blame others" is deeply ingrained and the public does not, apparently, have the acumen to correctly assess blame. Blaming the officer on the firing line is unethical, destructive, and a serious violation of principle.**

If a riot is under way all elected local government should be on duty, making the necessary community protection decisions and directing the police. Local government must ensure that police brass is directing the front-line officers and effectively making critical police operations decisions.

If elected officials and police brass were on the job and performing, how could police officer on the line be accused of malfeasance? **Obviously, if an officer on the line was committing malfeasance, police brass was either nowhere near the riot, or was present there and failed to supervise.**

In either event, the police hierarchy, up the ranks to the Chief, did not do their jobs, which is to make sure that the front-line officers are performing as required. **And if the police brass did not do their jobs, including the Chief of Police, obviously, the Mayor and local government Council are to blame, because policing is a critical function it is their job to supervise.**

We repeat the old management adage: "If the worker did not work the manager did not manage." Blaming workers is not only the height of managerial incompetence, it is also the pinnacle of moral and ethical failure.

SECTION 3
CONSTITUTIONAL PROVISION PROPOSAL

Following is a draft of a proposed Constitutional section to replace the Right to Peaceably Assemble contained in the First Amendment. The draft is intended to be a discussion paper that addresses the considerations involved.

Bear in mind that proposed for a new Constitution, the people-elected Constitutional Convention must draft any proposed Amendment placed before the Well-Informed Electors for consideration. The Convention choices may be completely different from this proposal, and the choices of the Well-Informed Electors may be even more divergent. But, if accountability is not carefully structured, success will not be experienced.

This proposed solution focuses on pinpointing accountability among Peaceable Assembly participants and on the part of governments. Of highest priority is the accountability of local government for the actions of its police force by transferring to local government the public liability of individual police officers for actions taken when quelling riotous assembly and liability for losses suffered by people and businesses because of riotous behavior not controlled by local government.

PROPOSED CONSTITUTIONAL PROVISION

THE RIGHT PEACEABLY TO ASSEMBLE

Citizens shall have the right peaceably to assemble, and to petition the Government for a redress of grievances. The right is granted to ensure citizens can communicate their opinions concerning government or of activity they consider inappropriate or harmful to their welfare or to that of the public in general.

Peaceable Assembly is not advocated as the preferred means of communicating and resolving issues. Constitutional Authorities have been established to allow The People to control and direct government. Those Authorities shall provide convenient and appropriate means for The People to express concerns and initiate action on matters deemed important and requiring attention. With the establishment of those channels of communication, the need for citizens peaceably to assemble should sharply diminish.

    a)   The People note that peaceable assemblies too often devolve into mob rampages with substantial injury to the rights and property of innocent persons and, as such, represent a threat to domestic peace and tranquility. The Right to Peaceably

Assemble does not convey to participants any right to engage in illegal activity during assembly.

b) Local elected officials shall have the duty to declare an assembly in process as either "peaceable assembly" or "riotous assembly" and to take appropriate action thereafter. Designation decisions, sometimes made under riotous circumstances, shall not be subsequently questioned, but failure to decide shall. Local government and its police department management, which have primary responsibility for maintaining the peace and ensuring property rights are not violated, shall be held accountable for actions not taken. The latitude granted them to take action shall be directly proportional to their perception of the danger of a riotous assembly in progress.

c) Those who choose to peaceably assemble do so to make a point, communicate a position, or advocate an action. In return for that opportunity, they incur an obligation to disclose and validate who they are so that citizens and government can make a knowledgeable role evaluation. No person engaging in peaceable assembly has the right to hide identity but instead has an outright obligation to willingly disclose the identity and make it publicly visible during assembly.

d) The right of citizens to assemble peaceably, for those who avail themselves of its privilege, shall carry with it substantial personal accountability for actions. **The first responsibility of assembly participants is to immediately leave the assembly location if riotous activity is developing.** Failing to do so, they shall be deemed riot participants merely by their presence at the scene.

e) The right peaceably to assemble does not carry with it the right to destroy property, with its resultant cost to society, or to challenge law enforcement in any way. Aggression toward law enforcement by assembly participants shall be met with even more aggressive law enforcement responses. Property damage shall invite aggressive law enforcement.

Section 1

Permitting Requirements

Peaceable assembly shall require a permit issued by the local government of the place of assembly. Citizens shall not be unreasonably denied the right to peaceably assemble. Permits may not be withheld for reason or purpose of assembly or unnecessarily delayed in issuance. **However, applicants shall be required to submit proof they have utilized Constitutional facilities for complaint or redress and may only be granted a permit if the Constitutional vehicle for complaint or redress has failed to take action.**

a) Organizers of a proposed peaceable assembly shall provide permitting authorities with personal identification, declare its purpose, the time and place of assembly, and shall warrant that all participants will be informed of the rules applicable to the assembly, shall warrant in writing that they understand the meaning and implications of a declaration of riotous activity, and commit to conducting the assembly so it does not devolve into riotous activity. Permit-granting governments shall, solely for their own use and at the expense of the organizers, contract for and acquire a complete and comprehensive video record of assembly events, which shall be stored securely and retained for twenty-five years.

b) Permits shall be denied to applicants, and registration denied to participants, who have been involved in prior peaceable assembly that devolved into riotous activity. Law enforcement shall maintain a national data base of all individuals participating in assemblies turned riotous, together with video records, all of which shall be readily available to the public. Researching existing law enforcement records shall be a primary responsibility of permit-granting governments.

c) The public shall be informed regarding persons who have been granted a Right to Peaceable Assembly under this Provision of the date, time, and stated purpose of assembly, which shall be published by the permitting government prior to the Assembly date.

d) **Issued permits shall require that all assembly participants provide identification and register before the event and, while participating, prominently display permit-issued personal identification.** Participants shall not in any manner attempt to deny personal recognition, particularly by use of face covering, shielding, or disguise.

e) Governments issuing permits for peaceable assembly shall write into law descriptions of various acts common in riotous assemblies, and enact specific criminal penalties for each. They shall provide copies of the law and penalties to assembly organizers at the time of participant registration. Violations shall result in a negative rating on the Morals and Ethics records of individuals involved, but criminal penalties involving incarceration shall always be imposed for riotous behavior.

f) The Right Peaceably to Assemble does not extend to non-permitted assemblies. Spontaneous unpermitted assembly shall be confronted by law enforcement, verbally informed of permitting regulations, and ordered to disperse. Failure of those assembled to do so shall result in enforceable disbursement by law enforcement under the close direction of the responsible local government.

Section 2

No Contrarian Assemblies in the Same Vicinity

A permit, under appropriate conditions, shall be required by those who wish to peaceably assemble to present a message contrary to that being conveyed by a permitted assembly. Such contrarian assemblies shall not be allowed in the same place at the same time as another permitted assembly.

Section 3

Obligations and Accountability of Assembly Participants

The permit-issuing government is responsible for protecting the rights and properties of persons in the assembly area and shall be liable for property damage and personal injury that occurs during the assembly. Local government shall take all necessary steps to prevent property damage, bloodshed, aggression against law enforcement, looting, and other illegal activity and shall direct and supervise law enforcement control efforts.

a) Permit-issuing authorities shall approve or deny the right of each individual making an application to participate in an assembly to assure that unpermitted third-party factions do not take advantage for undeclared purposes **and shall retain and prosecute those not displaying permitter-issued identification.**

b) **Peaceable assembly organizers and participants shall be personally criminally liable for acts of civil disobedience transpiring during an assembly.** Video evidence, coupled with law enforcement testimony, shall be adequate proof of civil disobedience.

The investigation diligence and legal approaches utilized following the January 6, 2020, occupation of Congress shall be the model against which local government performance in individual cases of civil disobedience is measured.

c) Any assembly participant physically or verbally challenging or obstructing police officers shall be if observed, designated a "criminal participant." **No officer of the law may be prosecuted for enforcement actions taken against such criminal participant, including for his/her loss of life.**

d) Failure of local elected officials to control an assembly, whether spontaneous or permitted, shall result in their prompt removal from office by the State Government. Liability claims against local government for losses suffered during riotous assembly will be borne by the taxpayers, full information about which shall be published. Validated liability claims shall be prima facie evidence of local government incompetence. **An early election, within 60 days of a riotous event, allowing voters to consider the retention of such officials, shall be held.**

Section 4

Riotous Assembly Declaration

The Chief of Police or an official properly acting on his behalf of a permitting government shall declare an assembly "riotous" upon observation of participant actions deemed unlawful or dangerous. The declaration shall be announced by loudspeaker to those assembled, with consequences and instructions to immediately disperse. Upon such declaration, law enforcement officials shall be operating solely to protect citizens and property and are granted the widest latitude in acts deemed necessary to control and disperse the assembly.

Section 5

Accountability For Riotous Assemblies

Peaceable assemblies that turn riotous shall be deemed an act of egregious illegality. **The People intend that, when such an event occurs, full accountability shall be imposed on assembly participants for illegal behavior and on local governments for failure to govern effectively.**

a) Local government holds all authority over its law enforcement and is totally accountable for enforcement actions. Local government officials shall direct law enforcement decision-making during assemblies deemed riotous to ensure actions taken by police management are appropriate and shall be accountable to the citizens for that job performance.

b) Liability for inappropriate actions taken by law enforcement in quelling assemblies and for losses sustained by property owners may be pursued against the permit-issuing government, but personal accountability of assembly organizers and participants involved in those same actions and losses shall first have been invoked.

c) No officer of the law may be held liable by assembly organizers, participants, or others for enforcement actions taken during assemblies. **Actions, appropriate or otherwise, taken by individual law enforcement officers are and shall be deemed to be the authorized actions of the local government.**

d) The permitting government, accountable for the actions of law enforcement officers who policed an assembly, may investigate and take appropriate administrative action against individual officers for failing to follow orders or operating instructions but may not escape liability because such failures occurred or because appropriate administrative action was not subsequently taken.

e) State government is responsible for ensuring that local governments have performed their responsibilities properly in managing assemblies and have conducted necessary personnel administrative actions.

f) The President of the United States, responsible for seeing that the laws are faithfully executed, shall, within 90 days, commission an impartial review of the facts of every assembly turned riotous. He/she shall determine if the actions of governments were proper and conform to the requirements of this Article and shall institute punishment for failure as appropriate. If he/she determines a state or local government is incapable of maintaining the peace, he/she shall deploy appropriate force. He/she shall report all findings, together with accountability enforcement, to The People within two months. He/she shall take into account the message and activities of assembly participants and determine if further action is warranted. He/she shall evaluate the involvement of the Media and take appropriate action to punish and/or correct Media malfeasance.

Section 6

Media Accountability

Most peaceable assembly is undertaken to generate public attention and support. Media shall be held to the highest standards of impartiality in reporting assemblies, whether peaceful or riotous, may not support or denigrate assembly proponents or causes verbally or otherwise, may not publicly display video of assemblies in a manner favorable to any side or participant, may not fail to report observed actions of any participant, and must fairly and impartially report the actions of law enforcement and local government. Media commentators, in all instances, shall explain to the public that local government is responsible to the citizens for the actions of law enforcement.

a) Violations of these requirements by Media personnel shall subject them to job loss, criminal liability, and permanent banishment from the industry, The Media provider that permits reporting not in accordance with these requirements shall suffer loss of license.

CHAPTER 23

PUTTING "THE PEOPLE" IN CHARGE OF THE CONSTITUTION AND AUTHORITY STRUCTURE

CONTENT:

SECTION 1: BRIEF SUMMARY OF EXECUTION BARRIERS

SECTION 2: CONSTITUTIONAL ROUTES AVAILABLE FOR AMENDMENT APPROVAL

SECTION 3: BY-PASSING ARTICLE V ROUTES, INSTITUTING DIRECT ACTION BY THE PEOPLE

SECTION 4: PROPOSED CHANGES TO CREATE TRUE SELF-GOVERNED DEMOCRACY

FOREWORD

Readers who have struggled through the complex material about government organization, the constitutional provisions that laid the groundwork for our stresses, the actions of politicians and political parties, and all the other forces that brought us to our present condition are no doubt pondering the critical question:

"How are we, The People, going to get the needed changes made?"

There is no obvious answer to that question. It will be necessary to sort through what we know and what we have to work with to create a plan. And citizens have to wake up to the fact that supporting their favorite political party is working against the nation's best interest.

Rewriting our nation's constitution will require The People to come together in a way we have not experienced since World War 11. Those who remember that time saw a remarkable level of cohesion, with the nation's people focused on doing what was necessary to survive. What the future held in store wasn't clear then, either, but the threat certainly was. It brought The People together.

The survival threat today is internal, not external. It is not as clear to citizens as the obvious external threats, even though the level may be equally high. But the assumption that The People do not understand that our nation is in deep duress due to a failing government system may very well be proven dead wrong.

The organization, the planning, the selection of leadership, and the intelligence of approach will dictate the success of reconstitution. This Author's role is to attempt to stimulate the effort, here referred to simply as "Constitution 2."

It was said in the time of the Romans, "Fortune favors the brave." And the brave may finally provide an answer to Alexander Hamilton's concerns about whether the people of this nation are truly capable of self-government.

SECTION 1
BRIEF SUMMARY OF EXECUTION BARRIERS

THE EFFORT TO FORMULATE CONSTITUTION 2 WILL FACE VIGOROUS OPPOSITION

An effort to change the basic structure and operation of governance in our democratic republic will face instantaneous and intense opposition from those who now control it or have a stake in its continuity. Observers of the intense political-class reaction to Donald Trump's 2016-2020 "Drain the Swamp" presidency goals will rate reaction to that threat as mere child's play compared to what will occur when The People launch an effort to constitutionally change the nation's authority operations, from the political elite's entrenched "monarchy republic" to true focused and organized democratic self-government.

The political elite of our country control everything; the levers of government, the military, the political parties, the media and communications system, the Constitution. They do, in fact, govern as a monarchy. Possessed of a nice situation, they can be expected to react violently to what they will decide is their existential threat, and will employ every weapon at their disposal. They have everything to lose. Entrenched entitlement will prompt an immediate response, which it cannot be assumed will be rational.

There are a number of on-going, but futile, efforts to amend the constitution. Popular causes have included lengthening the term of elected representatives beyond the existing two-year cycle, doing away with the Electoral College to convey presidential voting advantage to population-heavy states, changing elections to the Senate for the same purpose, increasing the number of justices on the Supreme Court, and changing its political make-up to favor one political party. All of those efforts flow out of the party system, and are focused on attaining party political advantage.

What those efforts tell us is that the moment a new constitutional amendment movement launches, all of the self-interest antagonism of politicians will burst forth to attack those proposing changes. Our party-based politicians do not have a history of putting the nation first, nor do they evidence any meaningful concern for the rights and welfare of The People.

The leadership of The People's Movement will succeed only if their organization and effort are geared to anticipate and overcome the inevitable response.

OVERCOMING THE BARRIER OF THE PEOPLE'S COMPREHENSION LEVEL

Voters have been conditioned to view government as it exists, a self-contained party-politics system with voting the only process in which citizens are involved. They have been conditioned to that and to the necessity of attempting to institute change **through their party of choice**. Two-thirds of the voters of the nation are members of a political party**. We don't well understand the depth of loyalty attached to their party membership.**

The U.S. government may be the most complex organization on the planet. Citizen comprehension is made difficult by that reality. Citizen understanding is surface knowledge at best, picked up from biased media news and the exhortations of the party system since most have had little formal civics training. Their involvement has been voting in the election of officials, a decision that, in reality, is choosing a political party. The average citizen knows the names of chambers, some of the processes of government, and some politicians but does not know enough to be classified as "knowledgeable."

Even though much of this book's discussion may be beyond the present insight of many citizens, the new organization of government proposed is based on the fundamental principle that The People must perform functions they, as the owners of a self-governed nation, are obligated to carry out. That, also, may not be in keeping with notions of citizen responsibility. To participate in the true self-government model this book proposes, citizens will need insight far deeper than what is required to merely elect candidates or to decide which party to support.

These observations are in no way intended to suggest that our citizens are not capable of reaching the level of understanding needed to vote in a new self-government structure that requires citizen decisions more complex than candidate selection. The observations merely highlight the fact that the existing gap between the civics knowledge of the average voting citizen and the required knowledge of a citizen participating in true self-government decision-making is large.

YOU CAN CALL ME A "COCK-EYED OPTIMIST"
66

So, the first barrier is ourselves. *Isn't that always the case?*

This Author may rightfully be accused of being a "cock-eyed optimist" for choosing to bet on the American people. It has been known since the 1700s that democratic self-government requires an informed citizenry, and ours is certainly not that. Our citizens have been methodically 'dumbed-down" by the political parties and the media. Their low knowledge level is not their fault and is certainly not a measure of their capability. **It is the product of today's political environment.**

Sophisticated modern democratic self-government demands that voting citizens have much more than surface-level knowledge. We must either face and overcome that barrier or abandon a pure democratic self-government restructure as unachievable. **Abandonment will be a concession that The People are incapable of self-government, as Hamilton speculated might be the case.** This book proposes the task of preparing The People for true self-government is a mission that drives the reconstruction of the Media and puts that effort in a priority perspective. It also suggests that the organization of the reconstitution effort and the manner in which it is implemented will largely dictate its success prospects. Patience will be a very valuable attitude!

Because of the magnitude of the citizen comprehension barrier and the time required to overcome it, the effort could be begun unobtrusively, in an "underground" fashion, well in advance of the launch and disclosure of the Constitution 2 project.

SECTION 2
CONSTITUTIONAL ROUTES AVAILABLE

There are different routes that could be pursued to gain approval of a constitutional amendment that would remove existing Article V. and insert in its place a new provision formally establishing the sole right of The People to reconstruct the Constitution and manage its content. It will be advisable to undertake the project in steps that can be digested by The People. The first critical action is a selection of the guidance team.

Decisions required of the guidance team will outline the citizen comprehension plan, the selection of the content for the authorizing amendment, the selection of the best route and

---

[66] Music of Rogers and Hammerstein, stage show "South Pacific"

plan to gain its approval, and the development of the post-approval implementation plan of The People.

In this Section, we will examine the various amendment approval routes available to the guidance team, from which a selection must be made.

UTILIZING THE CONSTITUTION'S ARTICLE V AMENDMENT ROUTES

Article V rules regarding constitutional amendments are contained in one sentence of 90 words, separated by 12 commas. The text is so convoluted that understanding the alternatives it contains is an intellectual challenge. Following is a rough summary of the rules.

a. The Congress, **by a vote of two-thirds of both Houses**, may propose Amendments.

b. The States, **on application of two-thirds of their number**, may propose Amendments.

c. If the States make the application, the Congress shall call a Convention to propose Amendments.

d. Amendments proposed by Congress or by a Convention will become part of the Constitution **if ratified by the legislatures of, or conventions of, three-quarters of the States**. The Congress will propose the mode of ratification.

Consideration of the Article V rules brings forth the following thought:

After proposing an amendment or granting approval of a Convention following application by the States, Congress has no further involvement. Congress can subvert state-fostered amendments through the selection of people assigned to the Amendment-proposing Convention.

ALTERNATIVE 1 OPTIONS

(UTILIZING ARTICLE V AVAILABLE ROUTES)

ROUTE 1: ACHIEVE AMENDMENT VIA THE STATES

The States have the final approval of amendments proposed by Congress and can deny them by vote. But states can also lead the amendment approval process.

- Lining up the states and using their advantageous position may be the most direct amendment approval route available under Article V because it avoids Congressional pre-approval. Also, the requirement of approval by two-thirds of the states is lower than the ratification requirement of 75% of the states.

- The states have constitutional amendment control. In order to vest in The People's total control over future amendments, states will have to be induced to give up their existing amendment control. That is a barrier of tremendous consequence, and because of party influence, it will probably defeat any effort on the part of The People.

- Attempting to amend the constitution via Article V provisions will require immense political capability, skill, luck, and money. Following are additional routes available to the guidance team.

ROUTE 2: PRESSURE FEDERAL ELECTED PERSONS TO PASS THE REQUIRED AMENDMENT

Another route exists to pursue a constitutional amendment via the Congress, using the provisions of Article V, by developing enough voter amendment support to influence the re-election of sitting members of Congress. Those voters, in an organized campaign, would induce candidates to commit to vote in favor of the required amendment or face a losing election. Tremendous grass-roots political pressure from masses of voters could be mounted and would be needed.

This strategy has the advantage of direct simplicity. It could be executed in conjunction with a federal election involving the two existing political parties. The core problem of generating voter support dominates this path. In order to secure their vote, citizens would demand that sitting members and candidates publicly declare support for a constitutional amendment to replace Article V. Citizens would vote for or against candidates based upon that declaration. Based upon a survey of voter attitudes, candidates of both parties might decide to be supportive.

It should be noted that if Congressional members voted passage of the required amendment, voted support from three-quarters of the states would then be required. The grass-roots voter pressure would then have to be successfully refocused on state candidates in state elections.

ROUTE 3: FORM A SINGLE-PURPOSE "CONSTITUTION 2" POLITICAL PARTY

The United States does not need political parties, let alone one more political party, but utilizing the existing party system has some advantages. **Pursuing amendment under the existing provisions of Article V by forming a single-purpose political party is worth considering.**

This route would seek to speed up approval of The People's constitutional amendment control by inserting a new single-purpose political party into the federal and state government election process, formed for the sole purpose of achieving amendment approval.

The approach would convert the decision process from an altruistic stand-alone national deliberation to a politician-level voting contest within an election. The Constitution 2 Party would be competing for votes and, in the process, subject itself to political attack. That is the price to be paid for the wide political exposure from promoting the constitutional issue during an election.

If the Constitution 2 Party gains the required majority, it will be expected to form a government. That is a good news/bad news result. Having the Party-run government will be a total distraction from its purpose. On the other hand, there are tremendous advantages to simultaneously controlling the government. Readers should consider the possibility that the Constitution 2 party does not gain a majority but does elect sufficient officials to disturb the majority position of the existing parties. A coalition government might result, allowing the Constitution 2 party to achieve its goals.

Existing political parties will feel threatened by having to compete for votes against the Constitution 2 party. The approach will harden opposition. It might be possible for the Constitution 2 party to form an alliance with one of the two existing parties under the terms of which that party would run the government, while the Constitution 2 Party would run the Constitutional Amendment process.

The Constitution 2 Party will have to simplify its platform down to a constitutional amendment canceling the existing Article V provision and authorizing The People to approve all future amendments; however, it will be very difficult to avoid discussion of an overall reconstitution plan, which raises a range of questions.

The assumption is that elected by The People, the Constitution 2 party would be able to accelerate Article V State concurrence. At the end of the day, even if elected as a majority party, for the Constitution 2 party to move an amendment through Congress, it will need to line up the supporting vote of two-thirds of both Houses. It would be remarkable if the Constitution 2 party is successful in electing or negotiating a majority that large.

CONCLUSIONS REGARDING AMENDMENT PURSUIT UTILIZING AVAILABLE ARTICLE V ROUTES

A quick review of Article V of the constitution will remind readers that attempting to make constitutional changes using the existing Article V vehicles is likely to produce frustration. Since 1789, more than 11,000 constitutional amendments have been proposed, but only 27 have been enacted. That statistic states, loud and clear, the long odds of success from choosing that constitutional amendment road.

That is true because those routes require the co-operation of two groups of elected persons. Those who will feel most threatened by the effort would be Federal rather than State. If The People were successful in populating Congress with elected persons committed to supporting

The People's constitutional amendment, the barrier of gaining acquiescence from three-fourths of the States would be easier to overcome.

Article V was installed in the Constitution to protect the political elite's Monarchy Republic against just such an effort as is proposed. The provision permitting the States to control amendment approval was included to secure support from the thirteen then-existing states and, as such, was the result of a political bargain.

SECTION 3
BY-PASSING ARTICLE V ROUTES, INSTITUTING DIRECT ACTION BY THE PEOPLE

The People have the inalienable right, as owners of the nation, to take steps necessary to ensure government functions to their satisfaction. The third paragraph of the Declaration of Independence, dated July 4, 1776, states that right in the following words:

> **"We hold these truths to be self-evident, that all men are created equal, that they are endowed by their Creator with certain inalienable Rights, that among those are Life, Liberty, and the pursuit of happiness.**
>
> **- That to secure these rights Governments are instituted among Men, deriving their just powers from the consent of the governed.**
>
> **- That whenever any Form of Government becomes destructive of these ends, it is the Right of the People to alter or to abolish it, and to institute new Government, laying its foundation on such principles and organizing its powers in such form as to them shall seem most likely to affect their Safety and Happiness.**
>
> **Prudence, indeed, will dictate that Governments long established should not be changed for light and transient causes, and accordingly all experience hath shewn, that mankind is more disposed to suffer, while evils are sufferable, than to right themselves by abolishing the forms to which they are accustomed."**

The People can, by this declaration, decide that provisions of the existing constitution must be revoked, declaring the existing provisions no longer to have the consent of the governed. There are no constitutional procedures for The People to carry out such direct action, but if a majority of citizens so voted, denying them their rights would be very difficult and self-destructive for persons or organizations attempting denial.

The goal of such an effort would be to achieve, by a majority vote of all citizens, approval of an amendment to the constitution replacing Article V, which amendment would declare the sole right of The People to approve all amendments to the Constitution and define the procedure by which that is done. Because the United States is a democratic republic, the vote of a majority of the citizens must be deemed their exercise of will, which no existing authority should be able to legally refute.

RECONSTITUTION SUPPORT MUST BE AT LEAST EQUAL TO A MAJORITY OF THE NATION'S VOTERS

Constitutional Amendment can be accomplished through an undertaking of The People, with majority popular support, to nullify the existing Article V provisions and replace them with a provision whereby only The People may make changes to the constitution. No other way exists for The People to enforce their self-government rights. Constitutional changes will require not only the consent of a majority of the citizens but also their active and whole-hearted on-going involvement.

CREATING A GRASS-ROOTS SUPPORT MOVEMENT FOR ALTERNATIVE 2 APPROACH

On the assumption that the vote support of more than 50% of the nation's citizens will be needed, how can a successful campaign be undertaken to gain the support of that many people?

1. Leadership

The People of our nation are trained political followers. They will respond to leadership. The politically-active people in the nation are party-oriented and are an unlikely place to look for leadership of this cause. A successful movement will need leadership who can plan an effective campaign, pull the citizens together, and have the credibility to attract massive funding.

"Leadership" may be one or more persons. The person(s) who lead must be honorable, trustworthy, and have the nation's best interest at heart. Leadership must be well-known and exceptionally credible. Organization skills are of great importance because The People's Movement must be built from nothing.

2. Military-Quality Planning Will be Needed

The introductory section to this Chapter begins with the statement that, "The People's Constitutional Effort Will Face Vigorous Opposition." That assumption dictates the quality of planning needed for the Constitution 2 grass-roots movement to succeed.

The entire effort must be planned and executed with the precision of a military campaign. Attack plans, massive communication capabilities, specific counter-measures against ripostes by an entrenched political elite, plans to marshal the citizens, and all support requirements must be in place.

3. *Substantial Funding Will Be Required*

The many pieces to the effort described herein will require that substantial funding be available for Constitution 2 to succeed. The Media will be a pervasive cost factor. Political elite opposition will certainly have at their disposal not only massive media resources but also access to substantial resistance funding. It must be assumed that the fund-raising capabilities of both political parties will be forcefully brought into play.

A seat-of-the-pants estimate for The People's Movement funding will be in the range of $1 to $5 billion, expended over a period of several years.

Funding the venture will be the first and most important task of leadership, a critical factor in the selection of qualifications of leadership candidates. High on the list of funding alternatives is the option of writing the proposal in a manner that allows funding for it to be provided by the U.S. Treasury. As the proposal is an action of The People, who are the owners of the nation, if approved by a vote of The People, Treasury funding is totally justifiable.

4. *"Movement" Advertising and Promotion*

To implant immediate recognition in the minds of citizens, professional support will be needed to create the attention-getters that would draw citizens to Constitution 2 and keep it prominently in their minds.

Advertising and promotion tools such as slogans, attractive labeling, themes, reinforcement, and a range of messaging techniques must be brought into play.

Because electronic media must necessarily be heavily utilized to promote the movement, considerable media resources will be required. The movement should either firm a relationship with a prominent electronic media channel such as CNBC, CNN, or Fox or purchase or build a new channel solely to serve its own needs.

Citizen education must necessarily involve the Media. That route could be utilized early on in a concentrated effort to educate the citizenry on the issues involved.

5. *Create a Grass-Roots Educational Effort*

Because voter thinking will have to be modified, a focused grass-roots "study group" to examine the situation and its recommended solution would seem to be a necessary and productive route to building the needed support base. Although "educating the voters" is not a recommended term, the fact of the matter is that individual voters will not appreciate and support the movement without first absorbing a considerable amount of basic information and rationale not currently available to them.

Marshaling thousands of local leaders and supplying them with books and audio-visual training aids, training guides, and talking points would be a good approach. Training would be conducted in small groups assembled by local leaders, using audio-visual presentations and sections of text material to deliver foundation information.

Upon training completion, graduating group members would be expected to lead new study groups, bringing the multiplication factor into play.

On-going movement promotion activity by members must be planned and executed to maintain interest, vitality, and growth.

6. *Establish a Movement Member Data Base with Electronic Communication*

In the modern world, leadership of an effort such as proposed here has to evaluate the effort status at every point in time, and have the ability to communicate with all members at the drop of a hat.

That approach would require a membership data base coupled with an electronic communications system. Such a system immediately brings to mind concerns about hacking, with all the various risks involved. Those are indeed concerns, but the communication system benefits outweigh the risks. Perhaps the communications system can be a function of the electronic media it is suggested be acquired by the Movement.

Members graduating from training could be enrolled in the data base as "Well-Informed Electors" for future voting purposes.

7. *Emphasis Necessary: The "Form" of Government Will Not Change, but its "Organization and Process" will because of control by The People.*

The Framers were largely correct in their concept of government. The problems we face stem from their self-serving constitutional provisions that created the Monarchy Republic and their failure to deal properly and correctly with the rights and involvement of The People.

The Constitution 2 effort will build on the positive concepts provided by the Framers, such as Democracy, Freedom and Liberty, the one-person, one-vote rule, and self-government by The People.

The distinction between The People as owners and the Hired Management as employees will be the Constitution 2 organization strategy built around the achievement of accountability and a focus on decision excellence.

The People, utilizing Constitutional Authorities, will restructure all government organizations and procedures, eliminating processes that were built to serve the political class, such as the right of the Houses of Congress to manage their own proceedings and to form political parties. It will focus on guarantying the elected will do only what they are directed to do.

These are important emphasis points in the communication process. **The People need to understand that proposed changes are both "conceptual" and "operational."**

SECTION 4
PROPOSED CHANGES TO CREATE A HIGH-PERFORMANCE SELF-GOVERNED DEMOCRACY

It will perhaps be helpful to readers if the proposed actions sprinkled throughout this book are summarized in one list. Readers will understand the following summaries are not complete descriptions of the proposed actions, and a number are not included.

The size of this list should signal to readers the level of extreme disrepair to which our nation's government has fallen. This reveals there is almost nothing in it that functions properly.

1, Rewrite the Constitution and Maintain it Current

Make it a "living document" that is written and maintained under the direction of an elected body of The People called the Constitutional Convention. Establish the right of The People solely to make amendments to the constitution. Make it the principal citizenship education and training document of the nation, written in a manner that allows it to perform that function.

2. Create a new Authority Structure for the Nation

It will be made up of two organizations: Constitutional Authorities, executing The People's will and intentions, and Government, managing the affairs of the nation. The Constitutional Authorities will perform all check-and-balance on government and arrange or manage the processes that produce all decisions within the Authority Structure. The three-silo internal control structure of the Framers will be disbanded.

3. Establish and build the "Well-Informed Electors" Voting Body

It will have sole authority to vote approval, on behalf of all citizens, of national policy matters, including the provisions of the constitution. The critical "what we are going to do" decisions of the nation will be made for all The People by the Well-Informed Electors. The elected functions in government will decide "how to do it."

4. Posture The People as "Owners," Elected Persons as "Hired Management"

All elected persons will be contracted for a one-time specific period of service. All such service would be documented by employment agreements, heavily incentive-based, but no pension provided. All Federal elections will be organized and funded by the nation under the direction of an elected Federal group called The People's Election Commission, which will locate candidates and manage the election process.

5. Utilize Morals and Ethics Tabulation to Establish Individual Accountability

Establish personal accountability as a citizenship fundamental and as the price for individual freedoms. Install Morals and Ethics (currently available public records) as a readily-accessible information pool for public use. Make that principle a foundation for the nation's citizenship, education, and the court's legal structure. For low-level transgressions replace prison time, as a penalty, with public shaming. Establish a Morals and Ethics Rating system covering citizens and residents, modeled after the Credit Rating System, to tabulate lapses by individuals and make transgressions and scores available to all. Consider establishing classes of citizenship based upon morals and ethics tabulation score.

Rewrite all relevant legal codes, reviewing the legal penalty to enforce personal accountability.

6. Establish Decision Excellence as the Principal Strategy for Government Improvement

Abandon government by contention. Control the legal faction and its influence. Bet on the benefits to be derived from achieving decision excellence. As owners, The People, through The Guardians of the Constitution, will manage the entire Authority Structure decision process. Structure government organizations specifically to produce decisions of quality. All decisions must be made democratically, and each must reach a pre-determined demandingly-high voting majority.

7. Define and Counteract Self-Government Threats

Define our misdirected and weak government, inadequate control of the nation's finance, totalitarian attacks against our form of government, and the monopolistic and overly-dominant Communications Media as the major threats to our nation's future. Plan and execute correction and elimination of those threats.

8. Remove totalitarian practices in government. Establish Constitutional control over the media and transfer to The People's isolated control the news operations that collect and

transmit vital communication between The People and the Authority Structure. Dismantle and divide the media into components to eliminate its monopoly construction and its threatening political behavior. Organize the governance information to be made available to The People.

9. The People Will Dominate the Nation's Forward Planning

Utilizing the Well-Informed Electors, decide the forward-looking goals of the nation (National Imperatives) to be achieved by the government. In the same process, decide the key financial controls (Financial Measures) to be applied to the government. Those become the achievement responsibility of government, and The People's key "Control."

10. Eliminate Political Parties and Their Activities

Political parties are the source of most of our governance problems, a poor system of non-contributory factions, contention, and self-serving activities. Having achieved an unwarranted control position in Congress, they created the non-performing House processes.

Eliminate the elected official concept of "representation." Eliminate self-management in elected assemblies. The Constitutional Authorities will install a wide capability for The People to inform the government as a replacement for the "representative" concept.

11. Restructure the Job of The President, Making Him/Her the Chief Executive Officer of Government

All decisions affecting the nation and its people will be made by elected assemblies, with ratification by the Senate and the President. Use elected Vice Presidents, reporting to the President, through which he/she will control all government operations, including legislation.

The President will be the unitary head of all government, responsible for operations. Introduce planning-based management and decision-making to replace the current reactionary management under The President for all decision and legislation. The President will execute, and achieve the People-generated Financial Measures and National Imperatives.

12. Restructure the Lower House for Decision Focus and Overall Improvement

Replace the House of Representatives with 30 to 60 elected assemblies reporting to the President, each dedicated solely to making governance decisions respecting an explicit economic or social segment of America. Eliminate assembly self-management and the concept of representation. Utilize professional management supplied by the Guardians to control the work of the Assemblies and the Senate. Align the assemblies with existing departments and agencies utilizing a matrix organization. Limit the percentage of lawyers permitted.

Under the direction of the President but initiated by The People, develop and implement a repeating two-year plan system for legislation and needed decisions to be executed by the Assemblies, to ensure needed legislation is produced.

13. Broaden the Role of the Senate to "Senior Decision Body of the Nation"

Restructure the role and purpose of the Senate. Place it under the President, but Guardians of the Constitution specialists will manage its daily work and decision processes. Make it the validation body for all governmental decisions. Involve it in the President's planning.

14. Transfer "Vital Infrastructure" Organizations from Government to the Constitutional Authorities

Move the Elections System, the Judicial System, and the Communications System from government to Constitutional Authorities. Move control over communications between The People and the Authority Structure to the Constitutional Authorities. Make the Federal Government explicitly responsible for the democratic structure, accountability to The People, and specific performance of State and Local governments.

Enforce the "one person, one vote" concept. Establish tight Constitutional Authority control over political factions, disqualifying most, to squelch efforts to multiply voting power using political faction influence. Create Constitutional feed-back mechanisms to ensure communication from The People.

Place elections under the control of the People, managed and funded through The People's Election Commission. Pay for elections by taxation, allow no private money, and no involvement by government. The Commission will propose a range of pre-qualified candidates for each elected position and manage the election process. Move to "competence" election decision criteria to replace "popularity."

15. Through Constitutional Authorities, Plan and Remodel People/Authority Communications

Current government/People communications are controlled by third parties, and what is provided is heavily biased to protect the government from public criticism. The information provided does not build informed citizens, nor what is required for self-government.

Opinion surveys are privately arranged and patchy in coverage. An Authority unit is needed to ensure those self-government requirements are met professionally and under tight control. An example is regular independent evaluations by The People of Trust in Government. There are many others needed.

16. Update the Bill of Rights and the Definition and Penalties for Treason

Revise, broaden, and update the Bill of Rights, tying the rights to personal accountability and to citizenship.

Redefine Treason, bringing a range of personal and elected person behavior against the nation within its scope, and enhance treason penalties.

Set up entirely new constitutional provisions governing "the right peaceably to assemble," built on assembly permits and full disclosure of participants, and place directly on local government accountability for tight control over any such activities.

ACKNOWLEDGEMENTS

T his book is written to present a specific perspective to citizens concerned about the foundering condition of the U.S. Government and where it is taking the nation.

Possessed of some basic knowledge, some relevant specialized knowledge, and strong experience in management organization and strategic planning but no background whatsoever in politics or government, the author brings little to the table that constitutes an advantage for the task undertaken. His concern focuses on the perspectives and capabilities of the average citizen, the mass of whom are the only true solution route.

During the long course of research and investigation, he chose not to visit the nation's centers of governance or to interview the many politicians available.

The author hopes the confrontations with reality that emerge will guide the reader's response and will stimulate the much-needed grassroots corrective action.

Special contribution from the following people is acknowledged:

Daniel Laughry, a retired judge, for his cogent observations early-on that helped book development a great deal.

Michael Gibbert, computer specialist and valued son-in-law, without whose technical help the author would probably have abandoned the project.

www.ingramcontent.com/pod-product-compliance
Lightning Source LLC
Chambersburg PA
CBHW042337030426
42335CB00030B/3376